Pax Sinica

To

Kueh Yi Kai (郭貽凱)

Kueh Yi Ren (郭貽仁)

Kueh Yi An (郭貽安)

Pax Sinica

Geopolitics and Economics of China's Ascendance

Y. Y. Kueh

香港大學出版社
Hong Kong University Press

Hong Kong University Press
14/F Hing Wai Centre
7 Tin Wan Praya Road
Aberdeen
Hong Kong
www.hkupress.org

ISBN 978-988-8083-82-4 *(Hardback)*

British Library Cataloguing-in-Publication Data
A catalogue record for this book is available from the British Library.

10 9 8 7 6 5 4 3 2 1

Printed and bound by Kings Time Printing Press Ltd., Hong Kong, China

Contents

Preface

This volume is a collection of academic articles and commissioned research monographs completed at different critical junctures of China's opening up to the West. Taken together, the various chapters trace the major policy measures adopted for the country's integration with the global system of free trade and investment flows, and her accelerated ascendency as a global economic power. From the vantage point of the post-global financial crisis of 2008/2009, the study concludes with an interpretative assessment of the globally increasingly popular conjecture of a "Pax Sinica" being poised to help marginalize or mitigate the American hegemony, similar to Pax Americana emerging to overshadow Pax Britannica at the turn of the previous century.

Such a study necessarily involves geopolitics. China's increased integration with the global economy has indeed been marked, time and again, with geopolitical interfering, negative or positive. While Western powers generally embrace China's strategy of *gaige kaifang* (reform and opening up) and her consistent transition from a centrally planned and closed economy to a market-based and internationally opened system over the past three decades or so, by virtue of the country's sheer magnitude, her rapid economic advances have also, quite naturally, met with political suspicion and fear from outside. This study makes an attempt to show, however, how economic imperatives normally prevail over geopolitics in favour of closer regional synergy and integration within the global framework of trade and investment liberalization.

The study focuses, in particular, on China's complex relationships with the APEC (Asia Pacific Economic Cooperation Forum) economies. For the purpose, a distinction is made between North APEC and South APEC on the one hand, and APEC proper and APEC at large (Full APEC) on the other hand (which embraces all member economies including those on the American-Pacific coast, from Canada and the United States in the north to Chile in the south). It examines, in the first place, how China's new policy approach has triggered a wide-ranging realignment of the production network in the Asia Pacific to result in the country's remarkable rise in the region. The selected articles all fall into three major parts of the study, displaying largely a chronological order.

The first part deals with the emergence of the so-called Greater China economic circle; or more specifically, the pace and pattern—and as well, the underlying economic forces—of Hong Kong and Taiwan being forcefully drawn into the broader economic context of mainland China commencing in the early 1980s. It also resorts to the case of Guangdong, the Chinese province bordering Hong Kong and dubbed "the Fifth Dragon", to show how, the Greater China synergy has also helped to increasingly convert the coastal belt of China into a highly export-oriented entity, alongside the globally well-known "Four Little Dragons" (South Korea, Taiwan, Hong Kong, and Singapore).

The second part of the study examines how no sooner had the basic structural parameters of Greater China as an economic phenomenon been established than the Asian Financial Crisis erupted in 1997 to seriously probe into the integrity and resilience of the three constituent Chinese economies. It shows, namely, how despite enhanced integration in the real economic sphere, the financial crisis had brought the Chinese trio to bear on account of the remaining differences in institutional setting, financial and monetary policy regime, and the exchange rate system. Moreover, the disparate policy measures adopted for coping with the crisis are also critically compared and assessed as to their durability and desirability. Viewed differently, this second part, together with the first one, should indeed also be taken as a unique case study blending economic analysis of development with institutional and comparative economics.

The third consecutive part reveals how economic and trade relations between China and the South APEC countries have also been enhanced in tandem with the emergence of the Greater China economic circle, leading eventually to the signing of the ASEAN 10+1 (China) Free Trade Area (FTA) agreement in November 2002 for formal launching in 2010. It also shows how soon after the Early Harvest Programme of the framework agreement had been put in place, a similar formal FTA agreement with the Hong Kong SAR (Special Administrative Region), viz. CEPA (Closer Economic Partnership Arrangement), was signed by China in 2003; and how this was in turn, albeit for political reasons quiet latterly, followed by ECFA (Economic Cooperation

Framework Agreement) signed with the Taiwan authority in 2010, in the immediate aftermath of the global financial crisis. CEPA and ECFA have indeed helped to complete the thirty-year continuum of Greater China economic synergy, while together with ASEAN 10+1, the FTAs are all poised to encompass the other North APEC countries, namely, Japan and South Korea, by virtue of what may be considered as the spillover effect of "open regionalism". And in like vein, it seems that the inclusion of the American-Pacific countries—the United States and Canada, in particular—may be just a stone's throw away to complete the 1994 Bogor agenda for an overall trade and investment liberalization within APEC at large by 2020.

From a latitudinal perspective, the study discusses several major factors highly critical to the sequential metamorphoses as illustrated. The first is, of course, the sheer magnitude of the mainland China economy. This makes the virtually unilateral offer of CEPA for the HKSAR and ECFA for Taiwan extraordinarily effective as rescue packages from the painful economic doldrums associated with the 1997/1998 Asian financial crisis and the 2008/2009 global financial crisis respectively. In this way, China is also poised, alongside Japan, to be an "engine of growth" for South APEC by way of continuous expansion of trade and investment relations.

The second factor is China's accession to the World Trade Organization (WTO) in December 2001. This marks a significant watershed in the economic history of APEC and the world at large. ASEAN 10+1, CEPA, and ECFA as codified FTAs were all successively signed thereafter. The WTO accession has indeed greatly helped to unfold China's overwhelming comparative advantages and huge export capacity to Western markets, such as that of the US in particular. The upshot is a remarkably drastic regional restructuring of export supplies in the Asia Pacific in favour of China, as is rigorously verified by the electronics and IT industries in the third part of the study.

Another equally if not even more important factor relates to the United States and Japan, and for that matter, the European Union as well. Taken together, the highly industrialized trio—dubbed the Triad—carries absolutely unmatched economic weight to APEC proper, especially to China as an ascending economic giant. Setting aside EU, the US and Japan as APEC member states represent the single most important sources of technology transfer and advanced capital goods supplies, and at the same time, the largest export markets for foreign exchange earnings needed for financing the imports bills. Thus, as is consistently revealed throughout the three major parts of the study, trade and investment flows between China and the Triad, taken separately or as a whole, capture exactly the very gravity of economic integration within APEC proper. As a result, the South APEC economies all tended to be "marginalized", relative to the global trade of the rapidly expanding China.

Against this background, the ASEAN 10+1 FTA should perhaps be seen as a redress for the widening North-South APEC economic dichotomy. Ironically, however, the joint China-ASEAN initiative has lately (in 2010) met with an equally rigorous countervailing response from the American superpower but of a geopolitical nature, obviously for fear of ASEAN being eventually drawn into the Chinese sphere of influence. The irony is startling, given that it was precisely none other than the United States which engaged China in its global strategic interests against the Soviet hegemony in the early 1970s, and readily embraced the former arch-rival into its global economic axis. As a matter of fact, geopolitics persists amidst pervasive globalization and forceful economic integration within APEC.

Thus, it seems opportune to begin the study by featuring a geopolitical perspective. The Greater China nexus, for example, for promoting economic synergy without a bona fide political reunification under the tenor of "one country, two systems" may in itself be seen as a matter of geopolitical expediency. Needless to say, economic relations between China and Japan, and especially between China and the US have at times fallen prey to political manoeuvre across the Pacific. More than often, nevertheless, economic imperatives override politics to help enhance systemic industrial symbiosis, regionally and globally, as shown in the studies.

The book concludes with a summarized assessment of the quantitative significance of China rising as an economic giant, by referring to such increasingly popular perceptions as "G2" (juxtaposing China with the United States) to supercede the familiar G7 or G20 grouping, or a "Pax Sinica" replacing Pax Americana following the 2008/2009 global financial tsunami. The author argues that should it come to an era of "Pax Sinica", it would essentially be an economic-industrial phenomenon for the Asia Pacific or Asia at large, perhaps to be infused with some Confucius cultural traits, and hopefully not to the chagrin of any exclusive believers. But even such a scenario could not be easily sustained without being buttressed by the equally strong Japanese and American economies in the foreseeable future.

Acknowledgements

My gratitude is due to the following journals, publishers and research institutions for permission to use their materials: *The China Quarterly, The Pacific Review*, Oxford University Press, Hong Kong University Press, St. Martin's Press, The World Bank, United Nations University-Institute of Advanced Studies (Tokyo), International Development Research Center (Canada), University of Queensland (Brisbane, Australia), De La Salle University (Manila), Thailand Research Fund, and Asian Development Research Forum (Bangkok), among others, as noted in detail on the title page (bottom) of each chapter.

I am also grateful to Dr. Wong Shek-wah (黃石華), President of Cheong Man Wah (Wong King Sun) Foundation Ltd. (昌文華[黃金生]基金會) for a grant to support the indexing of the book, and to Professor Yao Dan of China Renmin University for suggesting the Chinese translation of the book title as “走向中華‘帝國’的昇平盛世：地緣政治經濟學視角”.

I must also thank Miss Isabel Xiaoyi Shen who, with her highly competent computer skills, graciously helped to convert several hard copies into rewritable versions for reworking, and proofread many chapters of the book.

Last but not least, I am most grateful to my wife, Hsiaohu, who has with great patience accompanied me through my academic life of research and teaching.

Y. Y. Kueh

Acknowledgements

Acronyms and Glossaries

The list comprises three parts: (1) Acronyms and glossaries, (2) Abbreviations (of documentary sources) common to most chapters, and (3) Abbreviations specific to Chapter 11.

Part 1: Acronyms and glossaries

ADB	Asian Development Bank
APEC	Asia Pacific Economic Cooperation (APEC) Forum, established in 1989
APEC at large*	APEC with all its member economies on both sides of the Pacific; or Full APEC
APEC proper*	APEC with the Asia-Pacific coast member economies only
ASEAN	Association of Southeast Asian Nations—an economic and geopolitical organization founded in 1967
ASEAN 5	The five founding countries of ASEAN: Thailand, Malaysia, the Philippines, Singapore and Indonesia (considered as the major 5)
ASEAN 10	ASEAN 5 plus the five newer member countries: Vietnam, Cambodia, Laos, Myanmar (Burma) and Brunei (considered as the minor 5)
ASEAN 10 + 1	ASEAN 10 plus China, with the latter originally serving as a 'dialogue partner', but a formal agreement for an ASEAN–China Free Trade Area (ACFTA), was eventually signed in 2002 and formally launched in 2010 between the ASEAN 10 and China

ASEAN 10 + 3	ASEAN 10 plus China, Japan and South Korea serving as 'dialogue partners', with a view to promoting further integration of the region, agreed upon in 1997
Bogor Declaration	APEC leaders declared the commitment at the Summit meeting held at Bogor (Indonesia) on 15 November 1994 that taking into account differing levels of economic development among APEC economies, the industrialized economies should achieve the goal of free and open trade and investment no later than the year 2010 and developing economies no later than the year 2020.
CEPA	Closer Economic Partnership Arrangement (Agreement between China and HKSAR, 2003)
Diaoyutai	Senkaku in Japanese; name of the island and adjacent islets off the East China Sea controversially claimed by both China and Japan
East Asia Summit	A forum held annually since 2005 in conjunction with the annual meeting of ASEAN Summit and ASEAN 10+3; other members include India, Australia, New Zealand; the United States and Russia first invited in 2011
ECFA	Economic Cooperation Framework Agreement (between China and Taiwan, 2011)
FDI	Foreign Direct Investment
Four Little Dragons	The four highly export-oriented economies: South Korea, Taiwan, Hong Kong and Singapore
FTA	Free Trade Area
FTAAP	Free Trade Area of the Asia Pacific—a long-term vision for APEC
G-0	'G-Zero', a term coined by Nouriel Roubini to refer to the lacking of global leadership for reigning in global affairs following the 2008/09 Global Financial Tsunami
G-2	'Group of 2', an informal term (attributable to Zbigniew Brzezinski and Fred Bergsten) referring to the emerging Sino-American cooperative partnership for dealing with significant global economic and political affairs

G-7	Group of 7, established in 1976 as an informal forum of seven major industrial economies: Canada, France, Germany, Italy, Japan, the United Kingdom and United States of America
G-20	Group of 20, set up in 1999 as a response to the 1997 Asian Financial Crisis and growing recognition that key emerging-market countries should also be embraced by the G-7 into the core of global economic discussion and governance
gaige kaifang	China's reform and opening-up strategy heralding the country's increased integration with the global economy
GMS	Greater Mekong Subregion cooperation programme established in 1992 with assistance from Asian Development Bank for promoting economic cooperation and development in the six riparian states of the Mekong River basin (Cambodia, Laos, Myanmar, Thailand, Vietnam and China as represented by its Yunnan Province and the Guangxi Zhuang Autonomous Region)
Greater China	An informal term referring to China plus HKSAR, Macao SAR, and the province of Taiwan, essentially a geo-economic complex
HKGSESB	Hong Kong Government Secretariat Economic Services Branch
HKGTD	Hong Kong Government Trade Department
HKMA	Hong Kong Monetary Authority
HKSAR	Special Administrative Region of Hong Kong
HKTDC	Hong Kong Trade Development Council
HSBC	Hong Kong and Shanghai Banking Corporation
IMF	International Monetary Fund
LMK Initiative	Lower Mekong Initiative (LMI), initiated by Secretary of State Hillary Clinton with the foreign Ministers of the four Lower Mekong Countries—Cambodia, Laos, Thailand and Vietnam at a meeting in Phuket in July 2009 for enhancing cooperation in the areas of environment (water management), health, education, and infrastructure evelopment

MOFTEC	Ministry of Foreign Trade and Economic Cooperation, China
NATO	North Atlantic Treaty Organization
North APEC*	APEC member economies located at both the Asia Pacific and American coasts including respectively China, HKSAR, Taiwan province, Japan, South Korea and the United States and Canada
North APEC proper*	North APEC member economies but excluding the United States and Canada
NPC	National Party Congress or National People's Congress (as appropriate)
RMB	The Chinese currency *renminbi*
SEATO	South East Asia Treaty Organization (The Asian version of NATO)
Shanghai Five	The 5-country grouping (China and the former four Soviet states: Russia, Kazakhstan, Kirghizia and Tajikistan) established in Shanghai, 1996, under the name Shanghai Cooperation Organization (SCO), Uzbekistan included in 2001
SOEs	State-Owned Enterprises
South APEC*	APEC member economies located south of HKSAR and Mexico
South APEC proper*	South APEC including ASEAN 10 plus Australia and New Zealand only
taoguang yanghui	A motto inked by Deng Xiaoping advocating literally for China to 'hide the light under the bushel' (*taoguang*), and to bide for the time (*yanghui*)
TCEPAD	Taiwan Council for Economic Planning and Development, Taiwan
TPP	Trans-Pacific Partnership, initially a FTA agreement signed among a few minor countries (Singapore, New Zealand, and Chile) in 1998 (Brunei joined in 2006); at the 2011 APEC Summit (held in Hawaii, 13-14 November), the United States initiated to negotiate with other interested APEC countries (Australia, Peru, Vietnam, and Malaysia) for a formal framework agreement to take effect from January 2012

TRIAD	USA, European Union and Japan combined, so dubbed for the Trio's overwhelming dominance as economic and trading powerhouse
UNCTAD	United Nations Conference on Trade and Development
USDC	Unites States Department of Commerce
USIS—Hong Kong	United States Information Services, Hong Kong
USTRO	United States Trade Representative Office
WB	The World Bank
WTO	World Trade Organization

**These are informal (unofficial) acronyms used in the book for ease of reference.*

Part 2: Abbreviations common to most chapters

ADB—*KIDAPC*	*Key Indicators of Developing Asian and Pacific Countries*
CQ	*The China Quarterly*
CSICSC	China Statistical Information and Consulting Center
CSICSC—*CLS*	*China's Latest Statistics*
CSICSC—*CMS*	*China's Monthly Statistics*
CTR	*China Trade Report*
FJDXM	*Fenjin de Xiamen* (Advancing Xiamen)(published by Xiamen Statistical Bureau)
FJSHTJZL	*Fujian Shehui Tongji Ziliao* (Fujian Social Statistics)
FJTJNJ	*Fujian Tongji Nianjian* (Fujian Provincial Statistical Yearbook)
GDTJNJ	*Guangdong Tongji Nianjian* (Guangdong Provincial Statistical Yearbook)
GDSGMJJHSHFZTJZL	*Guangdong Sheng Guominjingji He Shehui Fazhan Tongji Ziliao* (Guangdong Provincial Statistical Materials on National Economic and Social Development)

GZTJNJ	*Guangzhou Tongji Nianjian* (Guangzhou Municipality Statistical Yearbook)
HKG—*HKYB*	Hong Kong Government *Hong Kong Yearbook*
HKGCSD	Hong Kong Government Census and Statistics Department
HKGCSD—*ARHKET*	*Annual Review of Hong Kong External Trade*
HKGCSD—*AROT*	*Annual Review of Overseas Trade*
HKGCSD—*EGDP*	*Estimates of Gross Domestic Product*
HKGCSD—*HKADS*	*Hong Kong Annual Digest of Statistics*
HKGCSD—*HKMDS*	*Hong Kong Monthly Digest of Statistics*
HKGCSD—*QRHSLFC*	*Quarterly Report on Household Survey: Labour Force Characteristics*
HKTDC—*SHKDERETT*	*Survey on Hong Kong Domestic Exports, Re-exports and Triangular Trade*
HNTJNJ	*Hainan Tongji Nianjian* (Hainan Provincial Statistical Yearbook)
HSB—*HSEM*	*Hang Seng Economic Monthly* by Hang Seng Bank
IMF—*DTSYB*	*Direction of Trade Statistics Yearbook*
IMF—*IFSYB*	*International Financial Statistics Yearbook*
JJXXXB	*Jingjixue Xiaoxibao* (Economics Highlights Weekly), Beijing
JJYJ	*Jingji Yanjiu* (Economic Research Monthly) (published by Institute of Economics, The Chinese Academy of Social Science)
MOFTEC—*ACFERT*	*Almanac of China's Foreign Economic Relations and Trade*
QGGSZZLSTJZLHB	*Quanguo Gesheng Zizhiqu Zhixiashi Lishi Tongji Ziliao Huibian* (Compilation of Historical Statistics for Every Province, Autonomous Region and Directly-Administered Municipality in China)
QJZDGD	*Qianjinzhong De Guangdong* (Guangdong Advancing 1949–1988)
SCMP	*South China Morning Post*, Hong Kong
SHTJNJ	*Shanghai Tongji Nianjian* (Shanghai Statistical Yearbook)

SZSQIWUSQGMJJHSHTJZL	*Shenzhenshi Qiwu Shiqi Guomin Jingji He Shehui Tongji Ziliao* (National Economic and Social Statistical Materials for Shenzhen Municipality During the Seventh Five-Year Plan Period)
SZTJNJ	*Shenzhen Tongji Nianjian* (Shenzhen Statistical Yearbook)
SZTJSC	*Shenzhen Tongji Shouce* (Shenzhen Statistical Handbook)
TCEPAD—*TWSDB*	*Taiwan Statistical Data Book*
TKP	*Ta Kung Pao* (Impartial Daily), Hong Kong
TQJJ	*Tequ Jingji* (Special Zone Economy), Shenzhen
UN—*ITSYB*	United Nations *International Trade Statistics Yearbook*
UN—*SYBAP*	United Nations *Statistical Yearbook for Asia and the Pacific*
UNCTAD—*WIR*	United Nations Conference on Trade and Development *World Investment Report*
USDC—*SAUS*	US Department of Commerce *Statistical Abstract of the United States*
USTRO	United States Trade Representative Office
WB*WT*	*World Tables of the World Bank*
XINBAO	*Xinbao* (Hong Kong Economic Journal)
XMJJTQNJ	*Xiamen Jingji Tequ Nianjian* (Xiamen SEZ Yearbook)
ZGGDZCTZTJZL	*Zhongguo Guding Zichan Touzi Tongji Ziliao* (Statistical Materials on Fixed Assets Investment in China)
ZGSYWJTJZL	*Zhongguo Shangye Waijing Tongji Ziliao* (Statistical Materials Relating to China's Internal and External Trade)
ZGTJNJ	*Zhongguo Tongji Nianjian* (China Statistical Yearbook)
ZGTJZY	*Zhongguo Tongji Zhaiyao* (China Statistical Abstract)

Part 3: Abbreviations specific to Chapter 11

(Original titles all in Chinese, unless otherwise noted)

AMJRI	*Asia Monthly* (in English) (published by Japan Research Institute)
CAIYB	*China Automobile Industry Yearbook*, various years
CAMP	*China Automobile Market Prospects* (edited by China Information Centre and State Planning Commission, Office of Industrial Development, and published by China Machine Press, Beijing, 2003)
CCSYB	*China Custom Statistical Yearbook*, various years
CEIIAR	*China Electronics and Information Industry Annual Report*, published by the Ministry of Information Industry (Section on Economic System Reform and Operation), May 2002
CEITPERR	*China Electronics and Information Technology Products Exports—Research Report* (edited by Qu Weizhi and Li Zhiming, and published by Zhongguo Jingji Chubanshe, Beijing, 2001)
CEIYB	*China Electronics Industry Yearbook*, various years
CFETYB	*China Foreign Economic and Trade Yearbook*, various years
CHNTIDYB	*China High and New Technology Industry Development Yearbook*, 2002
CIDR	*China Industrial Development Report* (edited by Institute of Industrial Economics of the Chinese Academy of Social Science, and published by Beijing: Jingji Guanli Chubanshe), various years
CST	*China Securities Times* (Zhongguo Zhengjuan Bao)
CSYB	*China Statistical Yearbook*, various years
CSYBHTI	*China Statistical Yearbook on High Technology Industry 2002* (edited by National Bureau of Statistics, State Development Planning Commission, Ministry of Science and Technology, and State Economic and Trade Commission, and published by China Statistics Press, 2003)

ERMRI	*Economic Reports* (in English) (published by Marubeni Research Institute), Japan, October 2002 (available at www.marubenLco.jp/research/eindex/0210/body.html via www.google.com, accessed 31 January 2004)
ERT	*Economic Reference Times* (Jingji Cankaobao)
HSBC—CMR	*China Monthly Report* (in English) (published by Hong Kong and Shanghai Banking Corporation), Hong Kong, various issues
WTATLAS	*World Trade Atlas*, provided by Global Trade Information Service. Inc., and accessed via Business Infocentre of HKTDC

1
Introduction
Economic Imperatives versus Geopolitics

Geopolitical preamble to China's opening up

In a way, China's opening-up strategy started already as early as the launch of the "ping-pong diplomacy" in April 1971 and the following "whirlwind" visit to Beijing by Richard Nixon, President of the United States, in February 1972. Both events took place well ahead of the promulgation of the *gaige kaifang* (reform and opening up) strategy following the celebrated Third Plenum held in Beijing in December 1978 for the 11th National Party Congress. The "incidents", which then caught the world in great surprise, were undoubtedly initiated on the part of China as a response to the bloody military conflicts in 1969 with the former Soviet Union on the Zhenbao Island in Heilongjiang (or Amur River). Subsequent to the clashes, the former socialist superpower deployed massive ground forces to the Mongolian regions bordering China. For the Chinese leadership, the threat from the North was clearly much more immediate than from its arch-rival, the United States, which had subjected the entire coastal belt of China to long-term containment ever since the founding of the People's Republic in 1949, or at least, from the end of the Korean war in 1953. For the United States, however, wary of the unpredictable Moscow regime with its massive buildup of nuclear arsenals—especially since the Cuban Missile Crisis of 1962, the Chinese initiative for a rapprochement was clearly to be embraced as a windfall to help check the new and aggressive global power.

Upon returning from his secret visit to Beijing in July 1971 in preparation for Nixon's trip, Henry Kissinger, then Secretary of State, likened Premier Zhou Enlai—his counterpart negotiator while in Beijing—to the nineteenth century Austrian Chancellor, Clemens von Metternich, whose name is still often cited in standard political science textbooks for his master grip on power politics and regional balance of powers. Rightly, as Kissinger sees it, Premier

Zhou was fully confident about how to fit China—the weakest link—into the triangular global power constellation involving the two superpowers and the ancient oriental culture.

What almost immediately followed the 1972 Mao-Nixon encounter in Beijing is familiar: the emerging Sino-American political detente prompted China to quickly import, in a first ever attempt since 1949, a remarkable array of chemical fertilizer plants from the United States as early as 1973/1974. The about-face, ostensibly out of specific agricultural policy requirements, resembles in a way but falls far short of—in terms of quantitative scale of imports involved—the drastic trade reorientation towards Western Europe and Japan in 1962 following the abrupt withdrawal in 1960 of Soviet economic and technical aid to China. However, while the 1962 new policy plank of China was triggered by immediate economic imperatives rather than anything else, the modest venture of 1973/1974 signalled palpably a definitive and significant political gesture, which eventually led to the restoration of formal diplomatic relations between the two countries in 1978. This was to strongly help pave the way for accelerated bilateral trade growth and open up diverse and significant venues for China to rigorously expand trade with Europe, Japan and other countries, large and small, which were traditionally allied with the United States.

The rest is history. A brief revisit:

- China admitted as a member of both IMF (International Monetary Fund) and the World Bank in 1980, hardly a year into the *gaige kaifang* strategy;
- accelerated foray of FDI (foreign direct investment) accompanied increasingly by technology transfer into China from non-socialist countries since the early 1980s;
- fourteen major coastal cities declared open in April 1984 for foreign investment following the establishment earlier in 1979/1980 of the four Special Economic Zones (SEZs) in Guangdong and Fujian provinces, especially for export-oriented FDI from Hong Kong;
- first major reform blueprint announced by the Third Plenum (of the 12th National Party Congress) held in October 1984 for bifurcating Soviet-style central planning into a two-track (planned and market-oriented) resources allocation system, following the granting of expanded decision autonomy to state-owned enterprises (SOEs) in May;
- China applying for accession to WTO (World Trade Organization) in 1986, reflecting willingness of the country to be gradually subjected to the market-based rules of the Western system of free trade and investment flows;

- market-oriented reform experiments being further consolidated into the landmark resolution of the 13th NPC of October 1987 for "the state to regulate the market, and the market to guide the enterprises";
- in a single government decree given in early 1988, China's entire coastal belt covering eleven provinces from Liaoning in the north to Guangxi and Hainan in the south (comprising a total of 288 counties) designated for foreign investment and trade, in addition to the SEZs and the fourteen cities opened earlier;
- APEC coming into being in 1989, with China, Hong Kong and Taiwan all joining as member entities since 1991, bypassing the critical sovereignty issues;
- historic resolution by the 14th NPC held in October 1992 to formally establish a "socialist" market economic system, despite severe setback for the market-oriented reform following the June 4, 1989 incident;
- mandatory input and output targets for SOEs all abolished, immediately following the October 1992 resolution;
- concurrently, under Deng Xiaoping's 1992 strategic policy dictum of "[opening up domestic] market for technology exchange [from advanced Western countries]", remarkable intrusion of multinationals for import-substitution investment in China;
- China in the 1994 APEC meeting agreeing to the Bogor agenda to commit industrialized countries and developing economies to free and open trade and investment by 2010 and 2020 respectively;
- wide-ranging banking, fiscal, and foreign exchange reform conducted in 1994 to further realign China's institutions and policy measures with the global system, including the massive devaluation of the Chinese currency and the convergence of the two-track (officially fixed and market-regulated) exchange rates;
- consecutive price reforms rendered redundant both "import-regulatory taxes" and "export subsidies" (important culprits for US denial of China's accession to WTO), and helped to realign domestic prices with international price relatives towards the end of the 1990s;
- China finally resumed its WTO membership in December 2001, which has also helped to facilitate FTA (Free Trade Area) agreements with an increased number of countries, notably the ASEAN 10+1 agreement signed in 2002[1] and the China-New Zealand FTA of 2008;
- CEPA (Closer Economic Partnership Arrangement) Agreement signed with the HKSAR (Hong Kong Special Administrative Region) in 2003 and ECFA (Economic Cooperation Framework Agreement) with Taiwan in June 2010, bringing the Greater China triangle closer as an integrated economic entity; and
- ASEAN 10+1 FTA formally launched in 2010.

Imperatives for economic integration with the Triad

The grand strategic turnaround initiated by Chairman Mao and Zhou Enlai for a Sino-American political rapprochement and reconciliation from the 1970s belies indeed the compelling urgency for China to resort to the advanced industrialized economies of the West for import supplies in pursuit of her massive industrialization-cum-modernization programme. And it is clearly none other than this Mao-Zhou legacy that has given rise to the strategic, and much celebrated, motto of "*taoguang yanghui*" (韜光養晦) inked by Deng Xiaoping himself—the paramount post-Mao Chinese leader and architect of the opening-up strategy. Briefly, the motto advocates for the country to "keep a low profile (or literally, "hide the light under the bushel", i.e., *taoguang*), and conserve its strength and develop its potentialities (to bide for the time, i.e., *yanghui*)".

No doubt, Deng's motto has consistently and most coherently helped to shape the country's foreign policy in both spirit and practical approach, and in political as well as economic spheres, throughout the entire post-Mao era. Unfortunately, however, the classical Chinese overtones subtly inherent in the sagacious epigram of humbleness, self-restraint, and self-strengthening have more than often been simplistically construed as "buying time for a revenge". This has notably been the case with some influential Cold-War-minded US officials with half-baked knowledge of Chinese history and culture, who paid no regard to the aspirations of the Chinese leadership to a strengthening of national defence capabilities to hedge against another possible round of "imperialist plunder and humiliation", as occurring from the Opium War through to the Japanese invasion during the Second World War.[2]

Added to the American mindset of conventional "containment politics" is what has often been cited as the "insular mentality" of the Japanese. As Lee Kuan Yew, the founding father of the Singapore Republic once put it, Japan has been constantly fearful of Chinese vengeance; hence the fortified defence alliance with the United States with increased salvo over and across the East China Sea, which has lately, in 2010/2011, also strongly evoked resonance in the South China Sea from Vietnam and the Philippines.

Nonetheless, beyond the façade of at times shattering diplomacy, economic forces have remarkably and powerfully converged over the past two or three decades, in favour of an ever enhancing integration within APEC at large. For China, any practical schemes of national self-strengthening obviously cannot be enforced in defiance of Western technological supremacy, as during the Mao era. And evidently, it is also much more palatable for the country to shop for the necessary advanced technologies and capital goods from within the broader Western context of competitive market supplies than through dealing with the state trading monopolies of the former Soviet Union,[3] (the nightmarish experience of the early 1960s notwithstanding); or, after its collapse in 1991, with the disillusioned and disjointed Russian suppliers. China's import supplies from the United States, as well as from Japan and West Europe—the Triad taken together—have thus thrived profusely following the normalization of diplomatic relations with the US in 1978. At the same time, the United States and European Union, and latterly Japan since the early 2000s, have also become the overwhelming sources of foreign exchange earnings needed by the country for imports financing.

Thus, over the past three decades or so, China has become firmly knitted into the US economic fabric—especially by virtue of export linkages—more than anywhere else; save perhaps Hong Kong, which constitutes an integral part of the Greater China growth triangle. The backdrop to the metamorphosis is of course drastic decontrol of export-decision makings in China ever since the early 1980s, which helped to convert the provincial/local authorities and the producer enterprises themselves, instead of the state or the central authority, into the agents for maximizing foreign exchange earnings by resorting to the country's comparative advantages in labour-intensive manufacturing.

Since China's accession to WTO, however, there has also been a forceful trend for the country to increasingly relax import control to allow for imports other than those strictly destined for supporting the industrialization drive. In the aftermath of the 2008/2009 global financial crisis, the United States also seems prepared to relax, albeit marginally, control of "high-tech" exports to China. Perhaps this is an attempt on the part of the US government to redress the bilateral and international imbalances, in light of China's massive accumulation of trade surplus from bilateral trade with the United States; we do not know for sure. At any rate, it seems that one can anticipate the asymmetric export versus import relation between China and the United States (and indeed, the European Union as well), are poised to be increasingly mitigated as a result. It is hoped that this would allow for a silver lining to emerge from the horizon for a full economic integration between the two giant trading partners across the Pacific.

The strong Sino-American economic synergy has indeed not only helped to lend glamour to the rising China, but it has also been brought to bear on the relative fortune of many other economies of APEC proper. This particular aspect of dynamism in APEC economic integration represents an integral thread of the study, and resurfaces across virtually all the chapters of this volume.

Equally notably, however, the far-flung regional geo-economic power realignment within APEC has also caused, ipso facto, conflicting territorial claims among a number of APEC member countries in a competitive scramble for the increasingly scarce natural resources. The disputes over the *Diaoyutai*, as well as the *Xisha* (Paracel) and *Dongsha* (Spratly) *Qundao* (Islands) should obviously be viewed in this context as attempts made to edge out some compensatory grants from each other. Nonetheless, given that the highly enhanced economic synergistic relations among the various APEC stakeholders have now been firmly welded to be the hardest core of realpolitik, regional geopolitical controversies and frictions, alarming as they may sound at times, have usually turned out to be "storm in a tea cup", as is highlighted in the concluding chapter. A good case in point is the explosive wrangle initiated in July 2011 by Vietnam and the Philippines against China over the South China Sea issues. No sooner had the ASEAN 10+1 Foreign Ministers' Conference been convened in the Bali island of Indonesia than the dust from the wrangle had already basically settled.

Politics of the Greater China growth triangle

The Greater China circle as an economic phenomenon is also bound up with geopolitics. For Hong Kong, the handover to China in 1997 was clearly obliged by the rising sovereign power. But notably, the decision to grant the HKSAR the status quo of what the British were to largely leave behind under the rubric of "one country, two systems" had actually already been hammered out in the early 1980s, i.e., closely following the launch of the national opening-up strategy. That is to say, the Chinese approach to reclaiming the former British colony—by granting the HKSAR virtually full autonomy, save the sovereign's prerogative on the city's diplomatic and consular affairs—should essentially be seen as a matter of economic expediency. This is by any standard of world history and politics a truly unique episode. But before highlighting the underpinning economic rationale (for details see Chapter 5), the story of a "non-comparable" Taiwan should be briefly referred to.

It goes without saying that it is not in China's interest at all to pursue any military confrontation over the breakaway island—dubbed the "unsinkable aircraft carrier"—against the United States, or Japan in alliance, which the United Kingdom as an "Empire of the (Declining) Sun" is evidently no peer to, relative to Hong Kong—her formal tiny colonial enclave. Nonetheless, in defiance of the uneasy geopolitical equilibrium, but in compliance with the *taoguang yanghui* strategy, China's trade and investment flows have continued to flourish not only with the two mighty industrial-cum-military powers, the US and Japan, but most remarkably, also across the Taiwan Straits for more than two decades now.

The economics of the Greater China growth triangle is familiar: at the initial stage of China's opening up, the bulk of the country's export and import trade—with the US, in particular—was obligingly routed through Hong Kong to take advantage of the well-established harbour facilities and the highly experienced global marketing and sourcing expertise offered by the then still British-held enclave. At the same time, Hong Kong's export manufacturers scrambled to relocate their factories across the border to cash in the offer of cheap labour and land rentals, triggering an endless chain of foreign direct investment (FDI) in the Chinese mainland. Similar export-oriented Taiwanese investors quickly joined the spree commencing in 1987, perhaps not so much as a result of relaxed political control on the island vis-à-vis the Chinese mainland; but rather, being prompted by the increasingly lucrative opportunities available over there. By 1997 when Hong Kong was handed over to Chinese sovereignty, the Greater China growth triangle was already exhibiting all the hallmarks of a fully integrated economic entity, especially with respect to Hong Kong, through which Taiwan's trade with and investment in the Mainland were normally routed, as is elaborated in great detail in Chapters 2 to 4; and in Chapter 5 as well, which more specifically dwells on the crucial importance of the US connection in this regard.

As a matter of fact, upon the onset in July 1997 of the Asian financial crisis, which exactly coincided with the founding of the HKSAR, the growth triangle had already firmly turned out to be an "alliance in defence", with mainland China serving as a strong bulwark, by virtue of the sustainable stability and inconvertibility of renminbi, to help shield off and mitigate vulnerability from outside. Chapters 6 through 8 discuss how this bore upon both the HKSAR and Taiwan to varying degrees. Chapter 9 offers an analysis of how the "China factor" stood in relation to Hong Kong's well-established US dollar-linked exchange rate system (adopted since 1983) to bail out the SAR amidst the prolonged crisis. And with CEPA signed in 2003—which was closely followed for the next six years by consecutive supplementary agreements with virtually unilateral offers from the motherland of free access of goods and services to the hinterland—Hong Kong is now no doubt fully woven into the national economic fabric. And with ECFA now in place, Taiwan is clearly also poised to follow suit.

As I previously put in a Chinese treatise published in 2000, there should be a day when with high economic prosperity reigning on the Mainland and the income and living standards across the Taiwan Straits basically equalizing, let alone the island, even the neighbouring Mongolia might be motivated to vie for "statehood" in the People's Republic, like the remote Kingdom of Hawaii to the United States of America just some fifty years ago.[4] The long-awaited ECFA, which was essentially initiated by the Taiwan authority and signed in June 2010 with the Mainland for fear of the island being marginalized in the wake of the launching of the ASEAN 10+1 FTA in 2010, implies just such a move towards that direction, similar to Hong Kong's irreversible economic integration with the Chinese hinterland consequent upon the signing of CEPA nearly ten years ago.

Accelerated industrial agglomeration within North APEC proper

Given the peculiar political relationship between China and North Korea, the establishment of diplomatic relations between China and South Korea in 1992 was at the time certainly not less sensational compared to the signing of ECFA in 2010 between the two arch-rivals across the Taiwan Straits. In hindsight, however, the geopolitical breakthrough seems to have also been equally strongly grounded in economic diktat. Thus, South Korea's investment in, and bilateral trade with China started to abruptly accelerate from practically a zero base since 1992, in an attempt to emulate the frontrunner, Japan, for cashing in the huge market potentials offered across the Yellow Sea. Chapter 10 provides the necessary historical backdrop for appreciating the forceful trends of development from the broader APEC perspective.

As alluded to, Japan as a North APEC neighbour has long been a crucial trading partner, supplying China with the bulk of producer goods and necessary technologies ever since 1962. Especially since China's WTO accession in 2001, Japan has also been a major FDI provider through manufacturing in China, predominantly but not limited to electronic and information technology products for import substitution, and as well for exporting overseas, with a remarkable proportion to the Japanese domestic market itself.

Japan and South Korea, are each by virtue of their absolute GDP size, or relative to China's global trade volume, much more closely tied in with the Chinese economy than with South APEC proper comprising the ASEAN nations plus Australia and New Zealand. Interestingly, a substantial amount of Japan's exports to China—notably machinery and transport equipment, and such industrial raw materials as PVC (polyvinyl chloride)—has also been channeled through Hong Kong in conjunction with the SAR's relocation of export manufacturing plants to the Chinese hinterland since the early 1980s. This has indeed strongly helped to enhance the modus operandi of the Greater China growth triangle.

While through the 1990s, Japan had normally enjoyed surplus in trading with China, after WTO accession, however, China overtook the United States to become Japan's largest importer by 2002, as well as its largest export destination by 2009. The bilateral trade balance has consistently reversed to be in China's favour since around the advent of the new century. Presently, China still takes up one-fifth of Japan's total exports of iron and steel, and a quarter of its semiconductors destined to the global market, in exchange for clothing and apparel from China which makes up more than 80 percent of total Japanese imports for the category. And perhaps more remarkably, more than 10 percent of Japan's semiconductor imports are now from China, quickly closing in on the comparable figures for such electronics giants as South Korea (15%) and the United States (17%), although still falling well behind Taiwan's share (nearly 30%).[5] This all seems to signal intensifying intra-industrial trade typical among industrialized/industrializing countries, as opposed to the conventional north-south (i.e., industrialized versus less-developed countries) type of exchanges.

Moreover, since China's WTO accession, Japan's FDI foray into the country by the giant car manufacturers has also started to gain momentum. This is discussed at length in Chapter 11, and it should inevitably result in a wide-ranging reshuffle of the APEC proper production network for the automobile industry, likely at the expense of a couple of ASEAN countries, Thailand in particular. The latter has hitherto enjoyed the single largest regional concentration of foreign carmakers, including virtually all Japanese giants and a number of familiar American and European brand names.

Viewed together with the Greater China growth triangle, North APEC proper as a whole has thus become rather a closely agglomerated economic entity, standing in sharp contrast to South APEC proper. And it has indeed also proved to be quite a resilient structure, defying time and again serious geopolitical clashes over the years—the persistent nuclear crisis with the prodigal North Korea notwithstanding, as is revealed in the concluding chapter of the study.

Can ASEAN 10+1 FTA really help to redress the asymmetry?

As a result of the heightened South China Sea disputes, ASEAN, which may trace its origin to SEATO (South East Asian Treaty Organization) (1954–1977)—the Asian version of NATO (North Atlantic Treaty Organization)—appears to be increasingly inclined to resurrecting the founding aspiration of its predecessor to be a regional defence mechanism vis-à-vis the rising giant neighbour to the north. But apart from Vietnam and the Philippines, the other major stakeholders, notably Indonesia and Thailand, seem reluctant to confront China directly; noting also that the combined population of the two latter member states is nearly double that of the two former ones, which taken together, constitute less than one-third of the ASEAN total, and only 16 percent in terms of GDP share. More importantly, unlike SEATO in the 1950s and 1960s, ASEAN as a collective does not nowadays perceive China as a common enemy, as the US-inspired SEATO did in its staunch opposition to East Asian Communism, then encompassing both China and Vietnam. Thus, realpolitik eventually prevailed over what initially appeared to be an unavoidable military conflict in the latest (July 2011) row between China, Vietnam and the Philippines, as mentioned earlier.

In this context, more should be said to bring to light what is referred to as the economic core of the realpolitik within APEC proper.

First of all, ASEAN, as established in 1967, purports to help accelerate regional economic growth in peaceful cooperation. It failed remarkably, however, in its initial policy thrust of promoting "agreed specialization". As one prominent Swedish economist put it, "[the] attempts at 'agreed specialization' have [like all inward-looking integration] created centrifugal forces due to an unwillingness to assume the cost of trade diversion".[6] In other words, similar to factor endowments, ASEAN countries used to be commonly engaged in competitive exports to the industrialized West of such primary commodities as timber, rubber, palm oil and the likes at the pre-industrializing stage; and it had indeed proved to be difficult for the different sovereign member states to agree on any meaningful intraregional industrial specialization, without compromising each other's priorities of industrialization. Nonetheless, no sooner had they turned to emulate the four little dragons in promoting labour-intensive export manufacturing commencing in the early and mid-1970s than the attempts were closely followed by similar but massive competitive efforts made by China in conjunction with the opening-up strategy.

The upshot is, by the mid-1990s, and especially since accession to WTO in December 2001, China is clearly in a position to "crowd out" the global market shares of ASEAN exporters, as is shown in Chapters 10 through 12. Chapter 11, in particular, illustrates at length in what way enhanced accessibility for China to the US market has triggered a drastic realignment of the APEC proper production network. Thus, from 1995 to 2004, virtually for every single item of electronics and IT exports to the US (notably computers, display units, electric and video apparatuses, TV cameras, and increasingly, coloured TV sets), China had strongly outperformed both North and South APEC proper counterparts in terms of market share as well as "revealed comparative advantage" (RCA) index. The only notable exception relates to the integrated circuit—dubbed the "foodgrain" of the electronics industry—for which Korea, Taiwan, Malaysia and, to a lesser extent, Singapore, could still manage to keep a foothold in the vast US import market. But the question is for how long can this possibly be sustained, given that China's semiconductor manufacturing technology is seen by American authority itself as rapidly closing in on that of the United States.[7]

Similar developments may be observed with respect to the car manufacturing industry, also discussed in Chapter 11. Consecutive import tariff reductions following China's admission to WTO not only has prompted remarkable influx of foreign-made sedans, but with enhanced intellectual property rights protection under the WTO framework, virtually all major global brands, notably Volkswagen, General Motors, Audi, and Renault, have since rigorously continued to invest in capacity expansion in China to take advantage of the huge domestic markets. The investment spree has in turn been strongly enhanced by similar Japanese ventures, and is bound to cause displacement or restructuring (e.g., towards components production or assembling) among the established American, European, and Japanese stakeholders in such major ASEAN countries as Thailand and Indonesia.

In hindsight,[8] the ASEAN 10+1 FTA agreement (signed in November 2002, hardly a year after China's accession to WTO in December 2001), should perhaps be seen as a tacit Chinese initiative of a geopolitical nature, purporting to help the South APEC proper neighbours hedge against a "relative marginalization" of their economic standing within the broader APEC context. More specifically, it compensates ASEAN member countries for prospective losses in both FDI intake and export earnings, absolute or relative, incurred or to be expected, as a result of the ever strengthening position of China emerging as a global FDI destination and a highly competitive exporting country.[9]

As a matter of fact, China, being wary for decades of US containment to the East China coast, should have the least interest to see South APEC proper play herself as the "troublesome" South American "backyard" to the United States. It was probably under the same strategic aspiration that when ASEAN countries were seriously drawn into the 1997/1998 Asian financial crisis, China had, amidst the mounting pressures, made the critical decision not to devalue the renminbi, thus forestalling a potentially disastrous round of competitive devaluation of the falling ASEAN currencies. The incident, then globally hailed, may have been buried in oblivion in Vietnam, which was admitted as a new member state just shortly prior to the eruption of the crisis; but it should nonetheless still remain fresh in the memory of the leaders of major ASEAN countries.

In Chapter 12, I discuss how, subsequent to the signing of the ASEAN 10+1 FTA agreement in 2002 for formal launch in 2010, the ASEAN 10 as a trading bloc still largely managed to maintain its share in China's global trade over the past decade or so, thanks to the Early Harvest Programme which took effect from 2004. Hopefully the relative share may be sustained, or expanded, now that the ASEAN 10+1 FTA is firmly in place. Whatever the prospect may be in this respect, the South APEC proper regional conglomeration seems bound just to be ever more tightly embedded into the Chinese economy. There really is no reason why ASEAN should not be highly motivated to aspire for such an economic integration: starting as early as the late 1980s, Australia, as well as the "ANZAC clique"—i.e., the strongest US allies in Asia—had already unequivocally advocated for the country to "look East" and to "identify with

Asia", much to the chagrin of a dwindling number of residents traditionally heeding the British Crown.

No doubt, the high-profile industrial agglomeration within North APEC proper tends to make its southern counterpart pale in comparison. Nevertheless, since the signatory economies to both CEPA and ECFA were in a way prompted by ASEAN 10+1, as discussed in Chapter 12, to board the bandwagon of trade and investment liberalization, there seems to be no reason why ASEAN 10 would not now in turn seek to further take advantage of the enormous agglomeration economies spilling over from the north, in terms of investment flows from China and Japan being the "engines of growth" as well as the huge potentials of China, as destinations for exports. This is especially so in the view that, in the wake of the global financial crisis, the US and European Union markets have become increasingly vulnerable for all concerned.

This particular hard economic core of North-South APEC proper synergy will in all likelihood strongly help to shape the realpolitik in the Asia Pacific in many years to come, despite the vehement American rhetoric—lately per Secretary of State, Hillary Clinton in summer 2010—for resurrecting/reasserting US geopolitical interests in the region, for "fear" of China emerging as a global economic-political giant. This will be discussed in the concluding Chapter 13.

Concluding remarks: Economic imperatives prevailing over geopolitics

The various chapters of this volume were conceived and written basically in tandem with the development of the affairs involved. They were therefore all "current" at the time of writing. However, the focus was then all essentially on the economic aspects of regional cooperation and integration within the APEC system. The geopolitics of the economic dynamism was hardly made explicit, although it may have not entirely escaped the subtle mind. In retrospect, it seems desirable to bring to light the complexities involved in this respect. This introductory chapter attempts therefore to unravel with broad sweep the delicate interplay between economics and geopolitics during the process of regional economic integration or synergy, or the lack thereof. And as such, it helps to provide a coherent geopolitical perspective for reading through the different chapters of the volume.

With the benefit of hindsight, however, it seems also clear that, generally speaking, economic imperatives often, if not always, prevail over geopolitics in shaping the pattern and intensity of regional integration among APEC economies. Ignoring CEPA which the HKSAR readily embraces as a beneficiary option taker, ECFA for Taiwan, e.g., is a clear case in point. Fearful of being pushed to the very periphery of the APEC system, the breakaway island was finally compelled to initiate and sign the venture agreement in 2010, despite deep-rooted favouritism towards the United States, which has provided the government with a highly secure protective umbrella in all respects, political and economic, and foremost military, over the past six decades or so.

The abrupt rapprochement between South Korea and China in 1992 appears extremely bizarre, given the familiar oddity of the triangular relationship between China and the two Koreas. However, the highly accelerated growth in trade and investment flows between the two once rival countries, following the establishment of diplomatic relations, has just strongly helped to vindicate the equally compulsive economic rationale underpinning the rapprochement. In fact, circumstantial evidences emerging recently seem to suggest that North Korea would also be motivated to interact with APEC before long. Most importantly, never really have the ever growing Sino-Japanese economic and trade relations been disrupted to any noticeable extent by the highly sensitive *Diaoyutai* issue, which has at times threatened to bring the two countries to the brink of war.

With the pace of industrialization accelerating in China, the country is set to follow Japan in its footsteps as an engine of growth for South APEC proper. In this context, ASEAN 10+1 FTA represents indeed a porous media for bilateral investment and trade flows, which would only be enhanced by China's parallel geopolitical interest in the South Pacific. More than likely, the joint military rehearsals frequently conducted by the mighty US naval with some interested parties in the East and Southeast Asian littoral in 2010/2011, will, as usual, prove to be another round of mere fanfare for the APEC proper countries, north and south.

2

The Emergence of the Greater China Economic Circle*

Economic integration is essentially a process of unification—the means whereby coherence is imposed upon previously separate, even disparate, geographical regions. It may be pursued as a domestic or international goal, although the simultaneous attainment of both may prove elusive. Recent efforts towards the creation of formal transnational, regional economic identities, whether North American (NAFTA), European (EC) or Asian-Pacific (APEC), have sometimes been perceived as a threat to the establishment of a truly integrated global economy. By contrast, the remarkable degree of economic integration already achieved between southern China and Hong Kong (and, latterly, Taiwan) might ironically have a fissiparous effect on China's domestic economy. From this point of view, there is a danger that increasing economic integration within Greater China[1] could threaten China's national economic identity, or at least compel its redefinition.

Cultural and linguistic affinities have no doubt helped to facilitate the economic integration of China, Hong Kong and Taiwan. But international trade and foreign investment have been its most potent stimuli. The rapid development of trade has generated familiar static and dynamic gains, which have enhanced economic growth within the region. These have been complemented, especially for China, by the benefits of rapidly expanding foreign investment. Overcoming their technological backwardness is a cornerstone of developing countries' growth strategies, and it is no coincidence that the Chinese government has increasingly used foreign investment to encourage

---

* Reprinted with minor adaptation from "Economic integration within Greater China: Trade and investment flows between Hong Kong, Mainland China and Taiwan" (coauthored with Robert Ash), *The China Quarterly* (*CQ*), No. 136 (December 1993), pp. 711–45.

productivity-enhancing technical progress. After all, inflows of capital promise to obviate resource bottlenecks, especially capital shortages and skill deficiencies. China's willingness to accept such overseas participation, including foreign direct investment (FDI), in its domestic economic development is a measure of the real significance of its post-1978 open-door strategy.

The different resource endowments and levels of development of China, Hong Kong and Taiwan suggest how all stand to benefit from greater economic integration. Economic growth in Hong Kong and Taiwan has derived overwhelmingly from trade-orientated strategies, characterized by a decline in the export shares of resource-based goods in favour of those of labour-and (later) capital-intensive products. Such developments have been accompanied by worsening shortages of land and labour, which have generated upward pressure on rents and wages.

In China too, the export sector, originally dominated by resource-based goods, has shifted towards the production of labour-intensive commodities. But land and labour remain plentiful, and their accessibility has made the extension of Hong Kong and Taiwanese industrial facilities to the Chinese mainland an increasingly attractive proposition. For China, short of capital and technologically immature, such a relationship promises enormous benefits. This complementarity has generated an economic symbiosis between the constituent elements of Greater China.

Through their effects on resource allocation and their stimulus to technology transfer, the expansion of merchandise trade and investment has had a profound impact on the economies of Hong Kong, Taiwan and southern China. The same forces have generated new employment and production opportunities. They have also been the source of important structural changes, associated with the reallocation of resources. Above all, they have caused accelerated economic growth, in recent times unmatched almost anywhere else in the world.

These considerations define the main themes of this article. We seek to assess, through an examination of the pattern and level of trade and investment flows, the extent to which Greater China has become economically integrated. Another concern of ours is to analyse some of the economic implications of this process. For reasons of convenience, trade and investment are treated separately. The reality is of course more complicated and less cut and dried. Each component encourages and facilitates the other, and it is the combined effects of both which make their stimulus to economic growth so powerful.

Merchandise trade with greater China

Trends and patterns of exports and imports

The rapid expansion of China's foreign trade after 1978 is one of the most remarkable features of the impact of the reform programme (in this case, the open-door strategy). Between 1978 and 1991, China's merchandise trade grew, on average, by over 14% per annum—almost twice as fast as global trade, marginally faster than Taiwan's, but a little more slowly than that of Hong Kong.[2] The outcome was that all three regions dramatically increased their share of global trade during this period: China and Taiwan by almost 100% each, and Hong Kong by almost 200%. Imports and exports contributed about equally to Hong Kong's trade expansion, whereas the increasing contribution of China and Taiwan to world trade owed more to export expansion than to import growth.[3]

The historical context of the most recent (post-1978) expansion in Hong Kong's trade with China has been reviewed elsewhere[4] and will not receive detailed consideration here. Suffice it to say that between 1949 and the end of the 1970s, China's share of Hong Kong exports fell to a negligible level, although the latter's role as an major importer of Chinese goods remained significant. It is worth recording that by the beginning of the 1970s, Hong Kong's role as a channel for the re-export of Chinese goods had become insignificant.[5] In 1970, for example, the value of retained imports of Chinese products was 13 times higher than in the 1930s, whilst that of re-exported commodities was only 57% more.[6] A striking feature of developments during the 1980s was a reversal of this position to one approximating that of the prewar years.

Table 2.1 contains estimates of the average annual rate of growth of bilateral trade flows between 1980 and 1991. They highlight the process whereby Hong Kong and China have each become the other's most important trading partner.

Analysis of the data from which these estimates are derived suggests the critical contribution which China has made to Hong Kong's overall trade performance. For example, in 1978, exports[7] to China accounted for less than 1% of Hong Kong's total exports. By 1983, the corresponding figure was 11.45%, and by 1985 it had risen to 26.03%. Thereafter, after a temporary decline, it remained (on average) in excess of 26%. Without access to the Chinese market, Hong Kong's export growth in the 1980s would have been significantly slower,[8] although it would also have displayed a more sharply accelerating trend during the second half of the 1980s.

The symbiosis which has come to characterize the economic relationship between China and Hong Kong is highlighted in the British colony's role as a redistribution channel for goods passing through the territory.

Domestic exports and re-exports from Hong Kong to China grew strongly, but in tandem throughout the period. By contrast, the global picture reveals slower export growth, but a differential performance in favour of re-exports. The share of re-exports in Hong Kong's total shipments to China remained stable at around 75% throughout the 1980s, while the corresponding figure for countries other than China rose steadily from 30% to 70%.[9]

Hong Kong's import profile shows that the growth of imports from China consistently outstripped that from the rest of the world.[10] Moreover, in contrast to the pattern of export growth, the expansion of imports—already strong during the first half of the 1980s—accelerated quite sharply after 1985. The increasing share of imports from China subsequently re-exported from Hong Kong is particularly striking. Between 1980 and 1985, this rose from 31% to 47%; by 1991, it had reached an astonishing 86%.[11] The true measure of this transformation is indicated by the changing ratio between re-exports of imports from China and from elsewhere: in 1978 it was 0.35: 1.00, but by 1990 it had been reversed to 1.26: 1.00.[12] Meanwhile, not only has the share of Chinese imports retained in Hong Kong declined, but—since 1988—the absolute level of such shipments has also fallen.[13]

The growing importance of Hong Kong as a channel for the redistribution of goods originating from, or destined for, China is the single most significant finding to emerge from Table 2.1. This fact, perhaps more than anything else, highlights the integration of the region into the southern Chinese economy.[14]

Table 2.1 The Expansion of Trade between Hong Kong and China, 1980–1991 (Average annual growth rate in %)

	HK exports to China			**HK imports from China**		
	Total	**Domestic**	**Re-exports**	**Total**	**Retained**	**Re-exports**
1980–91	31.86	32.03	31.79	23.57	8.96	32.98
1980–85	45.65	44.95	45.88	19.76	14.38	28.34
1985–91	20.36	21.26	20.06	26.74	4.44	36.83

Sources: HKGCSD–*HKMDS*, various issues.

Between 1978 and 1983, Hong Kong's trade deficit vis-à-vis China increased from US$10.25 to US$24.42 million.[15] A sharp but temporary reversal took place in 1984 and 1985 (the only post-1978 year in which Hong Kong enjoyed a bilateral surplus), but thereafter, the deficit reasserted itself and steadily increased to reach US$85.63 million in 1991. During the same period, Hong Kong consistently enjoyed a surplus in its trade with the rest of the world.[16] This was not always sufficient to offset the bilateral deficit, the net result being that Hong Kong's global trade balance was sometimes in surplus, sometimes in deficit, without any clear pattern emerging.

Trade relations between Taiwan and the Chinese mainland were historically very close,[17] and at the beginning of the 1930s, during the Japanese occupation of the island, its trade with the mainland accounted for half or more of total trade with countries other than Japan.[18] Such relations were interrupted after the removal of the Kuomintang government to Taiwan in 1949 and only officially resumed some three decades later. But as the estimates in Table 2.2 suggest, two-way trade subsequently expanded rapidly.[19]

The estimates leave no room for doubt about the dramatic nature of trade expansion across the Taiwan Straits during the 1980s and into the 90s. At first it was subject to considerable instability, mainly because of strong annual fluctuations in Taiwanese exports to the mainland (only in 1985 did shipments in the opposite direction fail to record positive growth). Major increases between 1979 and 1981 gave way to absolute declines in 1982 and 1983, and recovery

Table 2.2 Changing Trends in Trade between Taiwan and the Chinese Mainland: Indirect Trade through Hong Kong, 1980–1991

	Taiwan exports			Taiwan imports		
	Annual growth rate of global exports (%)	**Annual growth rate of exports to PRC (%)**	**Exports to PRC as % global exports**	**Annual growth rate of global imports (%)**	**Annual growth rate of imports from PRC (%)**	**Imports from PRC as % global imports**
1980–91	12.25	26.90	3.41	10.55	24.22	0.99
1980–85	8.78	28.08	1.61	0.36	7.79	0.48
1985–91	15.14	25.92	4.09	19.04	37.92	1.17

Sources: HKGCSD–*HKMDS*, various issues; and IMF–*IFSYB* 1992, pp. 111 and 113.

during 1984 and 1985 was again halted in 1986. In short, only since 1987 has relatively stable growth become apparent.

Until mid-1981, a no-tariff policy was a major incentive to Taiwan exporters to the PRC. But it also encouraged market saturation by inviting others to disguise their products as being of Taiwanese origin. The subsequent abandonment of preferential treatment and imposition of stricter controls were the factors behind the negative growth of Taiwanese exports in 1982 and 1983. Recovery was, however, rapid and only momentarily interrupted in 1986, when import restrictions were introduced in an effort to halt the sharp decline in China's foreign exchange reserves.

For the post-1980 period as a whole, the average annual rate of growth of Taiwanese imports from the Chinese mainland almost matched that of exports to the PRC. However, legal restraints on such imports, especially during the early 1980s, were responsible for the much slower rate of expansion during the first half of the decade.

Table 2.2 also quantifies the increasing involvement of Taiwan and the PRC in each other's overall trade after 1980. At the start of the decade, mainland exports accounted for 1.22% of Taiwan's global exports, the corresponding figure for imports being less than 0.5%. By 1991 these figures had risen to 6.13 and 1.6% respectively.[20] From the mainland's perspective, Taiwan's share in total exports rose more modestly from 0.43% to 1.57% during 1980–91.

The indirect nature of trade between Taiwan and the PRC highlights the paramount role which Hong Kong has played in the evolution of bilateral trade relations. That it will continue to do this is suggested by the finding that, in 1992, almost 49% of shipments from Taiwan to Hong Kong were destined for the Chinese mainland, and 29.5% of goods exported to Taiwan from Hong Kong originated in the PRC.[21]

Since 1980, Taiwan has maintained a favourable balance in its indirect trade with the PRC, the second half of the decade witnessing a consistent increase in its surplus. Indeed, between 1985 and 1991, Taiwan's cross-Straits surplus rose from 8% to 27% of its global surplus.[22] Such estimates are one measure of the extent to which Taiwan's remarkable record in accumulating foreign exchange reserves has increasingly become linked to the expansion of trade with its neighbour.[23]

Measuring the intensity of trade within Greater China

Estimates of the trade intensity ratio (TIR) between two countries provide a formal measure of the changing strength of their trade relationship—the extent to which each is becoming more (or less) dependent upon the other.[24] A value of TIR greater than unity is significant in the sense that the share of country A's exports to country B in the former's export portfolio is higher than B's import share as a proportion of aggregated global imports. The larger the value of TIR, the stronger the trade links between any two countries.

Table 2.3 sets out TIR estimates in selected years for China, Hong Kong and Taiwan in the twin contexts of Sino-Hong Kong and Sino-Taiwanese merchandise trade. The figures highlight some of the implications of China's implementation of the open-door strategy after 1978. They suggest that from a Chinese export perspective, trade with Hong Kong has remained "significant",[25] albeit—especially in the early reform years—at a declining rate. From the Hong Kong perspective, the open-door policy had a marked impact, with the TIR rising sharply up to the mid-1980s and then stabilizing somewhat.

If, however, re-exports of Chinese goods are excluded, the calculations show China's TIR to have fallen more sharply and consistently.[26] This would seem to suggest that an increasingly small proportion of exports to Hong Kong was retained in the territory. The results of similar calculations based on Hong Kong as the exporting region are much more closely in line with those in Table

Table 2.3 TIR Estimates: China, Hong Kong and Taiwan, 1978–1991

	China—Hong Kong		**China—Taiwan**	
	With China as exporter	**With Hong Kong as exporter**	**With China as exporter**	**With Taiwan as exporter**
1978	24.43	0.62	0.53	0.0005
1980	20.92	6.23	0.43	1.20
1985	16.62	11.41	0.39	1.41
1989	17.68	13.21	0.64	2.24
1990	–	–	0.78	3.20
1991	–	–	0.90	3.48

Sources: HKGCSD–*HKMDS*, various issues; IMF–*IFSYB* 1992, pp. 111 and 113; and UN–*SYBAP* 1991, pp. 85 and 127–8.

2.3, and indicate an increasingly important role for the territory as both the direct and indirect supplier of goods to China after 1978.[27]

In the wake of the open-door strategy, China's trade ties with Taiwan rapidly assumed significance. But it is noteworthy that this process was driven more by the expansion of exports from Taiwan than from the PRC. With China (PRC) as the exporting country, the value of TIR has not yet reached unity, although if recent trends are maintained, attainment of this level cannot be long delayed.[28]

The changing composition of merchandise trade

The export experiences of countries in northeast Asia, including the constituent regions of Greater China, reveal a common pattern. In the early stages of economic development, exports derive largely from natural resource-based products. Only later is there an increasing role for labour-intensive manufactured goods—and ultimately for capital-intensive, high-technology commodities.[29]

The decline in the share of Chinese exports retained in Hong Kong is reflected in the changing structure of bilateral trade. One contributory factor has been the fall in food exports from the mainland, consequent upon rising per capita income.[30] More generally, Hong Kong consumers' perception of Chinese goods as cheap, but inferior in quality and design, has encouraged demand to shift towards other overseas sources of goods (especially manufactures).[31] Meanwhile, the share of re-exported Chinese goods has been rising. Between 1979 and 1987, for example, the ratios of retained to re-exported Chinese crude materials, chemicals and manufactures were reversed in favour of re-exports.[32]

Hong Kong's role as a direct supplier of goods to China has expanded markedly since 1978. The fact that domestic exports of producer goods (especially machinery and transport equipment) have outstripped those of consumer goods makes Hong Kong's trade with China unique, and reflects the increasingly important role of Hong Kong-based industrial operations on the Chinese mainland.[33] Thus, the expanding share of Chinese imports of Hong Kong-produced machinery and components highlights the growing importance of outward processing activities in southern China. This emerging pattern is further evidence of a cross-border economic symbiosis and growing regional integration.

Similar factors have determined the changing composition of Taiwan's exports to China. During 1985–90, for example, these were dominated by machinery, transport equipment and industrial materials for manufacturing purposes,[34] with the contribution of chemicals and related products also expanding rapidly.[35] These are precisely the goods needed by the subsidiaries of parent Taiwan companies, located in China. The simultaneous acceleration of exports and FDI from Taiwan to the Chinese mainland after 1987 suggests that the cross-Straits export expansion has been no less intimately related to investment considerations than in the case of Hong Kong.

The composition of Chinese exports to Taiwan has been limited by government restrictions emanating from Taipei.[36] But available evidence points to the declining importance of agricultural products, fuels and raw materials in favour of industrial materials for manufacturing, machinery and transport equipment, and miscellaneous manufactures.[37]

The role of Guangdong and Fujian in trade integration within Greater China

Hong Kong and Taiwan entrepreneurial activity has been heavily concentrated in Guangdong and Fujian provinces, and the nature and level of the trade flows analysed above have been critically influenced by the process of economic integration between Hong Kong, Taiwan and southern China. This process has dictated the changing composition of shipments of goods to and from the Chinese mainland, not least as outward processing activities have come to dominate the operations of Hong Kong and Taiwanese manufacturers in China.[38]

The economic rationale of the integration of Greater China lies essentially in the complementarity of factor endowments throughout the region. In recent years, the continued economic expansion of Hong Kong and Taiwan has been constrained by shortages of land and labour, and the associated pressures on rents and wages. In contrast to unemployment rates in these regions of well under 2%,[39] the labour force in Guangdong and Fujian was growing, respectively, by 2.85 and 3.35% during the second half of the 1980s.[40] Such figures mean access to cheap labour and land for overseas entrepreneurs who are prepared to re-site their operations in southern China.

Guangdong and Fujian's trade growth after 1978 was significantly faster than that of China as a whole, and of Hong Kong and Taiwan.[41] Such rapid expansion was reflected in an increasing contribution by both provinces to China's overall trade, even though Guangdong's share of national exports only re-attained the previous peak level (1970) in 1991.[42] Their contribution to China's trade balance throughout the 1980s was also positive and significant.[43] Meanwhile, one corollary of these regional developments was the spectacular decline of Shanghai's export role in domestic trade, its contribution to all exports falling from 23.55% to 7.98% between 1980 and 1991.[44]

Such figures set the trade performances of Guangdong and Fujian in a national context. They do not, however, show the debt which they owed to evolving relationships with Hong Kong and Taiwan. Table 2.4 seeks to encapsulate these emerging trade relations. Between 1980 and 1991, Guangdong's exports to Hong Kong grew by 21.2% annually—a performance which owed most to accelerated expansion after 1985.[45] The result was to raise Hong Kong's share in Guangdong's exports to so dominant a position that by 1991 such shipments constituted 85% of total provincial exports and accounted for more than one-third of all exports from China to Hong Kong. This remarkable expansion also brought about a dramatic improvement in Guangdong's trade balance, the figures in Table 2.4 indicating that a minor deficit in 1985 was transformed into a healthy surplus by the end of the decade.[46]

Hong Kong also became an important destination for goods from Fujian during the 1980s. During the first half of the decade, exports to the British colony grew by almost 11% per annum, but this figure accelerated to 28% between 1985 and 1991.[47] This differential performance no doubt reflects the availability of new markets in Taiwan, as restrictions on cross-Straits trade were relaxed and entrepreneurs increasingly exploited new investment opportunities on the Chinese mainland. The same factors are no doubt responsible for the marked impact which Hong Kong and, latterly, Taiwan, had on Fujian imports. Taken at face value, the figures in Table 2.4 suggest that Hong Kong's share of provincial imports doubled between 1980 and 1985, but thereafter stabilized; by contrast, imports from Taiwan grew by more than 34% annually during the next six years, their share rising almost three-and-a-half fold.[48]

The economic symbiosis inherent in integration counsels caution in interpreting these figures. Shipments of commodities between the Chinese mainland, Hong Kong and Taiwan do not all derive from self-contained, indigenous activities. Rather, they have increasingly reflected the integrative impact of FDI and outward processing operations. Such considerations make it desirable to distinguish between conventional merchandise trade and commodity

Table 2.4 Trade Flows between Guangdong, Fujian, Hong Kong and Taiwan, 1980–1991

	1980		1985		1989		1990		1991	
	Value US$ m.	**%**	**Value US$ m.**	**%**	**Value US$ m.**	**%**	**Value US$ m.**	**%**	**Value US$ m.**	**%**
Guangdong										
Total exports	2,194.72	100	2,952.67	100	8,167.67	100	10,560.24	100	13,687.87	100
Hong Kong	1,126.80	51.4	2,168.20	73.4	6,514.32	79.8	8,709.11	82.5	11,593.06	84.7
Taiwan	–	–	–	–	6.96	0.1	8.95	0.1	36.52	0.3
Total imports	356.12	100	2,426.64	100	4,831.21	100	5,748.88	100	8,510.09	100
Hong Kong	–	–	2,210.64	91.1	3,554.17	73.6	4,152.16	72.2	6,294.13	74.0
Taiwan	–	–	–	–	28.44	0.6	53.78	0.9	134.11	1.6
Fujian										
Total exports	363.66	100	491.48	100	1,661.77	100	2,238.13	100	2,925.67	100
Hong Kong	116.76	32.1	200.76	40.8	761.69	45.8	1,065.35	47.6	1,075.58	36.8
Total imports	141.77	100	599.90	100	735.31	100	933.24	100	1,407.76	100
Hong Kong	37.25	26.3	318.23	53.1	373.23	50.8	459.94	49.3	747.23	53.1
Taiwan	–	–	13.20	2.2	20.41	2.8	41.58	4.5	103.84	7.4

Notes: The figures shown here are based on export and import trade statistics. Notice that a different set of estimates of Fujian's total exports and imports are available from "customs statistics", as follows: exports: 1989—1,828.36, 1990—2,448.82, 1991—3,147.46; imports: 1989—1,594.45, 1990—1,897.18, 1991—2,608.51.

Sources: Guangdong: *GDTJNJ* 1992, pp. 343–45 (1980, 1985, 1990 and 1991); *GDTJNJ* 1991, pp. 303–5 (1989); and p. 334 (imports from Hong Kong, 1985). Fujian export and import trade statistics: *FJTJNJ* 1992, p. 330 (1980–85, 1989, 1990 and 1991) and pp. 332–3 (Hong Kong, exports and imports, 1980, 1985, 1989, 1990, and 1991; and Taiwan, imports, 1985, 1990 and 1991). Customs statistics: *FJTJNJ* 1991, p. 314; *FJTJNJ* 1992, p. 337.

Table 2.5 FDI-Related Exports and Imports of Guangdong and Fujian Provinces, 1980–1991

	1980		1985		1989		1990		1991	
	Value US$ m.	**%**	**Value US$ m.**	**%**	**Value US$ m.**	**%**	**Value US$ m.**	**%**	**Value US$ m.**	**%**
Guangdong										
Total exports	2,194.72	100	2,952.67	100	8,167.67	100	10,560.24	100	1,3687.87	100
Commissioned processing	82.33	3.8	272.50	9.2	578.17	7.1	583.32	5.5	799.72	5.8
Compensation trade	6.65	0.3	8.70	0.3	62.67	0.8	77.78	0.7	95.06	0.7
FDI ventures	–	–	221.16	7.5	2,276.71	27.9	3,723.83	35.3	5,327.48	38.9
Total imports	356.12	100	2,426.22	100	4,831.21	100	5,748.88	100	8,510.09	100
FDI ventures	–	–	336.56	13.9	1,950.92	40.4	3,297.44	57.4	4,513.02	53.0
Fujian										
Total exports	–	–	–	–	1,828.36	100	2,448.82	100	3,147.46	100
Commissioned processing	–	–	–	–	178.07	9.7	208.54	8.5	293.31	9.3
Compensation trade	–	–	–	–	12.49	0.7	11.29	0.5	5.53	0.2
FDI ventures	–	–	–	–	687.14	37.6	1,115.52	45.6	1,376.95	43.8
Total imports	–	–	–	–	1,594.45	100	1,897.18	100	2,608.51	100
Commissioned processing	–	–	–	–	163.54	10.3	161.87	8.5	251.25	9.6
Compensation trade	–	–	–	–	9.90	0.6	4.20	0.2	5.04	0.2

Table 2.5 (to be continued)

Table 2.5 (continued)

	1980		1985		1989		1990		1991	
	Value US$ m.	**%**	**Value US$ m.**	**%**	**Value US$ m.**	**%**	**Value US$ m.**	**%**	**Value US$ m.**	**%**
FDI ventures	–	–	–	–	168.35	10.6	237.63	12.5	282.80	10.8
Export processing	–	–	–	–	584.25	36.6	895.97	47.2	1,278.55	49.0

Notes: Guangdong: "Commissioned processing" is a translation of the Chinese phrase *lailiao jiagong*. It refers to the processing (*jiagong*) of materials from outside (*lailiao*) for re-export. This category usually includes assembly (*zhuanpei*) of product parts which have been similarly imported. Export through "compensation trade" (*buchang maoyi*) involves not only the provision of raw materials, semi-finished manufactures and/or parts, but also the supply of machinery and equipment, to be "compensated" for by reducing or relinquishing processing fees or land rents. Note that the term *sanlai yibu* embraces both *lailiao jiagong* and *buchang maoyi*. "FDI ventures" refer to the activities of the "three foreign-funded enterprises" (*sanzi qiye*): equity, contractual and wholly-foreign-owned ventures. Because of Chinese restrictions on domestic sales, the bulk of these enterprises' output is destined for the world market. A large proportion of exports generated through "commissioned processing" or "compensation trade" also involves FDI firms. Fujian: "Export processing" translates the Chinese phrase *jinliao jiagong* (literally "imported materials for processing"). The term is clearly similar to *lailiao jiagong*, although it is not clear whether the activities under this heading constitute a broader category, which also embraces "commissioned processing". "FDI equipment" refers to imports via FDI of machinery and equipment as part of their investment.

Sources: As Table 2.4. Estimates for Fujian are derived from customs statistics.

movements related to FDI (*sanzi*[49]) or outward processing and compensation trade (*sanlai yibu*[50]). The significance of these distinctions is highlighted in Table 2.5.

These figures highlight the changing structural composition of the two provinces' exports and imports, and thereby suggest the impact of regional integration with Hong Kong and Taiwan upon their foreign trade profiles. In the immediate wake of the new open-door policy, for example, virtually all Guangdong's exports remained conventional "merchandise exports" (*maoyi chukou*).[51] Their share fell from 96% to 83% during the first half of the 1980s, but thereafter declined much more rapidly to reach a mere 55% in 1991. Initially, the role of exports generated through *sanzi* funding took second place to those facilitated by *sanlai yibu* activities. But under the impact of China's strategy of export-orientated foreign investment, this relationship changed dramatically during the second half of the decade. Increased capital inflows were reflected in a rapid growth of *sanzi* exports (on average, by 53% per annum between 1985 and 1991). As a result, by the beginning of the 1990s, foreign sales of FDI-related products accounted for more than a third of all Guangdong's exports.[52] (On the import side, the dominance of FDI-related activities emerges even more dramatically.) Although a detailed breakdown of Fujian's exports and imports is only available for the most recent years, the evidence points to the emergence of a similar pattern. [53]

The symbiotic economic relationship between the constituent parts of Greater China is well reflected in their trading position vis-à-vis the United States. Figure 2.1 seeks to illustrate this by showing the changing trade surpluses of Hong Kong, Taiwan and China (including Greater China) with the United States between 1981 and 1991.[54] It is clear that since the mid-1980s, China's trade surplus with the United States has risen dramatically. By contrast, during 1987–91, the large surpluses enjoyed by Hong Kong and especially Taiwan declined no less significantly. There can be no doubt that these contrary trends precisely reflect the accelerated relocation, since the mid-1980s, of export-orientated Hong Kong and Taiwanese firms to mainland China (above all, to the Pearl River Delta).[55]

The impact of the relocation of Hong Kong manufacturing activities to China, and the associated outward processing operations for re-export through Hong Kong, are suggested by the estimates in Table 2.6. The figures reveal that, between 1989 and the first half of 1992, some 71–77% of Hong Kong's exports to China were destined for outward processing and

Figure 2.1 Annual Trade Surpluses of Greater China with the United States, 1981–1991

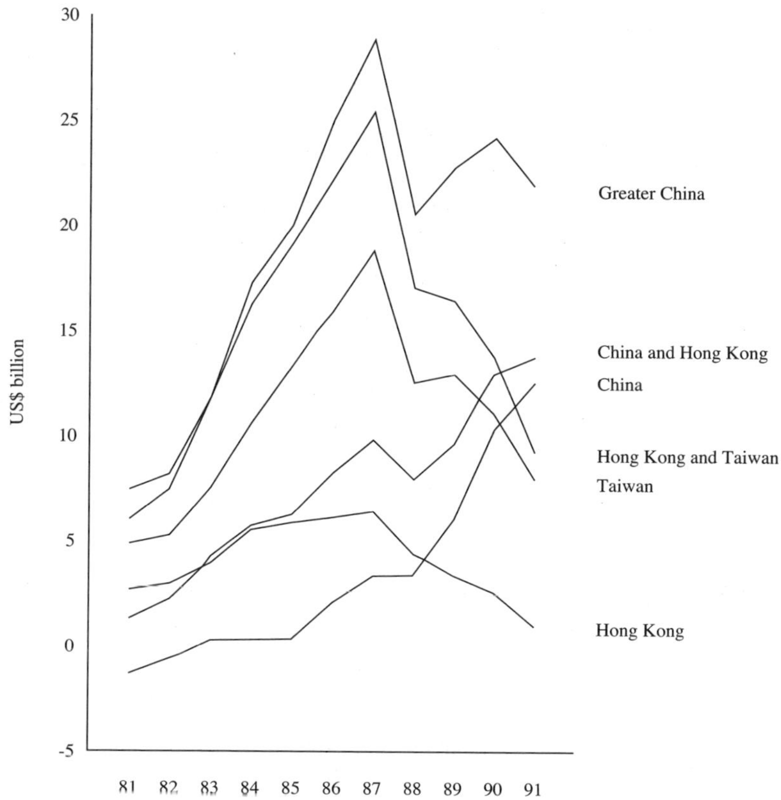

Sources: 1981–90: Ian K. Perkin, "Greater China trade area surplus with the US" in *SCMP*, 29 January 1992; Hong Kong and China 1991: *SCMP*, 21 February 1992; Taiwan 1991: TCEPAD–*TWSDB* 1992.

related to FDI ventures. On the conservative assumption that the processing fee (including transport costs) constituted 20% of the value of exports to China, the finished manufactures accounted, on average, for 68% of Hong Kong's total exports to the United States during the same period. This clearly reflects the transfer of Hong Kong manufacturing enterprises to mainland China during recent years.

The evidence presented in this section suggests that the open-door strategy has facilitated the establishment of a framework to accommodate increasing involvement by Hong Kong and Taiwan entrepreneurs in the southern Chinese

Table 2.6 The Implications of the Relocation of Hong Kong Manufacturing Enterprises in China

	Hong Kong exports to China (US$ million)	Hong Kong exports to China for outward processing (US$ million)	%	Hong Kong exports to United States (US$ million)
1988	38,043	–	–	72,884
1989	43,272	32,262	74.6	72,162
1990	47,470	36,418	76.7	66,370
1991	54,404	40,369	74.2	62,870
1992 Jan–June	28,499	20,323	71.3	28,038

Sources: *TKP*, 30 December 1992.

economy. The outcome has been to alter both the level and pattern of trade within Greater China. Especially striking are the changes which have taken place since the mid-1980s and which at present show no signs of abating. Such changes have of course had important implications for economic growth and structural change throughout the region. Before examining these implications in greater detail, however, further consideration must be given to the nature of investment flows from Hong Kong and Taiwan to Guangdong and Fujian.

Investment and capital flows within greater China[56]

Trend and pattern of investment and capital flows

Changes in the level of investment flows from Hong Kong and Taiwan to southern China provide a further measure of the growing economic integration of the region. Capital flows from mainland China to Taiwan for the time being remain largely non-existent, although accelerated increases in Chinese investment in Hong Kong—especially from Guangdong—have been a notable feature of the recent past. Political factors may have played a part in this recent expansion. But from an economic perspective, it is as well to remember that capital flows from Japan and the United States continue to dominate foreign investment in the colony. There is no question of the archetypal market economy of Hong Kong (or, for that matter, of Taiwan) becoming integrated with those of Guangdong and Fujian under the impact of increased Chinese investment in Hong Kong.

Table 2.7 summarizes trends in capital flows between Hong Kong and Taiwan and the Chinese mainland between 1985 and 1991. Where possible, estimates for Shanghai have also been included in order to introduce a comparative perspective. The table shows that Guangdong has remained by far the largest recipient of investment from Hong Kong, whether measured in terms of FDI (FDI plus capital borrowing for investment in China) flows or, more broadly, of AFI. Except for 1987, the provincial intake of FDI increased consistently after 1985, the gross stock rising on average by 51.2% per annum. The comparable percentage for AFI was 47.1, the slightly lower figure perhaps reflecting the downturn in 1990 as well as in 1987.

Fujian's intake of capital from Hong Kong has been much less impressive than that of Guangdong (cf. an average annual rate of growth of AFI of 41%). It is telling too that the cumulative level of AFI into Fujian from Hong Kong during 1985–91 was little more than half that received by the tiny enclave of Shenzhen Special Economic Zone (SEZ).[57] But Fujian's profile still compares favourably with most other FDI/AFI recipient provinces, including—see Table 2.4—Shanghai.

After 1985, Hong Kong investment in China as a whole grew even more rapidly than in Guangdong.[58] Such a comparison is, however, misleading in at least one important respect. As a pioneer in the search for foreign capital, Guangdong was by 1985 already well-established as a recipient of investment from the British colony. Subsequently, an increasing number of eastern coastal provinces emerged as competitors for the same pool of capital.[59] Even so, in 1991, Guangdong still accounted for more than half of total Hong Kong investment in China (54% of FDI, 59% of AFI). If Fujian were included (9% of FDI, 8% of AFI), the two provinces were in receipt of some two-thirds of foreign investment from the colony.

It is difficult to estimate with accuracy the level of Taiwanese investment in mainland China. The fragmentary data shown in Table 2.4 are all that can be found in official mainland publications. What is not in doubt is that Taiwanese investment in the two southern provinces has increased dramatically in recent years in the wake of informal contacts and, since 1991, the formal authorization by the Taipei government of "indirect investment" through third parties.[60] With US$469.89 million invested in 1991 (twice as much as in the previous year), FDI of Taiwanese origin accounted for some 10% of China's total intake.

Table 2.7 Shares of Guangdong, Fujian, Shanghai and All China in Realized Foreign Investment from Hong Kong and Taiwan, 1985–1991 (US$ million)

	1985	1986	1987	1988	1989	1990	1991	1985–91
From Hong Kong								
Guangdong								
FDI	450.20	622.65	502.67	836.54	952.72	1,018.59	1,448.60	5,831.97
	(47.11)	(46.86)	(27.79)	(34.45)	(40.68)	(48.08)	(54.42)	(42.75)
AFI	845.63	1,095.45	884.09	1,537.96	1,544.89	1,298.46	1,724.80	8,931.28
	(83.20)	(69.65)	(42.28)	(49.46)	(53.04)	(53.40)	(58.97)	(55.61)
Shenzhen								
FDI	146.05	328.87	219.54	225.61	212.66	177.99	227.81	1,538.53
	(15.28)	(24.75)	(12.14)	(9.29)	(9.08)	(8.40)	(8.56)	(11.28)
AFI	272.42	385.87	256.32	281.98	287.29	262.91	323.75	2,070.54
	(26.80)	(24.53)	(12.26)	(9.07)	(9.86)	(10.81)	(11.07)	(12.89)
Guangzhou								
FDI	–	–	–	–	–	125.71	187.07	–
	–	–	–	–	–	(5.93)	(7.03)	–
AFI	136.63	120.85	49.72	111.47	104.16	125.57	–	–
	(13.44)	(7.68)	(2.38)	(3.58)	(3.58)	(5.16)	–	–
Fujian								
FDI	95.07	–	–	80.56	195.25	160.91	225.77	–
	(9.95)	–	–	(3.32)	(8.34)	(7.60)	(8.40)	–
AFI	141.97	70.23	36.67	177.48	204.23	249.45	225.77	1,105.80
	(13.97)	(4.47)	(1.75)	(5.71)	(7.01)	(10.26)	(7.72)	(6.89)
Xiamen								
FDI	58.83	–	–	31.77	–	45.08	–	–

Table 2.7 (to be continued)

Table 2.7 (continued)

	1985	1986	1987	1988	1989	1990	1991	1985–91
	(6.16)	–	–	(1.31)	–	(2.13)	–	–
AFI	*	*	*	*	153.91	107.27	–	–
					(5.28)	(4.41)	–	–
Shanghai								
FDI	–	–	–	–	–	–	47.44	–
	–	–	–	–	–	–	(1.78)	–
AFI	–	31.30	312.83	–	178.96	–	–	–
	–	(1.99)	(14.96)	–	(6.14)	–	–	–
All China								
FDI	955.68	1,328.71	1,809.05	2,428.05	2,341.77	2,118.48	2,661.81	13,643.55
	(48.86)	(59.22)	(68.35)	(64.93)	(62.06)	(56.42)	(57.04)	(60.67)
AFI	1,016.37	1,572.85	2,091.24	3,109.44	2,912.78	2,431.68	2,924.96	16,059.32
	(22.78)	(21.67)	(24.74)	(30.40)	(28.96)	(23.63)	(25.32)	(25.95)
From Taiwan								
Guangdong								
FDI	–	–	–	3.24	22.72	70.33	109.56	–
	–	–	–	–	–	(31.36)	(23.32)	–
Shenzhen								
FDI	–	–	–	3.16	10.06	3.71	2.16	–
	–	–	–	–	–	(1.65)	(0.46)	–
Guangzhou								
FDI	–	–	–	–	4.37	22.69	28.79	–
	–	–	–	–	–	(10.12)	(6.13)	–
Hainan				–	–			
FDI	–	–	–	–	–	5.68	–	–
	–	–	–	–	–	(2.53)	–	–

Table 2.7 (to be continued)

Table 2.7 (continued)

	1985	1986	1987	1988	1989	1990	1991	1985–91
Fujian								
FDI	–	0.57	0.72	11.01	106.66	–	–	–
	–	–	–	–	–	–	–	–
Shangshai								
FDI	–	–	–	–	–	–	–	–
	–	–	–	–	–	–	–	–
All China								
FDI	–	–	–	–	–	224.26	469.89	–
	–	–	–	–	–	(5.97)	(10.11)	–

Notes: The asterisk* indicates that the cumulative total AFI for 1985–88 was US$240.46 million (3.09%). FDI = foreign direct investment; AFI = all foreign investment (including FDI and loans). Figures in brackets show the percentage share of total investment to China from Hong Kong and Taiwan, except for those under "All China", which show the share of Hong Kong and Taiwan in China's total intake for foreign capital. Some of the absolute USD estimates for Hong Kong have been obtained by applying the FDI or AFI ratio to the total FDI or AFI intake for the relevant region. For example, Shenzhen's FDI (1991) is derived from the AFI ratio and total FDI (from Hong Kong and elsewhere). For some areas—notably Guangzhou (1985–88) and Shanghai (1986–87)—the ratio from the pledged, rather than realized, investment series has been used. The figures for Taiwan are all from official mainland Chinese sources. For Fujian the estimates appear to constitute a complete series. The source from which they are taken (*FJTJNJ* 1990) also gives a cumulative total for 1979–89 as US$120.19 million. This is only marginally more than the US$118.96 million cited for 1986–89. It is curious that annual estimates for 1990 and 1991 are absent from the 1991 and 1992 editions of *FJTJNJ*—precisely when the National Statistical Yearbook (*ZGTJNJ*) made available such estimates for the country as a whole. The estimates for Shenzhen for 1988–91, which generated a cumulative total of US$19.09 million, seem to constitute another complete series, since the figure is almost identical to that given in *SZTJSC* 1991 (p. 43).

Sources: Hong Kong: Y. Y. Kueh, "Foreign investment and economic change in China", *The China Quarterly*, No. 132 (September 1992), pp. 674 and 682–3; *GZTJNJ* 1992, p. 315; and *SHTJNJ* 1992, p. 358. Taiwan: *GDTJNJ* 1992, p. 360; *SZSQIWUSQGMJJHSHTJZL* 1986–90; p. 405; *SZTJNJ* 1992, p. 397; *GZTJNJ* 1991, p. 305; *GZTJNJ* 1992, p. 315; *HNTJNJ* 1991, p. 433; *FJTJNJ* 1987, p. 331; *FJTJNJ* 1988, p. 429; *FJTJNJ* 1990, p. 295; and *ZGTJNJ* 1992, p. 642.

Although this was far behind the contribution of Hong Kong, it placed Taiwan only marginally behind Japan as a supplier of FDI to the Chinese mainland. By the end of 1992, Taiwan had in fact overtaken Japan to rank second as a source of FDI to the PRC.[61]

Estimates of Fujian's intake of FDI from Taiwan in 1991 are apparently not available. But assuming that it was no smaller than the US$109.56 million invested in Guangdong, there can be little doubt that the combined share of the two provinces in FDI flows from Hong Kong and Taiwan was no less than 60%—and cumulatively (1985–91) much more. Such figures demonstrate clearly the locational choice made by Hong Kong and Taiwanese entrepreneurs and signal the trend towards greater economic integration within Greater China.

There is, however, a qualification to be entered here. A survey conducted by the Ministry of Economic Affairs (MOEA) in Taipei in April 1991 suggested that the level of Taiwanese FDI in mainland China was more substantial than that indicated in official PRC sources. The survey, based on the responses of 2,503 firms which had voluntarily registered their investment interests with the government in Taipei, revealed a cumulative FDI stock of US$750 million.[62] Although it is impossible to reconcile the statistical discrepancy, there is no doubt that a significant part of FDI flows to China from Hong Kong, Japan, the United States and Southeast Asia reflect the activities of Taiwanese firms in disguise. It is unlikely, however, that such flows from places other than Hong Kong have exceeded the colony's own investment involvement, and we are confident that the combined contribution of FDI from Hong Kong and Taiwan to mainland China (or Guangdong and Fujian) shown in Table 2.7 requires little modification.

In line with the findings of official PRC statistics, the MOEA survey reveals that accumulated FDI stock of Taiwanese origin was, as of April 1991, heavily concentrated in Guangdong and Fujian (see Table 2.8). On the basis of such evidence, the distribution of Taiwanese FDI between the two provinces seems less unbalanced than that of Hong Kong (see Table 2.7), although it remains heavily skewed towards Guangdong. In any case, current press reports indicate that new FDI from Taiwan continues to favour Guangdong ahead of Fujian.

Impact of investment flows on economic growth

It is difficult to estimate exactly how foreign investment from Hong Kong and Taiwan has translated into economic growth in Guangdong and Fujian

Table 2.8 Distribution of Cumulative FDI of Taiwanese Origin within Mainland China (as of April 1991)

	FDI		No. of firms	
	US$ m.	**%**	**Units**	**%**
Guangdong	342.6	45.7	1,253	50.1
Shenzhen	111.6	14.9	378	15.1
Guangzhou	55.9	7.5	146	5.8
Fujian	179.5	23.9	598	23.9
Xiamen	92.2	12.3	275	11.0
Shanghai	87.0	12.3	78	3.1
Others	140.9	18.8	574	22.9
Total	750.0	100.0	2,503	100.0

Sources: Charles H. C. Kao, Joseph S. Lee and Chu-chia Steve Lin, *Taiwan tupuo: liangan jingmao zhuizhong (An Empirical Study of Taiwanese Investment in Mainland China;* hereafter *Taiwan Tupuo),* Taipei: Taipei Commonwealth Publishing Company Ltd., p. 12.

provinces.[63] As a proxy, it is likely that Hong Kong contributed no less than 16% of total fixed capital formation in Guangdong between 1985 and 1990—and 28% in Shenzhen. The comparable figure for Fujian is probably around 7%.[64] Even more important is the fact that every dollar of foreign investment will generate a multiplier effect in terms of complementary domestic investment expenditure (expressed in *yuan*). In short, the overall level of investment associated with FDI and AFI has become very substantial.[65]

A summary of the growth performance of Guangdong and Fujian since 1980 is given in Table 2.9. For comparative purposes, data for Hong Kong, Taiwan and Shanghai are also included. Most foreign investment (FDI and AFI) has been directed towards high growth sectors, and it is reasonable to suppose that the impressive GNP growth recorded in Guangdong and Fujian (including Shenzhen, Guangzhou and Xiamen) after 1985 owed much to capital contributions from Hong Kong and Taiwan. The contrast between Hong Kong and Taiwan—both, after all, mature economies with a sustained record of high growth—and the two southern Chinese provinces is less significant than that between those same provinces and Shanghai. It is no coincidence that Shanghai has fallen far short of Guangdong and Fujian as a recipient of

Table 2.9 The Growth Performance of Hong Kong, Taiwan and Selected Areas of China—Trends in Gross Domestic [National] Product, 1980–1991 (Average Annual Rates of Growth %)

	1980–85	1985–91	1980–91
Hong Kong	5.60	7.20	6.47
Taiwan	6.71 [7.09]	8.34 [8.63]	7.69 [7.92]
Guangdong	12.16	13.30	12.80
Shenzhen	54.54	25.95	38.22
Guangzhou	12.71	10.83	12.51
Fujian	11.91 [11.93]	9.71 [9.96]	10.71 [10.85]
Xiamen	16.24	29.00	23.04
Shanghai	9.08	5.90	7.34

Sources: Hong Kong: HKGCSD–*HKMDS*, September 1992, p. 10. Taiwan: TCEPAD–*TWSDB* 1992, p. 25. Guangdong: *GDTJNJ* 1992, p. 83. Shenzhen: *SZTJNJ* 1992, p. 170. Guangzhou: *GZTJNJ* 1992, pp. 14 and 20. Fujian: *FJTJNJ* 1992, p. 20. Xiamen: *FJTJNJ* 1992, p. 447; Xiamen Statistical Bureau, *FJDXM* 1989, p. 46. Shanghai: *SHTJNJ* 1992, p. 34.

foreign capital. The data in Table 2.9 thereby suggest the influence of overseas involvement in the Chinese economy and its impact upon domestic growth.

Trends towards economic integration

Structural realignment in GDP and employment

The factors which have led Hong Kong and Taiwanese firms to relocate their manufacturing activities to mainland China are already the subject of a considerable literature. The most familiar argument is that against the background of high indigenous wage costs and land rents, entrepreneurs have sought increasingly to transfer their labour-intensive operations across the border, or Taiwan Straits, in order to take advantage of an abundant supply of cheap labour and land. The accelerated appreciation of the NT Dollar against the US dollar since the mid-1980s has been a further contributory factor, prompting many Taiwanese firms to move to the mainland in an attempt to reduce export costs. More stringent government legislation to control pollution, as well as greater self-awareness and even militancy on the part of the labour force, have been further reasons for the accelerating trend, especially amongst Taiwanese entrepreneurs.

In an attempt to measure the impact of the transfer of manufacturing activities from Hong Kong and Taiwan to the Chinese mainland, estimates of sectoral contributions to national income and employment in all three countries and regions, as well as of labour productivity, are set out in Table 2.10. There is no doubt that the relocation of manufacturing operations from Hong Kong and Taiwan to the Chinese mainland has been a catalyst in effecting remarkable structural changes in national income and employment within the constituent economies of Greater China. In 1991, for example, Hong Kong investors were reported to be employing some three million workers in Guangdong (especially in the Pearl River Delta).[66] This constituted a labour force about 4.5 times greater than the colony's own manufacturing workforce. Transferring industrial activities across the Shenzhen River meanwhile resulted in a decline in manufacturing employment in Hong Kong in both absolute and relative terms. Table 2.10 (Panel A) shows that the employment share of the industrial sector (including building construction) fell from 50% (1980) to 44% (1985) to a mere 36% (1991), whilst that of services rose from 48% to 54% to 63%.

The corresponding changes in Taiwan's employment structure appear at first glance to have been less spectacular. But the reality is that employment in many branches of light industry (notably electrical engineering, footwear, plastics and textile production) has fallen dramatically as a result of the transfer of such labour-intensive activities to the PRC. Indeed, at times the government in Taipei has expressed its concern about a "hollowing out" of the island's industrial structure.

The relocation of manufacturing firms to China has also been accompanied by striking changes in the structure of output in Hong Kong and Taiwan. Table 2.10 (Panel A) shows that the service sector's share in Hong Kong GDP increased by almost 8% between 1980 and 1991, mostly at the expense of industrial activity. Similar structural "upgrading" has apparently taken place in Taiwan, although the smaller scale of its FDI involvement may mean that the principal reason for this lies elsewhere. The more significant consequence for Taiwan may have been in terms of changes in its intra-industrial structure. According to the Head of the Industry Bureau in Taipei, the large-scale transfer of "sunset industries" to the PRC has more than anything else accounted for the rapid increase of heavy industry's share in total manufacturing output in recent years (from 47% to 56% between 1986 and 1991).[67]

There is no doubt that Guangdong and Fujian have benefited most from the increased economic integration of Greater China. As a result of accelerated GDP (GNP) growth and more rapid industrialization, the structure of output and employment in both regions—but above all, in subprovincial units such as Guangzhou, Shenzhen and Xiamen—has changed markedly. This process of structural change has been characterized by gains for the industrial and service sectors at the expense of agriculture, and by a reduction in inter-sectoral relative levels of labour productivity (see Panels A and B of Table 2.10). The significance of the latter achievement is highlighted by the experience

Table 2.10 Measuring the Impact of Relocating Manufacturing Activities to the Chinese Mainland, 1980–91

A. The Changing Contributions of Agriculture (A), Industry (I) and Services (S) to Gross Domestic Product (GDP) and Employment in Greater China (%)

	1980			**1985**			**1991**		
	A	**I**	**S**	**A**	**I**	**S**	**A**	**I**	**S**
GDP									
Hong Kong	1.0	31.8	67.2	0.7	29.6	69.7	0.3	24.9	74.8
Taiwan	7.7	45.7	46.6	5.8	46.3	47.9	3.7	42.3	54.0
Guangdong	33.8	41.1	25.1	31.1	40.8	28.1	23.4	42.1	34.5
Shenzhen	28.9	26.0	45.1	7.9	46.8	45.4	4.6	60.2	35.2
Guangzhou	10.9	54.5	34.6	9.7	52.9	37.4	7.3	46.5	46.2
Fujian	37.2	41.5	21.3	35.7	38.0	26.3	31.2	39.8	29.0
Xiamen	21.1	58.6	20.3	12.7	56.3	31.0	10.4	53.7	35.9
Shanghai	3.2	75.7	21.1	4.2	69.8	26.0	4.0	64.3	31.8
Employment									
Hong Kong	2.0	49.6	48.3	1.8	43.8	54.4	1.0	35.9	63.1
Taiwan	19.5	42.4	38.1	17.5	41.4	41.1	12.9	40.1	47.0
Guangdong	73.7	13.9	12.5	60.1	21.3	18.6	51.0	25.9	23.1
Shenzhen	–	–	–	–	–	–	6.1	69.8	24.1
Guangzhou	40.2	33.6	26.2	31.3	37.7	31.1	27.6	36.8	35.6
Fujian	73.0	11.8	15.2	61.5	19.4	19.0	57.8	20.9	21.3
Xiamen	–	–	–	46.6	26.8	26.6	42.4	28.8	28.8
Shanghai	29.6	48.7	22.1	16.6	57.9	25.5	10.7	60.0	29.3

B. Relative Product per Worker (RPW) in A, I, and S compared

	1980			1985			1991		
	A	I	S	A	I	S	A	I	S
Hong Kong	0.50	0.64	1.39	0.39	0.68	1.28	0.30	0.69	1.19
Taiwan	0.39	1.08	1.22	0.33	1.12	1.17	0.29	1.05	1.15
Guangdong	0.46	2.96	2.01	0.52	1.92	1.51	0.46	1.63	1.49
Shenzhen	–	–	–	–	–	–	0.75	0.86	1.46
Guangzhou	0.27	1.62	1.32	0.31	1.40	1.21	0.26	1.26	1.30
Fujian	0.51	3.52	1.40	0.58	1.96	1.38	0.54	1.90	1.36
Xiamen	–	–	–	0.27	2.10	1.17	0.25	1.86	1.25
Shanghai	0.11	1.55	0.95	0.25	1.21	1.02	0.37	1.07	1.09

C. Total Inequality Amongst Sectors (TIAS)

	1980	1985	1991
Hong Kong	0.37	0.30	0.24
Taiwan	0.24	0.24	0.18
Guangdong	0.80	0.58	0.55
Shenzhen	–	–	0.22
Guangzhou	0.59	0.43	0.41
Fujian	0.72	0.52	0.53
Xiamen	–	0.68	0.64
Shanghai	0.54	0.25	0.14

Notes: RPW = (% share in GDP) ÷ (% share in employment); TIAS = $\Sigma[1 - Y_{(i)}] \cdot W_{(i)}$ (ignoring the minus sign); where $Y_{(i)}$ = RPW at sector i, and $W_{(i)}$ = % share in employment of sector i.

Sources: Hong Kong: HKGCSD—*EGDP* 1966–91, p. 38; HKGCSD—*HKADS* 1991, p. 34; Yin-ping Ho, *Trade, Industrial Restructuring and Development in Hong Kong* (London: Macmillan Press, 1992), p. 36. Taiwan: TCEPAD—*TWSDB* 1992, pp. 17 and 41. Guangdong: *GDTJNJ* 1992, pp. 85 and 142. Shenzhen: *SZTJNJ* 1992, pp. 161 and 182; *SZSQIWUSQGMJJHSHTJZL* 1979–85, pp. 10–11; *SZTJNJ* 1992, pp. 168–69; *ibid.* 1986–90, p. 21. Guangzhou: GZTJNJ 1992, pp. 28 and 358. Fujian: *FJTJNJ* 1992, pp. 15 and 53; *FJSHTJZL* 1986, p. 43. Xiamen: *FJDXM*, p. 44; *FJTJNJ* 1992, p. 447; *FJSHTJZL* 1986, p. 48; *XMJJTQNJ* 1990, p. 171. Shanghai: *SHTJNJ* 1991, pp. 34 and 72; *SHTJNJ* 1992, pp. 33 and 86.

of China's pre-reform era, when—accelerated industrialization notwithstanding—agriculture carried almost the entire burden of absorbing increases in labour supply, thereby exacerbating inter-sectoral productivity differentials.[68]

The tertiary sector's increased share of total output and employment since 1980 has been a noteworthy feature of the recent development experience of both Guangdong and Fujian.[69] This no doubt reflects the increased provision of banking, insurance and financial services, transport and telecommunication facilities, and expertise in processing export and import orders. An expansion of tourism and rise in real estate transactions also underlie the same trend. The growing contribution of the tertiary sector in the southern Chinese economy is of course paralleled in the experience of other industrializing countries.

Issues, problems and prospects

The experience of economic integration in Greater China differs significantly from that which has occurred elsewhere in the world. For example, the European Commission (EC) and ASEAN are two economic groupings which have sought to create a single common market, designed to enhance the free movement of goods and factors of production to members' mutual advantage. By contrast, the establishment of closer ties between Hong Kong, Taiwan and the Chinese mainland is the result of the internationalization of manufacturing production, based on joint production and/or the division of labour, and is geared towards third-party countries (rather than the member countries themselves). A large proportion of output so generated has been destined for overseas locations and most inputs similarly derive from abroad. The movement of factors of production, as well as of finished products, within Greater China meanwhile remains limited; and much Hong Kong and Taiwanese FDI is still heavily concentrated in SEZs, geographically isolated from the rest of the PRC. Backward and forward linkages have thereby been minimized.[70]

The creation of closer trade and investment ties between Hong Kong, Taiwan, Guangdong and Fujian and the process of economic integration which it has facilitated are, in any case, not free of risk. An example is that associated with the vulnerability of the Hong Kong and southern Chinese (especially Guangdong) economies to their export dependency on American markets. From this perspective, an increase in export tariffs following the cancellation of China's most-favoured-nation (MFN) status would have serious consequences for both regions. It has, for example, been estimated that the loss to Hong Kong could be as much as US$15.7 billion in overall trade and 60,000 jobs; re-exports from China might meanwhile fall by US$4.6–6.2 billion, leading to massive job losses in Guangdong.[71] Such data highlight the importance to China *and Hong Kong* of a resumption of Chinese membership within the General Agreement of Tariffs and Trade (GATT). They also suggest how failure to resolve trade issues between China and the United States could undermine the very process of regional economic integration by leading investors to lessen their involvement in the southern Chinese economy and redirect their investment elsewhere (say, to other countries in Southeast Asia).

If the rapid expansion of cross-Straits trade has boosted Taiwan's export growth, it has also led to increasing dependence on Chinese markets. This has obvious dangers in a situation in which cross-Straits political relations remain uncertain. Meanwhile, Taiwanese enterprises must face up to increased competition from their overseas subsidiaries, now sited in southern China. Other things being equal, the access to cheaper land and labour which such firms enjoy should enable them to produce cheaper goods, and may thereby threaten parent firms' competitiveness in international (and even local) markets.[72]

Nevertheless, as the estimates in Table 2.11 suggest, there also remains considerable scope for even closer economic integration within Greater China. The marked economic differences between Hong Kong, Taiwan and southern China in terms of the major measures shown above suggest that before full integration and equalization of per capita income, productivity and degree of industrialization[73] can be achieved, many economic and political barriers to cross-border labour mobility will have to be removed. However, the political unification which such an outcome would seem to demand is clearly far beyond anything conceivable within the foreseeable future.

The data in Table 2.11 indicate that within China, only Shenzhen can lay claim to approaching the advanced standards of Hong Kong and Taiwan in terms of per capita income, productivity and degree of industrialization. But even that gap remains considerable, and in any case, Shenzhen SEZ can perhaps be more usefully regarded as a "satellite town" of Hong Kong than an integral part of Guangdong.[74] If the SEZ's "second line", north of the enclave, replaced the Shenzhen River as the border with Hong Kong, no doubt economic equalization would rapidly come about. Whether or not this would be to the benefit or detriment of the British colony is an open question.

In any case, with or without Shenzhen, Hong Kong has now become inseparable from the economy of Guangdong. With the tertiary sector now contributing about three-quarters of its GDP (see Panel A of Table 2.10), its process of "de-industrialization" seems to have reached a point at which it has become irreversible. The most unequivocal evidence of the two regions' inseparability are the estimates of the potential economic impact of a withdrawal by the United States of China's MFN status, cited earlier.

If Hong Kong has wholly succumbed to the principle of comparative advantage in pursuing regional economic specialization, Taiwan has adopted a more cautious approach vis-à-vis the Chinese mainland. Various econometric studies have been undertaken in an attempt to assess the security implications of its closer trade and investment relations with the PRC. One of these suggested that against the background of increased exports to mainland China in recent years, an embargo by the authorities in Beijing would, on average, have reduced Taiwan's GDP and total employment by 1.46% and 3.42% respectively (1987–91).[75] Such losses would have to be regarded as fairly minor in their impact. By contrast, another study has argued that the reduction in Taiwan's GDP consequent upon reduced domestic capital formation might offset FDI-related exports to the PRC to generate a significant net income loss. To those who would use such estimates to highlight the threat posed by Taiwan's allegedly increasing dependency, it has, however, been argued that in the absence of investment opportunities on the Chinese mainland, Taiwanese entrepreneurs would merely have directed their funds elsewhere. Nor could there be any guarantee that the funds involved would have been used for productive purposes on Taiwan itself.[76]

Clearly, it is not easy to estimate the economic costs and benefits associated with Taiwanese investment in mainland China. But it would be surprising if the government in Taipei were not to act prudently to safeguard its security. To this extent, it is significant that when "indirect investment" to the PRC was officially sanctioned in 1991, it was deliberately restricted to 3,679 product categories. It was also specified that such investment should only involve labour-intensive undertakings to which the PRC could contribute necessary raw materials and in areas which, in terms of the domestic Taiwanese economy, had low inter-industrial linkages; and should embrace the production of goods which might enjoy a competitive advantage against Taiwanese exports.[77]

Whether Taiwanese investors will be able to overcome what are essentially political restrictions on their activities as successfully as they circumvented earlier restraints on investment contacts with mainland firms—and if so, how—remains to be seen. What is not in doubt, however, is the potentially

Table 2.11 Economic Disparities within Greater China, 1991

	Population (m.)	GNP (US$ m.)	Per capita GNP (US$)	GVIO (US$ m.)	Per capita GVIO (US$)	Capital labour ratio (US$)	Trade volume (US$ m.)	Trade/GNP ratio
Hong Kong	5.82	81,157	13,945	–	–	4,339	107,439	1.32
Taiwan	20.56	180,270	8,815	155,000	7,546	4,832	139,035	0.77
Guangdong	63.49	33,452	527	47,422	747	2,597	22,198	0.66
Shenzhen	2.39	3,284	1,491	5,303	2,223	4,951	5,967	1.82
	(1.20)	(2,546)	(2,306)	–	–	–	–	–
Guangzhou	6.02	7,265	1,214	10,887	1,808	3,998	5,382	0.74
	(3.62)	(5,977)	(1,660)	–	–	–	–	–
Fujian	30.39	10,480	340	12,378	402	1,761	4,334	0.41
Xiamen	1.15	1,169	1,016	1,936	1,683	–	2,406	2.06
Shanghai	13.40	16,114	1,203	36,583	2,730	2,822	8,044	0.50

Notes: Bracketed figures are for Shenzhen and Guangzhou cities "proper", i.e., excluding the outlying counties. Population: the estimates for Shenzhen embrace "temporary" and "permanent" residents. GNP: the figures for Hong Kong, Shenzhen, Guangzhou and Xiamen are measures of GDP. Per capita GDP estimates for Shenzhen and Guangzhou are given independently in Chinese sources and are slightly different from figures which can be obtained from the estimates of population and GDP shown in Table 2.11. GVIO: gross value of industrial output. Capital-labour ratio: this refers to capital stock (K) per industrial employee (L). For Hong Kong and Taiwan, K means, respectively, gross domestic capital formation and gross fixed capital formation. For China, K is the net value of fixed assets (i.e., net of depreciation); and K/L refers to industry in general in Guangdong, Fujian and Shanghai, but only those enterprises which have an independent accounting (*duli hesuan*) identity

Table 2.11 (to be continued)

Table 2.11 (continued)

in Shenzhen and Guangzhou. Trade volume: this embraces only domestic exports and imports (i.e., it excludes exports originating from, and imports destined for, other places). However, the data for Xiamen appear to include re-exports. Exchange rates: US$1.00 is assumed to equal HK$7.80 (under the linked system), NT$25.75 (interbank closing rate, December 1991) and RMB 5.323 (official annual average, 1991).

Sources: Hong Kong: HKGCSD—*EGDP* 1966–1991, p. 10; HKGCSD–*HKMDS*, August 1992, p. 105 and September 1992, pp. 1–2 and 19. Taiwan: TCEPAD—*TWSDB* 1992, pp. 1, 17, 49 and 192. Guangdong: *GDTJNJ* 1992, pp. 68, 183 and 341. Shenzhen: *SZTJNJ* 1991, p. 2; *SZTJNJ* 1992, p. 163; and *GDTJNJ* 1992, pp. 81, 93 and 105. Guangzhou: *GDTJNJ* 1992, pp. 91, 93, 104, 138 and 199; *GZTJNJ* 1992, p. 307. Fujian: *FJTJNJ* 1992, pp. 8–9, 53 and 146. Xiamen: *FJTJNJ* 1992, pp. 444–8; Y. Y. Kueh, "Foreign investment and economic change", pp. 689–90. Shanghai: *ZGTJNJ* 1992, p. 79; *SHTJNJ* 1992, pp. 33, 86, 112, 144 and 349.

explosive nature of the current situation, should continuing embargoes on direct commercial, navigational and postal links (the *san tong*) be lifted. If this were to happen, a dramatic realignment of investment and trade flows within Greater China would certainly result. Such a prospect may at present seem remote. But it behoves the government and business community of Hong Kong to be on constant alert and ready to adjust their plans in anticipation of such an eventuality.

The various problems outlined in this final section suggest that the undoubted benefits of closer economic integration within Greater China are not to be taken for granted. The experience of the 1980s is evidence enough of the substantial gains to be derived from closer economic—and by implication, political—relations. But many obstacles remain to be overcome if the growth and structural benefits are to be sustained. To the extent that the economic well-being of Guangdong and Fujian determines the economic direction and health of the rest of the Chinese economy, resolving these issues assumes the greatest urgency in China itself.

3

Hong Kong Surviving the Open-Door, Reforming Chinese Economy*

With scarcely four years to go before sovereignty reverts to China, the British enclave of Hong Kong on the South China coast has greatly benefitted from the open-door policy of China and its celebrated move from a centrally planned Soviet-style system to a market-type economy. Trade, investment, and financial flows across the 18-mile land border have greatly increased over the past decade or so. Particularly spectacular is the massive relocation of the colony's manufacturing activities to the Pearl River Delta in neighbouring Guangdong province to take advantage of cheap labour and land costs. The allocative resource realignment has brought about an intricate process of "de-industrialization" in Hong Kong in favour of the tertiary sector. But it has nonetheless hardly helped to mitigate the acute labour shortage which has faced the colony since the mid-1980s.

Over the past few years, Hong Kong has thrived on the limitless opportunities offered by the hinterland, with a robust annual Gross Domestic Product (GDP) growth of 5–6% (amidst worldwide recession), against the backdrop of a mere 1% growth of labour force per year. If anything, the GDP measure only helps to conceal the real magnitude of economic gains, because profit repatriation and similar net capital inflow from investment in the mainland or elsewhere cannot be adequately captured by the government's statistical department for a Gross National Product (GNP) measure for the territory, since it is an entirely free port in the most classical sense.[1]

---

* Reprinted from "Whither Hong Kong in the open-door, reforming Chinese economy", (coauthored with Yin-ping Ho), *The Pacific Review*, Vol. 6, No. 4 (December 1993), pp. 333–51.

The Hong Kong-China symbiosis, which has emerged in the past decade, is beyond the wildest possible imaginings of any dependency theorists or development structuralists. For "economic integration" theorists or proponents—the late Professor Bela Balassa in particular—the bewilderment must have been compounded by the high import barriers imposed by China, which is not presently a contracting party to the General Agreement on Tariffs and Trade (GATT), and the glaring lack of labour mobility southward across the border. Free capital flow is also basically a one-way traffic, notwithstanding increased illicit or semi-licit transfers from the mainland as witnessed in the recent past. The economic symbiosis represents, therefore, a rare phenomenon which defies any textbook elaboration, in either theoretical construct or empirical terms, of regional economic integration under a free trade regime.

The question is whether the observed Hong Kong phenomenon can be sustained beyond 1997 with its conversion to a Special Administrative Region (SAR) under the People's Republic of China. At present, the capitalist enclave enjoys a per capita GDP of US$16,380 for its 5.8 million residents who are crammed into a tiny total land area of 1,076 square kilometres with virtually no natural resources.[2] By contrast, GNP per head stands at a mere US$550 for Guangdong province, or no more than US$2,500 (the highest in China) in the Special Economic Zone (SEZ) of Shenzhen, just across the border river, which is more a satellite town of Hong Kong than a Chinese economic entity.[3] There is no doubt that this sharp contrast appears very odd in the light of the imminent reversion of Hong Kong's sovereignty.

The question raised about the real crux of Hong Kong's post-1997 future appears therefore to be political rather than economic in nature. There is no point in questioning the integrity of the Dengist design for the "one country, two systems" scheme under which Hong Kong as a SAR should be allowed to retain the status quo for fifty years. There is also no doubt that the border checkpoints would remain strictly guarded to prevent any massive influx of immigrants who could cause the system to disintegrate. Nonetheless, the fundamental economic question remains whether, given the present trend and pattern of economic integration with the motherland without political reunification, the highly industrialized and commercialized Hong Kong economy would be eventually reduced to a Chinese outpost for trading, banking, shipping, telecommunication and tourist business; and how such a transformation would affect the long-term economic vitality and economic welfare of Hong Kong people.

This article attempts to shed some light on these questions by examining the various aspects of the economic interaction between the two sides of the Shenzhen River. We shall focus essentially on import and export relationships, with a particular reference to the unique phenomenon of trade-bound outward processing investment undertaken by Hong Kong manufacturers in South China. The analysis will be preceded by a description, in broad contours, of the changing overall economic structure in Hong Kong in terms of GDP and employment structure in the past decade. This helps to provide a frame of reference for assessing the implications of trade and financial flows across the border. We shall begin by highlighting the changing basic economic and institutional parameters in China itself in order to place the economic involvement of Hong Kong in a proper and broader historical context. The latter part of the article evaluates the relative degree of Hong Kong's economic dependence on the Chinese mainland and points to possible courses of development in the future.

The changing environment

The history of Hong Kong's contemporary economic development has been one of continual change. Since its inception as a British trading post in 1843, the island economy of Hong Kong (whose original acquisition bewildered the young Queen Victoria and annoyed her foreign secretary, Lord Palmerston) had been shattered during the Second World War when the Japanese occupied the territory from 1941 to 1945, and then deluged by successive waves of immigrants from across the border. Yet, beyond all expectations, it survived. As a dependent enclave, Hong Kong's economic development since 1945 has been accompanied by solicitude and uncertainty about its political future. There is no doubt that the post-war development of Hong Kong's political economy has revolved around the interplay of Britain's and China's shared interest in the prosperity and stability of Hong Kong and the Sino-British struggles over the object and management of the city's economy.

Apart from the problem of how the British government of Hong Kong and Hong Kong's populace can successfully prepare the capitalist economy for the new political regime after reversion in 1997, Hong Kong's trade-dependent economy is today faced with the challenges of a changing international division of labour and of growing capacity constraints domestically. Without question, the external orientation of Hong Kong's economy and its exposure to changing international circumstances have made flexibility necessary. Indeed, Hong Kong has succeeded in the postwar decades because its export-oriented enterprises, both large and small, have been quick to exploit changing market conditions and to capture speciality niches. Over the long haul, however, the very success of Hong Kong's export industrialism has, on balance, become a double-edged sword. For one thing, export success has engendered stringent quantitative restrictions and other forms of harsh trade barriers in overseas markets. At the same time, rising costs of labour and land have meant that Hong Kong's export-led economy has reached a point where growth can no longer be dependent on sheer domestic factor inputs alone. In a world of continual change and international competition—and Hong Kong is, of course, fully in that world—the international division of labour keeps changing.

So far as the global economic transition is concerned, world development during the last decades of the twentieth century should have made us aware that virtually nothing in development economics can be predicted with certainty, particularly not the miraculous economic development of China in the 1980s and its engagement in gradualist reform for transforming a basically Soviet-type planned economy to a market-oriented system.[4] Since the open-door policy and economic reforms began in late 1978 in China, rapid economic growth has followed. By contrast, all the former Soviet republics and all the East European economies, without exception, have experienced substantial declines in aggregate output. Over the past couple of years, the contrast between China's economic performance and that of the former planned economies of the Soviet bloc has become so large that it is now widely argued that the Chinese gradualist reform has been a success, whereas the shock therapy, otherwise known as the "big bang", is in big trouble.[5]

In 1992, while the West still struggled with recession, China's real GDP grew by a staggering 12.8%, definitely the fastest rate in the world. That China has now the most dynamically growing economy can hardly be doubted. Indeed, over the lengthy period of 1978–92, real GDP in China grew at an average rate of some 9.5% per annum, stop-go cycles notwithstanding. *Per se,* this growth record has been high not only by China's own historical standards but also internationally. Rhetorically, China's growth performance during the last reform decade would not look out of place amongst the records of the legendary "hyper-growth" East Asian NIEs of the 1960s and 70s. The achievement stands out all the more if one takes into account the fact that China has the most populous and diverse economy on earth.[6] All of this has led to predictions by Western experts that China's domestic economy could become the world's dominant economy by the turn of the twenty-first century. For instance, Lawrence H. Summers, a former chief economist of the World Bank, recently extrapolated that, if the growth differential between China and the United States during the 1980s continues, China could surpass the United States to become the world's largest economy in eleven years.[7]

Yet, in contrast to the pre-reform and closed-door era, no sector in the Chinese economy has undergone as dramatic a change as foreign trade and the international production of tradables via direct inward investment, otherwise known as foreign direct investment (FDI). Since December 1978, when the history-making third plenary session of the 11th Central Committee of the Communist Party of China was held, China has made tremendous headway in attracting FDI capital. Between 1979 and 1992, China had approved 84,000 FDI projects with an agreed investment from them amounting to some US$100 billion,[8] mostly in industrial processing and export-oriented manufacturing. Correspondingly, in the relatively short span of fourteen years, China has emerged as an important trading nation exporting and importing a wide range of products in volumes substantial enough to cause concern over problems of industrial adjustment in the world's major industrial countries. By 1992, China's foreign trade volume totalled US$165.6 billion, ranking it eleventh in the world, an impressive surge from thirty-second in 1979. Arguably, foreign trade and FDI have now become the twin engines of growth behind China's rapid economic advance, accelerating not only the speed of industrial development but the pace of economic transformation as well.[9] It would seem obvious that the Dengist 1978 open-door policy—while open to some conflicting interpretations of export promotion, trade liberalization (albeit still modest in scope), the attracting of foreign capital and utilization of foreign loans—has played a central role in this growth and transformation process.

The implications of such a reforming Chinese economy on the industrial structure of Hong Kong's small, open, city-state economy are far-reaching. In the first place, attracted by the liberalization of FDI regulations and other economic reforms under way in China since the late 1970s, many an energetic industrialist in Hong Kong has shifted a substantial share of his labour-intensive operations across the border to neighbouring regions in South China, where basic wage and land costs are a fraction of those in Hong Kong. The ease of shifting Hong Kong's labour-intensive manufacturing industries across the Shenzhen border to the coastal areas in mainland China has contributed much to the FDI proliferation in China and to the rise of China as a trading power. Reportedly, between 1979 and 1992, some three-fifths of all FDIs in China were made by Hong Kong entrepreneurs. In particular, as high as 80% of FDIs in Guangdong Province have come from Hong Kong.

On Hong Kong's part, these developments have no doubt led to significant economic changes involving inter-sectoral shifts of resources. In fact, many have argued that a process of "hollowing out", or "de-industrialization" (a somewhat better known, if not less ambiguous, term) has been occurring for rather more than a decade now as Hong Kong firms keep shifting out of manufacturing domestically and into service industries. That Hong Kong is undergoing rapid structural changes towards a more service-oriented economy is revealed below.

Structural changes in the Hong Kong economy

The development and changing structure of Hong Kong's economy as reflected by the relative shares of major industrial sectors in total GDP for the past ten years or so is outlined in Table 3.1. As can be expected, given the geographical formation and non-factor resource endowment of the territory, primary products have never been important in Hong Kong. Even more, their relative contribution to the total domestic product has dwindled from a meagre 1% of the GDP in 1980 to only 0.2% of the GDP in 1991.

At the same time, the contribution of the manufacturing sector to the GDP declined steadily from about 24% in 1980 to some 15.5% in 1991. This reflects what has been called a de-industrialization process. At its height in 1970, manufacturing accounted for 31% of Hong Kong's GDP. In terms of employed labour force by the industrial sector, such a de-industrialization process is also clearly reflected in a steady decline in the share of manufacturing employment.

As Table 3.2 shows, the share of manufacturing employment fell from about 42% of the total workforce in 1980 to some 25% in 1991, and to less than 23% in 1992. In other words, over this period, employment in the manufacturing sector saw a relative drop of over 19 percentage points, which is even more pronounced than the decline in its relative contribution to GDP. In fact, since the early 1980s, manufacturing employment in Hong Kong has continued to edge downward not only in relative terms but also in absolute numbers. In September 1992, there were 41,937 manufacturing concerns in Hong Kong employing 571,181 persons. This level of employment was some 37% below the peak of 904,646 recorded in September 1981. On the other hand, the share of the tertiary sector as a whole in the total workforce increased from about 49% in 1980 to over 65% in 1991, and further to nearly 68% in 1992. This development signified a growing structural orientation of the economy towards services, in line with Hong Kong's continued expansion as a financial and trading centre and its increasing economic integration with South China.

So far as Hong Kong's status as a financial centre in the Asia-Pacific region is concerned, there are now 515 banks (including representative offices of foreign banks) and deposit-taking companies in the territory. Of the world's top 100 banks, 83 have established a presence in Hong Kong, 79 of which operate with a full banking licence. Thanks to the favourable geographical and time zone location, strong links with China and other economies in East and Southeast Asia, and, above all, the absence of any restrictions on capital flows in and out of the territory, a substantial proportion of the banking transactions in Hong Kong are international in nature. In 1992, more than 60% of aggregate assets and liabilities of the banking sector were external, spreading over more than 100 countries. With an average daily turnover of around US$61 billion, according to a global foreign exchange market survey conducted in April 1992, Hong Kong's foreign exchange market, which forms an integral part of the global market, is among the largest trading centres in the region. Moreover, particularly through the syndication of loans and fund management, Hong Kong serves as an important centre for the financial intermediation of international flows of savings and investment. It is reported that between 70% and 80% of syndicated loans for China as well as Southeast Asia are arranged in the territory.[10] Tangible evidence of Hong Kong's significance as the region's financial centre is also provided by its gold market, which is the largest in Asia and the third largest in the world, and its bustling stock market. The local stock market, with a total market capitalization of HK$1,332 billion (US$171 billion) at the end of 1992, ranked second in Asia after Japan's.

Alongside its continued expansion as a major financial centre in the Asia-Pacific region, another robust development that occurred in the 1980s was the re-emergence of Hong Kong as a centre for China trade. In large measure, this upsurge has been activated by the opening up of China since the late 1970s, which has not only led to a dramatic revival of Hong Kong's traditional role as an entrepôt for China, but also generated an inlet for outward processing trade which we shall consider later. And, unlike the early postwar period,

Table 3.1 Percentage Contribution by Major Industrial Sectors to GDP, 1980–1991

Sector	1980	1985	1990	1991
Primary sector	1.0	0.7	0.3	0.2
Secondary sector	31.8	29.6	25.1	23.0
Manufacturing	23.8	21.9	17.2	15.5
Construction	6.7	5.0	5.6	5.3
Tertiary sector	67.2	69.7	74.6	76.8
Financial services	22.8	16.3	20.8	23.0
Trading services	20.4	21.8	24.3	25.4
Transport and communication	7.5	8.1	9.4	9.7

Notes: Financial services include banking, finance, real estate and business services; trading services include wholesale, retail, import and export trades, and hotels and restaurants; transport includes storage.

Sources: HKGCSD—*EGDP* 1966–1992.

Table 3.2 Percentage Distribution of Working Population by Major Industrial Sectors, 1980–1992

Sector	1980	1985	1990	1991	1992
Primary sector	1.4	1.8	1.1	1.0	1.0
Secondary sector	49.8	43.8	36.8	33.7	31.5
Manufacturing	41.7	35.6	28.0	25.3	22.6
Construction	7.6	7.5	8.4	8.2	8.4
Tertiary sector	48.8	54.4	62.1	65.3	67.5
Financial services	4.9	5.8	7.3	8.4	8.6
Trading services	20.0	22.9	26.1	26.8	28.0
Transport and communication	7.0	8.2	9.9	10.0	10.8

Sources: HKGCSD—*QRHSLFC*, relevant issues.

Hong Kong's new entrepôt function has added significant value to trade with banking, transportation, insurance and other business services.

Resulting largely from dynamic outward processing and re-export trade, Hong Kong has witnessed a steady proliferation of trading entities in its industrial structure. In mid-1991, according to Hong Kong Trade Development Council (TDC) data,[11] there were 68,659 trading firms in Hong Kong, almost five times the number of 1978, the year China started to open up its economy. During the same period, gainful employment in these trading firms rose by four times to some 367,800. In analysing contributions by the trading sector to the local economy, however, one has to consider that the kind of trading activity currently undertaken by Hong Kong companies has far exceeded the traditional entrepôt trade, as the TDC rightly argues. It actually embraces a lot of production-related services such as product design, sample making, quality control, packaging, transportation and warehousing. More important still, many companies declared as trading entities in Hong Kong have industrial undertakings, in one form or another, outside the territory. The most common and easiest form is an outward processing venture in South China. As a result, the real distinction between manufacturing and trading activities in Hong Kong, as well as their respective value-added contributions to the economy, has been blurred over the years.

Indeed, with the continual transfer of an increasingly large part of Hong Kong's manufacturing capacity across the border, not only is the nature of business difficult to define, the geographical boundary of production activity performed by many Hong Kong companies has likewise dissolved. This trend of outward processing development has given rise to an oft-heard question about the appropriateness of GDP as a measure of Hong Kong's aggregate income. As yet, Hong Kong has no national income or gross national product (GNP) statistics. Certainly, with the increasing importance of outward processing trade, net factor income earnings from across the border loom large, and more importantly so with the passage of time, in the determination of the total value added and factor income of Hong Kong residents.

After all, given its comparative advantage—arising from both physical and man-made conditions—in entrepôt trade, financial and shipping services, Hong Kong's city-state economy has traditionally had a large service sector when compared with other economies at a similar stage of development. Today, with its booming tertiary sector accounting for almost 77% of its total GDP, Hong Kong has perhaps the most service-oriented economy in the world. Conceivably, as China's principal trading partner, middleman, financier and facilitator,[12] the output and employment of Hong Kong's tertiary sector as a whole are likely to see further surges in the years to come.

Yet, despite its relative decline over the past decade, manufacturing industry has remained one of the most important economic sectors in the territory. To be sure, the significance of export manufacturing in Hong Kong goes far beyond the relative GDP contribution and employment statistics. Amongst other valuable characteristics, there are direct and indirect linkage effects, such as the demand for intermediate and secondary supporting services including banking, insurance, and legal services. It is in this light that we should watch Hong Kong's trade-dependent, service-oriented economy as it goes into the last decade of the twentieth century.

Changes in trade structure

Hong Kong has always had a highly trade-dependent economy, and increasingly so since the launch of economic reforms and the adoption of the open-door policy by China in the late 1970s. The changing degree of Hong Kong's reliance on imports and its export propulsion between 1980 and 1992 can be seen from the increased import and export ratios in relation to Hong Kong's GDP. As shown in Table 3.3, the import-GDP ratio reached a record high of nearly 129% in 1992, compared to about 122% in 1991 and 82% in 1980. On the other hand, export ratios rose even more markedly from about 72% in 1980 to nearly 120% in 1991 and further to approximately 125% in 1992, indicating an increasing degree of export propulsion over the years. This robust export growth was mainly attributable to the structural shift from domestic exports to re-exports made possible by the availability of outward processing facilities in South China along with the rapid increase in China's exports through Hong Kong. Taken together, the volume of Hong Kong's two-way external trade in merchandise rose from about 1.5 times GDP in 1980 to well over 2.5 times GDP in 1992. With the possible exception of Singapore's city-state economy, such a high and increasing foreign trade proportion is rarely seen, even among the family of small, open economic entities.

By any standard, the growth of Hong Kong's foreign trade volume has been little short of phenomenal. The money value of Hong Kong's merchandise exports in 1992 of HK$925 billion was about 9.4 times that of HK$98 billion in 1980, representing a compound growth rate of 20.5% per year; while imports in 1992 of HK$955 billion were about 8.6 times the HK$112 billion in 1980, at a compound growth rate of 19.6% per year. All together, the combined volume of Hong Kong's merchandise trade grew from HK$210 billion in 1980 to HK$1,880 billion in 1992, at an average growth rate of 20% a year, more than three times as fast as world trade. Despite its size, in value terms Hong Kong is now among the top ten traders in the world.

Table 3.3 Changes in Merchandise Trade Structure and Foreign Portions, 1980–1992

Year	1980	1985	1990	1991	1992
Value (at HK$ billion)					
Total exports (X)	98.2	235.1	639.9	765.9	925.0
Domestic exports (DX)	68.2	129.9	225.9	231.0	234.1
Re-exports (RX)	30.1	105.3	414.0	534.8	690.8
Total imports (M)	111.6	231.4	642.5	779.0	955.3
Total trade (X+M)	209.9	466.6	1,282.4	1,544.9	1,880.3
Total GDP (at market prices)	136.8	261.1	558.9	641.1	742.6
Proportion (in percentages)					
DX/X	69.4	55.2	35.3	30.2	25.3
RX/X	30.6	44.8	64.7	69.8	74.7
RX/DX	44.1	81.1	183.3	231.5	295.1
X/GDP	71.8	90.0	114.5	119.5	124.6
M/GDP	81.6	88.6	115.0	121.5	128.6
(X+M)/GDP	153.5	178.6	229.5	241.0	253.2

Sources: HKGCSD—*AROT* and —*ARHKET*, relevant issues; and HKGCSD—*EGDP* 1966–1992.

In respect of trade balance, Hong Kong has had a chronic deficit in trade in merchandise, at least up to the mid-1980s. Deficits in merchandise trade, however, have not been a matter of grave concern in Hong Kong, as in most years these deficits have been amply compensated for by net income from invisible trade in services. In 1992, Hong Kong had a trade deficit on merchandise of HK$30.3 billion, or HK$33.5 billion when adjusted for imports of gold for industrial and commercial use. Combined with an invisible trade surplus of HK$46.3 billion, there was an overall trade account surplus for the year of HK$12.8 billion.[13] The continued expansion in trade in services in recent years was in line with the growing importance of Hong Kong as a regional trading, financial, business services and tourist centre.

Meanwhile, capitalizing on increasing economic integration with South China through outward direct investment and production, the structure of Hong Kong's merchandise tradables has continued to evolve, with more tilting towards those re-exports involving China in both directions. Enlarged production capacity aside, the lower production costs in South China helped to maintain the external competitiveness of Hong Kong's exportables in the world market. By relocating the more labour-intensive production processes across the border, Hong Kong manufacturers have been able to concentrate on the higher value-added and more human capital-intensive production processes, thereby contributing to the upgrading of the manufacturing sector. Concurrently, it has also facilitated the release of a good portion of the local manufacturing workforce to the service sector, thereby underpinning its continued growth.

Having said this, we now turn to the significance of the close economic links between Hong Kong and China that have developed in the years following China's adoption of a more open economic policy in relation to Hong Kong's changing merchandise trade flows with China and other major trading partners.

Re-exports

One of the most visible signs of Hong Kong's increasing economic integration with South China is the rise in re-export growth in the territory. In 1988, for the first time in over thirty-odd years, the volume of Hong Kong re-exports exceeded that of domestic exports. By 1992, around three-quarters of Hong Kong's total exports were re-exports. Spurred by the robust growth in outward processing activities, as well as the continued expansion of international trade in China, the distributive shares of Hong Kong's domestic exports and re-exports as a percentage of its total exports have been more than neatly reversed between the late 1970s and early 1990s.

Hong Kong entrepôt trade in relation to major places of origin and of consignment is listed in Tables 3.4 and 3.5 respectively. As shown, China was the largest source of, as well as the largest market for, Hong Kong's re-exports. Yet, as regards Hong Kong's re-exports to China, it is of interest to note that, as late as the early 1970s, Hong Kong's re-exports to China remained at a very low level, amounting to a few percent of its total re-exports. This scene changed dramatically when China's open-door policy came into being. Since 1980, China has replaced the United States and Japan as the largest market for Hong Kong's re-exports in addition to its more traditional role as the largest source of goods re-exported through Hong Kong. Despite the relative decline since the mid-1980s, China accounted for about 31% of all goods re-exported

Table 3.4 Origin of Re-Exports, 1980–1992 (HK$ billion)

Origin	1980	1985	1990	1991	1992
China	8.4	34.6	240.4	315.7	403.8
	(27.9)	(32.9)	(58.1)	(59.0)	(58.4)
Japan	5.9	22.5	42.3	57.2	85.0
	(19.6)	(21.4)	(10.2)	(10.7)	(12.3)
Taiwan	2.1	9.6	30.3	41.7	54.4
	(7.1)	(9.1)	(7.3)	(7.8)	(7.9)
United States	3.2	9.5	24.5	26.6	32.1
	(10.5)	(9.0)	(5.9)	(5.0)	(4.6)
South Korea	0.9	3.7	11.6	15.0	19.4
	(2.9)	(3.5)	(2.8)	(2.8)	(2.8)
Germany	0.5	2.0	5.5	6.8	9.1
	(1.6)	(1.9)	(1.3)	(1.3)	(1.3)
Singapore	0.3	0.9	4.7	6.2	8.3
	(0.9)	(0.9)	(1.1)	(1.2)	(1.2)
United Kingdom	0.5	1.7	4.6	5.8	7.4
	(1.6)	(1.6)	(1.1)	(1.1)	(1.1)

Notes: Figures in parentheses are percentage shares of the corresponding total re-export trade. As the Federal Republic of Germany (West Germany) and German Democratic Republic (East Germany) were unified on 3 October 1990, entries for Germany before that date refer to West Germany and those from 1990 onwards refer to the trade with the unified Germany.

Sources: HKGCSD—*AROT* and —*ARHKET*, relevant issues.

through Hong Kong in 1992, compared with a meagre share of less than 2% in 1977. Hong Kong has now recovered as a fully-fledged entrepôt, with China playing the role of the leading trader, accounting for over 89% of Hong Kong's two-way entrepôt trade.

Apart from China, the other major re-exports' markets were the United States, Japan, Germany, Taiwan, South Korea and Singapore. In general, the relative importance of Japan and that of Singapore have been declining and that of the United States, like China, has been increasing very rapidly. The implications of the rapid growth in Hong Kong's entrepôt trade involving China on the one hand and the United States on the other on Hong Kong's status as an

Table 3.5 Destination of Re-Exports, 1980–1992 (HK$ billion)

Destination	1980	1985	1990	1991	1992
China	4.6	46.0	110.9	153.3	212.1
	(15.4)	(43.7)	(26.8)	(28.7)	(30.7)
United States	3.1	14.7	87.7	110.8	148.5
	(10.3)	(14.0)	(21.2)	(20.7)	(21.5)
Japan	2.2	5.5	24.4	29.6	37.5
	(7.3)	(5.2)	(5.9)	(5.5)	(5.4)
Germany	0.7	1.5	23.4	32.1	33.1
	(2.2)	(1.5)	(5.7)	(6.0)	(4.8)
Taiwan	2.2	4.3	21.2	24.8	26.2
	(7.4)	(4.1)	(5.1)	(4.6)	(3.8)
United Kingdom	0.8	1.2	12.1	14.7	20.6
	(2.7)	(1.2)	(2.9)	(2.7)	(3.0)
Singapore	2.5	4.4	12.6	12.1	13.9
	(8.4)	(4.2)	(3.0)	(2.3)	(2.0)
South Korea	0.9	3.9	13.0	14.6	13.6
	(3.0)	(3.7)	(3.1)	(2.7)	(2.0)

Notes: Figures in parentheses are percentage shares of the corresponding total re-export trade.

Sources: As Table 3.4.

international entrepôt are far-reaching. In particular, the issue of the United States' annual renewal of China's most-favoured-nation (MFN) status casts a shadow. With regard to the origin of the re-exports, the other major suppliers were Japan, Taiwan, the United States and South Korea. In 1992, 86% of Hong Kong's re-exports originated from these five leading suppliers, compared to some 68% in 1980. As destinations, however, they accounted for around 63% and 43% in 1992 and 1980, respectively.

At this juncture, it is worth pointing out that because of Taiwan's ban on direct economic ties with China, Hong Kong has played a pivotal role as an intermediary handling much of the trade flow between the two sides of the Taiwan Strait. By dint of this, indirect trade between Taiwan and mainland China has been one of the fastest growing components in Hong Kong's entrepôt trade.[14] Between 1978 and 1990, indirect trade across the Strait grew at an average annual rate of 51%. It reached US$5.8 billion and US$7.3 billion in 1991 and 1992, respectively. This entrepôt trade now makes up around 45% of Hong Kong's bilateral trade with Taiwan. On top of this, as much as 50% of Hong Kong's imports from Taiwan are destined for China. Conversely, around 30% of Hong Kong's total exports to Taiwan are made up of products of mainland origin, and these China-made re-exports now exceed Hong Kong's domestic exports to Taiwan.

Correspondingly, Taiwan became China's seventh largest trading partner in 1991, and the fifth largest in 1992. Meanwhile, Taiwan was China's fifth largest importer in 1990, and the fourth largest in both 1991 and 1992. Much of this increased trading interaction was attributable to the rapid upsurge of Taiwan's outward direct investment and processing activities across the Strait. In 1992, Taiwan stood second in the number of FDI projects in China and third in contract value after Hong Kong and the United States.[15] This is noteworthy as an obvious reflection of the deepening economic relations between Taiwan and the mainland. Apparently, the increasing economic integration and cooperation between the "giant dragon" of China and the two "small dragons", namely Hong Kong and Taiwan, have signalled the coming of a Greater China economic community that is bidding to become a significant player in the global economy of the twenty-first century. Certainly, if the next century is going to be the Asia-Pacific era, the continuing economic integration and cooperation of the three Chinese economies must be the cornerstone.

Domestic exports

Apart from the booming entrepôt trade, Hong Kong's domestic exports to China increased by leaps and bounds over the past decade or so. In 1977, only about 0.1% of Hong Kong's domestic exports found their way into China. But this has changed dramatically since China launched its economic reforms and adopted the open-door policy in late 1978. In 1984, for the first time in postwar years, China overtook Britain and Germany to become the second largest market for Hong Kong's domestic exports. As shown in Table 3.6, which outlines the performance of Hong Kong's domestic exports in major markets, by 1992, China's share had risen to an all-time high of 26.5%, more than the combined total of the British and German intakes. However, it is important to note that, although an increasing proportion of Hong Kong's domestic exports

Table 3.6 Domestic Exports by Major Importing Economies, 1980–1992 (HK$ billion)

Destination	1980	1985	1990	1991	1992
United States	22.6	57.7	66.4	62.9	64.6
	(33.1)	(44.4)	(29.4)	(27.2)	(27.6)
China	1.6	15.2	47.5	54.4	62.0
	(2.4)	(11.7)	(21.0)	(23.5)	(26.5)
Germany	7.4	8.0	18.0	19.3	16.0
	(10.8)	(6.2)	(8.0)	(8.4)	(6.8)
United Kingdom	6.8	8.5	13.5	13.7	12.5
	(10.0)	(6.6)	(6.0)	(5.9)	(5.4)
Japan	2.3	4.5	12.1	11.7	11.0
	(3.4)	(3.4)	(5.3)	(5.0)	(4.7)
Singapore	1.8	2.2	7.8	8.8	10.4
	(2.6)	(1.7)	(3.5)	(3.8)	(4.4)
Taiwan	0.8	1.2	5.7	6.1	6.5
	(1.2)	(1.0)	(2.5)	(2.6)	(2.8)
Canada	1.8	4.4	5.4	5.0	5.0
	(2.6)	(3.4)	(2.4)	(2.2)	(2.1)
Netherlands	1.6	2.1	5.0	5.2	4.9
	(2.3)	(1.6)	(2.2)	(2.3)	(2.1)
France	1.4	1.8	3.6	3.7	3.2
	(2.1)	(1.4)	(1.6)	(1.6)	(1.4)

Notes: Figures in parentheses are percentage shares of the corresponding total domestic exports.

Sources: As Table 3.4.

to China was to meet its local demands for finished goods, the bulk of these exports consisted of raw materials, parts and semi-manufactures, and were related to outward processing arrangements commissioned by Hong Kong companies, amid the tight labour market situation in Hong Kong.

Despite its relative decline in recent years, the United States was nevertheless still the largest market for Hong Kong's domestic exports, accounting for 27.6% of the total value in 1992, compared with the record high of over 44%

in 1985. For historical reasons, the United Kingdom was traditionally one of Hong Kong's most important market outlets. But its relative importance has been declining. In the early 1960s, its share still stood at over 20%, second only to the United States, whereas Germany's share was less than 4%. By 1992, the British intake had declined to only 5.4%, while Germany's share was 6.8%. Although Japan has been Hong Kong's fourth largest export market for most of the postwar years, its relative intake has seen little improvement over time. It accounted for less than 5% of the total value in 1992.

As to other important markets, in the early 1960s, a number of economies in Southeast Asia, including Malaysia, Thailand and Indonesia, were still among the list of Hong Kong's top ten markets. But by 1970s, only Singapore remained on the list. The shares of these Southeast Asian countries were replaced by Canada, the Netherlands, France and, more recently, Taiwan. At any rate, the direction and level of Hong Kong's domestic export trade and their changes over time have been much influenced by the changing economic conditions and commercial policies in major importing countries.

Imports

To meet the needs of its teeming populace and the requirements of its diverse industries, Hong Kong is almost entirely dependent on imported resources. Under free trade these supplies come from all over the world. What is imported from different exporting economies largely reflects their competitive supply conditions. Because of geographical proximity, it is only natural that Hong Kong often turns first to China for competitive supply. Aside from the usual merchandise imports, around 75–80% of fresh water now consumed in Hong Kong is imported from China.

As Table 3.7 shows, China's share of Hong Kong merchandise imports increased from about 20% in 1980 to over 37% in the past two years. One can surmise that a large part of this rapid import growth in recent years has been derived from the upsurge in Hong Kong's re-export trade, which was, in turn, partly due to the continued migration of Hong Kong's manufacturing base in the form of outward processing activity across the border, and partly due to the increase in exports from China, a significant proportion of which was channelled through Hong Kong to overseas markets, especially to the United States.

Table 3.7 Imports by Major Source Economies, 1980–1992 (HK$ billion)

Source	1980	1985	1990	1991	1992
China	21.9	59.0	236.1	293.4	354.3
	(19.7)	(25.5)	(36.8)	(37.7)	(37.1)
Japan	25.6	53.3	103.4	127.4	166.2
	(23.0)	(23.1)	(16.1)	(16.4)	(17.4)
Taiwan	8.0	20.9	58.1	74.6	87.0
	(7.1)	(9.0)	(9.0)	(9.6)	(9.1)
United States	13.2	21.9	51.8	58.8	70.6
	(11.8)	(9.5)	(8.1)	(7.6)	(7.4)
South Korea	3.9	8.3	28.2	34.9	44.2
	(3.5)	(3.6)	(4.4)	(4.5)	(4.6)
Singapore	7.4	11.3	26.1	31.5	39.1
	(6.6)	(4.9)	(4.1)	(4.0)	(4.1)
Germany	2.9	6.7	14.8	16.6	21.9
	(2.6)	(2.9)	(2.3)	(2.1)	(2.3)
United Kingdom	5.5	8.4	14.1	16.5	19.2
	(4.9)	(3.7)	(2.2)	(2.1)	(2.0)
Italy	1.4	3.6	10.9	11.7	14.8
	(1.2)	(1.5)	(1.7)	(1.5)	(1.6)

Notes: Figures in parentheses are percentage shares of the corresponding total imports.

Sources: As Table 3.4.

At the start of the 1980s, Japan was still the largest supplier of merchandise goods to Hong Kong. But with the opening up of China and the subsequent closer economic ties between China and Hong Kong, since 1982 China has regained its traditional number-one position. Since the mid-1980s onwards, Hong Kong has obtained around 50% of its imports from China and Japan, with the former being the most important source of foodstuffs and the latter supplying industrial materials, parts and components. The two are approximately equally important as suppliers of consumer goods. Despite the relative decline of imports from Japan, the combined share of these two traditional sources reached a record high of nearly 55% in 1992, compared with some 43% in 1980.

The other major sources of Hong Kong's imports were Taiwan, the United States, South Korea, Singapore, Germany and the United Kingdom. The importance of the United States and the United Kingdom in particular has been declining. On the other hand, Taiwan and South Korea have emerged as important sources of supply to Hong Kong. In fact, not only has Taiwan surpassed the United Kingdom as Hong Kong's major supplier since the mid-1970s, it has also replaced the United States since 1987 to run a distant third as an import source. As in the rise of Taiwan, the growth momentum from South Korea in recent years has been supported by a substantial amount of re-exports to China.

At this point, we should note that, due to the large proportion of re-exports, Hong Kong's official import trade statistics *per se* can be misleading at large, especially when analysed by end-use categories. In 1990, for example, industrial raw materials and semi-manufactures accounted for some 39%, consumer goods another 39%, capital goods 15%, foodstuffs 6%, and fuels 2%, respectively, of Hong Kong's gross import payment. But as much as some 51% of these raw materials and semi-manufactures, 89% of the consumer goods, 57% of the capital goods, 31% of the foodstuffs, and 17% of the fuels were later re-exported. With this caveat in mind, one has to look into retained imports (gross imports net of re-exports) for information on Hong Kong's own import requirements.

The surge of "outward processing" trade

For obvious factor-endowment reasons, Hong Kong's industrial development had to concentrate on light industries, as dictated by the comparative advantage doctrine. Yet, comparative advantages are never static assets. Since the late 1970s, as noted earlier, Hong Kong's price competitiveness in light export manufacturing has begun to erode as a result of increases in wages and land costs and the emergence of lower-cost regional competitors. The opening up of the Chinese economy and the subsequent setting up of four SEZs, including in particular the Shenzhen SEZ which is just across the Hong Kong border, in the early 1980s, have provided new and competitive outlets for Hong Kong's hard-pressed manufacturers. As also noted earlier, attracted by the much lower costs of production in the open coastal areas of South China, many Hong Kong industrialists shifted their production facilities or part of their production processes over there. This development gives rise to a large volume of what is called "outward processing trade" between Hong Kong and China.[16]

In this outward processing trade, there were exports (both domestic exports and re-exports) of raw materials and semi-manufactures, including near-finished goods, from or through Hong Kong to China (normally import duties exempted) for processing. This is accompanied with a contractual arrangement for subsequent reshipment of the processed goods to Hong Kong for final packaging and further processing if necessary, or else for re-export to third countries. On the other hand, there were imports from China of which all or part of their raw materials and semi-manufactures, including near-finished goods, were under contractual arrangement previously exported from or through Hong Kong. The development of outward processing activities has been stimulated by a host of push and pull factors. At the risk of oversimplification, however, the push factors in Hong Kong, especially on the question of labour, mirror closely the pull factors in South China. Over the past ten years, experience has now proved that highly favourable factor-resource conditions exist for complementary development and inter-territory division of labour under the outward processing arrangements, leading to dynamic economies of a scale and scope that are mutually beneficial.

In many ways, especially in terms of GNP measures, the continued migration of the territory's manufacturing base across the border has effectively enlarged Hong Kong's productive capacity. Today, in addition to the almost four-fifths of Hong Kong manufacturers who have transferred production to the mainland, around 25,000 factories in the Pearl River Delta region of Guangdong alone are engaged in outward processing for Hong Kong companies, while between three and four million workers there are directly or indirectly employed by these firms.[17] When it is noted that the entire employed labour force of the manufacturing sector in Hong Kong was less than 0.6 million at the end of 1992, the magnitude of the outward processing counterpart, which was about five to seven times as large as Hong Kong's own manufacturing workforce, becomes quickly apparent. Following the relocation of more labour-intensive processes across the border, many Hong Kong workers who were previously on the production line have become responsible for, among things, much of the training, supervision, and quality control. For those still on the production front, the tasks involved have become more skill and knowledge intensive. Meanwhile, the local manufacturing sector has been able to release a good portion of its labour resources to other sectors

Table 3.8 Percentage Share of Trade of Outward Processing Nature to Total Trade with China by Commodity Groups, 1989 and 1992

	Domestic exports		Re-exports		Imports	
Commodity group	**1989**	**1992**	**1989**	**1992**	**1989**	**1992**
Textiles	84.8	87.4	71.5	81.9	12.8	23.0
Clothing	85.1	93.2	87.3	76.0	84.5	84.4
Plastic products	83.9	77.5	58.0	64.5	73.4	89.3
Machinery and electrical appliances	56.7	59.7	24.9	27.3	77.8	81.0
Electronic products	94.6	92.7	43.1	41.4	85.2	92.7
Watches and clocks	98.5	98.6	93.5	97.7	94.6	94.3
Toys, games and sports goods	96.4	91.9	60.1	80.1	94.1	96.9
Metals and metal products	64.2	69.0	37.8	34.8	30.2	43.6
All commodities	76.0	74.3	43.6	46.2	58.1	72.1

Sources: HKGCSD—*ARHKET*, relevant issues.

which are likewise faced with the problem of labour recruitment in a very tight overall labour market situation. As mentioned earlier, the tertiary service sector in general, and trading, finance and business services in particular have been absorbing these labour resources and their relative contributions to the domestic economy have been rising as a result.

To provide a better understanding of Hong Kong's trade with China, the Hong Kong Census and Statistics Department began to compile statistics on domestic exports and re-exports to China for outward processing purposes in the third quarter of 1988; and statistics on imports from China related to outward processing in the first quarter of 1989. Apart from providing an indirect indication of the growth in outward processing activities on a quarterly basis, these statistics serve to confirm the general impression that much of the phenomenal increase in Sino-Hong Kong trade during the past decade can be attributed to the expansion in such activities. On this basis, over 72% of Hong Kong's imports from China were related to outward processing in 1992, compared to some 58% in 1989. The corresponding proportions in 1992 were 74% for domestic exports and 46% for re-exports, compared to 76% and 44% in 1989. Altogether, in 1992, over 52% of Hong Kong's total exports were related to outward processing arrangements.

Analysed by broad commodity categories, the outward processing content of all imports from China, as shown in Table 3.8, was generally high except for textiles. As regards domestic exports, the percentage of outward processing trade with respect to most individual commodity groups was no lower than their import equivalents. The ratio for machinery and electrical equipment, however, was somewhat lower than the others. In large measure, this is due to the existence of a strong demand for such Hong Kong products in China. The same was true for re-exports as there was a large market in China for foreign machinery, electrical equipment, consumer electronics such as television sets and sound recorders, as well as metals and metal products. In a nutshell, a large volume and variety of commodities in the trade between Hong Kong and China were associated with outward consignment or commissioned processing businesses. As a corollary, Hong Kong's manufacturing mix has been altering. Instead of expanding horizontally as in the past, the city economy has had to respond vertically by raising its own skill levels and productivity by moving into higher value-added activities.

As to the major locations in China where outward processing activities were domiciled, in 1992 more than 93% of Hong Kong's import trade of this nature had processing work carried out in Guangdong Province, according to the latest Census and Statistics Department's estimates. Through the aggressive outward processing activities of Hong Kong industrialists, the city economy of Hong Kong has been involved in a process of economic integration with South China centred on the Pearl River Delta region for more than a decade now. With the benefit of hindsight, it would not be too far-fetched to describe this process, which has now progressed to a point of virtually no return, as the "Hongkongization" of South China. In fact, the growing interdependence of the Hong Kong and Guangdong economies has now actually gone beyond the domain of real economic aggregates. Concurrent with the growth of cross-border investment and trade, an increasing pool of Hong Kong dollar notes has been used as a second medium of exchange in Guangdong and elsewhere in China. According to a recent study by the Hong Kong and Shanghai Banking Corporation, the amount of Hong Kong dollar notes in circulation in South China increased from HK$0.7 billion in 1980 to as much as HK$15 billion in 1992, representing some 30% of the total currency issued in Hong Kong.[18] Against this backdrop, several key ratios of Hong Kong's monetary aggregates have become less indicative of the state of the local economy and, in some case, even misleading.

Issues and problem areas in the Sino-Hong Kong trading nexus

Since China initiated its economic reforms and opened up its doors to foreign trade and investment some fourteen years ago, Hong Kong's economic fortunes have become increasingly enmeshed with those of China. Today, the most dynamically growing component in Hong Kong's overall external trade is the re-exports of products from Guangdong and elsewhere in China. Hong Kong and China are now each other's largest external investment and trading partner. Over the years, however, the growing integration of Hong Kong's manufacturing and outward processing trade flows with South China has become something of a new double-edged sword for Hong Kong's externally-oriented economy. On the plus side, China's diverse economy and labour abundance have provided Hong Kong with a vast hinterland of cheap land and low-wage labour just as its own external competitiveness in world tradables was gradually eroding. Economic integration, however, has made Hong Kong inherently vulnerable to the vagaries and vicissitudes of China's external commercial relations with the rest of the world. Most damaging to Hong Kong is the prospect of US trade action against China, both in the form of a revocation of China's MFN trade status with the United States and Section 301 of the United States Trade Act of 1974, or the so-called "Super 301" action of the United States Omnibus Trade and Competitiveness Act of 1988. For obvious political and economic reasons, trade between China and the United States has been conducted over troubled waters in recent times. Amidst this, the importance of the MFN status to China and its implications for Hong Kong could hardly be overstressed.

Under the Jackson-Vanik Amendment to the United States Trade Act of 1974,[19] as a non-market economy country, China's MFN status must be certified annually by a presidential determination stipulating that China meets the requirements for emigration freedom, or by a presidential waiver of the certification. The decision by the US president to extend MFN is automatically implemented unless both Houses of Congress pass a resolution of disapproval. The president can veto such a resolution, and China's MFN status then continues unless the veto is, in turn, overthrown by a two-thirds majority vote in both Houses of Congress. Beyond question, the yearly debate over renewal creates a high level of uncertainty which is damaging to the long-term business prospects of all parties concerned. For the purpose of seeing the extension of MFN status, over the past two years or so China has made a great deal of effort towards resolving a number of trade disputes with the United States, leading to the subsequent signing in 1992 of three memoranda of understanding on protection for US intellectual property rights, on the prohibition of the export of forced-labour products, and on US access to the Chinese market. So far as the market-access agreement is concerned, China has pledged to reduce or eliminate a wide range of trade barriers over the next five years, including tariffs, quotas, import licences, import substitutions, and other forms of non-tariff trade restrictions.

The stakes in the Sino-United States MFN trading nexus are high. On Hong Kong's part, the economic effects of a loss in China's status would be no less significant than for China itself. The arithmetic is simple: China and the United States, when taken together, now account for almost half of Hong Kong's total foreign trade volume. Take away China's MFN, and the United States import tariffs on Hong Kong's re-exports from China would go up as much as ten-fold. Put another way, without the MFN, around two-thirds of China's exports to the United States, much of which originated in Hong Kong-owned plants in South China, would be cut off, dealing a heavy blow to Hong Kong's entrepôt economy. In addition to the loss of the profits arising from outward investment in China, Hong Kong would lose considerably in the re-export markup, which includes profits and the cost of transportation, insurance, packaging and warehousing, and which is very substantial and is earned by Hong Kong middlemen. While estimates of the re-export markup which Hong Kong companies earn vary, conservative survey findings put the average figure for Chinese goods at no less than 16%.[20]

In fact, according to the most recent estimates by the Hong Kong government, the loss of China's MFN status would cost Hong Kong up to 70,000 jobs and up to three percentage points of Hong Kong's annual GDP growth.[21] There is, however, more to this than meets the eye. For one thing, Hong Kong's loss would increase significantly if China were to retaliate against the United States. For another, the casualties would not be confined to China and Hong Kong. Reportedly, the withdrawal of China's MFN status would also cost United States consumers some US$14 billion because of higher tariffs, while retaliation by China would put at risk over 150,000 jobs in the US.[22]

So far as United States external commercial policy is concerned, with the passage of the Omnibus Trade and Competitiveness Act of 1988, as the world trading community knows, the United States Congress has given *de facto* legitimacy to unilateralism in defining US trade rights, determining their violation and meting out punishment to secure satisfaction. As such, even leaving aside political factors such as human rights, missile sales, and the proliferation of nuclear material and technology, China still risks losing its MFN status in the medium term. The simple fact is that, according to United States Department of Commerce statistics, China already has one of the largest trade surpluses with the United States of any exporting economy in the world. Closely related to the trade imbalance issue is the problem of discrepancies between US and Chinese trade data. Official Chinese customs statistics differ widely from US reckoning. The Chinese figures do not take into account the export of goods through Hong Kong. The United States Department of Commerce statistics, in contrast, consider Chinese goods re-exported through Hong Kong to be Chinese exports, but count US goods trans-shipped through Hong Kong as exports to Hong Kong. Correspondingly, China claims to suffer trade deficits with the US, but US trade officials say that the reverse is true. According to the United States Department of Commerce, the country's bilateral deficit with China was US$3.5 billion in 1988. By 1992 it had risen to over US$18 billion, making China's trade imbalance with the United States second to Japan's and surpassing Taiwan's surplus with the United States. By and large, China's surplus, as recorded by the United States Department of Commerce, has become unpalatable to Americans because of its growing magnitude, and, therefore, works against the smooth continuation of its MFN status.

To a considerable extent China's rapid export expansion to the United States and the world market at large since the early 1980s has been spurred by the burgeoning outward processing activity of Hong Kong manufacturers in Guangdong and elsewhere in China. This has enabled Hong Kong to hold down its trade surplus with the United States by shifting a substantial part of the surplus onto China's trade ledgers. Following in the footsteps of Hong Kong, since the mid-1980s many manufacturing concerns in Taiwan have also shifted their production bases to the coastal areas in China, thereby reducing Taiwan's controversial trade surplus with the United States. Taken together, these developments could well threaten to blow up China's surplus with the United States to such a size that protectionist lobbying groups in the United States would become fiercely enraged. Arguably, then, China's MFN status and ultimately Hong Kong's trade prospects are more likely to be jeopardized by economic developments than by political controversy.

More pertinently, within these ongoing trends of outward investment from the two small dragons to mainland China, what is in fact emerging is a new economic entity: the Greater China triangle. As noted earlier, the implications of the advent of the Greater China economic community for the global economy are far-reaching. For one, because of the massive transfer of manufacturing capacity from Hong Kong and Taiwan to China over the past decade, the Greater China combined trade deficit with the United States, perhaps, gives a truer picture. In fact, while there is increasing attention focused on China's trade imbalance with the United States, the US combined trade deficit with the Greater China trio actually declined by some US$3 billion during 1987–91.[23] In the main, the growing US trade imbalance with China must be looked at from a broader regional perspective rather than in isolation.

How far with economic integration

The interdependence and economic integration of two economies, be they large or small, relatively poor or rich, are clearly not a one-way street. Beyond question, the Hong Kong factor in China's reforming economy is, to a greater or lesser extent, the mirror image of the China factor in Hong Kong's evolving economy, and all the discussion in this article must be seen in that light. Yet, while the China factor is beyond the control of Hong Kong, the converse is clearly not true.

Concurrent with the strong growth in money and capital funds from Hong Kong to China, the open-door policy and economic decentralization have encouraged many provincial and municipal entities in China to set up their own companies in Hong Kong. Over the past reformist decade, China's investment in Hong Kong has not only increased rapidly, but also proliferated into practically all major economic sectors. Besides the traditional banking, trade and trade-related activities such as transportation and warehousing, newer areas of investment range from manufacturing, stock market, real estate and property development, construction and infrastructural projects, tourism and tourist-related facilities such as hotels and restaurants, to the operation of taxi fleets and supermarkets. In particular, reflecting the increasing financial links between Hong Kong and China, the Bank of China Group now forms the second largest banking group in Hong Kong, after the Hongkong Bank Group, in terms of deposits and the number of branches.

Today, with more than 3,000 mainland companies operating in the city, China-related businesses are now involved in virtually everything that makes Hong Kong's bustling economy work. It is likely that no one, including the highest ranking officials in Beijing, knows just how much China has invested in Hong Kong. Even granted that the large state-run mainland firms are well charted, the puzzling question is how much capital is funnelled in by uncontrolled businesses and wealthy Chinese mainlanders. In all, while the total value of China's external investment in Hong Kong is a matter of conjecture, an oft-quoted figure these days is of US$15–20 billion,[24] well outpacing that of Japan and the United States.

On balance, there is little question that the China factor has emerged as the single most important factor underlying Hong Kong's robust economic growth in the 1980s. In this regard, a recent study by the Hang Seng Bank is informative for making an overall quantitative assessment about the contribution of

Table 3.9 Percentage Contribution to the Hong Kong Economy by the China Factor

	Contributive share	
GDP sectors	**1980**	**1990**
Primary sector	0.0	0.0
Secondary sector		
Manufacturing	0.0	10.6
Construction	0.0	5.0
Electricity, gas and water	2.7	7.0
Tertiary sector		
Financial services	0.8	6.5
Trading and entertainment services	8.9	33.7
Import and export trades	17.4	48.4
Wholesale and retail trades	0.0	5.9
Hotels and restaurants	0.0	13.2
Transport, storage and communication	12.0	20.5
Direct contribution	2.7	12.8
Total (direct and indirect) contribution	5.3	25.7

Sources: Hang Seng Bank, "The current state of the Chinese economy and its impact on Hong Kong", *HSEM*, June 1993.

the China factor in relation to Hong Kong's aggregate domestic output, as Table 3.9 shows. In 1980, at the dawn of the Dengist economic reforms, business with China contributed only about 5% to Hong Kong's economy; by 1990, just a decade later, that share had risen to nearly 26%. Without doubt, given the extensively growing economic links between the two places, China's direct and indirect contributions should have increased further in the past two years. The corollary is: without the Dengist reforms for more liberal trade and investment policies, Hong Kong's GDP growth during the 1980s would have averaged only 4.6% in real terms instead of the actual 7.1%.[25]

Looking ahead, the Hong Kong economy is bound to be even more intimately tied in with the mainland's in the years to come. And given the anticipated political parameters by way of the promised "one country, two systems" framework, any further economic integration with the hinterland appears likely to be for better rather than worse for the future SAR, which, as a separate independent economic entity as prescribed in the Sino-British Joint Declaration of 1984 and the promulgated Basic Law, would not be obliged to share, for example, its budget revenue with Beijing or the Guangdong authority.

With the exception of possible disturbance from the MFN-status wrangle, the hinterland will clearly continue to provide an unlimited labour supply for Hong Kong's manufacturers to fall back on. In a way, this expedient recourse may forestall the pressures for a technological upgrading in Hong Kong in the long run, but the potential losses in this respect will probably be outweighed by the continuous structural shift of the Hong Kong economy towards the modern services sector, such as banking, finance, and telecommunications, with higher value-added contributions.

There are other favourable factors at work as well, the foremost being China's prospective readmission to the GATT family. The expected wide-ranging industrial deregulation, just to make China compatible with GATT's market economy regime, will almost certainly help to open up many hitherto untapped trading opportunities to the outside world, let alone the abolition of the various non-tariff import barriers and the reductions in import tariffs.[26] Already, amidst the GATT euphoria which has emerged strongly in China since the summer of 1992, many Hong Kong industrial and business conglomerates are strongly poised to move into the vast Chinese service sector, including retail business, real estate, and transportation. Likewise, any early measure taken to make the Chinese currency—renminbi—fully convertible will only help to make China even more attractive as an investment proposition for Hong Kong businessmen.

To conclude, Hong Kong's economic prospects and the solutions to its problems are now intimately tied to both economic performance and political developments in China. Under the Sino-British Agreement, the direction of Hong Kong's capitalist economy towards one increasingly integrated with China, especially South China, is a fact of life in Hong Kong. While the China factor now forms the main impetus of Hong Kong's prosperity and stability, Hong Kong's usefulness to China's modernization also goes without saying. Rhetorically, tiny Hong Kong and the Chinese giant have more or less become Siamese twins. It is tempting to argue, therefore, that Hong Kong and China are going to be in the same boat, and for the dependent Hong Kong not to go under in a sea of incessant changes, China must be kept afloat. All said, the growing interdependence and increasing economic integration between Hong Kong and China underlines the need to maintain a concordant relationship in the years to come.

4

Guangdong Province Ascending as the "Fifth Dragon"*

Guangdong's economic aspiration is to catch up with the "four dragons" of East Asia within fifteen to twenty years.[1] Many theoretical simulations purport to show how export promotion or other strategies might enable the province to achieve this goal and attain the income and consumption standards prevailing in these regions. Such exercises may vary in econometric sophistication, but they share a bullish confidence based on accelerated economic growth in the province since the early 1980s.

It is true that in recent years, Guangdong has outpaced virtually every other province in almost every aspect of economic performance. Many factors have contributed to this achievement. Foremost among them is the preferential treatment accorded by the central government since 1980, which has enabled the provincial authorities to retain fiscal revenue and foreign currency receipts in excess of obligatory—and fixed remittances to the central government. This marks a sharp departure from previous confiscatory practices.[2]

Such financial privileges have enhanced provincial autonomy in the allocation of resources, especially in the foreign trade sector. But Guangdong's heightened economic independence has not only strengthened allocative efficiency within the province. It has also facilitated its increased integration into the world economy, paving the way for its competitive involvement in export and import markets, and generating improvements in productivity in indigenous manufacturing.

---

* Reprinted from "The fifth dragon: Economic development" (coauthored with Robert Ash), in Brian Hook (ed.), *Guangdong: China's Promised Land,* Hong Kong: Oxford University Press, 1996, pp. 149–92.

The role of the Special Economic Zones (SEZs) is an important dimension of Guangdong's economic success. Three of the four original SEZs were located in the province[3] and, at least until 1988, these absorbed almost all foreign direct investment (FDI) into China—most of it coming from neighbouring Hong Kong. Such inflows of FDI have brought in their wake fundamental changes in business attitudes and practices in Guangdong, and increasingly have acted as a catalyst in initiating structural changes in its economic system.

Such are the bare bones of recent economic development in Guangdong. In what follows, we seek to highlight the salient aspects of this process against the background of institutional and policy adjustments since the early 1980s. After considering the economic significance of Guangdong vis-à-vis China and the four East Asian dragons, we will analyse the nature and impact of economic growth and structural change both within the province itself and relative to the country as a whole. We will also look at the roles of investment and foreign capital, foreign trade, and Guangdong's links with Hong Kong. Finally, we will briefly assess the future prospects for the aspiring fifth little dragon.

The economic significance of Guangdong Province

With a population of 65 million in 1992, Guangdong is the fifth largest province in China, accounting for 5.5% of the national total. It is also one of the most densely populated provinces, its surface area of 0.18 million square kilometres constituting a mere 1.9% of the national figure.

Table 4.1 shows that in terms of its population and land base, Guangdong is a much larger entity than the four East Asian dragons.[4] But the economic gap between Guangdong and the other regions remains very wide.[5] Unadjusted estimates of per capita gross domestic product (GDP) show the province lagging far behind—a finding which is not materially altered, if an adjusted "purchasing power parity" base estimate is substituted for the official figure. The contrasts in terms of trade volume and intensity, which are based on original US dollar accounting and are therefore less problematic, are even more striking.

This static picture conceals, however, the progress which the aspiring Chinese dragon has made since the early 1980s. The inherent difficulties in making purchasing power parity estimates counsel caution in giving wholesale

Table 4.1 Major Economic Measures in Guangdong Province and the Four Little Dragons Compared, 1978–1992

	Population (million)	Land (100 sq. km.)	GDP (US$100 million)	GDP/head (US$)	Commodity trade volume (US$100 million) Exports	Imports
	(1)	(2)	(3)	(4)	(5)	(6)
South Korea	43.66	990	2,939	6,732	752	773
Taiwan	20.75	360	2,049	9,925	815	720
Hong Kong	5.81	11	966	16,615	1,195	1,234
Singapore	2.82	6.4	460	16,331	616	665
Guangdong	64.63	1,780	422	654	184	112
(Adjusted purchasing power parity [PPP] estimate)			(2,806)	(4,348)		

Notes: 1. The year-end exchange rate of the respective currency is used for converting into US dollars, except for Singapore for which the annual average exchange rate is applied. For Guangdong, the figures are based on the official rather than the swap-market exchange rate. Since January 1994, however, the two-tier system has been abolished and the official RMB rate readjusted to the level of the prevailing market rate in order to create a unified exchange rate system under an officially managed, floating exchange rate regime. The *de facto* RMB devaluation implies that the actual GNP/GDP figures for China in US dollars should be lower than estimates shown here.

2. The two figures in parentheses for Guangdong are derived by applying to the given official figures the ratio of the World Bank's GDP figure for China as a whole (US$2,460 per capita) based on the "purchasing power parity" (PPP) estimates to the official Chinese figure (US$370 per capita) obtained by conversion at the official exchange rate. The two GDP figures will be lower (US$193,892 million and US$3,005, respectively) if the PPP figure of US$1,700 per capita as estimated by the International Monetary Fund (IMF) is used.

Sources: IMF—*IFSYB* 1993, pp. 326 and 472 for South Korea. HKGCSD—*HKADS* 1993, pp. 4, 16, 95, 109, and 135 for Hong Kong. Ministry of Information and the Arts, Singapore, *Singapore* 1993, pp. 14, 259, 275, and 313 for Singapore. TCEPAD—*TWSDB* 1993, pp. 5, 6, 25, 30, and 152 for Taiwan. *GDTJNJ* 1993, pp. 61–2 and 64–5 for Guangdong. *The Economist*, 15 May 1993 and *TKP*, 18 May 1993 for the World Bank's and IMF's GDP figures.

Table 4.2 Major Economic Indicators of China (Nat'l) and Guangdong (GD) Compared, 1978–1992

	Population (10,000)			GDP (100 million yuan)			GVIO (100 million yuan)			GVAO (100 million yuan)			Grain output (10,000 tons)		
	National	GD	Ratio (%) (2)/(1)	National	GD	Ratio (%) (5)/(4)	National	GD	Ratio (%) (8)/(7)	National	GD	Ratio (%) (11)/(10)	National	GD	Ratio (%) (14)/(13)
	(1)	(2)	(3)	(4)	(5)	(6)	(7)	(8)	(9)	(10)	(11)	(12)	(13)	(14)	(15)
1978	96,259	5,064.15	5.26	3,588.1	184.73	5.15	4,237	200.25	4.73	1,397	85.89	6.15	30,477	1,509.51	4.95
1979	97,542	5,140.50	5.27	3,998.1	207.17	5.18	4,681	217.64	4.65	1,698	100.46	5.92	33,212	1,605.36	4.83
1980	98,705	5,227.67	5.30	4,470.0	245.71	5.50	5,154	223.02	4.33	1,923	122.18	6.35	32,056	1,681.91	5.25
1981	100,072	5,323.50	5.32	4,775.1	284.24	5.95	5,400	270.09	5.00	2,181	139.32	6.39	32,502	1,521.00	4.68
1982	101,654	5,415.32	5.33	5,182.3	331.27	6.39	5,811	293.95	5.06	2,483	170.08	6.85	35,450	1,795.72	5.07
1983	103,008	5,494.14	5.33	5,787.0	357.43	6.18	6,461	329.23	5.10	2,750	173.57	6.31	38,728	1,817.48	4.69
1984	104,357	5,576.59	5.34	6,928.2	441.81	6.38	7,617	405.98	5.33	3,214	201.87	6.28	40,731	1,819.33	4.47
1985	105,851	5,655.59	5.34	8,527.4	553.05	6.49	9,716	532.71	5.48	3,619	245.34	6.78	37,911	1,604.37	4.23
1986	107,507	5,740.71	5.34	9,687.6	637.72	6.58	11,194	631.10	5.64	4,013	279.16	6.96	39,151	1,567.00	4.00
1987	109,300	5,832.15	5.34	11,307.1	807.70	7.14	13,813	878.29	6.36	4,676	348.61	7.46	40,298	1,701.81	4.22
1988	111,026	5,928.31	5.34	14,074.2	1,098.61	7.81	18,224	1,318.92	7.24	5,865	473.78	8.08	39,408	1,636.70	4.15
1989	112,704	6,024.98	5.35	15,997.6	1,311.67	8.20	22,017	1,647.23	7.48	6,535	548.60	8.39	40,755	1,817.21	4.46
1990	114,333	6,246.32	5.46	17,681.3	1,471.84	8.32	23,924	1,902.25	7.95	7,662	600.71	7.84	44,624	1,896.29	4.25
1991	115,823	6,348.95	5.48	20,188.3	1,780.56	8.82	28,248	2,524.12	8.94	8,157	654.82	8.03	43,529	1,873.50	4.30

Table 4.2 (to be continued)

Table 4.2 (continued)

	Population (10,000)			GDP (100 million yuan)			GVIO (100 million yuan)			GVAO (100 million yuan)			Grain output (10,000 tons)		
	National	GD	Ratio (%) (2)/(1)	National	GD	Ratio (%) (5)/(4)	National	GD	Ratio (%) (8)/(7)	National	GD	Ratio (%) (11)/(10)	National	GD	Ratio (%) (14)/(13)
	(1)	(2)	(3)	(4)	(5)	(6)	(7)	(8)	(9)	(10)	(11)	(12)	(13)	(14)	(15)
1992	117,171	6,463.17	5.52	24,020.2	2,293.54	9.55	37,066	3,479.39	9.39	9,085	737.11	8.11	44,266	1,810.40	4.09
Average															
1978–85	100,931	5,362.18	5.31	5,407.03	325.68	6.02	6,134.63	309.11	5.04	2,408.13	154.84	6.43	35,133.4	1,669.34	4.75
1986–92	112,552	6,083.51	5.41	16,136.61	1,343.09	8.32	22,069.43	1,768.76	8.01	6,570.43	520.40	7.92	41,718.7	1,757.56	4.21

Notes: All yuan figures refer to the current prices. GDP = Gross Domestic Product; GVIO = Gross Value of Industrial Output; GVAO = Gross Value of Agricultural Output.

Sources: Columns 1, 4, 7, 10, 13: *ZGTJNJ* 1993, pp. 31, 50, 81, and 364. Columns 2, 5, 8, 11, 14: *GDTJNJ* 1991, pp. 57 and 132, and 1993, pp. 75, 77, 135, and 167; *QJZDGD* 1949–1988, p. 235; *GDSGMJJHSHFZTJZL* 1949–1989, p. 4 (section on balance statistics), and p. 36 (section on rural sector).

credence to the finding that Guangdong's adjusted per capita GDP in 1992 was only 35% behind that of South Korea. But there is no reason to question the impressive momentum of its recent economic growth, relative to the national performance and that of each of the four East Asian dragons.

Table 4.2 reflects this momentum. For example, Guangdong's share of national GDP increased from 5.5% to 9.6% between 1980 and 1992.[6] At a more disaggregated level, during the same period the province's share in national sectoral GDP rose as follows: from 4.6% to 9.1% (industry); from 6.1% to 8.1% (agriculture) and from 6.7% to 11.6% (services).[7]

The grain sector is one area in which Guangdong seems to have performed disappointingly, its contribution to national output having declined from 5.3% to 4.1% between 1980 and 1992.[8] In recent years, grain purchases from neighbouring provinces (especially Hunan) have offset falling output, thereby facilitating the transfer of labour and arable land to industrialization and export expansion. In any case, grain production is a narrow measure of agricultural performance. Broader measures, such as RSVO and GVAO, indicate that the poor growth record of the grain sector conceals both increased agricultural and rural economic diversification, as well as a greater degree of inter-regional specialization.[9]

Trends in GDP and sources of growth

Table 4.3 shows average annual GDP growth rates in Guangdong, China, and the East Asian dragons. The estimates further underline the province's strong momentum of growth. During the post-1978 reform period, Guangdong's economic growth easily outpaced that of China (13.28% and 8.97% per annum, respectively, between 1979 and 1992). But it also exceeded—and by an even greater margin—that of South Korea, Taiwan, Hong Kong, and Singapore.

If estimates for the more recent period offer a more appropriate basis for comparison, they also provide no less telling evidence of Guangdong's remarkable growth record.[10] For example, its annual GDP grew by 15% between 1986 and 1992, compared with 9% in South Korea and 8% in Taiwan. Such data provide a *prima facie* case in favour of the ability of the province eventually to catch up with its Asia-Pacific rivals.

The most striking indication in Table 4.3 is the acceleration of GDP growth (total and per capita) in Guangdong between 1979 and 1985, and 1986 and 1992.[11] Although this pattern of growth mirrored that of the four dragons, it

Table 4.3 Growth Rates of Total and per Capita Gross Domestic Product (GDP) in China, Guangdong, and the Four Little Dragons, Selected Periods, 1979–1992 (in %)

	GDP Total						
	China			**Four Little Dragons**			
	National	**GD**	**Ratio (2)/(1)**	**Hong Kong**	**S. Korea**	**Singapore**	**Taiwan**
	(1)	**(2)**	**(3)**	**(4)**	**(5)**	**(6)**	**(7)**
1985	12.9	20.08	1.56	0.2	6.93	–1.64	5.0
1986	8.5	11.32	1.33	11.1	12.40	1.84	11.6
1987	11.1	17.71	1.60	14.5	12.04	9.45	12.3
1988	11.3	15.57	1.38	8.3	11.48	11.15	7.3
1989	4.3	6.98	1.62	2.8	6.15	9.24	7.6
1990	3.9	11.33	2.91	3.2	9.15	8.34	4.9
1991	8.0	17.30	2.16	4.1	8.46	6.72	7.2
1992	13.2	22.00	1.67	5.3	4.79	5.80	6.6
1979–85	9.39	12.07	1.29	7.15	6.60	7.12	7.00
1986–92	8.56	14.51	1.70	6.98	9.18	7.46	8.20
1979–92	8.97	13.28	1.48	7.06	7.88	7.29	7.60

	GDP / Capita						
	China			**Four Little Dragons**			
	National	**GD**	**Ratio (9)/(8)**	**Hong Kong**	**S. Korea**	**Singapore**	**Taiwan**
	(8)	**(9)**	**(10)**	**(11)**	**(12)**	**(13)**	**(14)**
1985	11.37	18.36	1.61	–0.9	5.88	–2.79	4.1
1986	6.90	9.72	1.41	9.7	11.41	0.66	11.3
1987	9.33	15.91	1.71	13.4	10.92	8.61	10.7
1988	9.52	13.73	1.44	7.4	10.42	9.47	6.6
1989	2.71	5.25	1.94	1.8	5.18	7.61	6.2
1990	2.39	8.44	3.53	2.9	7.88	8.34	3.9
1991	6.54	14.32	2.19	3.2	7.53	4.00	6.1
1992	11.82	19.94	1.69	4.2	3.80	3.62	5.1
1979–85	7.92	10.30	1.30	4.79	5.16	5.82	5.46
1986–92	6.97	12.39	1.78	6.02	8.13	5.99	7.08
1979–92	7.44	11.34	1.52	5.40	6.63	5.90	6.27

Notes: All figures are based either on comparable prices (in the case of China and Guangdong), or constant prices—South Korea and Singapore (1985 as base); Hong Kong (1980); and Taiwan (1986). Column 14 refers to GNP rather than GDP.

Sources: Columns 1 and 8: *ZGTJNJ* 1993, pp. 31–32 and 81. Columns 2 and 9: *GDTJNJ* 1991, pp. 48 and 57; 1993, p. 79; *QJZDGD* 1949–88, pp. 44 and 54. Columns 4 and 11: *HKADS* 1988, p. 109; 1991, p. 109; and 1993, p. 109. Columns 5, 6, 12, and 13: UN—*SYBAP* 1990, pp. 371–2 and 210–11; IMF—*IFSYB*, November 1993, pp. 326 and 472. Columns 7 and 14: TCEPAD—*TWSDB* 1993, pp. 25 and 30.

was a remarkable achievement given the economic retrenchment and deceleration which were taking place nationally.

Several factors contributed to the contrasting provincial and national economic performances. Perhaps most important was the foundation for sustained growth and the exploitation of scale economies which had been laid in Guangdong during the first half of the 1980s and which facilitated subsequent economic expansion. The role of foreign direct investment (FDI) was critical in this respect, Guangdong being the single largest recipient of such capital inflows.[12] Many of the investment projects initiated at this time did not reach maturity until after the mid-1980s. Thus, as FDI continued to flow into the province, output growth accelerated.

By contrast, a different pattern emerged elsewhere in China. The initial net impact of early post-1978 reforms was beneficial throughout the country. But in the absence of substantial inflows of FDI, such as characterized the experience of Guangdong and other coastal regions, the effect in many interior provinces was not lasting, and the boost to economic expansion given by the early reforms weakened during the second half of the 1980s.

Guangdong's spectacular performance cannot, however, simply be attributed to the financial impact of FDI. Through access to new technology and modern production techniques which it has also provided, FDI has been a vehicle for improvements in the managerial efficiency and competitiveness of domestic enterprises. From such sources have come the allocative realignments and rationalization mentioned earlier.

These remarks highlight the extent to which productivity improvements have increasingly become the engine of economic growth in Guangdong. As Table 4.4 shows, they also set the provincial experience apart from that of the country as a whole, where physical increases in inputs have continued to be the major source of growth.

During the Maoist era, the contribution of productivity improvements to net material product growth in Guangdong showed a sharply declining trend, reaching a mere 21% during the Cultural Revolution decade (1966–76). Against this background, to have raised this figure to 49% (1977–85) and 53% (1986–92) is an outstanding achievement. It is all the more striking when compared with the corresponding national figures, which show a fall in the productivity contribution to net material product growth from 43% to 32% between 1977 and 1985, and 1986 and 1992.

The role of physical capital formation in recent economic growth offers another interesting contrast. In Guangdong, the contribution of increases in capital to net material product growth declined from 37% to 34% between 1977 and 1985, and 1986 and 1992, whereas nationally it rose from 38% to 51%. Such estimates suggest that in much of China, in the absence of any significant productivity improvement, the growth momentum has only been maintained through increasing dependence on the physical expansion of the capital base.

At the same time, both national and provincial estimates in Table 4.4 indicate that the contribution of labour to income growth has consistently been in decline since the late 1950s.[13]

This finding highlights the move away from traditional sources of output expansion, as an increasingly capital-intensive process of industrialization has taken place.

The accelerated growth, at a very high level, of per capita GDP growth is another noteworthy aspect of Guangdong's recent economic performance. Average per capita growth rose from 10% to 12% per annum between 1979 and 1985, and 1986 and 1992, whilst the corresponding national figure fell from 8% to 7%.[14] What is more, this buoyant performance was accompanied by an above-average expansion of population (see Table 4.2). This is the background to a demographic phenomenon which has attracted much attention in recent years: namely, the migration of large numbers of people from all parts of China in search of employment in Guangdong.

In short, far from adhering to the image of a labour surplus economy, Guangdong has now begun to display the attributes of labour shortage. In making this transformation, it has distanced itself from the rest of China, where surplus labour conditions persist, and is following the path of the other East Asian dragons.

Structural changes in income and employment

Empirical evidence suggests a strong correlation between rapid income growth, accelerated industrialization, and structural economic change. The figures in Tables 4.5 and 4.6 seek to highlight these changes, as they have taken place in Guangdong and China as a whole.

Both the national and provincial estimates show that under the impact of new economic priorities emerging out of the Third Plenum of the 11th CCP

Table 4.4 Sources of Net Material Product (NMP) Growth in China and Guangdong Compared, 1953–1992

	Growth of NMP			Contribution to NMP growth								
				Labour			Capital			Productivity		
	National	GD	Ratio (2)/(1)	National	GD	Ratio (5)/(4)	National	GD	Ratio (8)/(7)	National	GD	Ratio (11)/(10)
	(1)	(2)	(3)	(4)	(5)	(6)	(7)	(8)	(9)	(10)	(11)	(12)
1952–57	6.61	9.05	1.369	1.67	2.33	1.395	0.84	0.64	0.762	4.10	6.08	1.483
				(25.26)	(25.75)		(12.71)	(7.07)		(62.03)	(67.18)	
1957–65	2.09	3.43	1.641	1.63	0.47	0.288	1.87	1.35	0.722	–1.41	1.61	–1.142
				(77.99)	(13.70)		(89.47)	(39.36)		(–67.46)	(46.94)	
1965–76	5.11	4.36	0.853	1.68	1.62	0.965	2.81	1.83	0.651	0.62	0.91	1.463
				(32.84)	(37.16)		(54.99)	(41.97)		(12.17)	(20.87)	
1977–85	8.78	10.25	1.167	1.69	1.48	0.876	3.30	3.77	1.142	3.79	5.00	1.319
				(19.25)	(14.44)		(37.59)	(36.78)		(43.16)	(48.78)	
1985–92	8.75	14.75	1.686	1.52	1.82	1.197	4.47	5.06	1.132	2.76	7.87	2.851
				(17.37)	(12.34)		(51.09)	(34.31)		(31.54)	(53.35)	

Notes: NMP and capital are deflated figures in 1980 prices obtained by using the methodology of D. H. Perkins, as explained in his "Reforming China's economic system", *Journal of Economic Literature*, Vol. 26, No. 2 (June 1988), pp. 628–9; except for Guangdong's capital figures which are given in comparable prices. Labour force are year-end figures. Figures in parentheses are percentage shares in the contribution to NMP growth.

Sources: Columns 1, 4, 7, and 10: Perkins, *ibid*., for 1952–85, and *ZGTJNJ* 1983, pp. 33–5, 48, and 97 for 1985–92. Columns 2, 5, 8, and 11: *GDTJNJ* 1991, p. 115; 1993, pp. 76, 82, and 129; *GDSGMJJHSHFZTJZL* (section on balance statistics), pp. 1–2, 19–20, 25–26, 31–32, and 53–54.

Table 4.5 Contrasting Changes in GDP Structure in China and Guangdong 1978–1992 (in %)

	Agriculture			Industry			Services		
	National	**GD**	**Ratio (2)/(1)**	**National**	**GD**	**Ratio (5)/(4)**	**National**	**GD**	**Ratio (8)/(7)**
	(1)	**(2)**	**(3)**	**(4)**	**(5)**	**(6)**	**(7)**	**(8)**	**(9)**
1978	28.4	29.9	1.05	48.6	46.4	0.95	23.0	23.7	1.03
1979	31.5	32.2	1.02	47.9	43.8	0.91	20.6	24.0	1.17
1980	30.4	33.8	1.11	49.0	41.1	0.84	20.6	25.1	1.22
1981	32.4	33.2	1.02	47.2	41.7	0.88	20.4	25.1	1.23
1982	34.0	35.7	1.05	46.0	40.2	0.87	20.0	24.1	1.21
1983	33.9	33.9	1.00	45.7	41.9	0.92	20.4	24.2	1.19
1984	33.1	32.9	0.99	44.8	41.6	0.93	22.1	25.5	1.15
1985	29.8	31.1	1.04	45.3	40.8	0.90	24.9	28.1	1.13
1986	28.5	29.6	1.04	46.4	39.0	0.84	25.1	31.4	1.25
1987	28.3	28.8	1.02	46.5	39.4	0.85	25.2	31.8	1.26
1988	27.2	27.9	1.03	46.8	40.4	0.86	26.0	31.7	1.22
1989	26.4	26.8	1.02	45.5	40.3	0.89	28.1	32.9	1.17
1990	28.4	26.1	0.92	43.7	39.9	0.91	27.9	34.0	1.22
1991	26.2	23.4	0.89	45.2	42.1	0.93	28.6	34.5	1.21
1992	23.9	20.3	0.85	48.2	45.9	0.95	27.9	33.8	1.21
Average									
1978–85	31.8	32.9	1.03	46.5	41.8	0.90	21.7	25.3	1.17
1986–92	26.6	24.9	0.94	46.0	41.8	0.91	27.4	33.3	1.22

Sources: Columns 1, 4, and 7: *ZGTJNJ* 1993, pp. 31–2; Columns 2, 5, and 8: *GDTJNJ* 1991, p. 57; 1993, pp. 77–79; and *QJZDGD* 1949–88, p. 54.

Central Committee (December 1978), the contribution of agriculture to GDP increased between 1978 and 1982. Thereafter, this trend was reversed, but much more sharply in Guangdong (from 36% to 20% between 1982 and 1992) than in the rest of the country (from 34% to 24%). The contraction in the agricultural share reflected a major expansion in those of both industry and services. This pattern is common to both Guangdong and China, although since 1982 it has been more pronounced in the former. The rapid expansion of the service sector is another striking feature of structural change in Guangdong throughout the post-1978 reform period.

The changing structure of employment during the same period is illustrated in Table 4.6. The general trends apply at both the national and provincial level, although changes in the distribution of the labour force between the major sectors have been more pronounced in Guangdong. Thus, the percentage decline in agricultural employment in favour of increases in industry and services has been sharper in Guangdong than in China as a whole.[15] Suffice to say that the structural changes revealed in Tables 4.5 and 4.6 are similar to those which took place in South Korea, Taiwan, Hong Kong, and Singapore at comparable periods in their economic development.[16]

The real significance of these trends is, however, in their implications for productivity. Table 4.7 presents estimates of relative product per worker in agriculture, industry, and services in Guangdong and all of China. It provides convincing evidence of converging trends in labour productivity between the three sectors.

The more rapid growth in relative product per agricultural worker in Guangdong no doubt reflects accelerated outflows of labour from farming into industry and services—a process which helped mitigate labour pressures associated with provincial economic development.[17] These transfers dampened potential rises in per worker income in non-agricultural sectors of the province. They also exerted an equalizing influence on relative product per worker within all three sectors.

This finding is underlined by the estimates of total inequality shown in Table 4.7. They show a consistent decline in provincial inequality from 0.88 (1978) to 0.58 (1985) to 0.53 (1992). The corresponding figures for China (0.84, 0.65, and 0.69) also reflect a decline after 1978, but one which was not as sharp, nor as consistent. The convergence in sectoral productivity in Guangdong during the reform era is likely to be unprecedented anywhere else in China since 1949.

Table 4.6 Changes in Employment Structure in China and Guangdong, 1978–1992 (in %)

	Agriculture			Industry			Services		
	National	**GD**	**Ratio (2)/(1)**	**National**	**GD**	**Ratio (5)/(4)**	**National**	**GD**	**Ratio (8)/(7)**
	(1)	**(2)**	**(3)**	**(4)**	**(5)**	**(6)**	**(7)**	**(8)**	**(9)**
1978	70.5	73.68	1.05	17.4	13.75	0.79	12.1	12.57	1.04
1979	69.8	71.98	1.03	17.7	16.53	0.93	12.5	11.49	0.92
1980	68.7	70.68	1.03	18.3	17.10	0.93	13.0	12.22	0.94
1981	68.1	70.13	1.03	18.4	16.91	0.92	13.5	12.96	0.96
1982	68.1	68.35	1.00	18.5	17.74	0.96	13.4	13.91	1.04
1983	67.1	67.30	1.00	18.8	17.85	0.95	14.1	14.85	1.05
1984	64.0	63.68	0.99	20.0	18.89	0.94	16.0	17.43	1.09
1985	62.4	60.14	0.96	20.9	21.14	1.01	16.7	18.72	1.12
1986	60.9	57.76	0.95	21.9	22.68	1.04	17.2	19.56	1.14
1987	59.9	55.14	0.92	22.3	24.19	1.08	17.8	20.67	1.16
1988	59.3	53.66	0.90	22.4	24.84	1.11	18.3	21.50	1.17
1989	60.0	53.67	0.89	21.7	24.59	1.13	18.3	21.74	1.19
1990	60.0	52.97	0.88	21.4	27.21	1.27	18.6	19.82	1.07
1991	59.8	50.48	0.84	21.4	28.62	1.34	18.8	20.90	1.11
1992	58.5	47.35	0.81	21.7	30.44	1.40	19.8	22.21	1.12
Average									
1978–85	67.16	68.01	1.01	18.79	17.79	0.95	14.05	14.20	1.01
1986–92	59.72	52.83	0.88	21.83	26.23	1.20	18.45	20.94	1.13

Sources: Columns 1, 4, and 7: *ZGTJNJ* 1993, p. 101. Columns 2, 5, and 8: *GDTJNJ* 1989, p. 114; 1993, p. 129.

Table 4.7 Changes in Relative Product per Worker (RPW) for Agricultural, Industrial, and Services Sectors, and Total Inequality among Sectors in China and Guangdong, Selected Years 1978–1992

	Relative product per worker		
	National	**GD**	**Ratio (2)/(1)**
	(1)	**(2)**	**(3)**
1978			
Agriculture	0.40	0.41	1.01
Industry	2.79	3.37	1.21
Services	1.90	1.89	0.99
1985			
Agriculture	0.48	0.52	1.08
Industry	2.17	1.93	0.89
Services	1.49	1.50	1.01
1992			
Agriculture	0.41	0.43	1.06
Industry	2.22	1.51	0.68
Services	1.49	1.50	1.01
	Total inequality		
	National	**GD**	**Ratio (5)/(4)**
	(4)	**(5)**	**(6)**
1978	0.84	0.88	1.04
1985	0.65	0.58	0.89
1992	0.69	0.53	0.77

Notes: See Table 2.10 (Panels A and B) in Chapter 2 for the formulae for estimating RPW and total inequality.

Investment and the role of foreign capital

Estimates presented in the previous section showed that in Guangdong after 1978, the declining contribution to income (net material product) growth of physical increases in capital and labour was offset by higher factor productivity (that is, improved input efficiency). That the annual average rate of net material product growth in Guangdong rose from 10% (1977–85) to 15% (1986–92) illustrates the impact of such productivity improvements.

Attempting to identify and measure the sources of productivity growth is notoriously difficult.[18] In Guangdong's case, apart from technological progress embodied in imported hardware, the list would surely include improvements in workers' incentives and in managerial know-how associated with the establishment of Sino-foreign joint ventures. Dynamic forces arising out of increased competition in international markets and growing marketization of the domestic economy have also generated a more rational pattern of inter-provincial specialization, and so of resource allocation, within the province. It is true that all these factors have also been at work elsewhere in China, especially in the coastal regions. But more than any other region of the country, Guangdong has come to epitomize the dynamism inherent in post-1978 reforms.

Table 4.8 highlights the role of capital—especially foreign investment—in the buoyant economic performance of Guangdong.

The estimates show that just as Guangdong's GDP growth exceeded the national average, so too did the expansion of fixed capital formation. As a result, the province's share in national fixed investment increased almost three-fold, from 4.2% (1980) to 11.7% (1992). The inference is that favourable incentives and investment opportunities encouraged the re-investment of profits and tax revenue, thereby sustaining the continued expansion of the capital stock.

An interesting aspect of this process has been the active involvement of the state-owned sector in Guangdong. Between 1979 and 1985, and 1986 and 1992, this sector's average share in gross investment increased from 65% to 72%, compared with a corresponding *decline* (from 68% to 65%) in China as a whole. This finding is at first glance surprising. It is, after all, at variance with the familiar perception of Guangdong as a region in which heavy industries have been in decline and the state sector has contracted in favour of expanded private and collective economic activities. The state sector's continued strength derives in fact from two major factors. One is the provincial government's increased investment in large-scale infrastructural projects (construction of road and rail links, port facilities; installation of sophisticated telecommunications networks in order to accommodate burgeoning industrial and commercial activities). The other is the fact that most Sino-foreign joint venture investment projects in the province have been undertaken with the participation of state enterprises.

Guangdong has been the largest single recipient of foreign capital (especially foreign direct investment) in China. Between 1985 and 1992, on

Table 4.8 Fixed Investment Expenditure in China and Guangdong: Growth Rates and Share of the State-owned Sector Compared, 1978–1992

	Gross investment (100 million yuan)			Growth rates (%)			Share of stated-owned sector (%)		
	National	GD	Ratio (2)/(1)	National	GD	Ratio (5)/(4)	National	GD	Ratio (8)/(7)
	(1)	(2)	(3)	(4)	(5)	(6)	(7)	(8)	(9)
1978	–	27.23	–	–	–	–	–	73.60	–
1979	–	28.29	–	–	3.89	–	–	70.91	–
1980	910.85	38.29	4.20	–	35.35	–	81.89	67.17	0.82
1981	961.00	60.40	6.29	5.51	57.74	10.49	69.46	57.30	0.82
1982	1,230.40	84.73	6.89	28.03	40.28	1.44	68.70	61.10	0.89
1983	1,430.10	88.71	6.20	16.23	4.70	0.29	66.57	63.04	0.95
1984	1,832.90	130.37	7.11	28.17	46.96	1.67	64.66	61.86	0.96
1985	2,543.20	184.59	7.26	38.75	41.59	1.07	66.08	71.03	1.07
1986	3,019.60	216.50	7.17	18.73	17.29	0.92	65.52	73.25	1.12
1987	3,640.90	251.01	6.89	20.58	15.94	0.77	63.12	71.30	1.13
1988	4,496.50	353.59	7.86	23.50	40.87	1.74	61.44	71.90	1.17
1989	4,137.70	347.34	8.39	–7.89	–1.77	0.22	61.28	72.89	1.19
1990	4,449.30	372.59	8.37	7.53	7.27	0.97	65.60	73.05	1.11
1991	5,508.80	478.20	8.68	23.81	28.34	1.19	65.86	71.73	1.09
1992	7,854.98	921.75	11.73	42.59	92.75	2.18	67.14	65.45	0.97
Average									
1978–85	1,484.74	80.33	5.41	22.80	31.44	1.38	68.21	65.34	0.96
1986–92	4,729.68	420.14	8.88	17.48	25.83	1.48	64.62	71.50	1.11

Notes: Figures in yuan are all in current prices. Gross investment refers to total fixed assets investment of the whole society, covering investment made by different sectors including Sino-foreign joint ventures and private/collective undertakings.

Sources: Columns 1, 4, and 7: *ZGTJNJ* 1991, p. 143; 1993, p. 145; and *ZGGDZCTZTJZL* 1950–85, p. 5. Columns 2, 5, and 8: *GDTJNJ* 1993, p. 236.

average, it absorbed 22% of all foreign capital entering the country (including borrowing from overseas governments and financial institutions), and 34% of total realized FDI (see Table 4.9). It is noteworthy that in the wake of Deng Xiaoping's "southern tour" (*nanxun*) during January and February 1992, the rate of growth of both total foreign capital and FDI inflows accelerated sharply in 1992 and 1993.[19] However, the decline (from 42% to 32%) in Guangdong's share of national FDI in 1992 suggests that the predicted dispersal of foreign investment from South China along the coast to East and North China may now have started to take place.[20]

The national preeminence of Guangdong as a recipient of foreign capital itself suggests the significance of such resource flows in financing gross capital formation in the province. The estimates in Tables 4.8 and 4.9 indicate that in recent years FDI contributed more than 20% of provincial gross capital formation.[21] Even more telling is the finding that every US dollar of foreign investment has required the expenditure of some three yuan in complementary investment.[22] Such calculations leave no room for doubt that the growth of fixed asset investment in Guangdong has been closely related to the expansion of foreign investment.

We have already indicated that increased supplies of capital contributed around 34% of average provincial net material product growth of 15% per annum during 1986 to 1992 (Table 4.4). Set in this context, the 30% share of foreign capital in gross fixed investment translates into a 10% contribution to such growth. But for a variety of reasons, this is likely to underestimate the true impact. First, the concept of net material product is narrower than that of GDP, and use of the latter would reveal further additions to income growth associated with FDI in such forms as the construction of tourist hotels and recreational facilities. Second, the most potent—albeit unquantifiable—contribution of FDI is probably concealed in our earlier finding that productivity improvements were the source of 53% of net material product growth between 1986 and 1992. Finally, FDI has also served provincial economic development through its ability to ease foreign exchange constraints—a point taken up in the next section.

Foreign trade as a catalyst of growth [23]

Dramatic as the expansion of China's foreign trade has been since the inception of the open-door strategy, the pace of growth in Guangdong has been even more spectacular.[24] As shown in Table 4.10, the provincial share of national exports rose from 12% to 22% between 1980 and 1992. By the end of 1993, it had reached 29%.[25] The increase in its import share, from less than 2% to 14%, was no less impressive.

The massive, widening gap between national and provincial trade ratios during the reform period reveals the spectacular nature of Guangdong's foreign trade growth. In Guangdong, the combined value of exports and imports as a proportion of GNP increased from 16% to 71% between 1980 and 1992, compared with figures of 13% to 38% for China. Even allowing for distortions in the data,[26] there can be no doubt that Guangdong has become the most open province in the country.

In the absence of sophisticated input-output analysis, it is difficult to quantify precisely foreign trade's contribution to GNP growth in Guangdong. Instead, we offer the following estimates (admittedly, based on highly aggregative measures) as pointers to the changing role of the external sector since the beginning of the 1980s (Table 4.11).

The figures suggest that in the first half of the 1980s, the pattern, though not the absolute values, of the relative contributions of exports and domestic demand to GDP growth were similar in Guangdong and China. During the latter 1980s, however, the situation changed. The direction of such changes was the same,[27] but the strength with which they occurred was not. As a result, by the beginning of the 1990s, the role of exports dominated GDP growth in a way unparalleled throughout the country as a whole. To state the same point differently, Guangdong's GDP growth had become increasingly export-led during the 1980s.

Most FDI is export-orientated, and the role which such investment has played in the export-led economic expansion of Guangdong has been correspondingly important. The figures in Table 4.12 show, for example, that FDI-related exports (including commissioned export processing, most of it on behalf of Hong Kong entrepreneurs) accounted for half of Guangdong's total exports in 1992, compared with a mere 17% in 1985.[28]

Most FDI has been directed towards light industrial manufacturing activities. It therefore comes as no surprise to find that between 1980 and 1992, the combined share of light industrial goods and textiles in total provincial exports should have risen from 32% to 58% (see Table 4.13). During the same period, the share of farm-related exports fell from 41% to 23%.

Table 4.9 Realized Intake of Foreign Capital and Contributions to Fixed Capital Formation in China and Guangdong, 1985–1992

	Realized Intake (US$100 million)					
	Foreign Direct Investment			**All Foreign Capital**		
	National	**GD**	**Ratio (%) (2)/(1)**	**National**	**GD**	**Ratio (%) (5)/(4)**
	(1)	**(2)**	**(3)**	**(4)**	**(5)**	**(6)**
1985	16.61	5.15	31.01	46.47	9.19	19.78
1986	18.74	6.44	34.36	72.58	14.28	19.67
1987	23.14	5.94	25.67	84.52	12.17	14.40
1988	31.94	9.19	28.77	102.26	24.40	23.86
1989	33.92	11.56	34.08	100.59	23.99	23.85
1990	34.87	14.60	41.87	102.89	20.23	19.66
1991	43.66	18.23	41.75	115.54	25.82	22.35
1992	110.07	35.52	32.27	192.02	48.61	25.32
1985–92	312.95	106.63	34.07	816.87	178.69	21.87

	Contributions to Fixed Capital Formation (%)					
	Foreign Direct Investment			**All Foreign Capital**		
	National	**GD**	**Ratio (8)/(7)**	**National**	**GD**	**Ratio (11)/(10)**
	(7)	**(8)**	**(9)**	**(10)**	**(11)**	**(12)**
1985	1.92	8.20	4.27	5.37	14.64	2.72
1986	2.14	10.26	4.79	8.29	22.76	2.74
1987	2.36	8.80	3.72	8.64	18.04	2.09
1988	2.64	9.67	3.66	8.46	25.67	3.03
1989	3.08	12.51	4.06	9.14	25.97	2.84
1990	3.75	18.73	5.00	11.05	25.95	2.35
1991	4.22	20.28	4.81	11.16	28.72	2.57
1992	7.73	21.25	2.75	13.48	29.08	2.16
1985–92	4.07	15.99	3.93	10.17	25.74	2.53

Notes: All US dollar figures are converted into yuan, by using the official annual average exchange rate, to be related to all fixed assets investment expenditure to arrive at the percentage contribution figures. "All foreign capital" covers FDI, foreign borrowings, and other types of foreign investment.

Sources: Columns 1 and 4: *ZGTJNJ* 1993, p. 647. Columns 2 and 5: *GDTJNJ* 1991, p. 316; 1993, p. 363. Columns 7 to 12: Table 8 for the underlying fixed assets investment figures. Exchange rates used for conversion: Nicholas R. Lardy, "Chinese foreign trade", *The China Quarterly*, No. 131, p. 706 (Table 6); and *ZGTJNJ* 1993, p. 646.

Table 4.10 Exports, Imports, and Trade Ratios of China and Guangdong, 1978–1992

	Exports (US$100 million)			Imports (US$100 million)			Trade/GNP (GDP) Ratio (%)			
							Exports		Imports	
	National	GD	Ratio (%) (2)/(1)	National	GD	Ratio (%) (5)/(4)	National	GD	National	GD
	(1)	(2)	(3)	(4)	(5)	(6)	(7)	(8)	(9)	(10)
1978	97.5	13.88	14.24	108.9	2.04	1.87	4.67	12.62	5.22	1.85
1979	136.6	17.02	12.46	156.7	2.43	1.55	5.30	12.74	6.08	1.82
1980	181.2	21.95	12.11	200.2	3.56	1.78	6.07	13.40	6.68	2.17
1981	220.1	23.73	10.78	220.2	6.65	3.02	7.70	14.27	7.70	4.00
1982	223.2	22.56	10.11	192.9	8.01	4.15	7.97	12.87	6.88	4.57
1983	222.3	23.85	10.73	213.9	9.31	4.35	7.55	13.21	7.26	5.16
1984	261.4	24.87	9.51	274.1	11.17	4.08	8.34	13.12	8.91	5.89
1985	273.5	29.53	10.80	422.5	24.26	5.74	9.45	15.70	14.70	12.98
1986	309.4	42.51	13.74	429.0	25.58	5.96	11.16	23.00	15.45	13.84
1987	394.4	54.44	13.80	432.2	36.28	8.39	13.01	25.07	14.28	16.71
1988	475.2	74.84	15.75	552.8	51.10	9.24	12.56	25.34	12.56	17.30
1989	525.4	81.86	15.58	591.4	48.31	8.17	12.23	23.41	13.76	13.85
1990	620.9	105.60	17.01	533.5	57.49	10.78	16.87	34.30	14.55	27.64
1991	718.4	136.88	19.05	637.9	85.10	13.34	18.91	40.90	16.80	33.40
1992	850.0	184.40	21.69	806.1	111.79	13.87	19.41	44.34	18.49	26.88

Table 4.10 (to be continued)

Table 4.10 (continued)

	Exports (US$100 million)			Imports (US$100 million)			Trade/GNP (GDP) Ratio (%)			
							Exports		Imports	
	National	GD	Ratio (%) (2)/(1)	National	GD	Ratio (%) (5)/(4)	National	GD	National	GD
	(1)	(2)	(3)	(4)	(5)	(6)	(7)	(8)	(9)	(10)
Average										
1978–85	201.98	22.17	10.98	223.68	8.43	3.77	7.25	13.57	8.05	5.16
1986–92	556.24	97.22	17.48	568.99	59.38	10.44	15.13	32.32	15.13	21.59

Notes: Figures for Guangdong 1978–80 include Hainan, which became an independent province in 1986.

National trade figures for 1978–79 are from the Ministry of Foreign Economic Relations and Trade; from 1980 onwards, they are Customs statistics. US dollar figures are converted into yuan, by using the official annual average exchange rate, to be related to the GNP/GDP in yuan to arrive at the trade ratio. Instead of GNP, GDP is used as base for Guangdong's trade ratio.

Sources: Columns 1, 4, and 7: *ZGTJNJ* 1993, pp. 31 and 633. Columns 2, 5, and 8: *GDTJNJ* 1991, pp. 57 and 303; 1993, pp. 77 and 349; and *QJZDGD* 1949–88, p. 182. Exchange rates used for conversion: Nicholas R. Lardy, "Chinese foreign trade", *The China Quarterly*, No. 131, p. 706 (Table 6); and *ZGTJNJ* 1993, p. 646.

Table 4.11 Contributions of Exports, Imports, and Domestic Demand to Gross Domestic Product (GDP) Growth in China and Guangdong Compared, 1981–1990 (in %)

	Growth of GDP			Contributions to the Growth of GDP								
				Exports			Imports			Domestic Demand		
	National	GD	Ratio (2)/(1)	National	GD	Ratio (5)/(4)	National	GD	Ratio (8)/(7)	National (1)–(4)–(7)	GD (2)–(5)–(8)	Ratio (11)/(10)
	(1)	(2)	(3)	(4)	(5)	(6)	(7)	(8)	(9)	(10)	(11)	(12)
1981	4.45	8.20	1.84	1.91	2.62	1.37	–1.26	–2.30	1.82	3.80	7.88	2.07
1982	8.49	11.50	1.35	1.51	1.75	1.16	–0.82	–2.12	2.66	7.78	11.87	1.53
1983	10.18	6.39	0.63	1.58	3.59	2.27	–3.05	–2.46	0.81	11.65	5.26	0.45
1984	14.58	14.78	1.01	2.69	3.48	1.29	–4.32	–2.90	0.67	16.21	14.20	0.88
1985	12.93	19.56	1.51	5.11	11.05	2.16	–14.25	–17.49	1.23	22.07	26.00	1.18
1986	8.51	11.19	1.32	7.27	22.86	3.14	–4.69	–5.47	1.17	5.93	–6.20	–1.05
1987	11.10	17.37	1.56	5.41	12.80	2.37	–2.52	–13.89	5.52	8.21	18.46	2.25
1988	11.28	15.23	1.35	2.19	12.13	5.54	–0.06	–3.61	56.11	9.15	6.71	0.73
1989	4.34	6.97	1.61	0.72	1.60	2.23	2.15	6.06	2.82	1.47	–0.57	–0.39
1990	3.73	11.21	3.01	11.02	30.73	2.79	–7.12	–18.10	2.54	–0.16	–1.52	9.76
Average												
1981–85	10.07	11.99	1.19	2.61	4.66	1.79	–5.13	–5.83	1.14	12.59	13.16	1.05
1986–90	7.74	12.34	1.59	5.51	16.38	2.97	–2.50	–7.14	2.86	4.73	3.10	0.66

Notes: All value figures are in constant 1980 prices. See Perkins, "Reforming China's economic system", op. cit., pp. 628–9 for method of deriving the implicit deflators of GDP. The exports (X) and imports (M) price indexes from the *Chinese Yearbook of Foreign Economic Relations and Trade* 1991 (p. 321) are used for deflating both the national and Guangdong's trade figures. Contributions of X and M to GDP growth are estimated as: absolute change of X (M) / absolute change of GDP ∗ annual growth rate of GDP.

Sources: As Tables 4.2 and 4.10.

Table 4.12 Foreign Direct Investment-related Exports and Imports of Guangdong Province, 1980–1992 (US$ million and %)

	FDI-related Exports (US$ million)								FDI-related Imports (US$ million)	
	Commissioned Exports Processing		Compensation Trade		FDI Ventures		Total Value		FDI Ventures	
	Value	Share (%)	Value	Share (%)	Value	Share (%)	Value (1)+(3)+(5)	Share (%) (2)+(4)+(6)	Value	Share (%)
	(1)	(2)	(3)	(4)	(5)	(6)	(7)	(8)	(9)	(10)
1980	82.33	3.75	6.65	0.30	–	–	88.98	4.05	–	–
1985	272.5	9.23	8.70	0.29	22.16	7.49	303.36	17.01	336.56	13.87
1989	578.17	7.10	62.67	0.77	2,276.71	27.90	2,917.55	35.77	1,950.92	40.40
1990	583.32	5.52	77.78	0.74	3,723.83	35.26	4,384.93	41.52	3,297.44	57.36
1991	799.72	5.84	95.06	0.69	5,327.48	38.93	6,222.26	45.46	4,513.02	53.03
1992	999.23	5.42	96.69	0.52	8,159.06	44.25	9,254.98	50.19	6,014.96	53.80

Notes: All figures in columns 2, 4, 6, and 8 refer to the percentage shares in total exports; and similarly, figures in column 10 are percentage shares in total imports. The other components of Guangdong Province's total exports (other than FDI-related exports), as implied in columns 1 to 8, are commodity exports (see Table 4.13).

Sources: *GDTJNJ* 1991, p. 304; 1993, p. 351.

Table 4.13 Composition of Commodity Exports of Guangdong Province, 1980–1992

	Commodity Exports		**Commodity Export Composition (Total = 100%)**			
	Value (US$ million)	**Share in Total Exports (%)**	**Farm & Subsidiary**	**Farm Processing**	**Light Industry & Textile**	**Industrial and Minerals**
	(1)	**(2)**	**(3)**	**(4)**	**(5)**	**(6)**
1980	2,105.74	95.95	31.50	9.80	32.12	26.58
1985	2,450.31	82.99	32.65	8.84	39.44	19.07
1989	5,250.12	64.20	19.40	7.60	53.10	19.90
1990	6,175.31	58.48	17.02	8.13	54.80	20.05
1991	7,465.61	54.45	16.60	7.40	55.67	20.33
1992	9,184.46	49.81	14.36	8.11	57.59	19.94

Notes: The declining trend of commodity exports reflects the growing importance of FDI-related exports as shown in Table 3.12.

Sources: *GDTJNJ* 1991, p. 304; 1993, p. 351.

The changing commodity composition of exports revealed in Table 4.13 reflects changes in the level of economic development in Guangdong. It is a commonplace that industrialization brings about fundamental structural change, as an economy shifts from primary product (especially agricultural) domination to a new stage characterized by an expansion of manufacturing activities. Industrialization, of course, had been underway in Guangdong since the early 1950s. What is striking about the post-1978 developments is the accelerated nature of the process and its emphasis on export-promotion rather than import-substitution.

Special Economic Zones and the Hong Kong connection

No discussion of economic development in Guangdong can be considered complete without some reference to the SEZs[29] and the critical role played by Hong Kong. The preceding analysis has highlighted the enormous economic changes that have taken place from the perspective of the province as a whole. But further investigation of the regional dimension of these changes would reveal that the economic gains of the past fifteen years have been distributed unequally and skewed towards a few growth poles. These include the three original SEZs, Guangzhou, and several other municipalities, all of which were granted special economic privileges during the 1980s.[30] We have already investigated some aspects of the economic significance of such growth poles elsewhere.[31] In this section, we shall focus our attention on the role of the Guangdong–Hong Kong connection.

First, the role of Hong Kong as a source of capital: Table 4.14 reveals that Guangdong absorbed 42% of all foreign direct investment flowing from Hong Kong into China during the period 1985–92.[32] Viewed differently, Hong Kong was the immediate origin of 84% of Guangdong's total FDI intake during the same period. If "indirect" foreign investment (that is, capital borrowing from abroad) is included, the picture remains basically the same.

There is, however, an important qualification. Apart from several large-scale infrastructural projects (notably, the construction of the Guangzhou-Shenzhen highway and installation of major power-generation plants—all of them involving Hong Kong capital), a high proportion of FDI originating in Hong Kong reflects the relocation of manufacturing enterprises from the territory to Guangdong (especially the Pearl River Delta).[33] A characteristic of such FDI is that it also generates trade flows. In other words, on the input side, the establishment of joint ventures normally involves the export of machinery and equipment, raw or semi-finished materials from Hong Kong to Guangdong; at the same time, most joint-venture output returns to Hong Kong for re-export to North America and Western Europe. It follows that most of Guangdong's FDI-related imports and exports have been, and still are, dominated by Hong Kong-based manufacturing firms operating within the province.

Table 4.15 gives a comprehensive picture of the role of Hong Kong in the foreign trade of both Guangdong and China as a whole since 1985. It shows an increasing trend in the provincial share of national exports to the territory, reaching 41% in 1992. In the same year, 84% of Guangdong's exports were shipped to Hong Kong. Guangdong's dependence on its colonial neighbour for its imports also emerges clearly from Table 4.15.

Juxtaposition of the estimates of Guangdong's FDI-related exports and imports (Table 4.13) with the US dollar estimates of total provincial trade (Table 4.15) reveals that trade relations with Hong Kong reflect much more than investment in the Pearl River Delta. Clearly, non-FDI-related trade flows between Guangdong and Hong Kong are sizeable and have increased in recent years. No doubt a major contributory factor has been the need, against the background of accelerated export-based industrialization, to make use of Hong Kong's well-established port facilities, banking and financial services, telecommunications networks, and marketing skills in order to expand into international export markets. Hence the spectacular increases in Hong Kong's re-exports of goods of Chinese origin during the past decade.[34] The advantages of Hong Kong's international links and sourcing skills have no doubt similarly contributed to the surge in non-FDI-related imports through Hong Kong into Guangdong since the beginning of the 1990s.

In short, Hong Kong has been critical in transforming Guangdong into a major Chinese export base. It also promises to make the single most important contribution to fulfilling Guangdong's aspiration to become the fifth East Asian dragon.

The role of the state and prospects for sustained growth in Guangdong

The state has already made a significant contribution to Guangdong's recent economic transformation, and it will no doubt continue to be a critical determinant of the economic future of the province. We suggested earlier some of the factors which contributed to the rising share of the state-owned sector in provincial gross fixed investment during the 1980s. Large-scale infrastructural projects apart, there is a widespread presumption that economic activities conducted under the aegis of state ownership are inherently inefficient and should be phased out. Condemnation of this kind, however, is too facile and may deflect attention from other more important considerations. In Guangdong, one of these is the increasing extent to which state industrial enterprises, as well as Sino-foreign joint ventures, have become market-orientated. In this context—and against the background of an economic system which before 1978 was characterized by excessive centralized control and bureaucratic inertia—the distinction between different forms of ownership may be less significant than the efficiency-enhancing effects of greater competition.

Caution is needed in using the ratio between state budget and GNP as an accurate measure of the state's involvement in economic activities. The early stage of development is likely to be characterized by an increase in government spending in support of infrastructural construction. Subsequently, consumer pressures and demands for better social welfare shift government

Table 4.14 Hong Kong's Share in Realized Intake of Foreign Capital in China and Guangdong, 1985–1992

	Foreign Direct Investment					
	Total from Hong Kong (US$ million)			**HK's Share in Total Intake (%)**		
	National	**GD**	**Ratio (%)**	**National**	**GD**	**Ratio (%)**
	(1)	**(2)**	**(3)**	**(4)**	**(5)**	**(6)**
1985	955.68	450.20	47.11	57.53	87.37	151.87
1986	1,328.71	603.10	45.39	70.90	93.66	132.10
1987	1,809.05	502.67	27.79	78.17	84.63	108.26
1988	2,428.05	836.54	34.45	76.01	91.02	119.75
1989	2,341.77	952.72	40.68	65.03	82.38	119.33
1990	2,118.48	1,018.59	48.08	60.75	69.77	114.85
1991	2,661.81	1,448.60	54.42	60.97	79.47	130.37
1992	7,908.94	3,162.27	39.98	71.85	89.04	123.92
1985–92	21,552.49	8,974.69	41.64	68.87	84.17	122.22

	All Foreign Capital					
	Total from Hong Kong (US$ million)			**HK's Share in Total Intake (%)**		
	National	**GD**	**Ratio (%)**	**National**	**GD**	**Ratio (%)**
	(7)	**(8)**	**(9)**	**(10)**	**(11)**	**(12)**
1985	1,016.37	845.63	83.20	21.87	92.02	420.71
1986	1,572.85	1,095.45	69.65	21.67	76.71	353.99
1987	2,091.24	884.09	42.28	24.74	72.65	293.60
1988	3,109.44	1,537.96	49.46	30.41	63.03	207.29
1989	2,912.78	1,544.89	53.04	28.96	64.40	222.39
1990	2,431.68	1,298.76	53.41	23.63	64.20	271.64
1991	2,924.96	1,724.80	58.97	25.32	66.80	263.87
1992	8,689.95	3,623.25	41.69	45.26	74.54	164.70
1985–92	24,749.27	12,554.83	50.73	30.30	70.26	231.90

Notes: All investment figures refer to realized intake from both Hong Kong and Macao.

Sources: Columns 1, 4, 7, and 10: *ZGTJNJ* 1986, p. 580; 1987, p. 604; *ZGTJNJ* 1988, p. 734; 1989, p. 646; 1991, p. 630; and 1992, p. 648. Columns 2, 5, 8, and 11: *GDTJNJ* 1991, pp. 317 and 321; and *ZGTJNJ* 1993, pp. 364 and 368. Columns 4, 5, 10, and 11: Table 4.9.

Table 4.15 Hong Kong's Role in the Foreign Trade of China and Guangdong, 1985–1992

	Exports to Hong Kong					
	Value (US$100 million)			Percentage Share		
	National	GD	Ratio (%) (2)/(1)	National	GD	Ratio (%) (5)/(4)
	(1)	(2)	(3)	(4)	(5)	(6)
1985	72.04	21.27	29.53	26.34	72.03	273.46
1986	97.85	29.55	30.20	31.63	69.51	219.80
1987	137.78	37.51	27.22	34.93	68.90	197.23
1988	182.69	57.25	31.34	38.44	76.50	198.98
1989	219.16	63.66	29.05	41.71	77.77	186.43
1990	266.50	85.43	32.06	42.92	80.90	188.48
1991	321.37	113.69	35.38	44.73	83.06	185.67
1992	375.12	155.58	41.47	44.13	84.37	191.18
1985–92	1,672.51	563.94	33.72	40.14	79.42	197.89

	Imports from Hong Kong					
	Value (US$100 million)			Percentage Share		
	National	GD	Ratio (%) (8)/(7)	National	GD	Ratio (%) (11)/(10)
	(7)	(8)	(9)	(10)	(11)	(12)
1985	47.97	21.43	44.67	11.35	88.33	778.02
1986	56.00	18.74	33.46	13.05	73.26	561.23
1987	84.37	28.95	34.31	19.52	79.80	408.77
1988	119.73	40.89	34.15	21.66	80.02	369.45
1989	125.40	34.97	27.89	21.20	72.39	341.38
1990	142.58	41.16	28.87	26.73	71.60	267.89
1991	174.63	62.30	35.68	27.38	73.21	267.42
1992	205.34	82.68	40.26	25.48	73.96	290.29
1985–92	956.02	331.12	34.64	21.70	75.27	346.83

Notes: Columns 4, 5, 10, and 11 show Hong Kong's percentage shares in total export and import volumes of China and Guangdong Province, respectively.

Sources: Columns 1, 4, 7, and 10: *ZGTJNJ* 1987, p. 594; 1989, p. 636; 1991, p. 620; and 1993, p. 638. Columns 2, 5, 8, and 11: *GDTJNJ* 1987, p. 334; 1989, p. 334; 1991, p. 305; and 1993, p. 352. Columns 4, 5, 10, and 11: See sources of Table 4.10.

expenditure increasingly towards "non-productive" investment in such areas as health, education, and housing. Both categories of expenditure necessarily imply a higher state budget share in GNP, even though the direct implications of each for economic growth may be very different.

In any case, the experience of Guangdong since 1978 in these regards is less than impressive. The estimates in Table 4.16 show that as a proportion of GNP, the combined total of state budgetary revenue and expenditure in Guangdong (for that matter, China too) generally declined after 1978. In both cases, this trend reflects the impact of widespread decentralization. Prior to 1978, under the system of Soviet-style, centralized planning, the state budget was a comprehensive financial instrument: that is, it not only embraced the financing of fixed investment and working capital requirements, but also provided for recurrent expenditure on non-productive items such as education, health, and national defence. Implicit in such financial arrangements was a system of compulsory profit remittances to the state budget, side by side with pervasive price and wage-fixing designed to allow the state to siphon off income in excess of subsistence needs.

Amongst the reforms initiated after 1978 were the introduction of a profit-retention scheme for state enterprises and the implementation of measures designed to decontrol wages and prices. These initiatives were bound to have impact on existing financial arrangements, and as Table 4.16 shows, both nationally and in Guangdong the state budget/GNP ratio fell sharply. Although relatively speaking, the degree of budgetary curtailment was almost the same in Guangdong as in the country as a whole,[35] in reality the provincial impact was more severe because of its low base ratio of revenue/expenditure to GNP in 1978.[36]

Guangdong's budget/GNP ratio has also been consistently lower than the national average for the years under study.[37] Unlike Shanghai and Liaoning, Guangdong has not been subject to enforced, large-scale financial transfers by the centre. The inference is that the budgetary privileges extended to the provincial authorities by Beijing have helped remove excessive fiscal obligations from industries under their jurisdiction. In this way, industrial incentives have been significantly enhanced.

Nevertheless, at the beginning of the 1990s, Guangdong's budget/GNP ratio was significantly lower than that of many developing countries—and certainly lower than that of each of the four East Asian dragons. This cannot simply be attributed to the impact of reform upon earlier excessive centralization. Rather, the relatively low ratio may reflect fiscal constraints on the capacity of the provincial government to involve itself in infrastructural construction and social welfare programmes.[38]

Such considerations counsel caution in predicting when, or even if rising per capita GNP will enable Guangdong to set aside a major and increasing proportion of budgetary revenue in order to promote further growth and enhance social welfare.

This, in turn, begs the even more fundamental question of whether Guangdong can sustain its recent powerful momentum of economic growth in the immediate future. Major projects currently under construction or in the planning stage—the Shenzhen-Guangzhou highway, the Yantian Port project, and the new international airport for Shantou, Jieyang, and Chaozhou cities—attest to the high level of confidence in the province. Indeed, given the development experience of the four East Asian dragons, there is no reason why Guangdong should not maintain sufficient growth to fulfil its objectives. After all, South Korea's long-term GNP growth averaged only 8.6% per annum in the thirty years after 1962—considerably less than that of Guangdong during the post-1978 reform period.[39] Barring any major unexpected disturbance—and even allowing for some slowing in provincial growth in the years to come—it seems reasonable to suppose that Guangdong's recent impressive record will, in the foreseeable future, enable it to emulate the successful performance of the other dragons since the 1960s.

There are, however, important qualifications to such a sanguine prognosis, two of which may be mentioned here. The first concerns the ability of Guangdong to maintain its recent growth momentum. Fulfilment of provincial GDP targets for the years 2000 and 2010 originally required average growth rates of 13.4% and 12.4% per annum during the 1990s and the first decade of the next century.[40] It is true that average growth during the early 1990s remains well ahead of such requirements.[41] But some would argue that Guangdong is already close to a growth ceiling, and that structural and other bottlenecks will make it increasingly difficult to maintain the recent momentum of development. Even official sources concede the existence of serious obstacles to modernization. The production structure remains irrational;[42] regional growth is still uneven;[43] heavy infrastructural capital requirements place a heavy burden on the provincial budget; and the technical and scientific base is weak.

The second qualification emerges from the earlier experience of the East Asian little dragons. The economic transformation of all four was a function

Table 4.16 Budgetary Ratio of China and Guangdong, 1978–1992 (in %)

	Revenue/GNP			**Expenditure/GNP**			**Total Budget/GNP**		
	National	**GD**	**Ratio (2)/(1)**	**National**	**GD**	**Ratio (5)/(4)**	**National**	**GD**	**Ratio (8)/(7)**
	(1)	(2)	(3)	(4)	(5)	(6)	(7)	(8)	(9)
1978	33.75	21.36	0.63	30.97	14.63	0.47	64.72	35.99	0.56
1980	24.28	14.69	0.61	27.13	10.15	0.37	51.41	24.84	0.48
1985	21.81	11.84	0.54	21.56	11.00	0.51	43.37	22.84	0.53
1986	23.31	12.92	0.55	24.04	14.04	0.58	47.35	26.96	0.57
1987	20.96	11.50	0.55	21.67	11.13	0.51	42.63	22.63	0.53
1988	18.68	9.79	0.52	19.24	10.49	0.55	37.92	20.28	0.53
1989	18.43	10.43	0.57	19.01	10.76	0.57	37.44	21.19	0.57
1990	18.72	8.90	0.48	19.51	10.24	0.52	38.23	19.14	0.50
1991	17.84	9.96	0.56	18.85	10.25	0.54	36.69	20.21	0.55
1992	17.28	9.71	0.56	18.26	9.58	0.52	35.54	19.29	0.54

Notes: For Guangdong Province, GDP, rather than GNP, is used as base for the respective ratios. Total budget refers to the combined total of revenue and expenditure.

Sources: *ZGTJNJ* 1993, pp. 31 and 217 for national figures; and *GDTJNJ* 1987, p. 367; 1989, p. 367; 1993, p. 383 for Guangdong's figures. See sources of Table 4.2 for the underlying GNP/GDF data.

of the sustained economic growth of advanced Western countries (notably Japan and the United States). Japan, for example, provided large-scale imports of industrial equipment and raw materials; in addition, the United States and Western Europe provided markets for manufactured exports.[44] Whether the global economic environment will be conducive to the future growth requirements of the aspiring fifth dragon is a matter of judgment. But it is likely that through their impact upon Guangdong's exports, the US government and economy will continue to exert significant influence on the region's economic future. Even if the decision to delink the renewal of China's most-favoured-nation (MFN) status from political and human rights considerations marks a significant step forward, the uncertainty which still surrounds Sino-US relations highlights Guangdong's potential vulnerability from this source.

5

The US Connection of Hong Kong in China's "One Country, Two Economies" System*

Introduction: A new perspective

Hong Kong has traditionally been a very important source of China's foreign exchange earnings. Prior to the 1980s, generally about one-quarter to one-third of the country's hard foreign currency earnings were generated from exports to Hong Kong. Tiny as the British enclave may be in geographic terms, and with a population of only six million, it has nonetheless always been a very important market for China's food and food-processing industries, as well as textile and clothing manufacturers. Sales to Hong Kong have earned the Chinese government the bulk of the hard currency needed to finance her enormous import bills incurred with major Western suppliers of steel, machinery and high-tech products. This specific role played by Hong Kong in financing China's industrialization programme is of course widely understood. Yet hardly any observers have come to realize that the bulk of China's food and clothing exports to Hong Kong represent none other than Hong Kong's wage outlay on labour inputs necessary for sustaining its production of exports, which are, as is well known, overwhelmingly destined for the major Western markets, the United States in particular.

An intellectually interesting point may be made on this China-Hong Kong synergy: an essential part of Hong Kong's foreign exchange earnings may itself be seen as China's indirect export to the West. Viewed this way, there

---

* Reprinted with minor adaptation from "The role of Hong Kong in Sino-American economic relations" (coauthored with Thomas Voon), in Y. Y. Kueh (ed.), *The Political Economy of Sino-American Relations—A Greater China Perspective*, Hong Kong: Hong Kong University Press, 1997, pp. 61–92.

is obviously something wrong with the widely held view that in the case of a complete takeover of Hong Kong by its sovereign power, China would kill the "gold-laying goose" and forfeit all her direct foreign exchange earnings from Hong Kong. China has a pronounced interest in maintaining the economic status quo for Hong Kong—an interest apparent in the entire strategic design of the future Special Administrative Region under the concept of "one country, two systems".

The fallacy of this popular argument is clear enough. With a full-fledged socialist-style takeover, the present foreign exchange earnings as held by Hong Kong's exporters would, by implication, inevitably be entirely accruable to the government of the People's Republic of China (PRC), after allowing perhaps for certain proportion of "transaction costs" incurred as a result of, say, impaired export incentives, reduced efficiency and loss of competent marketing and sourcing expertise. It should also be clear that under such a complete socialist takeover, the present "direct" export earnings by China from Hong Kong would naturally become China's own liability, that is, the input costs needed for sustaining the export earnings of Hong Kong.

Interesting as the issues raised may be, intellectually speaking, we do not think it is worthwhile to pursue the matter further, because a socialist takeover of Hong Kong is clearly not on the agenda. Nonetheless, increased economic interaction and integration between Hong Kong and mainland China under the country's open-door policy in the past decade has lent some new dimensions to their trade relations that seem not entirely irrelevant to the questions posed for a fully-fledged political takeover of Hong Kong.

At least to the mind of many Americans, Hong Kong seems to have already become part of China proper. Any re-exports from Hong Kong of Chinese origin should thus be treated by the United States as Chinese exports, be it in terms of most-favoured-nation status (MFN) renewal, protection of intellectual property rights or otherwise. Rightly or wrongly, what is at stake is particularly the tens of thousands of Hong Kong manufacturers who prefer to have their export production contracted out, by way of what Hong Kong government statistics term as "outward processing" (or what in official Chinese parlance is referred to as *sanlai yibu*) to the Pearl River Delta basin, in order to avoid exorbitant land rental and labour cost pressures in Hong Kong.[1]

The relocation of Hong Kong's export manufacturing activities to the Pearl River hinterland is not entirely dissimilar to a socialist takeover, because in terms of trading relationship and foreign exchange accruable, it has become explicit that the land and labour inputs for Hong Kong's export products are now very much a matter of direct Chinese rather than Hong Kong contribution. Ignoring for the time being the interpretative complexities with capital contribution which very often is dominated by the Hong Kong investors' share, Hong Kong's role in this new context seems to have become very much one of export intermediary, important as this role may be.

It is obviously against this background that the familiar Sino-American dispute has arisen in recent years as to the absolute size of their trade balance with each other. To the United States, Hong Kong's exports with an "outward processing" element are Chinese by origin, and have helped to aggravate the US trade deficit *vis-à-vis* China. The Chinese maintain, however, that they only earn a very marginal fee for processing on behalf of Hong Kong's export manufacturers. This has in turn prompted some US government officials to argue that "China routinely calculates exports according to value-added as opposed to internationally accepted accounting method".[2] The dispute is clearly not just a matter of interpretative nuance. The fact that *sanlai yibu* exports have very much tilted, in the eyes of the Americans, the trade balance against their favour, already speaks for the sheer magnitude involved. *Sanlai yibu* Chinese exports may therefore be regarded as a phenomenon *sui generis*.[3]

The crux of the problem involved is obviously a matter of how one should estimate and interpret the appropriate relative shares of both the mainland Chinese and their Hong Kong counterparts in the total export margin earned from US importers. This is by no means a simple, straightforward technical matter. In addition to land and labour, capital input is involved from varying mainland Chinese and Hong Kong investors' contributions. There is also the touchy issue of how to assign weights to the different input categories. The difficulty is further compounded by the fact that apart from the voluminous "outward processing" contracts, there is a large number of *sanzi qiye* (literally, the "three foreign-funded enterprises": equity joint ventures (EJV), contractual joint ventures (CJV), and wholly-foreign-owned ventures (WFV) in China—hereafter *sanji* enterprises in this chapter). These are heavily dominated by Hong Kong capital input;[4] they are well established and engage themselves not only in output of proper Chinese origin for export, but also in outward processing from Hong Kong as well.

This chapter represents a first attempt to isolate the relative contributions of Hong Kong manufacturers and exporters to the export earnings from their joint ventures based in China, be they in the form of *sanlai yibu* (outward processing) or *sanji qiye* manufacturing proper. We focus naturally on exports that are physically channelled through Hong Kong, with a view to determining the relative share of exports from China to the United States (or the rest of the world at large) which should be accounted for by Hong Kong manufacturers rather than mainland Chinese exporters. Our work is of course made against the political backdrop that there is still, and will continue to be, a line drawn between Hong Kong and China, given that post-1997 Hong Kong will retain its membership in the World Trade Organization (WTO) and many other international bodies, as a separate customs entity.

Rough as our exercise may appear to be, particularly in terms of the various assumptions made for the analysis and the statistics used (as will become apparent during the course of our discussion), we hope to at least be able to provide an innovative methodology as a basis for further verification and refinement. We hope that this will eventually contribute to solving the conflicting claims between China and the United States on their trade gains or losses against each other.

The role played by Hong Kong within the broader context of Chinese economic relations with the United States, or with the rest of the world at large, is evidently much more than a matter of facilitating and mediating Chinese trade as illustrated. Interestingly, US exports through the port of Hong Kong to China have also experienced steady increases in the past fifteen years or so. Further, as an international financial centre, Hong Kong plays an important role in channelling overseas financial and banking resources, many of US origin, to China for financing its infrastructure projects. Hidden behind the capital and trade flows is, of course, the associated technology transfer from the West to China through Hong Kong.

Nonetheless, these are more or less familiar aspects of Hong Kong's contributions to China. They all deserve further analysis, but in this chapter we mainly concentrate on the unique phenomenon of *sanlai* or *sanji* Chinese exports, in order to isolate the possible size of the Hong Kong components as a contribution to resolving the conflicting claims between China and the United States on trade deficits against each other. In what follows, we first take stock of Hong Kong's export and import relations with both China and the United States, and give an account of its quantitative importance in linking China's dealings with the US and the rest of the world at large. This provides the necessary framework for looking at the specific issues involved in reconciling the Sino-American discrepancy.

Following statistical reconciliation of the conflicting US and Chinese trade deficit claims, we offer an overall evaluation of the possible economic and income benefits that Hong Kong has been drawing from serving as a trade mediator between the two economic giants. This helps to highlight, from a different perspective, to what extent the US-China discrepancy is actually a matter of Hong Kong's gains. The chapter concludes with a short remark about how Hong Kong may continue to play its third-party role beyond 1997 within the broader context of Sino-US economic relations.

Hong Kong in Sino-American trade: The new context

There are two major aspects of the role played by Hong Kong as a trade facilitator or mediator. The first is that Hong Kong itself serves as an important market for China's exports. The exports have been dominated by food and clothing supplies to sustain Hong Kong's export production for the United States. From the early 1980s, industrial material, machinery and equipment have come onto the Chinese supply list as well, as the country adjusted its development strategy in favour of light industry, thus giving the heavy industry sector excess capacity to produce producer goods for export. The changes as observed over the years reflect a universal trend in export commodity composition compatible with the pace and pattern of industrialization of developing countries.

The second aspect refers to the mainland's exports to Hong Kong that are not retained for domestic consumption but rather are re-exported to the United States and other Western importers. This category of Hong Kong's imports from the mainland comprises increased re-exports of truly Chinese origin, and especially the *sanlai yibu* of Chinese exports of essentially "Hong Kong origin" by way of outward processing to the Pearl River Delta. Part of the latter subcategory of Chinese exports to Hong Kong may of course be retained for local consumption,[5] but there is clear evidence that the bulk is destined for re-export to overseas market. It is clearly the second category of Chinese exports, particularly *sanlai yibu*, that has gained an enormous importance to Hong Kong in the past decade.

Hong Kong's imports from China and re-exports to the United States

The figures in Table 5.1 (Panel A) reveal that in 1993, 73% of all Hong Kong's merchandise imports from China were *sanlai yibu*, compared with 64% in 1991 or 58% in 1989, when, after nearly a decade of growth (starting the early 1980s), this type of Chinese export to Hong Kong was already entering a mature stage.

Sanlai yibu statistics are not available prior to 1989.[6] But their value for the early 1980s is virtually zero. Nonetheless, for 1989 to 1994 alone, *sanlai yibu* export from China to Hong Kong increased at a startling annual average rate of 26%. Amidst this spectacular growth, however, conventional Chinese exports to Hong Kong, comprised of Chinese domestic exports and re-exports proper, have also continued to thrive steadily. As is also revealed in Panel A of Table 5.1, this latter category in Hong Kong's imports from China increased at an annual rate of 13% in 1980 to 1994, although the growth slowed down substantially to 6.9% per year in the more recent period of 1989 to 1994. To the extent that Chinese domestic exports constitute, in turn, the backbone of Hong Kong's own domestic exports by way of input supply for export production, the long-term growth of conventional Chinese exports to Hong Kong (at the rate of 13% per annum in 1980 from 1994), seems to be basically in line with the pace of Hong Kong's own domestic exports to the United States (at the corresponding rate of 7.4%), or to the world at large (9.6%), as shown in Panel C of Table 5.1.

Likewise, to the extent that conventional Chinese exports also are comprised of re-exports via Hong Kong, the observed discrepancy in the long-term growth rate (that is, 13% versus 7.4% or 9.6%), may be accounted for exactly by the re-export component of truly Chinese origin. There is no doubt that amidst the massive Chinese export drive of the past fifteen years or so, a considerable proportion of increased Chinese exports proper simply has to be channelled through Hong Kong as a matter of expediency, because the mainland could not build port facilities and export service capabilities quickly enough to cope with the increased export demand.

Unfortunately, available Hong Kong government statistics do not distinguish re-exports of Chinese origin between *sanlai yibu* and re-exports of conventional exports for the period under study.

Table 5.1 Hong Kong's Merchandise Trade with China and the United States, 1979–1994

A. Hong Kong's Imports from China and Re-export to the United States (HK$ million)

	Total Imports	***Sanlai yibu* Share Value (2)/(1)*100**		**Conventional Value (4)/(1)*100**		**Total Re-export to US Value (6)/(1)*100**	
	(1)	(2)	(3)	(4)	(5)	(6)	(7)
1979	15,130	0	0.00	15,130	100.00	735	4.86
1980	21,948	0	0.00	21,948	100.00	1,690	7.70
1981	29,510	0	0.00	29,510	100.00	2,814	9.54
1982	32,935	–	–	–	–	3,574	10.85
1983	42,821	–	–	–	–	5,510	12.87
1984	55,753	–	–	–	–	8,778	15.74
1985	58,963	–	–	–	–	11,256	19.09
1986	81,633	–	–	–	–	18,667	22.87
1987	117,357	–	–	–	–	27,748	23.64
1988	155,634	–	–	–	–	43,242	27.78
1989	196,676	113,581	57.75	83,095	42.25	65,993	33.55
1990	236,134	145,103	61.45	91,031	38.55	81,645	34.58
1991	293,356	187,384	63.88	95,972	32.72	103,955	35.44
1992	354,348	254,013	71.68	100,335	28.32	139,977	39.50

Table 5.1 (to be continued)

Table 5.1 (continued)

	Total Imports	*Sanlai yibu* Share Value (2)/(1)*100		Conventional Value (4)/(1)*100		Total Re-export to US Value (6)/(1)*100	
	(1)	(2)	(3)	(4)	(5)	(6)	(7)
1993	402,161	295,203	73.40	106,958	26.60	168,331	41.86
1994	470,876	354,912	75.37	115,954	24.63	195,794	41.58
Annual Growth (%)							
1989–94	19.58	25.59	–	6.89	–	24.30	4.39
1980–94	24.48	–	–	12.63	–	40.62	12.80

B. Hong Kong's Exports and Re-export from the United States to China (HK$ million)

	Total Exports			*Sanlai yibu* Share in				US Share in			
	Domestic	Re-export	Total	Domestic Export Value (4)/(1)*100		Re-export Value (6)/(2)*100		Total Export Value (8)/(3)*100		Re-export Value (10)/(2)*100	
	(1)	(2)	(3)	(4)	(5)	(6)	(7)	(8)	(9)	(10)	(11)
1979	603	1,315	1,918	0	0	0	0	0	0	131	9.96
1980	1,605	4,642	6,247	0	0	0	0	0	0	337	7.16
1981	2,924	8,044	10,968	0	0	0	0	0	0	567	7.05
1982	3,806	7,992	11,798	–	–	–	–	–	–	1,034	12.94
1983	6,223	12,183	18,406	–	–	–	–	–	–	1,474	12.10
1984	11,283	28,064	39,347	–	–	–	–	–	–	2,932	10.45

Table 5.1 (to be continued)

Table 5.1 (continued)

	Total Exports			*Sanlai yibu* Share in				US Share in			
	Domestic	Re-export	Total	Domestic Export Value (4)/(1)*100		Re-export Value (6)/(2)*100		Total Export Value (8)/(3)*100		Re-export Value (10)/(2)*100	
	(1)	(2)	(3)	(4)	(5)	(6)	(7)	(8)	(9)	(10)	(11)
1985	15,189	46,023	61,212	–	–	–	–	–	–	4,476	9.73
1986	18,022	40,894	58,915	–	–	–	–	–	–	4,422	10.81
1987	27,871	60,170	88,041	–	–	–	–	–	–	6,179	10.27
1988	38,043	94,895	132,933	–	–	–	–	–	–	9,588	10.10
1989	43,272	103,492	146,764	31,962	73.86	44,906	43.39	76,868	52.38	10,265	9.92
1990	47,470	110,908	158,378	36,418	76.72	55,496	50.04	91,914	58.03	10,283	9.27
1991	54,404	153,318	207,722	40,369	74.20	73,562	47.98	113,931	57.74	13,302	8.68
1992	61,956	212,105	274,061	44,271	71.46	97,368	45.91	141,639	51.68	18,183	8.57
1993	63,367	274,561	337,928	45,141	71.24	115,037	41.90	160,178	47.40	24,601	8.96
1994	61,009	322,835	383,844	41,959	68.78	139,221	43.12	181,180	47.20	28,662	8.88
Average Growth (%)											
1989–94	7.11	25.55	21.20	9.01	–	25.39	–	18.71	–	22.80	–
1980–94	29.67	35.39	34.20	–	–	–	–	–	–	37.35	–

Table 5.1 (to be continued)

Table 5.1 (continued)

C. Hong Kong's Exports to the United States (HK$ million)

		Domestic Export							Re-export		
	Value	World Total Net of *Sanlai yibu* to China	Value	US Share (3)/ (1)*100	World Total (3)/ (2)*100	US Share Value	Value	(7)/ (6)*100	Chinese Origin Share (9)/ (6)*Value	100	US share %
	(1)	(2)	(3)	(4)	(5)	(6)	(7)	(8)	(9)	(10)	(11)
1979	55,912	55,912	18,797	33.62	33.62	20,022	1,995	9.96	5,663	28.28	12.98
1980	68,171	68,171	22,591	33.14	33.14	30,072	3,085	10.26	8,394	27.91	20.13
1981	80,423	80,423	29,200	36.31	36.31	41,739	4,785	11.46	12,834	30.75	21.93
1982	83,032	–	31,223	37.60	–	44,353	5,615	12.66	14,694	33.13	24.32
1983	104,405	–	43,802	41.95	–	56,294	8,028	14.26	19,680	34.96	28.00
1984	137,936	–	61,374	44.49	–	83,504	12,109	14.50	28,107	33.66	31.23
1985	129,882	–	57,687	44.41	–	105,270	14,705	13.97	34,628	32.89	32.52
1986	153,983	–	64,219	41.71	–	122,546	22,362	18.25	51,597	42.10	36.18
1987	195,254	–	72,817	37.29	–	182,780	32,456	17.76	84,266	46.10	32.93
1988	217,664	–	72,884	33.48	–	275,405	49,483	17.98	131,525	47.76	32.88
1989	224,104	192,142	72,162	32.20	37.56	346,405	72,033	20.79	188,271	54.35	35.05
1990	225,875	189,457	66,370	29.38	35.03	413,999	87,752	21.20	240,410	58.07	33.96
1991	231,045	190,676	62,870	27.21	32.97	534,841	110,800	20.72	315,689	59.02	32.93
1992	234,123	189,852	64,600	27.59	34.03	690,829	148,500	21.50	403,782	58.45	34.67

Table 5.1 (to be continued)

Table 5.1 (continued)

			Domestic Export						Re-export		
	Value	**World Total Net of *Sanlai yibu* to China**	**Value**	**US Share (3)/ (1)*100**	**World Total (3)/ (2)*100**	**US Share Value**	**Value**	**(7)/ (6)*100**	**Chinese Origin Share (9)/ (6)*Value**	**100**	**US share %**
	(1)	**(2)**	**(3)**	**(4)**	**(5)**	**(6)**	**(7)**	**(8)**	**(9)**	**(10)**	**(11)**
1993	223,027	177,886	60,292	27.03	33.89	823,224	180,349	21.91	474,007	57.58	35.51
1994	289,000	247,041	61,419	21.25	24.86	1,239,000	210,077	16.96	545,831	44.05	35.87
Annual Growth (%)											
1989–94	6.56	5.15	–3.9	–	–	29.03	23.87	–	23.72	–	–
1984–94	7.68	–	0.00	–	–	30.96	33.02	–	34.53	–	–
1980–94	10.87	9.63	7.40	–	–	30.42	35.19	–	34.74	–	–

Notes: For section A, *sanlai yibu* imports from China may be assumed to be zero or negligible in the early 1980s; hence conventional imports are equal to imports from China for those years, comprising both retained imports and imports destined for re-export to third destinations. For B, *sanlai yibu* shares in domestic exports and re-exports are assumed to be zero or negligible in 1979–81. For C, the same assumption applies; hence no distinction is made between columns 1 and 2. The underlying HK dollar figures for column 11 are given in A, column 6.

Sources: HKCSD—*HKADS*, —*HKMDS*, and —*ARHKET*, various issues.

Beyond our attempt to disentangle the intriguing triangular trade relationship between China, Hong Kong and the United States, however, the most noteworthy point to be made from Table 5.1 (Panel A) is that a drastically increasing share of total Chinese exports to Hong Kong (comprising both the *sanlai yibu* and conventional categories) has been re-exported to the United States. The US share increased from 7.7% in 1980 to 19% in 1985 when outward processing consignments from Hong Kong to China (especially Guangdong) started to gain momentum. By 1994, the share stood at 42%, representing virtually an exponential growth from the early 1980s.

In absolute value, total Chinese exports (*sanlai yibu* and exports proper combined) via Hong Kong to the United States increased at an annual rate of 24% from 1989 to 1994. This is higher than the growth rate of Chinese *sanlai yibu* exports to Hong Kong, that is, 6% per annum for the same period. Thus, there is no doubt that Hong Kong's outward processing consignments to China represent very much a business conducted by Hong Kong manufacturers on behalf of their US clients.

We note also that the total volume of Hong Kong's imports from China that is re-exported to the United States has become increasingly larger than the "conventional" type of Chinese exports to Hong Kong. In the past few years, such exports have indeed increasingly approached the value of Chinese *sanlai yibu* exports to Hong Kong in total (see Panel A of Table 5.1). This clearly signifies that Hong Kong has been able to increasingly expand its export production base into the Chinese hinterland, thereby being freed from serious land and labour supply constraints encountered in Hong Kong.

Hong Kong's exports and re-exports from the Unites States to China

The economic breakthrough for Hong Kong for an accelerated integration with China is also clearly reflected in Hong Kong's exports to China. Thus, while the territory's domestic exports to China have increased at a startling annual growth rate of 30% from 1980 to 1994, or just 7% from 1989 to 1994, there is no doubt that the lion's share has been taken up by domestic exports in the form of outward processing consignments. The share has consistently exceeded 70% since 1989, when the Hong Kong government began to publish such statistics (see Panel B of Table 5.1).

Interestingly enough, the volume of re-exports through Hong Kong to China has been growing even faster than Hong Kong's domestic exports to China (averaging at 35% per year from 1980 to 1994, or 26% from 1989 to 1994). Re-exports have indeed remained, in absolute terms, a multiple of domestic exports. The corresponding *sanlai yibu* share in total re-exports to China has also been very substantial, ranging from 42% to 50% from 1989 to 1994. Compared with the *sanlai yibu* share in domestic exports of 69% to 77% during the same period, these percentage shares may not look as impressive. Yet in absolute terms, the *sanlai yibu* size in Hong Kong's re-exports to China (totaling HK$526 billion for the period 1989–94 taken as a whole), is in fact more than double the size of *sanlai yibu* share (HK$240 billion) of Hong Kong's domestic exports to China for the same period. More remarkably, the absolute gap between the two different *sanlai yibu* shares has widened markedly in the past few years in favour of the *sanlai yibu* share in re-exports via Hong Kong to China.

Reference should now again be made to the role played by the United States in Hong Kong's exports to China. The figures in Table 5.1 (Panel B) show that as a country of origin, the US share in Hong Kong's overall re-exports to China has basically been growing in tandem with the total, with both averaging around 37% per year in the whole period from 1980 to 1994; or respectively 23% and 24% for the years from 1985 to 1994. However, while the declining annual growth rate for total re-exports reversed to 28% per year since 1989, that for the corresponding US share stagnated at 23%. As a result, the US share in Hong Kong's total re-exports to China declined from a high of 13% in 1982 (11% in 1986), to below 9% consistently for the four years from 1991 to 1994.

The decline in the US share in Hong Kong's total re-exports to China may not appear to be too remarkable, but it certainly stands in sharp contrast to the accelerated increases in the share of re-exports of Chinese origin to the United States from 5% in 1979, or 19% in 1985, to 42% in 1994 (Panel A of Table 5.1). The implications of these divergent trends should be clear enough. US exports through Hong Kong to China probably deal mostly with finished manufactures, embodying advanced industrial technology and representing a heterogeneous mix of such producer and consumer goods as machinery and equipment, pharmaceuticals, computer software, CDs, CD-ROMs, laser discs, cassette tapes, video games and the like. These are commodities in high demand that are also prone to intellectual property rights infringement.

It seems very likely that these re-exports are primarily destined to cash-rich South China, Guangdong Province in particular, which customarily resorts to experienced marketing experts in Hong Kong for the necessary import sourcing overseas.

Other than customers from South China who, compared with their northern and interior counterparts, have enjoyed considerable privileges in terms of foreign exchange retention schemes, and relatively easy access to hard currency transactions, it is difficult to visualize how demand from the central authority or elsewhere in China could sustain such an impressive growth rate of imports of such "luxurious" commodities from the United States.

At any rate, US exports via Hong Kong to China are likely to be dominated by finished manufactures, rather than raw materials or semi-manufactures, for the purpose of reprocessing for exports. By contrast, exports originating from overseas, which in the past used to be destined for Hong Kong, have in the past decade been increasingly shipped through Hong Kong and, on behalf of Hong Kong manufacturers rather than Chinese end-users, across the Shenzhen border for reprocessing for the purposes of re-exporting; hence the exponential growth of Hong Kong's re-exports of Chinese origin to the United States.

Hong Kong's economic relations with the United States and the world at large

We may now turn to Hong Kong's overall exports to the United States against the backdrop of the emerging Hong Kong–Guangdong economic synergy. Several important points may be made from the data in Panel C of Table 5.1.

Firstly and most remarkably, the US share in Hong Kong's total domestic exports, discounting the *sanlai yibu* export share to China which is essentially for reprocessing for the purposes of re-export, has virtually remained constant in the past fifteen years or so, despite the entire fanfare of "outward processing". The share has indeed been hovering around 35% from 1979 to 1994. This indicates that not only has Hong Kong continued to be heavily dependent upon the United States as a market outlet, but also that China has remained, by virtue of her overwhelming share in input supply to sustain Hong Kong's production for export, vulnerable to the vagaries of US import demand.

Secondly, both Hong Kong's domestic exports (net of *sanlai yibu* exports to China), and its US share tend to be shrinking, in absolute dollar terms, increasingly from the mid-1980s. This reflects clearly the accelerating relocation of

Hong Kong's export manufacturing activities to the Chinese hinterland. The trend is also mirrored in the expanding share of Hong Kong's re-exports of Chinese origin (which covers *sanlai yibu* exports), as well as the US share therein, since the early or mid-1980s. That is to say, the increased shares have compensated exactly for the decline in Hong Kong's conventional domestic exports to the United States and the world at large.

Thirdly, taken together, the observed trends in Hong Kong's domestic exports and re-exports suggest that the Hong Kong-Guangdong synergy with respect to export processing is to a considerable measure a matter of trade diversion (from Hong Kong to China). There is no denying, of course, that with the vast Pearl River Delta hinterland being increasingly converted into a Hong Kong export production base, thereby easing Hong Kong's land and labour supply constraints, the *sanlai yibu* invention is bound to be trade-creating as well. However, the relative contributions of both aspects, trade creation versus trade diversion, deserve further examination.

We have hitherto confined our attention strictly to the triangular China-Hong Kong-US trade relationship. Looking from a broader global perspective, however, it should be noted that the share of China, as a country of origin, in Hong Kong's re-exports (outward processing type included) to all countries has more than doubled from 28% in 1980, to 58% in 1993 at the expense of virtually all other countries. For example, in the case of Japan the share has declined from 20% in 1980 to only 13% in 1993.[7] The decline has taken place despite the fact that, among other things, a considerable proportion of Japanese car exports to China has continued to be shipped through Hong Kong.

Furthermore, the bulk of Hong Kong's global re-exports is indeed destined increasingly to the US market. The US share has increased from 10% in 1980 to 14% in 1985, and has stayed at 21% since 1990, at the expense of almost all other countries, except China. For China as a destination for Hong Kong's re-exports, the share has also more than doubled from some 15% in 1980 to 43% in 1985, to stabilize at between 27% in 1990 and 33% in 1993.[8] The increases should, however, be understood against the background that it has been increasingly dominated by outward processing consignments.

These trading relationships point to the fundamental role of Hong Kong as an international "export processing centre". Put simply, Hong Kong has to make use of machinery and equipment imports from Japan, and increasingly China, to convert the supply of cotton yarn from Pakistan and Egypt, wool from Australia, and, say, PVC and TV tubes from Japan into textiles, fabrics, apparel, toys and sports requisites, and TV sets, with, above all, Chinese supplies of wage food and clothing to feed and clothe its workers, for exports to the huge US consumer market. And these days, the overwhelming proportions of export processing activities are indeed being subcontracted to the Pearl River Delta manufacturers by way of "outward processing".

It should be of interest to note that prior to 1985 when *sanlai yibu* was just beginning to pick up momentum, the US share in Hong Kong's domestic exports still stood at around 45%. Thereafter, however, it declined steadily to the level of 27–29% between 1990 and 1993, before being further reduced to 21% in 1994. The relative decline in the US share is evidently very much a matter solely of accelerated increases in favour of China, from a mere 2.4% in 1980, to 12% in 1985, 21% in 1990, and 28% in 1993, as a result of increased Hong Kong "domestic" exports to China for the very purpose of "export reprocessing" on behalf of import clients in the United States and other major Western markets.[9]

Taking domestic exports and re-exports together, 23% of Hong Kong's total merchandise exports was absorbed by the US market in 1993 or 18% in 1994, compared to 26% in 1980, or 31% in 1985. Bearing in mind, however, that the bulk of Hong Kong's domestic exports are also inextricably linked to wage food and clothing supplies from China, it is clear that after China's opening up to the outside world since the late 1970s, both Hong Kong and China have continued to be substantially dependent, albeit not as markedly as before, on the US market for their export earnings. Within this context, Hong Kong in particular has actually become an adjunct to the Chinese export economy.

From an import-financing perspective, it is significant to note that Hong Kong is indeed of paramount importance to China as a source of foreign exchange earnings, direct or indirect, for financing China's massive import bills from the US, Japan, as well as the world at large. The figures given in Table 5.2, which tell the Chinese story of the trade balance, reveal that for 14 years out of the total of 15 from 1979 to 1993 for which China incurred a total trade deficit to the tune of US$23 billion with the United States, the shortfall could be effectively offset by an accumulated trade surplus of US$142 billion with Hong Kong, that is, at a multiple of 6.15. For the United States and Japan combined, both being the single most important trade creditors for China, the corresponding multiple still stands at a startling high of 2.09.

That is to say, China's total export earnings from Hong Kong alone, net of the corresponding import expenditure, are more than sufficient to finance

China's net import bills incurred with the United States and Japan, or the world at large, for the entire period from 1979 to 1993. Even if the *sanlai yibu* component is taken out of China's exports to Hong Kong, the Chinese trade surplus with Hong Kong is still more than sufficient to cover the country's combined deficits with the US and Japan from 1989 to 1993. This unequivocally speaks for the pivotal importance of Hong Kong in Sino-American and also Sino-Japanese trade relations, as well as beyond, in the entire Chinese foreign trade system.

To the extent, however, that Chinese exports to Hong Kong have been increasingly dominated by *sanlai yibu* components, we have yet to determine whether the bulk of Chinese earnings from Hong Kong really is of Chinese or Hong Kong origin, as the issue may bear on the conflict between the United States and China over the size of trade deficits.

Sino-American trade balance dispute: The Hong Kong link

Table 5.3 shows that both Chinese and American statistics consistently understate or overstate their exports or imports to or from each other. That is to say, they either overstate their bilateral trade deficits or understate their trade surplus. The discrepancy has indeed widened quite substantially since 1986, pointing again to the implication of the massive Chinese *sanlai yibu* exports through Hong Kong to the United States.

Part of the conflicting Chinese and American claims may be explained by the standard international statistical practice of reporting a country's own exports at FOB price and taking imports from the other at CIF price. For the earlier years, say from 1979 to 1985, the discrepancy is indeed rather limited, and may therefore essentially be accounted for by the FOB/CIF difference. However, from 1985 to 1986 onwards, the Chinese *sanlai yibu* exports via Hong Kong to the United States have undoubtedly changed the relative scale of the discrepancy quite drastically, with US government statistics claiming accelerated increases in trade deficits by many times against similar but basically declining Chinese claims (see Table 5.3).

Background to the conflicting trade deficit claims

The background to the conflicting Sino-American trade deficit claims is clear enough. Both countries have interpreted differently the growth of *sanlai yibu*

Table 5.2 China's Trade Balance with Major Trading Partners, 1979–1984 (US$ 100 million)

Year	All Countries	USA	Japan	Hong Kong		Ratio 1	Ratio 2	Ratio 3
				Gross of *Sanlai yibu*	Net of *Sanlai yibu*			
	(1)	(2)	(3)	(4)	(5)	(4)/(1)	(4)/(2)	(4)/[(2)+(3)]
1979	–20.10	–12.62	–11.80	33.33	–	1.66	2.64	1.36
1980	–19.00	–28.48	–11.37	40.34	–	2.12	1.42	1.01
1981	–0.10	–31.49	–13.95	40.33	–	403.30	1.28	0.89
1982	30.30	–25.23	9.07	38.67	–	–	1.53	2.39
1983	8.40	–10.45	–9.83	41.05	–	–	3.93	2.02
1984	–12.70	–16.05	–30.86	39.60	–	3.12	2.47	0.84
1985	–149.00	–27.51	–89.26	24.07	–	0.16	0.87	0.21
1986	–119.60	–20.85	–76.59	41.75	–	0.35	2.00	0.43
1987	–37.80	–17.94	–36.76	53.41	–	1.41	2.98	0.98
1988	–77.60	–32.86	–31.41	62.93	–	0.81	1.92	0.98
1989	–66.00	–34.54	–21.39	93.76	46.69	1.42	2.71	1.68
1990	87.40	–14.09	14.23	123.96	55.67	–	8.80	–
1991	80.50	–18.49	1.88	146.74	39.36	–	7.94	8.83
1992	43.50	–3.07	–20.04	169.79	24.61	–	55.31	7.35
1993	–121.90	–12.13	–74.74	241.95	115.91	1.918	19.95	2.79
1994	53.46	74.91	–47.48	229.08	–	–	–	–8.35
Total	–320.24	–230.89	–450.30	1420.76	282.24	4.44	6.15	2.09

Table 5.2 (to be continued)

Table 5.2 (continued)

Year	All Countries	USA	Japan	Hong Kong		Ratio 1	Ratio 2	Ratio 3
				Gross of *Sanlai yibu*	Net of *Sanlai yibu*			
	(1)	(2)	(3)	(4)	(5)	(4)/(1)	(4)/(2)	(4)/[(2)+(3)]
Average								
1979–85	–23.17	–21.69	–22.57	36.77	–	1.59	1.70	0.83
1986–94	–17.56	–8.78	–32.48	129.26	56.45	7.36	14.72	3.13
1979–94	–20.02	–14.43	–28.14	88.80	56.45	4.44	6.15	2.09

Notes: Figures for 1981–83 are converted from RMB yuan to US dollars by using the official annual average exchange rates. The two 1993 figures for the trade balance with Hong Kong (HK) are tentative estimates, and could be very problematic. The reasons are as follow: the year 1993 saw curiously both Chinese exports (US$22.1 billion) to and imports (US$10.5 billion) from HK being drastically curtailed from the previous year's highs of US$37.5 billion and 20.5 billion respectively. A likely explanation for the precipitous drop is that the 1993 figures do not include the *sanlai yibu* components with HK. This is because HK government statistics show that both *sanlai yibu* (outward processing) consignments (US$20.7 billion) to China and *sanlai yibu* imports (US$38.2 billion) from China in 1993 (as given in Table 4.1, panels A and B) are themselves very substantially larger than the given Chinese total exports to and imports from HK. Thus, barring any other better explanation, we simply regard the original Chinese export and import figures as net of the *sanlai yibu* component. This results therefore in the trade balance with HK of US$11.6 billion for 1993 as given for the net series. This figure is, of course, not directly comparable to those for 1989–92 (which are derived from HK government statistics) and seems to be biased upwards. For the 1993 trade balance (with HK) figure, we have in turn added Hong Kong's outward processing-related exports and imports to the original Chinese figures to derive the trade balance gross of the *sanlai yibu* components. In the estimates, HK's *sanlai yibu* import figure of US$38.2 billion is adjusted downwards by 10% and the comparable export figure adjusted upwards by 5% to account for the possible FOB/CIF discrepancy. This gives therefore, for trade balance, the figure of US$24.2 billion for 1993.

Sources: *ZGTJNJ*, various issues.

Table 5.3 Conflicting Chinese Versus US Claims on Exports (X), Imports (M), and Trade Balance, 1979–1994 (US$ billion)

Year	Chinese Statistics			US Statistics			Relative Discrepancy		
	M	X	X–M	M	X	X–M	(1)/(5)	(4)/(2)	(6)+(3)
	(1)	(2)	(3)	(4)	(5)	(6)	(7)	(8)	(9)
1979	1.86	0.60	–1.26	0.70	1.70	1.00	1.09	1.17	–0.26
1980	3.83	0.98	–2.85	1.16	3.76	2.60	1.02	1.18	–0.25
1981	4.66	1.51	–3.15	2.06	3.60	1.54	1.29	1.36	–1.61
1982	4.28	1.76	–2.52	2.50	2.91	0.41	1.47	1.42	–2.11
1983	2.77	1.72	–1.05	2.48	2.17	–0.31	1.28	1.44	–1.36
1984	4.04	2.43	–1.61	3.38	3.00	–0.38	1.35	1.39	–1.99
1985	5.09	2.34	–2.75	4.22	3.86	–0.36	1.32	1.80	–3.11
1986	4.72	2.63	–2.09	5.24	3.11	–2.13	1.52	1.99	–4.22
1987	4.83	3.04	–1.79	6.91	3.50	–3.41	1.38	2.27	–5.20
1988	6.67	3.38	–3.29	9.26	5.02	–4.24	1.33	2.74	–7.53
1989	7.86	4.41	–3.45	11.99	5.76	–6.23	1.36	2.72	–9.68
1990	6.59	5.18	–1.41	15.24	4.81	–10.43	1.37	2.94	–11.84
1991	8.01	6.16	–1.85	18.97	6.28	–12.69	1.28	3.08	–14.54
1992	8.90	8.59	–0.31	25.73	7.42	–18.31	1.20	3.00	–18.62
1993	10.69	9.48	–1.21	31.54	8.77	–22.77	1.22	3.33	–23.98
1994	13.97	13.55	–0.42	38.00	8.80	–29.20	1.59	2.80	–29.62

Table 5.3 (to be continued)

Table 5.3 (continued)

Year	Chinese Statistics			US Statistics			Relative Discrepancy		
	M	X	X–M	M	X	X–M	(1)/(5)	(4)/(2)	(6)+(3)
	(1)	(2)	(3)	(4)	(5)	(6)	(7)	(8)	(9)
Total									
1979–85	26.53	11.34	–15.19	16.50	21.00	4.50	1.26	1.40	–10.69
1986–94	72.24	56.42	–15.32	162.88	53.47	–109.41	1.36	2.76	–125.23
1979–94	98.77	67.76	–31.01	179.38	74.47	–104.91	1.32	2.17	–135.92
Average									
1979–85	3.79	1.62	–2.17	2.36	3.00	0.64	1.26	1.40	–1.53
1986–94	8.03	6.27	–1.76	18.10	5.94	–12.16	1.36	2.76	–13.91
1979–94	6.17	4.24	–1.94	11.21	4.65	–6.56	1.32	2.17	–8.50

Notes: The Chinese figures for 1981–83 are converted from RMB yuan to US dollars using the official annual average exchange rates. The 1993–94 Chinese export figures are adjusted values net of re-exports (including the outward processing components).

Sources: Chinese statistics are from *ZGTJNJ*, various issues, except for the 1994 figures which are China's Customs Statistics from *CTR*, June 1995. US statistics are from USDC—*SAUS* 1994.

re-exports and, relatedly, the crucial intermediary role of Hong Kong as the port through which their exports and imports flow to each other. The Chinese recorded their direct exports to the United States in their current account, but their indirect exports to the US through Hong Kong (*sanlai yibu* included) were regarded as Chinese exports to Hong Kong. The United States, on the other hand, claimed Chinese goods shipped through Hong Kong to be Chinese exports, but nonetheless deemed US goods trans-shipped to China through Hong Kong as exports to Hong Kong. Both Chinese and American statistics have therefore underreported their exports to each other and overstated their bilateral trade deficit.[10]

Given the enormous importance of *sanlai yibu* exports, it is therefore essentially a matter of how to determine Hong Kong's contribution to their total costs of production relative to the comparable Chinese share. The possible methodology may help to apportion the entire *sanlai yibu* export volume between the Chinese and Hong Kong shares accordingly.

Before we attempt to reconcile the Sino-American trade statistics, a few words should be said about the nature and scope of *sanlai yibu*, or outward processing (OP) activity from a Hong Kong perspective. Table 5.4 shows the Hong Kong government's statistics on the estimated value of OP-type flow of goods from China to Hong Kong by broad commodity groups from 1991 to 1994. Clearly, they cover a wide range of manufactured goods which, prior to the mid-1980s, were traditionally produced in Hong Kong with varying degrees of labour intensity. Note that foodstuffs and agricultural products, which are virtually non-existent in Hong Kong, are not listed as a category of OP-type imports. Of particular interest also is the fact that the OP-type flow of goods makes up an overwhelming share of Hong Kong's total imports from China. The overall share in 1989 when the Hong Kong government began to compile such statistics, already stood at 58.1%. It has increased to 76% in 1994 (see Table 5.4). In general, products which are based on supply of primary commodities, or those with lower value added (for example, yarn, fabrics, and base metals and metal products), tend to exhibit smaller OP proportions. On the other hand, for manufactured products such as clothing, electronic and electrical goods, watches, toys, plastic goods, ornaments, and machinery, the shares are well over 80%.

As a matter of fact, the bulk of *sanlai yibu* output is produced by *sanji qiye* (*qiye* meaning "enterprises") with Hong Kong interests, or by the hundreds of thousands of small-scale township and village enterprises commissioned

Table 5.4 Value and Proportion of OP-Related Goods Flowing from China to Hong Kong, 1991–1994

Commodity	Value (HK$ million)				OP Proportion (%)			
Group	1991	1992	1993	1994	1991	1992	1993	1994
Textile materials, textile articles other than textile garments	7,684	8,863	10,020	13,242	20.5	23.0	27.3	30.3
Articles of apparel and clothing accessories (textile garments)	51,003	59,830	67,351	70,128	86.6	84.4	83.1	83.1
Plastic articles	5,641	7,884	9,361	11,584	84.8	89.3	90.4	87.1
Machinery and appliances; electrical equipment	23,742	32,313	36,668	48,348	78.7	81.0	76.4	82.2
Television image recorders and reproducers	26,338	31,103	37,586	50,005	89.7	92.7	91.5	94.7
Clocks and watches	8,262	9,682	11,331	12,724	96.4	94.3	95.8	96.4
Toys, games and sports requisites; parts and accessories	17,332	25,301	27,289	32,847	92.1	96.9	96.0	94.2
Base metals and metal products	3,253	5,189	6,964	7,965	29.6	43.6	52.3	51.2
Others (including commodities and transactions not classified according to kind)	54,129	73,848	88,633	108,069	59.5	65.9	69.3	71.5
Total	197,384	254,013	295,203	354,912	67.7	72.1	73.8	75.9

Notes: The percentage figures are OP (*sanlai yibu*) shares in total exports to Hong Kong.

Sources: HKGCSD—*HKADS*, various issues.

by Hong Kong manufacturers to take up the processing in China, especially Guangdong Province. The Hong Kong Trade Development Council (HKTDC) estimates that 19,000 out of 25,000 (roughly 76%) enterprises of Hong Kong origin in China producing for Hong Kong are involved in *sanlai yibu* activities. A Chinese source reports that over 300,000 enterprises are engaged in *sanlai yibu* activities in Guangdong Province, employing more than two million local Chinese workers, earning a total processing fee (*gongjiao fei*) income of more than US$1.5 billion from a *sanlai yibu* exports total of US$15.1 billion in 1994. This presumably makes up 83% of the national total of *sanlai yibu* exports.[11]

HKTDC also reported that the predominant share of Chinese *sanlai yibu* products is exported indirectly via Hong Kong to the outside world, as shown in Table 5.5. The share rose, however, by only a very small margin from 82% in 1988 to 86% in 1991. This indicates that from the very early stage it is in fact Hong Kong manufacturers who have been directly involved with, and who represent the single most important clients of, Chinese *sanlai yibu* production. Needless to say, Hong Kong also commands, *vis-à-vis* other Chinese ports, absolute advantages in export shipping and related banking and insurance services to be the logical entrepôt for *sanlai yibu* exports of other sources as well. In fact, in the absence of direct navigational links with the mainland, Taiwanese manufacturers have increasingly channelled their own outward processing through Hong Kong to South China. And it is certainly very difficult, if not entirely impossible, for Hong Kong government statistics to distinguish OP-type re-exports between Hong Kong and Taiwanese sources.

Tables 5.5 Shipping Arrangement for OP-Related Products Made in China (% of year total)

	Indirect Exports through Hong Kong	Direct Shipment from China
1988	82	18
1991	86	14

Notes and sources: All Chinese indirect exports through Hong Kong are customs-declared, but direct shipments (termed by HKTDC as triangular trade) are not. The figures are from HKTDC—*SHKDERETT* (November 1991); see text and endnote 11 for explanation of possible sources of discrepancy with Chinese statistics.

Reconciliation and implications

We may now turn to examine how Hong Kong's contribution to Chinese *sanlai yibu* exports to the United States can be reasonably separated out from the Chinese share. A number of conceptual and methodological issues should first be dealt with briefly. Firstly, in the context of *sanlai yibu* (or OP-type) re-exports, it is obviously not correct to take the conventional re-export margin earned by Hong Kong (on account of its entrepôt facilities and services) as the only stake accruable to Hong Kong as a whole. This simple method omits the important capital input and current expenditure contributed by Hong Kong investors and manufacturers towards outward processing in the form of *sanji* enterprises. To rectify the downward bias, we should therefore, for the purposes of our estimates, define a "re-export margin" as a fraction of export value accruable to Hong Kong, based on Hong Kong's contribution to production and internal marketing of the *sanlai yibu* export goods.

Secondly, the FOB price of an export commodity is equivalent to the per unit cost of production, including the internal cost of marketing. This covers, in our case, the movement of goods within the common China-Hong Kong production zone. The unit price of a product embodies therefore: (1) the factory production cost pertaining to capital cost (for example, building, machinery and fixtures), labour, rental/rates, raw materials, fuel/electricity/water and any related fixed and variable costs of production, and (2) the marketing cost, which comprises the internal costs of handling, transportation, insurance, and payments for port, financial and other trade related services.

Thirdly, the proportional utilization of local and imported inputs by *sanlai yibu* enterprises is dependent on the type of industry. For example, the textile industry would use domestic cotton or silk produced in China (noting, however, that chemical fibre can be more popular these days), thereby raising the real cost/margin to be shared by the Chinese. In the case of Hong Kong investors contributing entirely to the production costs, the entire Chinese re-export volume may theoretically be taken as Hong Kong exports. Where an export production involves cooperating Chinese partners and the use of local labour and land resources, a proportion of the export margin should clearly accrue to them. Therefore, the production plus marketing margin as a part of the total export proceeds to be shared between the mainland Chinese and Hong Kong-based enterprises must be taken into account in adjusting the disputed trade balance statistics between China and the United States.

Fourthly, in the case of indirect exports from the United States to China via Hong Kong, it is appropriate to consider the re-export margin earned by Hong Kong just in terms of the entrepôt and brokerage fees charged by Hong Kong trade mediators. This is usually perceived to be not more than two percent of the total value of exports. However, if US export revenue registered in the American current account is calculated using the FOB price, then adjustment of the export margin will be unnecessary since the re-export margin earned by Hong Kong has already been netted out.

The statistical process for adjusting the Sino-American trade balances comprises several steps. Firstly, we estimate the total value of Chinese *sanlai yibu* exports and the proportion of these exports which were shipped directly and indirectly via Hong Kong to the United States.[12] These values are tabulated in Table 5.6 and Table 5.7. The Chinese direct and indirect (via Hong Kong) exports to the world in total constitute, respectively, around 14% and 86% of total Chinese *sanlai yibu* exports. Chinese *sanlai yibu* exports to the United States are assumed to be similar in proportion. China's total *sanlai yibu* re-exports via Hong Kong to the United States are estimated to be HK$104.6 billion in 1993, as shown in Table 5.6. This represents 12% of Hong Kong's gross domestic product and 50% of its direct investments made in China in 1993 (see Table 5.7), pointing to the sheer importance of OP-type re-exports flowing from China via Hong Kong to the United States.

The second step involves categorizing the important production inputs, fixed and variable, used in light manufacturing into capital (11),[13] rental (12), labour (13), raw materials (14), fuels/charges (15), and distribution (16), and then estimating the expected percentage use of each category of inputs relative to the total usage of inputs. The estimates are based on actual cost data obtained during our survey of five enterprises in Shenzhen specializing in *sanlai yibu* activities. The estimated percentage shares for the various input cost categories are tabulated in Table 5.8. On average, Hong Kong contributed 71.5% and China 28.5% to the aggregate production costs.[14]

Finally, the adjustment of the bilateral balance of trade figures between China and the United States may be made by resorting to the estimated re-export margin earned by Hong Kong (0.715) and China (0.285). We first deduct the OP-related re-export value (OP-RX) from the unadjusted Chinese value of indirect exports to the United States to derive China's exports proper to the United States. We then add to China's exports proper the Chinese share of OP-RX (that is, 0.285 (OP-RX)) to obtain total Chinese real (actual) exports to the United States (that is, exports of truly Chinese origin). China's adjusted trade balance with the United States is Chinese total real exports to the United States less Chinese imports from the United States.[15] The adjusted figures for 1991 to 1993 are shown in Table 5.9.

The adjusted estimates show that the flows of real Chinese production (exports of 100 percent Chinese origin) to the United States are substantially smaller than those originally recorded in US statistics, after netting away the re-export margin earned by Hong Kong. Overall, the unadjusted US deficits with China were approximately overstated by 93.65%, 90.03% and 132.98% in 1991, 1992 and 1993, respectively. As a matter of fact, the adjusted US trade deficits for the three years, 1991 to 1993, have turned out to be very close to the adjusted Chinese trade balances which now show a surplus instead of a deficit against the United States. They are HK$50.3 billion (US deficit) versus HK$56.4 billion (Chinese surplus) for 1991; and respectively HK$71.2 billion versus HK$87.4 billion in 1992, HK$74.7 billion versus HK$84.8 billion in 1993; and HK$105.7 billion versus HK$89.0 billion in 1994. The relative discrepancy for the three years stands respectively at only 12%, 23%, 14% and 16%, using the US deficits as the base measure.

Rough as our adjusted estimates may appear to be, they reveal nonetheless that US trade deficits with China have continued to persist through recent years. This is clearly related to a discernible shift in the direction of China's trade, particularly on the export side, with the United States becoming an increasingly important market for its manufactured goods. China's exports to the US, including the entire OP proportion through Hong Kong, have increased as a share in US global imports from 6% in 1979 to 14% in 1985 and 26% in 1992.[16] Such a shift can primarily be explained by China's evolving competitiveness, coupled in particular with the emerging comparative advantage associated with the China-Hong Kong economic synergy in light manufacturing and outward processing. Put differently, the increased Sino-American trade imbalances should essentially be seen "as a result of the catching-up industrialization of China following the flying geese pattern of development" of other Asian newly industrialized countries.[17]

A more fundamental point which emerges from our reconciliation of the conflicting Sino-US trade deficit claims is that the size of China's surplus as claimed by the United States can now be scaled down very substantially, and that the netted-out balances clearly imply that the overwhelming proportion of China's trade surplus with the United States really represents none other than

Table 5.6 China's Trade with the United States via Hong Kong, 1978–1994 (HK$ billion)

	Chinese Re-exports to the US			US Exports to China		
	All products	**OP-type only**	**(2)/(1)*100**	**Direct exports**	**Re-exports via Hong Kong**	**(5)/[(4)+(5)]*100**
	(1)	**(2)**	**(3)**	**(4)**	**(5)**	**(6)**
1978	0.3730	0.0003	0.1	8.5051	0.3199	3.6
1979	0.7353	0.0079	1.1	18.7098	0.1307	0.7
1980	1.6899	0.0685	4.1	20.1636	0.3368	1.6
1981	2.8136	0.1644	5.8	17.7015	0.5669	3.1
1982	3.5739	0.2575	7.2	15.7998	1.0337	6.1
1983	5.5099	0.4441	8.1	23.4810	1.4735	5.9
1984	8.7781	1.2101	13.8	30.1080	2.9316	8.9
1985	11.2558	1.9150	17.0	24.2704	4.4759	15.6
1986	18.6668	3.2918	17.6	27.2930	4.4221	13.9
1987	27.7480	4.6564	16.8	27.3210	6.1786	18.4
1988	43.2419	9.2742	21.4	39.1861	9.5883	19.7
1989	65.9928	20.7779	31.5	44.9280	10.2652	18.6
1990	81.6445	33.9013	41.5	37.4699	10.2832	21.5
1991	103.9551	47.2561	45.5	48.8082	13.3016	21.4
1992	139.9767	70.2564	50.2	57.4382	18.1827	24.0

Table 5.6 (to be continued)

Table 5.6 (continued)

	Chinese Re-exports to the US			US Exports to China		
	All products	**OP-type only**	**(2)/(1)*100**	**Direct exports**	**Re-exports via Hong Kong**	**(5)/[(4)+(5)]*100**
	(1)	**(2)**	**(3)**	**(4)**	**(5)**	**(6)**
1993	168.3313	104.5966	62.1	67.8447	24.6010	26.6
1994	195.7943	127.6630	65.2	68.0064	28.6615	29.6

Notes: Column 2 figures are indirectly estimated using OP (*sanlai yibu*) plus *sanji qiye* outputs from Guangdong, considering the growth rate of OP in Guangdong (bearing in mind that Guangdong produces more than 85% of all OP-type outputs in China) and the composition of Chinese re-exports to the United States via Hong Kong as a basis of exercising judgment. For instance, there was a negligible quantity of OP production in Guangdong in 1978. As a result, we expect little Chinese OP-related exports to the United States. On the other hand, there was a tremendous increase in OP-type outputs (both from *sanji* and township enterprises) in 1993, constituting about 62% of Guangdong's total exports. This percentage is smaller than the figure listed in Table 5.4, which shows that 76% of the goods flowing from China to Hong Kong in 1994 is OP-related. Besides, we also observe that about 86% of Chinese total re-exports to the United States is manufactured products in 1993, a large percentage of which is believed to be OP-related.

Sources: HKGCSD—*HKADS*, various issues.

Table 5.7 Percentages and Values of Direct and Indirect OP-Related Exports from China to the United States in 1993

	% of OP–XV	OP–XV (HK$ billion)	OP–XV as % FDI	OP–XV as % GDP
Direct	14	14.6435	6.94	1.65
Indirect	86	89.9531	42.60	10.13
Total	100	104.5699	49.54	11.78

Notes: OP-XV denotes outward processing-related export value. GDP and FDI stand respectively for Hong Kong's gross domestic products (HK$887.614 billion in 1993) and realized foreign direct investment in China (HK$211.1364 billion).

Sources: Table 5.6 and author's own estimates as explained in text.

Table 5.8 Hong Kong's Average Proportional Contribution of Each Input to Total Production Value based on a 1995/1996 Survey of Eight Different Industries in Guangdong

	I_1	I_2	I_3	I_4	I_5	I_6	π	Total
Hong Kong	0.094	0.021	0.027	0.326	0.016	0.131	0.113	0.728
China	0.010	0.029	0.078	0.068	0.045	0.030	0.012	0.272
Total	0.104	0.050	0.105	0.394	0.061	0.161	0.125	1.000

Notes: I denotes input and subscripts 1, 2, 3, 4, 5 and 6 denote, respectively, capital, rental, labour, raw materials, fuels/charges, and distribution (refer to the Appendix to this chapter). π denotes the profit margin earned by the surveyed firms. The figures are computed using survey data collected from eight different Guangdong-based joint ventures engaging in various outward processing activities. The labour cost was estimated to be about 10.5% of the total export value, using the sample data. This figure is lower than that quoted by "Hong Kong investment in China: Riding high", *Hong Kong Industrialist,* monthly magazine published by The Federation of Hong Kong Industries, May 1995.

Sources: Table 5.11 in the Appendix to this chapter.

the fact that Hong Kong, and in fact also Taiwan, have been able to successfully export (by way of outward processing) the US trade deficits incurred with them to the Chinese hinterland. As we have noted elsewhere, China's increasing trade surplus with the US since the mid-1980s is clearly a mirror image of the comparable but consistently shrinking trade balances of both Hong Kong and Taiwan *vis-à-vis* the United States.[18]

Table 5.9 Trade Balance: American and Chinese Statistics 1991–1994 (HK$ billion)

	US			China		
Year	**X**	**M**	**X–M**	**X**	**M**	**X–M**
	48.3039	145.6785	–97.3746	47.5372	61.3383	–13.8011
1991	(13.3016)	–	(–84.0730)	(103.9551)	–	(90.1542)
	–	{111.2761}	{–49.6706}	[69.5527]	–	[55.7516]
	57.5513	197.2090	–139.6577	65.9921	68.2942	–2.3021
1992	(18.1837)	–	(–121.4750)	(139.9767)	–	(137.6746)
		{146.0623}	{–70.3283}	[88.8302]	–	[86.5279]
	67.5030	241.6032	–174.1272	73.2989	82.0776	–8.7787
1993	(24.6010)	–	(–149.5262)	(168.3313)	–	(159.5526)
	–	{165.4569}	(–73.3529)	[92.1850]	–	[83.4063]
	68.0064	293.6640	–225.6576	92.4825	107.9602	–15.4777
1994	(28.6615)	–	(–196.9961)	(195.7943)	–	(180.3166)
	–	{200.7253}	{–104.0574}	[102.8556]	–	[87.3779]

Notes: Figures in round brackets include the indirect US-China trade in the form of HK re-exports. Figures in square brackets show the OP-adjusted exports, denoting total re-exports minus OP-related re-exports (which is equal to China's traditional domestic exports) plus China's share of OP-related re-exports, imports from China minus the re-export margin earned by Hong Kong. Figures in { } indicate the flow of real Chinese production to the US, denoting US total imports from China minus the re-export margin earned by Hong Kong.

Sources: As explained in text.

It should also be of interest to note that China's favourable trade balance with the United States is occasionally explained as being brought about by the Chinese ability to manipulate the RMB/USD exchange rate for promoting exports. There is of course a good case for such an argument, bearing in mind that the RMB/USD rate has been rising steadily, and at times quite drastically, in nominal and real terms ever since the early 1980s. However, a regression analysis for the years 1978 to 1993 based on the unadjusted China trade balance figures reveals that changes in the RMB exchange rate in real terms do not really bear to any significant extent on the growth of China's trade surplus with the United States.[19] A possible explanation is that the bulk of OP-type export and import flows between Hong Kong and China is, by the nature of the transactions, not at all vulnerable to fluctuations in the RMB/HKD exchange rate, and is even less so with the Hong Kong dollar having been pegged to the US dollar ever since late 1983.

The stake of Hong Kong in a Sino-American crossfire

By virtue of the highly enhanced symbiotic relationship between Hong Kong and China, it is clear that any US-initiated trade sanctions against China will seriously affect Hong Kong as well. In the past several years, the Hong Kong government, wary of an abrupt withdrawal by the United States of China's MFN status, has painstakingly estimated each year, ahead of the June deadline for MFN renewal, the possible impact on the Hong Kong economy in terms of trade, income and job losses.

As shown in Table 5.10, Hong Kong's exports of Chinese origin to the United States could be easily slashed by up to nearly 50% or a minimum of one-third, in the event of MFN withdrawal. It is not clear how exactly the statistics are compiled. But given that US demand for the export commodities involved are all highly price-elastic, the estimated magnitude of re-export losses seems to be quite reasonable. At any rate, according to the same Hong Kong government estimates, if MFN sanctions were implemented, the multiplier effect of a shortfall in re-exports to the US would have led to the expected Hong Kong GDP growth rate of around 5.5% for both 1993 and 1994 to be curtailed by 2.2% to 3.1%, and employment reduced by a massive component of up to 69,000 and 75,000 persons respectively in the two years involved. This is indeed nothing short of a doomsday forecast for Hong Kong.

An independent estimate of the possible magnitude of GDP losses in Hong Kong, as a result of a US withdrawal of MFN status for China, may also roughly be made on the basis of the adjustments we have made to Chinese re-exports through Hong Kong to the United States. Take the year 1993 for example, for which Chinese *sanlai yibu* or OP-type exports to the United States are given to be HKD 105 billion in total (see Table 5.6). With an estimated Hong Kong share of 71.5% (relative to its contribution to capital input and current expenditure on *sanlai yibu* production; see Table 5.8), the figure of HKD 105 billion translates into an absolute share of HKD 75.1 billion to the credit of Hong Kong, as compared to HKD 29.9 billion for Chinese counterparts involved in *sanlai yibu* production.

Table 5.10 Economic Impact on Hong Kong of a Withdrawal by the US of the MFN Status for China: Hong Kong Estimates of Trade and GDP Losses, 1991–1994

	1991	1992	1993	1994	1995
Losses in RXc %	–	35–47	34–47	–	2.3
Value (HK$ billion)	–	36–49	47–66	55–77	4.5
Losses in Related Trade	–	6–8	6–9	–	–
As % of total trade	35	91–123	118–166	133–187	–
GDP Losses Growth %	0.7	1.8–2.5	2.2–3.1	2.2–3.1	0.14
Value (HK$ billion)	–	12–16	16–23	19–26	–
Job Losses (1000 Persons)	16.6	44–60	49–69	54–75	4.7

Notes: RXc stands for re-exports of Chinese origin. The 1995 figures are not comparable to the ones for 1991–94. They refer to the possible impact of a US trade retaliation against China on account of Chinese "infringement" of US intellectual property rights. The scope of sanctions by way of imposing punitive tariffs on selected target commodities is much more limited, compared to a blanket denial of MFN status. The "hitlist", which amounted to US$1.08 billion in total, as announced in early 1995 covers such OP-type products as electrical and plastic products, telephone answering machines, wireless telephones, furniture, ceramic products, footwear and sporting goods.

Sources: HKGTD as quoted in the media in Hong Kong.

Assuming that MFN withdrawal would, in line with Hong Kong government's elasticity estimates, curtail the OP-type exports on account of the Hong Kong share, by 34–47% (see Table 5.10), this would give an effective export loss of HK$25.5–35.3 billion. If we further assume that for every Hong Kong dollar of OP-type exports, Hong Kong earns a value added of say, HK$0.5, then the net GDP losses will stand at a total of HK$10.2–12.8 billion or alternatively HK$14.1–17.7 billion respectively. These estimated losses fall behind the Hong Kong government estimates of HK$16–23 billion for 1993, but if the multiplier income effect is taken into consideration in our independent estimate, the two sets of outcomes would probably come quite close to each other.[20]

The estimated dollar-by-dollar losses should be placed in the broader context of the Hong Kong-China economic synergy, if one is to understand the full scale of economic losses which could incur to Hong Kong in the case of MFN non-renewal. There are two aspects to the economic synergy. The first is that with the massive relocation of Hong Kong's manufacturing undertakings to the Pearl River Delta, Hong Kong's industrial structure has basically been hollowed out in the past decade, so much so that one may rightly speak of a "Manhattanization" of Hong Kong in terms of its changing economic function. Specifically similar to New York City proper, Hong Kong has these days become very much an international centre of banking, finance, shipping, insurance and global communications, serving increasingly and linking the vast industrial Chinese hinterland to the outside world.

The second related aspect of the Hong Kong-China synergy is that in the past ten years or so, Hong Kong has also increasingly been transformed from an important manufacturing centre into an entrepôt of global scale. This has occurred on account of not only the increasing share of Chinese re-exports of OP-type outputs (in relation to Hong Kong's shrinking domestic exports per se), but more importantly, also a substantial and rising proportion of Chinese imports and re-exports of Chinese origin proper being continually channelled through Hong Kong. Note especially that US exports via Hong Kong to China alone have increased, as a share of total China-bound US exports, from 1.6% in 1980 to 16% in 1985, and then further to a most impressive high of 30% in 1994 (see Table 5.6). This speaks for the very importance of Hong Kong as an international hub of marketing, sourcing, financing and shipping services. In addition, Hong Kong also provides well-established and excellent port facilities.

Perhaps the most important point which should be made in this context is that contrary to the narrower perception of the Hong Kong-China synergy being no more than "trade diversion" (from Hong Kong to China for exports to the US), the Hong Kong economy has in fact been growing at a rate (generally five percent per year) significantly faster than that of any established industrialized country in the past decade or so. This has taken place against the backdrop of a labour supply in Hong Kong which could increase at the rate of only around one percent per year—and hence, until recently, mounting pressure from a labour shortage in the territory. Clearly, the Chinese industrial backbone is more than strong enough to support the now predominantly service-based, Manhattan-type economy of Hong Kong. Viewed against this new context, it becomes clear that the China factor will play an increasingly crucial role in the economic prosperity of Hong Kong towards and beyond 1997, and that any crossfire between the two economic giants—China and the United States—would have a wounding effect on the fortunes of Hong Kong.

Conclusion: Beyond 1997

Any speculation to be made about the economic fate of Hong Kong beyond 1997 is bound to be more a matter of academic exercise in political science rather than economics. In economic terms, any adaptations and adjustments made are necessarily marginal in scale. Clearly, the source of any significant disturbance will be political in nature. What the political balance between China and the United States will hold for the Hong Kong economy is beyond the realm of economic analysis. However, given that MFN renewal has been delinked from the human rights issue since 1994, it seems that an important stage has already been set in the depoliticization of Sino-American economic relations. It is, of course, far too early for anyone to predict that Sino-American economic relations—and with it the prosperity and stability of Hong Kong—will be free from further political influence. But given the sheer size of the present-day Chinese economy, its enhanced international linkages, as well as the importance of Hong Kong as an international economic phenomenon, US decision makers/policymakers would be wise to think twice before taking policy measures which could potentially exert severe economic consequences.

One should nonetheless be prudent enough to remain a realist: initiatives of a political nature from the US government will almost inescapably come to disturb the equilibrium from time to time with varying scales of damage, whether for reasons of trade imbalances with China, China's market inaccessibility, or otherwise. A critical example of side evidence sustains such a perception: the US has incurred, for more than two decades now, persistent and massive trade deficits with Japan, South Korea and Taiwan as well, but never really have their trade frictions assumed such a political tone as in the case of the US dispute with China. Perhaps, given the important stake both the United States and China are perceived to have in Hong Kong either in economic or, more importantly, political terms, one could hope for Hong Kong to serve as a stabilizer in Sino-American relations.

Appendix

Table 5.11 Percentage Input Contribution to Production by China and Hong Kong for the Eight Surveyed OP-Related Firms in Guangdong

	Survey Companies															
	A		B		C		D		E		F		G		H	
	HK	CN	HK	CN	HK	CN	HK	CN	HK	CN	HK	CN	HK	CN	HK	CN
Capital	13.0	0	13.0	0	13.0	0	11.5	0	9.0	0	6.8	3.2	8.8	2.2	0	2.4
Rental	2.0	5.0	3.0	5.0	1.5	0	1.5	0.5	5.0	10.0	2.4	0	1.0	0.8	0	1.5
Labour	2.5	5.0	4.0	8.0	2.0	15.0	2.0	1.0	6.0	6.0	2.3	6.5	0.5	2.8	2.0	18.0
Raw Material	45.0	0	16.0	16.0	30.0	0	40.0	0	0	–20.0	39.7	10.6	51.4	5.7	38.6	3.3
Fuel/Charges	1.5	2.0	2.0	3.5	2.0	12.0	1.5	12.0	2.5	2.5	2.7	2.0	0.5	1.5	0.3	0.5
Distribution	10.0	1.5	15.0	3.5	15.5	3.0	20.0	2.5	17.0	8.0	6.0	2.5	9.5	1.8	12.0	0
Total	74.0	13.5	53.0	36.0	64.0	30.0	76.5	16.0	39.5	46.5	59.9	24.8	71.2	14.8	52.6	25.7

Note: (1) HK and CN denote Hong Kong and China's share of input contribution. Conpanies A, B, C, and D relate, respectively, to printing, electronics, textile and household goods production.

(2) Companies E, F, and G, relate, respectively, to production of processed food, spectacle frames, and watches. Company H is a village enterprise, specializing in exports of clothes and household curtains. Each entry represents the percentage of the respective company's turnover (gross margin). Profit margin for each company can be derived from the last row of the table. For example, company A's profit margin is 12.5%, that is, (100–74–13.5)%.

Sources: Surveys conducted by Thomas Voon.

Table 5.12 Average Percentage Input Contribution by China and Hong Kong and the Profit Margin of the Surveyed Companies

Hong Kong	China	Profit margin (HK)	Profit margin (CN)	Total
61.5	26.0	11.3	1.2	100

Notes: Capital includes interest repayment, depreciation and bank fees/charges. Rental includes land and warehouse charges. Labour includes salary and wages. Raw materials and semi-manufactured products imported from the rest of the world and subsequently brought into China are treated as costs incurred by Hong Kong. Fuel/Charges include heating, electricity, water, insurance and sundry expenses. Distribution includes advertising, handling, transportation, travelling, postage, telecommunications, packaging and quality control.

6
Hong Kong Weathering the Asian Financial Storm*

Could the British have done better?

Hardly had Hong Kong wound up the fanfare of celebrating its return to Chinese sovereignty, on 1 July 1997, than the Asian financial crisis erupted. The next day, in a sudden collapse, the Thai baht fell precipitously in value against the US dollar. Within months, the financial disaster claimed several major "dominos" in Southeast and East Asia including, notably, Malaysia, Indonesia, and South Korea.[1] It spared no one, not even the newly installed Chinese Special Administrative Region (SAR) of Hong Kong. By October 1998, it became apparent that, after years of sustained growth at an annual rate of 5–6%, the SAR's Gross Domestic Product (GDP) for the year would be curtailed by a hefty 5%. By November 1998, the unemployment rate had already reached a postwar high of 5.3%. Just a year or so before, a rigorous labour importation programme had been launched to relieve the enormous labour shortage pressures impinging on Hong Kong for over a decade, following increased economic integration with the Chinese mainland. [2]

Now, how does the ongoing economic meltdown in the HKSAR stand in relation to the main theme of the book—*Hong Kong the Super Paradox: Life After Return to China* (edited by Professor James C. Hsiung, from which this chapter is reprinted)? While it is obvious that the drastic economic downturn had nothing whatsoever to do with the territory's reversion, it is worth noting, however, that prior to 1997 both domestic and external apprehensions

* Reprinted from "Weathering the Asian financial storm in Hong Kong", in James C. Hsiung (ed.), *Hong Kong the Super Paradox: Life After Return to China*, New York: St. Martin's Press, 2000, pp. 235–64.

about Hong Kong's future under Chinese sovereignty generally focused on domestic affairs, rather than on its external economic relations. Specifically, there were concerns as to whether Hong Kong would truly be granted full autonomy, as promised, under the "one country, two systems" model. Another fear was whether under increased Chinese influence the highly efficient public administration system in Hong Kong would be eroded, giving way to bureaucratic inertia, laxity, and corruption. In addition, there were also worries whether the integrity of the British common law-based legal system would be compromised by the socialist version of jurisprudence and justice, and whether press freedom would be impaired, and democracy and civic liberty (including the right of staging street demonstrations) suppressed in favour of a Chinese-style "law and social order".

While such politically inspired fears have now largely subsided, as discussed in the various chapters of this study,[3] the attack from the outside by the Asian financial storm caught all Hong Kong people by surprise. Prior to the sovereignty transfer, even the pessimists had foreseen Hong Kong's future economic relations as a major bright spot that would be free of possible political interference from its new sovereign. Most people expected the economic prosperity to continue after the handover. The reasons for the optimism were manifold, some quite obvious, others not so, as I will lay them out below.

1. Being a regional business and financial centre, Hong Kong would remain as an indispensable "window" for China to access the global market of information, technology, and finance.
2. Hong Kong, as the region's headquarters for many major international banking corporations from advanced Western countries, would continue to be an important banking centre for making large syndicated loans to China.
3. The SAR would itself continue to be the single most important source of foreign direct investment (FDI) flows to China, with virtually all its manufacturing plants having relocated to the Chinese hinterland in the past two decades or so.
4. While the prospects of Taiwan's reunion with the mainland remained remote, Hong Kong would continue to serve as a natural bridge for Taiwanese compatriots investing in and trading with the mainland—a link so much treasured by Beijing.
5. By virtue of its geographic proximity and cultural affinity, Hong Kong, with a sizable population of 6.5 million with high income and consumption power, would remain an absolutely significant client for Chinese exports of

foodstuff, clothing, and similar daily necessities for local consumption—a market that has in the past several decades consistently earned China the bulk of its foreign exchange sufficient to pay for the huge Chinese trade deficits incurred from Japan and Western Europe combined. It is also a market that has, from 1979 through the mid-1990s, helped to generate a cumulative total trade surplus more than enough to pay for all the bills from the United States for imports of machine and equipment, aircraft, and grains, and for technology transfer as well, during the same period.[4]

6. Complete with state-of-the-art facilities in banking, finance, insurance, telecommunications, and shipping, as well as a well-established pool of international marketing and sourcing expertise, Hong Kong would remain for many years to come the single largest trading port for China, irreplaceable by Shanghai, Tianjin, or any other major Chinese coastal metropolis. This is noting that the SAR's total re-exports, combining both those of Chinese origin destined to the various overseas markets, (notably North America and Western Europe), and those from these advanced industrialized markets to the various mainland destinations, have increased spectacularly by 40-fold within the past two decades to surpass domestic exports as the absolutely overwhelming source (86% in 1998, as compared with 31% in 1980) of Hong Kong's overall exports.
7. The status of Hong Kong as a "non-sovereign" but independent actor in the global economic arena was already firmly sealed, prior to the 1997 handover, by way of international treaty arrangements. The arrangements guaranteed the SAR to retain its privileges as a separate customs entity within the World Trade Organization (and thus free of potential trade restrictions and discriminations), as well as its separate membership in the International Monetary Fund, the World Bank, Asian Development Bank, APEC, and the like (alongside China's own membership).
8. Pending a resolution of the Taiwan issue, the Chinese government would certainly be keen to promote HKSAR as a role model for Taiwan—noting that international economic linkages are crucial for both Hong Kong and Taiwan for sustaining long-term economic growth and well-being.
9. And, finally, the statutory guarantee as given in the "Basic Law", the SAR's mini-constitution, that Hong Kong would be allowed to retain its own currency under the "one country, two systems" model, is by any measure unparalleled in modern world history. The guarantee means that the Hong Kong dollar would continue to be the most fully convertible currency in the

world, as it has been, entirely free of any restrictions, with respect to both current account and capital account transactions.

Taken together, there is, therefore, no doubt that Hong Kong is more closely integrated with the global economy rather than with that of its motherland. And China itself treasures enormously these particular global economic linkages of the SAR. Yet, paradoxically, it is exactly on account of its total openness to the outside world that the SAR economy was almost brought to its knees in 1998, as a result of renewed speculative attacks by international hedge funds on the Hong Kong dollar since August 1997.

Now, the question is whether the British administration would have been better able to lead Hong Kong through the Asian financial typhoon. History of course cannot be replayed just to verify a hypothesis like this. However, two important points can be made, perhaps not as a rebuttal of the familiar "doomsday prophecies" widely circulating before the handover so much as prima facie evidence that the British would probably have had no other alternative but to respond similarly to the Asian crisis, as the new Hong Kong SAR government has done over the past year and a half.

First, the new SAR administration under Chief Executive C. H. Tung is actually inherited lock, stock, and barrel from the pre-handover British administration including, notably, the powerful chief secretary of administration, Mrs Anson Chan, the outspoken financial secretary, Mr Donald Tsang, and Mr Joseph Yam, the executive chief of the Hong Kong Monetary Authority (the quasi-central bank). Were they subject to intervention or influence by the Beijing authorities in handling the crisis? There is hardly any evidence of this. Martin Lee, chairman of the Democratic Party (the largest opposition party in Hong Kong) and the habitual critic, had openly suspected that the Chinese government must have had a hand in the heavy-handed purchases by the SAR government of all leading corporate shares in August 1998 to forestall a total collapse of the stock market. But, two days later, after a futile search for evidence, Lee was obliged to retract his allegation (*SCMP*, 14 September 1998).

Second, it was argued that under the new political context, the SAR government was deprived of the benefit of consulting the British government in London on how to combat the unfolding Asian crisis, while the new sovereign in Beijing was not at all experienced in dealing with matters concerning international currency attacks. However, as a prelude to his official visit to the SAR on 9 October 1998, the British Prime Minister Tony Blair wrote that he understood the decision of "the Hong Kong Administration [to stand] by its commitment to maintain the Hong Kong dollar peg, despite the buffeting in the markets over the past few months", adding: "They need to safeguard the long-term financial stability and economic success for Hong Kong" (*SCMP*, 9 October 1998). He also underscored "the important role [played by] their defence of the dollar peg in underpinning stability and confidence in Asia more widely" (*SCMP,* 9 October 1998), and said indeed that "by using the powers guaranteed in the Joint Declaration (for the defence), Hong Kong has proved to the world that its autonomy is a reality" (*SCMP*, 9 October 1998).

Sceptics may regard Prime Minister Blair's statements as mere diplomatic rhetoric. But, uncharacteristically, in a rare show of support for Beijing, former governor Chris Patten also "threw his weight behind Premier Zhu Rongji for his firm opposition to devaluing the yuan" (*SCMP*, 31 October 1998). Patten gave his positive comments after emerging from a discussion with Mr C. H. Tung, the HKSAR chief executive, during a private visit to the SAR shortly after Blair's, about the way the government responded to the backlash of the Asian financial crunch. There seems little doubt that Patten must know well that one of the main factors frequently cited for Premier Zhu's policy stance against a devaluation of the renminbi, the Chinese currency, was to support Hong Kong's defence of the US dollar peg.

As a matter of fact, Patten himself, in an interview on CNN in New York, on 8 September 1998, disclaimed that the British departure was a cause of Hong Kong's economic downturn and said he was "lucky" that his governorship coincided with the territory's "good economic times". He made the point again while in Hong Kong on 30 October 1998.

The economic logic underpinning the HKSAR's defence of the US dollar peg will become clear during the course of our discussion. But before we turn to the substantive issues, another important point should be made in this context. That is, the stakes for the Chinese government, watching Hong Kong's sustained economic prosperity degenerate into chaos on the heels of the handover, were formidable. That would be, to say the least, a harrying matter of "losing face" before the watchful eyes of the entire world.

Thus, when the first wave of speculative attacks was unleashed on the Hong Kong dollar, in late July 1997, the Chinese government stood up to the occasion, declaring in no equivocal terms that it would, with its massive foreign exchange reserves (at around US$120 billion, it had the world's second largest, next only to Japan's), stand by the Hong Kong Monetary Authority in its defence of the US dollar peg.[5] It is doubtful whether Dai Xianglong, the governor of the People's Bank of China, would have made the same pledge of support when Hong Kong remained under British colonial rule. Equally doubtful is whether the British government in London would have similarly stood up for Hong Kong, even assuming it had the financial resources to do so, if the British were still the rulers here.

Defending the US dollar peg: The Achilles' heel

The existing Hong Kong currency system of linking the Hong Kong dollar to the US dollar, at the fixed exchange rate of HK$7.8 per US dollar, was first established in October 1983. That was the time when, amidst the political crisis associated with the Sino-British negotiations over the future of Hong Kong, public confidence in Hong Kong was drastically deteriorating, sending the Hong Kong dollar tumbling from the previous market rate of around HK$5.6 to the record low of around HK$9.0 per US dollar. The new US dollar peg, specifically, commits the Hong Kong government to redeem, via the authorized note-issuing banks, any amount of Hong Kong currency with the foreign exchange reserves held by the Exchange Fund at the fixed rate specified. The other integral part of the system, dubbed the Currency Board, is that the note-issuing banks are entitled to issuing Hong Kong dollar notes only upon surrendering the proportionate amount of US dollars to the Exchange Fund in exchange for the necessary instrument called certificates of indebtedness. This ensures that all Hong Kong currency in circulation is fully backed by foreign exchange reserves, the amount of which is, of course, closely tied in with the performance of the highly export-oriented economy.[6]

There are two aspects to the US dollar peg mechanism that serve to ensure stability of the exchange rate and that should be briefly explained as a background for understanding the intricacies of the speculative attacks on the Hong Kong currency. The first is the process of notes arbitrage and, the second, of interest rate arbitrage. Notes arbitrage may set in when, for some reason, the value of the HK dollar drops to, say, 7.9 per US dollar. This will prompt the note-issuing banks to surrender their certificates of indebtedness to the Exchange Fund in exchange for US dollars at the official rate of HK$7.8, in order to cash in the premium of HK$0.1 per US dollar by reselling their US dollar holdings to the market. It is then hoped that increased US dollar supply may therefore help to revert the market rate back to the official par value.

The interest rate arbitrage should work similarly in that any substantial selling of the Hong Kong currency for US dollars would inevitably lead to a contraction in money supply in Hong Kong dollar terms and, hence, a rise in local interest rates. Higher interest rates may, in turn, induce capital inflow to offset the initial outflow, and consequently help to stabilize the foreign exchange market. However, both notes arbitrage and interest rate arbitrage proved to be powerless in the wake of the heavy speculative attacks on the Hong Kong dollar in 1997–98. For one thing, notes arbitrage has actually never proven to be effective for reasons of the potentially high transaction costs involved. Moreover, the Hong Kong Monetary Authority has made it a practice to consistently intervene at around HK$7.75, instead of HK$7.8, since the early 1990s, making it impossible for the notes arbitrage to take place, as is shown in Figure 6.1.[7]

More importantly, as interest rates were forced up to a record high as a result of heavy borrowing and dumping of the Hong Kong currency (short-selling) by international speculators to coerce a devaluation of the Hong Kong dollar, foreign capital continued, nonetheless, to shy away from the SAR, despite substantially increased interest rate differentials between Hong Kong and the United States. During the currency attacks in January and August 1998, for example, the three-month HIBOR (Hong Kong Interbank Offered Rate) rose to an average of 12.7% and 11.9% respectively, and was 7.7% and 7.0% higher

Figure 6.1 Monthly Fluctuations in Exchange Rate (HK$/US$) and Interest Rate Differential (HK$/US$) in Hong Kong, 1984–1998

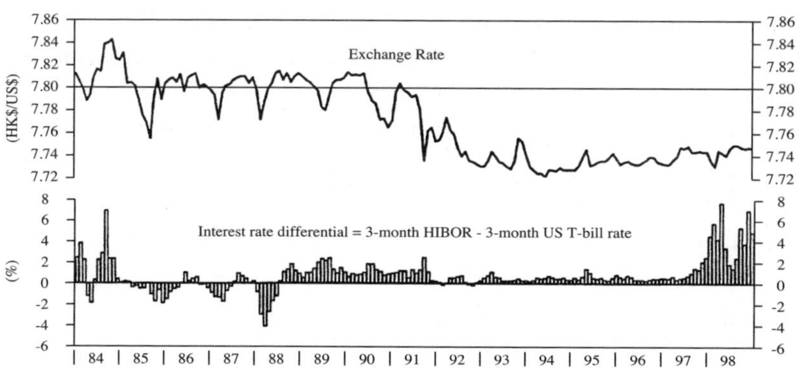

Sources: HKMA

than the respective three-month U.S. T-bills rates. These interest rate differentials between the HK and US dollars were unparalleled since mid-1984, and represented a sharp rise from the average interest premium of only 1.16% for the first nine months of 1997, as is also shown in Figure 6.1.

As public confidence in the US dollar peg was waning, US dollar deposits in Hong Kong jumped by 34% between September 1997 and August 1998, while HK dollar deposits rose by only 2.1% during the same period. The highly volatile and punitive interest rates not only caused the stock and futures markets to collapse, paving the way for speculators to reap huge profits from their short positions in the HK dollar forward market and Hang Seng Index futures, but also put enormous pressures on the local asset price bubble to burst. By late 1998, property prices in Hong Kong were generally reduced by 50–60% from the peak reached a year before. And the Hang Seng Index dropped from the record high of 16,673 achieved by the time of the sovereignty turnover to no more than around 6,500 in August 1998, when the SAR government's controversial rescue bid was introduced. The ensuing loss of investor and consumer confidence, coupled with a severe credit squeeze, penetrated deeply into the real sector, plunging the Hong Kong economy into its first recession in thirteen years.

The question now is why international currency speculators believed that they would win in betting against the US dollar peg in Hong Kong. This should, of course, be understood against the broader regional background of the currency crisis. With all the major Southeast Asian currencies and the South Korean won being greatly devalued against the US dollar under massive speculative attacks since July 1997, the Hong Kong dollar has indeed become excessively overvalued in relative terms, and hence vulnerable. This goes, of course, for the renminbi as well. Under such circumstances, it is only natural that pressures on both the SAR and Chinese currencies rapidly built up.

Two basic questions are involved here. The first is whether the attacks on the Hong Kong dollar were just a matter of "psychic mobility" in the market place; or, whether currency speculators were also seriously betting on a devaluation of both currencies on the grounds of real economic factors, say, the necessity for the HKSAR and Beijing governments to maintain their export competitive edge against their Asian neighbours. The second question is: why would a renminbi devaluation necessarily help to break the Hong Kong dollar peg to the US dollar, as widely assumed, which was the basis for the speculators' attacks on the Hong Kong currency?

The first question posed may, by itself, seem apparent as a matter of simple conventional wisdom, but in reality the answer is by no means a straightforward one. Before we take up the issue, however, a word or two should be said about the second question. Obviously the perception that the Hong Kong dollar is intricately linked to the renminbi has arisen from the fact that the SAR economy has one way or the other become inseparable from the Chinese hinterland, as a result of increased economic integration over the past two decades, in terms of capital and trade flows, quite apart from the political reunion of July 1997.

Nonetheless, it should be noted that the "one country, two systems" model also provides for two separate customs entities and, more importantly, two separate, independent currencies, viz., renminbi and Hong Kong dollar. Could it, therefore, not be the case that a devaluation of the renminbi would only benefit Hong Kong, in the same fashion as the United States has emerged as a major beneficiary from the Asian financial turmoil? Note also that while the Chinese government makes it explicitly clear that one of the reasons for not devaluing the renminbi is to help the HKSAR government to defend its US dollar peg system, the massive effort put up by the latter for the defence of the Hong Kong dollar is, however, entirely rooted, for better or worse, in considerations of its own merits in the minimization of domestic economic disturbance by forestalling massive and destabilizing capital flight from the SAR.

As a matter of fact, the HKSAR's own defence of the Hong Kong dollar against the backdrop of the Asian financial crisis has never been seen as a deliberate support of the prevailing value of the renminbi. This point should perhaps not be taken for granted, given that, dollar for dollar (i.e., without adjusting for the purchasing power parities between the HK dollar and the renminbi), Hong Kong's gross domestic product stood at around US$173.66 billion in 1997, which is, surprisingly, some 20 per cent of mainland China's GDP of US$901 billion, tiny as the former British enclave may be with a population of only 6.5 million, compared with 1.2 billion for the mainland. More remarkably, the Hong Kong government's budget expenditure alone, totalling US$22.4 billion in 1997, is equal to around 20% of China's national budget expenditure of US$111.39 billion. In addition, by the end of 1997, the SAR's foreign exchange reserves (at US$92.8 billion) were trailing quite closely behind mainland China's US$139.9 billion, which was next only to that of Japan (US$220.8 billion), the world's largest foreign reserves holder.

It seems necessary to look at the two questions raised at some length, with a view to disentangling the real dynamics underlying the speculative attacks on the Hong Kong currency in 1997–98. This will provide the necessary background for examining, in the subsequent section, the drastic steps taken by the Hong Kong SAR government to fend off the massive currency attacks in August 1998.

The Chinese connection: Asset or liability?

Since the fate of the Hong Kong dollar has been perceived as invariably bound up with the renminbi, it is necessary to examine, first of all, whether there really are tenable economic factors underlying the international speculations for a renminbi devaluation. What is at stake, in the first place, is clearly whether China, without a devaluation, would be able to maintain its competitive edge in major Western export markets (in particular, the United States and Western Europe) against the ASEAN countries and South Korea, which have all greatly depreciated their currencies within months of the onset of the Asian currency crisis in July 1997.

In his vigorous defence of the strong position of the renminbi, Dai Xianglong, the governor of the People's Bank of China, maintained in January 1998 that Chinese exports to the United States overlapped with those from Southeast Asia by not more than 15% of its total exports (*TKP*, 17 January 1998). A higher estimate, made by a senior economist at the Chinese Academy of Social Science in a CCTV (Beijing) interview in January 1999, put it between 20% and 30%. That is to say, the massive currency devaluations in Southeast Asia during 1997–98 may not have basically broken the established "flying geese pattern" of regional industrial specialization. Specifically, China could still take advantage of its relative abundance of labour supply and specialize in the conventional, more labour-intensive export processing trade, without competing head on against, say, Malaysia, which has increasingly upgraded its export structure by shifting to commodities with higher technology components, such as electronic products, including telephone sets and computers. Moreover, the bulk of Southeast Asian exports comprise essentially such primary commodities as rubber, timber, palm oil and the like, which are unavailable from China.

There is then also the question of whether a renminbi devaluation, if necessary, would really help to enhance China's export competitiveness, given that over half of the inputs required for export processing in China consist of materials supplied from overseas, and that a renminbi devaluation would also inevitably result in higher import costs to offset any potential monetary export gains that devaluation might bring. This point seems to have been borne out by the 1998 experience of some Southeast Asian countries, which have seen their export volume declining, despite massive currency devaluation.

On the part of the Chinese authority, there was obviously also concern that a renminbi devaluation may scare away foreign direct investments (FDI), since the end effect of any devaluations of the currency may, from the perspective of foreign investors, result in a curtailment of their earlier FDI value and their profit repatriation in foreign currency terms, from their existing investments in China. The economic logic for such considerations, of course, may not be entirely straightforward. For one thing, a renminbi devaluation may, nonetheless, help to reduce investment costs for foreign investors first and foremost.[8] And, for entirely export-oriented FDIs engaged in export processing (as is overwhelmingly the case with investors from Hong Kong and Taiwan), it does not really matter much whether the renminbi is devalued or not, so long as the overseas export market potentials are not impaired. The reason for this is simple, though not necessarily self-apparent for people not familiar with the Greater China context of economic cooperation, as I shall explain.

"Greater China context" refers to investments that involve complementary operations in two or all three places in the mainland-Hong Kong-Taiwan network. Specifically for this kind of investors from outside, export orders or letters of credit from overseas buyers are normally received in Hong Kong and Taiwan, instead of being channelled through the mainland Chinese banking system. Similarly, foreign exchange expenditure on imported materials and on the necessary processing machines and equipment are also normally incurred outside of China. In other words, both foreign currency receipts and expenditure on the part of Hong Kong and Taiwan investors in China are basically shielded off from the volatility of the renminbi.

Taken together, there seem, therefore, to be no compelling economic reasons why the Chinese currency would likewise be forced to devalue amidst the Asian currency crisis. That is, of course, not to say that China is entirely spared from the adverse impact of the regional crisis, in terms of capital inflows and trade flows. FDI inflows from Hong Kong did indeed slow down in 1998. But this seemed nonetheless more a result of the severe credit squeeze in Hong Kong associated with its massive efforts at defending the US dollar peg system (which has strongly boosted local interest rates), as well as the withdrawal of Japanese funds—upon which Hong Kong's FDI in the Chinese mainland substantially hinges—to meet domestic difficulties. Hence, it was not really a result of the concerns about the prospects of the value of the renminbi. As a matter of fact, FDI flows from elsewhere—the United States and Europe in particular—remained quite robust throughout 1998, to compensate for the relative decline in FDI inflows from Hong Kong and other Asian economies affected by the regional financial turmoil.[9]

Chinese exports in 1998 were clearly affected by the Asian crisis as well. Enhanced price competition from Southeast Asian countries for the "overlapping" export commodities to Western markets may partially account for this. But a more important source of export decline seems rather to be found in the impaired import capabilities of Southeast and East Asian countries, including Japan, which were all helplessly drawn, directly or indirectly, into the Asian financial whirlpool. Under such circumstances, a renminbi devaluation might not really help much in promoting Chinese exports to these countries. Besides, there seems to be considerable elbow room for the Chinese government to manoeuvre in (as indeed it did throughout most of 1998), such as resorting to policy alternatives like export value-added tax rebates, easy export credits and the like, capable of arresting the potential adverse trends in Chinese exports.

On balance, China's exports for the whole of 1998 still recorded a slight increase, from US$182.7 billion (1997) to US$183.76 billion (1998). Its total imports, on the other hand, declined slightly from US$142.36 billion (1997) to US$140.17 billion (1998), in part as a result of reduced imports for export processing by Hong Kong and Taiwan investors. Hence, the country could still score an impressive trade balance of US$43.6 billion for 1998. As a result, China's total foreign exchange reserves stood at US$144.9 billion by 31 December 1998, compared with US$139.9 billion a year earlier, not counting gold reserves and foreign earnings held by enterprises and other non-treasury entities.[10] This balance sheet clearly provides a strong backing for continuing confidence in the renminbi and, with it, in the Hong Kong dollar as well.

There are no clues for a possible deterioration in the internal financial balance in China that might eventually trigger a renminbi devaluation. Rather, with the inflation rate having been kept in the negative for more than 1.5 years (through early 1999), the Chinese government was able in 1998 to resort, time and again, to bond issuing to finance infrastructure investments, and to other fiscal and monetary reflationary policy measures for boosting domestic demand, as a means to achieving the much flouted GDP growth target of 8% for 1998.[11] And the public spending spree is clearly to continue well into 1999.

As a matter of fact, Zhu Rongji, the Chinese Premier, who frequently reiterated in 1997–98 that the renminbi would not be devalued for the sake of maintaining regional economic stability and, in particular, upholding Hong Kong's US dollar peg system, made it clear for the first time—at a meeting with the visiting Laotian premier in Beijing in late January 1999—that the Chinese government would only reconsider its position on the external value of the renminbi when the Chinese trade balance turns sour (*SCMP*, 26 January 1999). With this statement, we seem to see evidence of economic considerations in Chinese policy making. It should nonetheless be noted that in the established Chinese practice of maintaining external trade balance, imports seem to have always been used as an instrumental variable (rather than a target variable) for readjusting any imbalance. Whether this is a matter of financial prudence or political gimmick is, of course, subject to interpretation. And whether Zhu's reassurances about the robustness of the renminbi would effectively help to dispel any further doubts remains to be seen.

At any rate, with most of the Southeast Asian currencies having more or less regained their lost ground in the past several months, the pressures on the renminbi are bound to be easing gradually. Hopefully, in a year or two, the dust of the financial sandstorm will be settled, and the pre-crisis currency parity among the various currencies in Southeast and East Asian countries will be basically restored.

Let us now turn to the second set of questions, if only for theoretical interest, to see whether it makes sense, in economic terms, that in the unlikely event of a renminbi devaluation, the Hong Kong dollar should also fall simultaneously. Several points may be made briefly.

First, a renminbi devaluation may actually only help to lower Hong Kong investors' overheads and expenditure on the mainland, especially with regard to the costs of plant construction materials supplied from within China. Managerial and wage costs may or may not be affected, depending on whether these are denominated in renminbi yuan, Hong Kong dollar, or US dollar. Outlay on current input materials brought in from abroad for export processing in China, as well as foreign exchange earnings from export sales, would clearly remain unchanged, by virtue of the particular mode of operation adopted by Hong Kong investors engaged in export processing in China, as alluded to earlier.

Second, the bulk of import supplies from China to Hong Kong of wage foods, clothing, and other light industrial goods retained for local consumption should, theoretically speaking, become even cheaper in the absence of a concomitant Hong Kong dollar devaluation; although, in reality, this may not necessarily be the case. It depends really on whether Chinese suppliers are willing to pass on the price benefits to Hong Kong consumers by quoting their exports to Hong Kong in renminbi rather than Hong Kong dollar. The well-established convention over the past several decades has been for the supplies to be quoted in Hong Kong dollars.[12] Under such circumstances, it does not really matter whether the Hong Kong dollar would stay put in case of a renminbi devaluation. Rather, if the Hong Kong dollar were to follow the renminbi or to depreciate to an even greater extent, it would be entirely possible that Chinese suppliers would be prompted to quote higher export prices in Hong Kong dollars, in order to reach their expected level of renminbi receipts.

Third, even if a renminbi devaluation would help stimulate China mainland's exports to the West, the Hong Kong SAR—with or without a concomitant Hong Kong dollar devaluation—would clearly stand to gain handsomely. The obvious reason is that a very substantial amount of Chinese exports are channelled through Hong Kong, taking advantage of all the necessary facilities it offers, including international marketing skills, banking, finance, insurance, and shipping.[13] Of course, any gains to be made in this respect would have to be weighed against the potential revenue losses for Hong Kong, which may result as well from reduced Chinese imports after renminbi devaluation. Around 50% of the SAR's exports to China comprise goods (mostly of third-country origin) for final consumption on the mainland, rather than for export processing. However, it should also be noted that, irrespective of what the net balance may be, a concomitant devaluation of the Hong Kong dollar would only make things worse, as it would curtail the import capability of the SAR for re-exports to the Chinese hinterland.

The fourth point concerns the potential effect on capital flow from China to Hong Kong, which has over the past fifteen years or so played an increasingly important role in enhancing confidence in the territory and its economy. Would Chinese capital flow into Hong Kong be retarded if the Hong Kong dollar does not depreciate in tandem with a renminbi devaluation? This may not necessarily occur in the present context. So far as capital inflow of true mainland origin is concerned, few cases seem to have taken the form of hard currency repatriations obtained through conversion of renminbi sources. Apart from possible direct allocation of foreign exchange from the treasury, most "expatriations" probably represent funds raised by state or quasi-state agents (e.g., the itics)[14] from outside of the country or through direct "interception" of foreign exchange earnings in Hong Kong, by the familiar practice of "under-invoicing" exports to the SAR for re-exports to third countries at much higher prices.

Finally, the only venue that may unequivocally require a Hong Kong dollar devaluation to help mitigate curtailment in earnings following a renminbi devaluation would be the SAR's domestic exports to the Chinese mainland. But note that such exports of Hong Kong origin make up not much more than 10% of Hong Kong's total exports to the mainland (1997 figure), and the major proportion (around 75%) is indeed destined for further export processing, rather than for end-users in China. More seriously, perhaps, if the Hong Kong dollar were to devalue to a greater extent than the Chinese renminbi, then it would probably only help to thwart the emerging access to the domestic mainland market, something long sought after by investors from Hong Kong (and Taiwan as well). The devaluation of the NT dollar in Taiwan in late 1997 is a good case in point. In that particular case, as a result, many consumer goods industries of Taiwan origin operating on the mainland—food processing in particular, which relies extensively on Japan and Taiwan for imports of spices and packaging materials—simply had to suspend their production for not being able to withstand price competition from domestic producers.[15]

Taken together, therefore, it seems quite clear that there are no hard economic reasons why a renminbi devaluation will inevitably trigger the Hong Kong dollar to follow suit immediately. This leaves us with the conclusion that the renewed speculative attacks on the Hong Kong currency have been no more than a matter of international hedge funds managers attempting to capitalize on the "herd psychology" of small investors who are fearful of their savings capital being wiped out overnight by a totally unanticipated depreciation of the Hong Kong dollar. These hedge fund managers have sought to do so by speculating for the devaluation of the renminbi as an inevitable domino of the Southeast Asian currency crisis.

Viewed this way, the resolve of the Chinese government against devaluing the renminbi and the unparalleled strength of the Chinese economy (e.g., a most impressive GDP growth, negative inflation rate, negligible fiscal deficits at least for 1998, remarkable trade surplus, and huge foreign exchange reserves) have certainly helped to greatly boost the confidence in the HKSAR government's defence of its own currency.

Paradoxically, however, the solid Chinese hinterland backbone has, in a way, proved to be a liability to the tiny SAR: while mainland China's capital account is strictly closed to any outside manipulations, the fully convertible Hong Kong currency unfortunately became a target of international speculations, as when the Southeast Asian financial turbulence swept through the whole of East Asia in 1998.

Revamping the Currency Board: Has it really helped?

This is not the place for a detailed discussion of how the speculative attacks on the Hong Kong dollar evolved in 1997–98.[16] But, briefly, by mid-August 1998, it had become evident that a massive showdown was imminent. As Financial Secretary Donald Tsang put it, the evidence was a two-pronged attack on both the Hang Seng Index futures of the local stock market and the foreign exchange market. Specifically, international hedge funds were not only targeting the foreign exchange market by short-selling the Hong Kong dollar; but, more critically, by thus pushing up the local interest rates, they were also aiming at the much more lucrative Index futures market on which they had earlier accumulated huge short positions.

The decisive showdown came on 14 August 1998, when the HKSAR government acted decisively to rescue the local stock market. Funds from the Exchange Fund were used to buy 33 leading stocks. The Hang Seng Index was, as a result, massively pushed up by 564 points to 7,224.7, a rise of 8.5%. It seemed that Hong Kong had for the first time exerted, with such a dramatic turnaround in the Hang Seng Index, an impact on the global stock market. In London, the FTSE 100 Index closed 55.5 points higher at 5,455.0. And the Dow Jones Industrial Average was also raised by 18.03 points to 8,477.53 after mid-day in New York (*SCMP*, 15 August 1998).

It is clear that by intervening in the stock and futures markets, the SAR government opened another front in its defence of the US dollar peg system. It no longer just relies on raising the interest rates to fend off speculative attacks on the Hong Kong currency. As Secretary Tsang saw it, the simultaneous speculative activity in the futures and currency markets was "a double play" by people who were trying to "play around" in an attempt to "wreak havoc" on the linked exchange rate system. "We will", he added, "continue this action as long as it is necessary." The linked exchange rate is "paramount" and here to stay (*SCMP*, 15 August 1998).

The stock market intervention of 14 August 1998 was, of course, not entirely free of controversy, although the financial secretary strongly rejected suggestions that his action contravened Hong Kong's commitment to non-intervention. He explained the day after the event,

> I must emphasize that our long-standing policy of non-intervention in the stock and futures markets remains unchanged. No intervention may take place unless a sufficiently clear linkage exists between the currency play and the stock and futures markets play. I must make it clear that we are not against the shorting (short-selling) of Hang Seng Index futures by hedge funds. But we do not tolerate attempts by speculators to manipulate our interest rates so that they can benefit from the short positions they have built up in Hang Seng Index futures (*SCMP*, 15 August 1998).

In the subsequent months, Tsang had to make it part of his agenda for his overseas trips to explain to and convince his major foreign counterparts, including AIan Greenspan, chairman of the Federal Reserve Bank in the United States, about the rationale and necessity of the unprecedented interventionist move. Nonetheless, the conservative US-based Heritage Foundation announced in December 1998 that it would likely downgrade for 1999 the status of Hong Kong as the most free economy in the world, because of the government's unprecedented stock market intervention.

More seriously perhaps, voices were raised by local political parties and academics as well, on the question of whether the SAR government's uncompromising move, wrestling with giant international hedge funds, would not put the entire Exchange Fund at risk. As a matter of fact, the stake that the government invested in the 33 leading stocks was later officially confirmed to be a massive US$15.2 billion, against the initial speculative estimate of US$0.39 billion. In other words, about 16% of the Exchange Fund's reserves were literally put at risk in one stroke. A few more rounds of similar wrestling might eventually see the entire Exchange Fund rapidly depleted, should the government lose the battle against the speculators.

It is probably against this background that the Hong Kong Monetary Authority was obliged to embark, three weeks later (on 7 September 1998), on a major initiative of significantly revamping the existing Currency Board system as a new defence mechanism against international currency assault. The initiative comprises a seven-point package, but essentially they all converge on two major policy measures.

The first relates to the government's so-called "convertibility undertaking" (to convert the Hong Kong dollars into the US dollars). Originally, the conversion was limited to the "legal tender in circulation" at the rate of HK$7.80; but it is now extended to all Hong Kong dollars held by all licenced banks in their clearing accounts with the Exchange Fund at the more favourable fixed rate of HK$7.50. The second is to replace the restrictive "liquidity adjustment facility" with a "discount window". This allows the banks to repeatedly borrow from the Hong Kong Monetary Authority with their holdings of Exchange Fund bills and notes as collateral. In other words, it helps to greatly raise the liquidity of the entire banking system.[17]

Obviously, the new measures were adopted against the backdrop of a sizable foreign exchange reserve held by the Hong Kong government. As a matter of fact, despite the massive stock market buy-up by the government in August 1998, the reserve was still 3.5 times larger than the SAR's entire monetary base of US$23 billion. But has the new Currency Board really helped? The answer is a mixed one.

For one thing, the prime lending rate of the Hong Kong Association of Banks did indeed decline successively from the high of 10% to 9.25% within less than two months from October 1998. The gap with the comparable US interest rate also narrowed from 3% to 2.5%, although this still could not entirely prevent the interest rate arbitrage under the US dollar peg from taking place. Nevertheless, the reductions in Hong Kong's interest rate also seem to be a matter of a similar move by the US Federal Reserve Bank, as well as the withdrawal of the international hedge funds following their collapse in Russia, Brazil, and elsewhere. There also seems to be little doubt that the augmented financial manoeuverability arising from the bold Currency Board reform measures of early September 1998 had prompted both the stock market and the property market in Hong Kong to rebound quite remarkably, although similar recovery also took place in other Southeast Asian countries, which have likewise seen their currencies recover substantial ground against the US dollar, as international speculative currency attacks subsided.

As a matter of fact, the chief executive of the Hong Kong Monetary Authority, Joseph Yam, himself admitted that to effectively counter the international hedge funds, a new global financial system should eventually be put in place. He said: "We face a world crisis. If Hong Kong, with its sound fundamentals and prudent financial management, can be brought to the brink of a systemic breakdown by aggressive cross-border speculation, then something must be wrong with the world financial order" (*SCMP*, 6 January 1999). Specifically, Yam called for the regulation of international capital flows and the eventual creation of an Asian currency to prevent a repeat of the regional economic crisis (*SCMP*, 6 January 1999). This also seems to be the general consensus arising from the annual joint meeting of the World Bank and IMF held in Washington DC in October 1998.

Impact on external trade

This chapter is not the place for rehearsing how the real economic sphere in Hong Kong has been affected by the financial crisis. But, briefly, by early 1999 it was confirmed that the SAR's GDP was curtailed by a hefty 5.1% in 1998 from 1997. And earlier, by February 1999, the unemployment rate had reached a twenty-five-year high of 6%. Interestingly, however, the Hang Seng Index—the barometer of the local stock market—has been hovering in the region between 10,000 and 11,000 points since early 1999. This represents roughly a 60% gain from the trough of October 1997, and is only about 35% short of a full recovery to the all-time high of 16,670 points achieved in August 1997. Obviously, in relation to the remarkable magnitude of GDP decline in 1998, and the projected modest GDP growth of only 0.5% for 1999, Hong Kong stocks seem to be excessively overvalued once again. There is no doubt that the renewed "overheating" has been fuelled by the return of major international investors and stockbrokers.

Are the Hong Kong stock exchange and currency markets heading for another showdown? We really do not know for sure at this moment. But Joseph Yam warned explicitly that hedge funds might regroup in 1999 and renew attacks on the Hong Kong dollar's fifteen-year-old peg to the US dollar (*SCMP*, 6 January 1999). What seemed certain, nevertheless, was that amidst the renewed financial euphoria, there were, by the first quarter of 1999, still no signs of an early recovery in the real domestic sector. And this was in spite of the respectable efforts made by the SAR government, following tenets of Keynesian economics for the first time ever in Hong Kong, to revive the economy through large-scale public spending on large infrastructure projects.

In this context, the only spot that tends to offer a ray of hope and comfort seems to be external trade, which has always been the lifeline of the Hong Kong economy. For the whole of 1998, the territory's total exports declined by a relatively modest amount of 7.4%, as compared with 1997.

And, more importantly, as Figure 6.2 reveals, the major sources of export decline are the weakened position of the Southeast and East Asian trading partners that were hardest hit by the Asian financial crisis. Because of massive currency devaluations, all their import capabilities were seriously impaired. By contrast, Hong Kong's most significant export markets, the United States and Western Europe, have basically remained intact. The same goes for exports to the rest of world as a whole. Total exports to the Chinese mainland also declined by 8.7% from 1997 to 1998; but the reductions comprised essentially re-exports of third-country origin destined for end-users in China (rather than for export processing). Obviously, the decline was a result of a measured and deliberate Chinese curtailment of imports, instituted in order to maintain a favourable trade balance to hedge against the increased pressures for a renminbi devaluation.

Figure 6.2 Value of Hong Kong's Exports and Year-On-Year Changes by Major Regions and Trading Partners, 1997 and January to December 1998 (HK$ million and %)

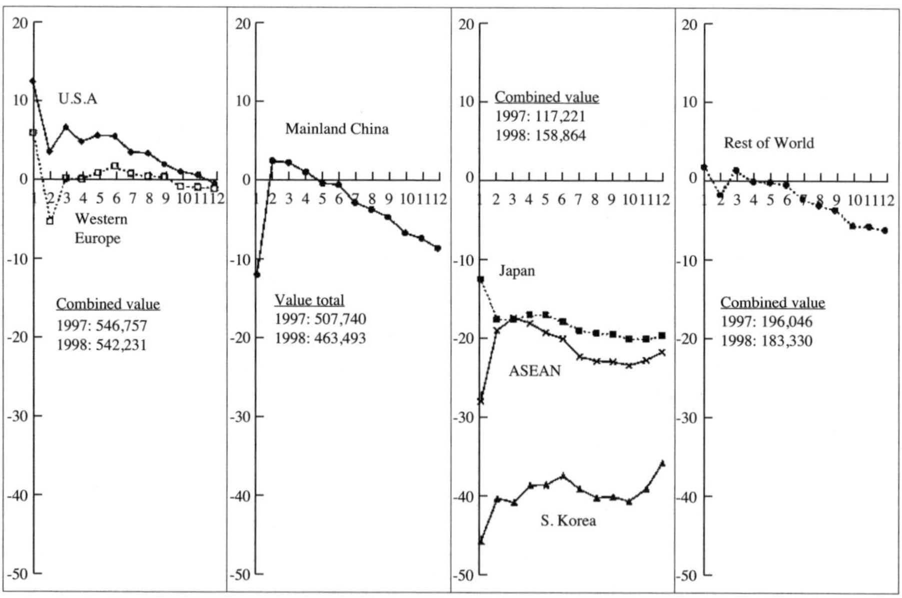

Sources: HKGCSD—*HKADS* and *HKMDS*, various issues.

The more important point that should be made in this context is that virtually all the SAR's exports to the United States and Western Europe represent re-exports from China on behalf of Hong Kong manufacturers based in the mainland and engaged in export processing. That is to say, as long as these major overseas markets can sustain their import demand, (as basically has been the case amidst the Asian financial crisis), Hong Kong will continue to enjoy the privileges of making use of the Chinese hinterland as its export processing base for enhancing its exports and GDP growth.

A word or two should be said about the invisible trade. Hong Kong does not really have any natural resources of any scale to build its economy on, apart from the beautiful landscape and perhaps some cultural relics. Traditionally, the SAR has had to rely on imports, not only for export processing, but also for maintaining the livelihood of its population. Visible trade has therefore been, as a rule, in the red, and it has had consistently to rely on tourism earnings to balance the trade deficits throughout the past several decades.

Unfortunately, however, the number of tourist arrivals dropped quite remarkably after the political handover to China on 1 July 1997—perhaps due to some global misperception about the nature of the historical event. Worse still, the difficulty has been greatly compounded by the Asian financial crisis, in that the massive devaluation of Southeast Asian currencies and the persistent recession in Japan have indeed made the SAR relatively too expensive a destination for tourists from these conventional Asian sources. As a result, rigorous efforts have been made by the tourist industry to court even such unlikely tourist sources as mainland China, to compensate for the losses from elsewhere. Nonetheless, total tourism receipts for 1998 still recorded a 14% decline in real terms.[18] Moreover, Hong Kong's exports of financial and other business services also fell by 6.6%, again in real terms, for 1998, because of a setback in regional demand.

Fortunately, under the full impact of the Asian crisis, Hong Kong's import demand also weakened substantially, resulting in a large reduction in the visible trade deficit. Coupled with a still sizable invisible trade surplus, the overall trade balance could still improve to a small surplus in 1998, from the deficits recorded for 1995–97. However, it is clear that for the Hong Kong government to bring the SAR economic growth back to the pre-crisis track, some extra efforts need be made, in addition to promoting conventional exports. It is against this background that an enormous initiative was made to attract the Disney Company to Hong Kong to set up its second theme park in Asia, next to Tokyo. Similar initiatives include the idea for the construction of a fisherman's wharf in Aberdeen (a familiar tourist attraction on Hong Kong Island) and, more importantly, the development of a "cyber-port" worth HK$13 billion to provide high-tech information services to businesses and the financial sector in Hong Kong and the region.

Concluding remarks

The major points made in this chapter are as follows:

First, there are no fundamental economic reasons to suggest that the Chinese currency, the renminbi, would have to be devalued under the impact of the Asian financial crisis. Nor are there any strong economic factors at work that would suggest that the value of the Hong Kong dollar would fall as well against the US dollar, should a renminbi devaluation take place as is widely speculated.

Second, the speculative attacks on the Hong Kong currency in 1997–98 seem, therefore, essentially a matter of premeditated attempts made by international hedge funds to coerce Hong Kong to be the next Asian financial domino, by exploiting the volatile market sentiments following the Southeast and East Asian crisis.

Third, an important reason why the fully convertible Hong Kong dollar has become the sole focus of international currency assault within Greater China is that the capital account of the Chinese mainland is strictly closed to outside manipulations. Nonetheless, the remarkable strength of the mainland economy (in terms of both internal and external balances) in 1997–98 has also greatly helped to boost confidence in the Hong Kong SAR's rigorous defence of its US dollar peg system.

Fourth, the unprecedented, massive government buy-up of leading stock shares in August and the significant Currency Board reform in September 1998 have proved to be effective in stabilizing both the stock and currency markets in Hong Kong. But the success was not without its external effects: it entailed the timely lowering by the US Federal Reserve Bank of interest rates, not to mention the withdrawal of the international hedge funds following their defeat in Russia, Brazil, and elsewhere.

Fifth, pending a long-term solution to the global financial system, Hong Kong will likely remain vulnerable to international speculators' attack on its currency, despite its well-organized and efficient banking and financial systems, as well as prudent fiscal and monetary policies.

Sixth, while, as a result of the collapse of investors' and consumers' confidence (coupled with high interest rate pressures and severe credit squeeze), the Hong Kong economy was nearly brought to the brink of collapse, it has been fortunate in being able to fall back on the Chinese hinterland as a base for generating exports to the resilient, most important export markets of the United States and Western Europe.

Is a full economic recovery in Hong Kong from the Asian financial meltdown around the corner? Donald Tsang, the financial secretary, in his 1999–2000 budget speech delivered on 3 March 1999, envisaged a modest GDP growth of 0.5% in 1999, to be followed by a marked acceleration of around 3.5–4% in 2000, and to appreciably above that in 2001 and 2002. That is to say, it will take four to five years for the SAR economy to restore its pre-crisis pattern of GDP growth. As Tsang aptly put it, "This in turn will depend on the external economic and financial situation turning progressively more favourable".

Assuming that the major United States and West European markets will be able to sustain their demand for imports from China and the SAR, the situation in ASEAN countries, and in South Korea and Japan as well, obviously holds the key to an early recovery in Hong Kong. Nonetheless, despite encouraging signs of a rapid recovery in some of these countries, both the renminbi and the Hong Kong dollar still remain "overvalued" to Southeast Asian currencies and the Korean won, in relation to the pre-crisis benchmarks. This undoubtedly will continue to be a source of uncertainty for the mainland and the HKSAR.

Appendix

Chronology of the Asian financial crisis in the HKSAR, July 1997 to January 1999

1997

July

2 Under heavy pressure from massive selling by foreigners, the Bank of Thailand floats the baht and raises the discount rate by 2 percentage points, to 12.5%. By the end of the day, the currency devalues 18% from the rate of 25 baht per US dollar.

27 First wave of speculative attacks on the Hong Kong currency takes place. Overnight HIBOR (Hong Kong Interbank Offered Rate) raised from 5.13% to 6.38% per annum, and the three-month HIBOR from 6.19% to 6.75%. It was confirmed later that the Hong Kong Monetary Authority (HKMA) spent around US$1 billion of its reserves (of US$81 billion) to defend the HK dollar.

21–27 The Indonesian rupiah, Thai baht, Malaysian ringgit, and Philippine peso all slump as confidence in the region rapidly deteriorates.

28 US Secretary of State, Madeleine Albright, criticizes Mohamad Mahathir, the Prime Minister of Malaysia, for blaming the West for a decline of Southeast Asian currencies.

August

19 The second wave of international speculative attack against the Hong Kong dollar takes place, sending overnight HIBOR up to 10% from the previous close of 6.81%, and the three-month HIBOR to 9% from 8.25%.

September

4 The baht falls to an all-time low of 38.4 to the US dollar.

8 On the eve of his trip to the United States, the chief executive of the Hong Kong Special Administrative Region (HKSAR), Mr C. H. Tung, reiterates that the HK dollar will remain pegged to the US dollar.

22 At the joint annual meeting of the World Bank and the International Monetary Fund (IMF), Mahathir lashes out against US financier George Soros and blames him for Malaysia's currency crisis.

October

18 The Central Bank of China in Taipei allows the New Taiwan Dollar (NTD) to fall, giving up defending the currency at NT$28.6 per US dollar.

23 The third wave of international speculative assault on the Hong Kong dollar forces the HKMA to push HIBOR overnight up to 100% (closing high) after reaching, at one point of the day, 280%, from the previous low of 6.25%. The three-month HIBOR also surges to 25% from 9.25%.

The Hang Seng Index drops to 10,426.30—a 10.4% decline from the previous close of 11,637.77, and a total reduction of 23% from previous Friday's close of 13,601.01.

Both China and the HKSAR governments subsequently promised to protect the HK dollar peg to the US dollar with their massive foreign reserves (US$88 billion in HK and US$120 billion in China).

November

19 The Central Bank of China in Taipei indicates that it will allow the market to determine the value of the NTD in the wake of sharp depreciation of the Korean won.

December

16 President Jiang Zemin announces, in his meeting with heads of ASEAN countries, that the renminbi will not be devalued.

1998

January

1 The fourth wave of speculative currency assault on the Hong Kong dollar forces HIBOR to climb to 12% from the previous close of 5.5%, and the three-month HIBOR to 13.5% from 12.5%.

16 People's Bank of China Governor, Dai Xianglong, reiterates that the renminbi will remain stable in light of China's favourable balance of payments.

23 The Indonesian rupiah falls to a low of 15,000 against the US dollar, leaving its banking sector on the verge of collapse.

February

2 Hong Kong stocks jump 14.33%, the second largest one-day points gain. Regional markets also advance.

10 The rupiah rebounds more than 30% at one stage, amid rumours that Indonesia is to adopt capital controls and a Hong Kong-style currency board exchange rate system.

15 IMF Managing Director Michel Camdessus threatens to cut off Indonesia's IMF-led US$43 billion bailout if the country pushes ahead with plans to peg the rupiah to the US dollar. Regional stocks and currencies fall sharply on the news the following day.

18 Financial Secretary Donald Tsang announces, in his first budget for the Hong Kong SAR, a HK$13.6 billion tax cut package to boost the sagging economy and comfort jittery financial markets. The unexpected tax cuts send the Hang Seng Index 4.29% higher.

20 The US credit rating agency, Moody's Investors Service, downgrades Hong Kong's short-term sovereign rating, the first since the agency assigned the same rating fourteen years ago.

March

7 Dai Xianglong reaffirms that China's increased foreign reserves will help to strengthen the renminbi.

19 The Chinese Premier, Zhu Rongji, guarantees that the renminbi will not be devalued.

April

2 During his visit to the United Kingdom, Chinese Premier Zhu Rongji emphasizes that there are only pressures for the renminbi to appreciate, rather than depreciate.

3 The yen plummets to a six-and-a-half-year low as Moody's downgrades Japan's outlook for country ceilings and domestic currency ratings from stable to negative.

18 The Chinese Finance Minister, Xian Huaicheng, reconfirms that the value of the renminbi will be maintained.

May

7 Chinese President Jiang Zemin tells Reuter's chief executive that he has full confidence in keeping the renminbi stable without following the devaluation of neighbouring countries.

13 Regional stock markets and currencies slide in the wake of days of intense anti-government protests and riots in various Indonesian cities. Indonesian stocks dive almost 7% as the rupiah crashes.

27 Government economists confirm that Hong Kong's economy shrank for the first time in thirteen years during the first quarter. Investor fears of a recession send the Hang Seng Index down 5.55% the following day.

29 HKSAR government announces a seven-point emergency economic rescue package as the economy is confirmed to have shrunk 2% in real terms during the first quarter of the year. The measures aim to stimulate the property, banking and tourism sectors and enhance the financial system's liquidity.

June

3 Jiang Zemin tells US President Clinton that the decision not to devalue the renminbi not only helps to maintain economic stability in China, but also supports economic stability in Asia and the world at large.

9 People's Bank of China Governor, Dai Xianglong, warns the falling yen is having a "very negative" impact on the mainland's foreign trade, capital inflows, and economic restructuring.

10 Hong Kong shares tumble 4.91% to their lowest level in more than three years, as the yen's fall triggers fears about a devaluation of the yuan.

11 HKMA decides to issue statements twice a day detailing aggregate balances in accounts it holds on behalf of banks for foreign exchange dealings for the next two days. By increasing transparency, the authority hopes to smooth out volatility in interbank rates, in a bid to stave off attacks on the currency peg.

12 Japan enters into the worst recession since World War II, as it is revealed that its economy shrank at an annualized rate of 5.3% in the first quarter, bringing real GDP down 0.7% in fiscal 1997.

15 Another round of assault by international hedge funds on the Hong Kong dollar pushes overnight HIBOR up to 12.5% from 8.25%, and the three-month HIBOR from 12% to 14%, with the Hang Seng Index tumbling by nearly 6% from 7,915.44 to 7,462.50.

17 Heavy intervention by the US and Japan in the foreign exchange market sends the yen rising more than 4% to 137.25 against the US dollar. This follows heavy selling from hedge funds on the previous day, which put an end to the yen's dramatic slide. The yen's rise triggers a 6.35% rebound by the Hang Seng Index to just over 8,000 points.

18 The rupiah plunges to near its January record low of 17,000, raising prospects of a possible collapse of Indonesia's banking system.

22 China's Minister of Foreign Trade and Economic Cooperation, Shi Guangsheng, announces once again on behalf of the Chinese government that the renminbi will not be devalued.

HKSAR Chief Executive, Mr C. H. Tung, announces a HK$44 billion rescue package for the economy, which includes a surprise plan to freeze land sales until March 31, a pay freeze for top civil servants, and a tax exemption for companies on interest earned on locally held deposits.

July

8 HKMA announces that it plans to repatriate "billions of dollars" in overseas deposits to the local banking system as part of its effort to ease the SAR's liquidity crisis.

17 China reports an economic growth of 7% in the first six months of the year, the slowest growth rate in seven years, underlining the difficulty Beijing would have in achieving its target of 8% for the year.

August

7 Dai Xianglong reiterates there will be no devaluation of the renminbi.

HKMA Chairman, Joseph Yam, calls speculation on the Hong Kong dollar peg a conspiracy. Chief Executive C. H. Tung reiterates the SAR government's willingness to defend the HK dollar. Hong Kong shares plunge to their lowest in more than three years amid renewed fears of a yuan devaluation. The Hang Seng Index teeters near 7,000 points, ending the week down 10.9%.

11 The yen tumbles to an eight-year low of 147.63 against the US dollar. The Economic Planning Agency says Japan is in a prolonged slump.

14 The SAR government launches a heavy, unprecedented market intervention in stock and derivative markets, which sends the Hang Seng Index soaring 8.47% to 7,224.69 points.

27 Sources close to the Quantum Fund, run by George Soros, confirm it has made sizeable bets against the Hong Kong dollar. Stanley Druckenmiller, the manager of the fund, says the Hong Kong government will lose its bet on the local currency.

28 In a further massive defence of Hong Kong's currency peg, the HKMA throws HK$70 billion at the markets, bringing the amount spent in the campaign to about 15% of the SAR's reserves.

The government confirms the SAR has fallen into recession, announcing a 5% second-quarter GDP contraction.

30 Taiwan authorities order a crackdown on what they say is illegal trading in the funds of George Soros.

Hong Kong shares slump 7.09% as the government halts its intervention.

September

2 Malaysia's central bank pegs the local currency at 3.80 ringgits against the US dollar. The rate peg sees Malaysian share prices soar 12%.

5 HKMA announces a seven-point package to strengthen the currency board and deter manipulation of local interest rates by speculators.

7 The Hong Kong stock market surges 7.85%, surpassing the 8,000 point level, on massive short covering by funds squeezed by a resurgent Japanese yen and falling interest rates.

Malaysian shares soar 22.45%, recording the country's largest one-day rise. Investors chase after stocks related to associates of Prime Minister Mohamad Mahathir, who appoints himself first finance minister.

10 Jiang Zemin says stability of the renminbi has greatly helped to stabilize Asian economies.

14 State Council spokesman, Bai Hejin, stresses that the renminbi will not be devalued in 1998 or in 1999.

24 The hedge fund company, Long Term Capital Management, receives an injection of US$3.75 billion from New York Federal Reserve Bank in a rescue bid.

October

6 The People's Bank of China closes down Guangdong International Trust and Investment Corporation. The investment vehicle has incurred losses of billions of yuan on overseas investment, mainly in derivatives and properties.

8 The US dollar slumps almost 8% to its lowest level in fifteen months against the yen, touching a low of 111.63 and recording the largest one-day drop in twenty-five years.

November

11 The government-appointed Committee on Singapore's Competitiveness puts forward measures to slash manufacturers' costs by 15%, in a bid to boost the country's international competitiveness.

17 The SAR government merges the HK$211.4 billion Land Fund and the HK$735 billion Exchange Fund to further enhance Hong Kong's defence against speculative attacks on its currency.

December

9 Zhu Rongji reiterates there will be no devaluation of the renminbi.

1999

January

13 Zhu Rongji says China is pursuing an active fiscal policy and an appropriate monetary policy for maintaining the stability of the renminbi.

28 Yuan devaluation angrily rejected by Dai Xianglong as unnecessary.

Sources: *SCMP*, 31 December and 13 January 1998, and 28 January 1999; *TKP*, 26 January 1999; and Kar-yiu Wong (ed.), *The Asian Crisis: What Has Happened and Why*, Seattle: University of Washington, October 1998, pp. 3–37 and 84–7.

7

The Greater China Growth Triangle in the Asian Financial Crisis*

This chapter focuses on the economic cooperation between Hong Kong, Taiwan, and mainland China to examine (a) the impact of the Asian financial crisis on trade and investment flows among the three entities and (b) their longer-term implications for China as a whole in the context of economic integration among nations. Throughout the chapter, the term Greater China will be used to refer to the three Chinese locations.

Greater China as a process of economic integration

Hong Kong and Taiwan, small as they are in population and geographic area, are by no means unequal economic partners of their huge mainland Chinese neighbour. Hong Kong's gross domestic product (GDP) per capita in 1997 stood at US$26,369 and Taiwan's was US$13,233, compared with probably not more than US$860 for mainland China. Dollar for dollar, that is, without adjusting for possible implications of the purchasing power disparities between the respective currencies, the combined GDP of Hong Kong and Taiwan is surprisingly some 51% of China's (in absolute terms, China's GDP was US$900.88 billion in 1997). The Hong Kong government's budget expenditure alone, totalling US$22.4 billion in 1997, is equal to around 20% of China's national budget expenditure of US$111.39 billion. In short, the remarkable economic importance of both Hong Kong and Taiwan has significant bearing on their economic relationships with China.

---

* Reprinted from "The Greater China Growth Triangle in the Asian Financial Crisis", in Shahid Jusuf, Simon Evenett, and Weiping Wu (eds.), *Facets of Globalization: International and Local Dimensions of Development,* Washington D.C.: The World Bank, 2001, pp. 57–77.

There are several important aspects to the emergence of Greater China as a regional economic growth triangle in the past twenty years or so.

First, economic integration within Greater China has taken place essentially by way of foreign direct investment (FDI) flows from Hong Kong and Taiwan to mainland China, especially to Guangdong Province. It is associated with the continuous relocation of export-oriented manufacturing activities from both Hong Kong and Taiwan to take advantage of low land and labour costs available across the border from Hong Kong, and hence has resulted in what Hong Kong government statistics refer to as outward processing trade flows to China. This is therefore a clear case of FDI and trade being "twin travellers", whereby together with FDI, industrial materials such as machinery and equipment as well as semi-manufactures are shipped to the Chinese hinterland for export processing.[1]

Second, the processing trade covers a wide range of export manufactures. Some are often regarded as sunset industries; some are relatively new lines of production, but all are labour-intensive manufacturing undertakings. They include garments, clocks and watches, toys, games and sport requisites, electrical appliances, and video recorders. Taken together they represent the traditional backbone of light industry in Hong Kong and Taiwan and, in each case, since the 1960s, have been the single most important source of foreign exchange earnings and employment.[2]

Third, virtually all export commodities processed on behalf of Hong Kong and Taiwanese investors are shipped back to Hong Kong for re-export, as this represents the most direct and cost-saving transport route to final overseas markets. In addition, under Taiwan's "third country" rule (intended to avoid any direct contact with the mainland authorities), virtually all mainland-bound FDI and processing trade flows have also been channelled through Hong Kong. Similarly, mainland Chinese exports to Taiwan, irrespective of the degree of control exercised by Taiwan in respect to commodity categories and quantities, also have to be routed via Hong Kong or elsewhere. Hong Kong therefore plays a pivotal role in linking Taiwan with the mainland Chinese economy.

Fourth, since 1979, an increasing volume of Chinese exports has also been routed through Hong Kong to overseas destinations to take advantage of the international marketing expertise of Hong Kong and its highly efficient banking, finance, insurance, and telecommunications services, as well as its highly advanced shipping and port facilities (Hong Kong is the largest container port in the world). This is in addition to the huge quantity of intermediate input supplies from various overseas countries en route to the mainland for export processing. Hong Kong has thus become the largest entrepôt of the entire Chinese economic complex, surpassing by far the importance of Shanghai.

Fifth, to take advantage of the many opportunities arising from the two-way trade flows between Hong Kong and mainland China, Chinese capital has also increasingly moved into Hong Kong. Traditionally, there has long been a Chinese presence in Hong Kong's banking, finance, commerce, and retail trade sectors, associated with the regular massive Chinese shipments to Hong Kong of wage goods and clothing for local consumption or re-export, and of industrial, chemical, and mineral materials needed for the region's own highly export-oriented industries.[3] From the 1980s, however, not only has China's visibility in such trade-related investment in Hong Kong been greatly raised, but mainland Chinese capital has also been diverted to a wide variety of activities, most notably to aviation (Cathay Pacific Airways and its affiliate, Dragon Air), power generation, highway construction, telecommunications, manufacturing, and real estate development. In addition to the highly visible China International Trust and Investment Corporation, which is a national agency, most major Chinese provinces also have their own international trust and investment corporations in Hong Kong, engaging in fund raising, portfolio investment, and equity sharing in large, long-term capital projects locally and abroad. These, together with internationally syndicated bank loans often arranged in Hong Kong for large Chinese national or provincial governments' infrastructure projects, have helped to make Hong Kong the financial centre of Greater China.[4]

The overall process of economic integration within Greater China has been so powerful that within a decade, from around 1985 when the relocation of Hong Kong's manufacturing activities to the Chinese hinterland started to gain momentum, the entire Hong Kong economy was radically transformed into a Manhattan-type services industry. By 1998, the manufacturing sector's contribution to GDP had fallen to a mere 6.2% from 22.1% in 1985 and 17.6% in 1990, while the share of the service sector had rapidly expanded to more than 84.7% in 1998, from 69.7% in 1985 and 74.8% in 1990.

Similar changes also took place in Taiwan, following political decontrol instituted by the Taipei authorities in 1987 that allowed residents to visit mainland China. Taiwanese manufacturers moved swiftly to imitate their Hong Kong counterparts in investing in China. However, by 1992 the government in

Taipei was already fearful of a "hollowing out" of the island's industrial structure through the relocation to mainland China of such export earning industries as electrical, engineering, footwear, plastics, and textile production, with the share of light industry in national income and employment having been markedly curtailed.[5] Note that since 1992, Taiwan has surpassed both Japan and the United States as the second largest FDI supplier to mainland China, although its accumulated FDI stock is still far behind that of Hong Kong.

Capital flows within Greater China during the Asian financial crisis

Capital flows within Greater China are overwhelmingly dominated by FDI flows from Hong Kong and Taiwan to mainland China. In 1998 their combined total made up nearly half of China's total FDI intake of US$45.6 billion (Table 7.1). Taiwan does not allow any mainland capital to be invested in the island. In 1997, the Taiwanese government recorded only a small amount of investment from Hong Kong, a mere US$73 million. By contrast, mainland China's investment in Hong Kong totalled US$14.6 billion by the end of 1996, US$337 million in manufacturing and US$14.3 billion in non-manufacturing industries.[6] This makes China the second largest outside investor in Hong Kong, after the United Kingdom. Dollar for dollar, the mainland's cumulative investment in Hong Kong amounted to as much as 11% of Hong Kong's cumulative FDI stock of US$135 billion in mainland China as of the end of July 1998. The figures do not include mainland-backed enterprises that have long been based in Hong Kong.

According to Chinese official estimates, more than 1,856 mainland-backed enterprises are registered in Hong Kong, with an estimated gross asset value of US$185 billion and a net asset value of US$23.5 billion at the end of 1996 and employing more than 53,000 employees by the end of 1997. These include such relatively new arrivals as the China International Trust and Investment Corporation (HK) Holdings, China Everbright, and Guangdong Investment, as well as traditional mainland-backed Chinese enterprises, such as the Bank of China and China Resources (the latter having operated in Hong Kong for many decades).

Portfolio capital flows within Greater China essentially involve listing China's 41 state-owned enterprises on the Hong Kong Stock Exchange. As of November 1998, total capital raised by these "H" share companies amounted to US$7.9 billion. Together with the 72 "red chips", mainland-backed enterprises accounted for 16% of the stock market's total market capitalization of US$343 billion at the end of October 1998. An index called the Hang Seng China-Affiliated Corporation Index was introduced on 16 June 1997, for all red chips listed in Hong Kong, alongside the familiar Hang Seng Index.

Under the full impact of the regional financial turmoil, the red chips have been as volatile as, if not more vulnerable than, the broader Hang Seng Index, which plummeted to as low as 6,500 from a record high of around 16,500 shortly before the Asian financial crisis. Amid persistent speculation in 1997–98 that a devaluation of the Chinese currency was imminent to maintain the country's export competitiveness against Southeast Asian rivals (whose currencies had been devalued by 40–70% against the US dollar since July 1997), red chip prices suffered severely. As a result, the anticipated flotation of a number of significant state-owned enterprises on the Hong Kong Stock Exchange had to be postponed.

Moreover, as a result of the extreme volatility of the stock market and the withdrawal of billions of US dollars from the Asia-Pacific region because of the financial crisis, Hong Kong's role as a leading centre for arranging syndicated loans in Asia (mostly for large government infrastructure projects in China) has also been seriously eroded. The total value of syndicated loans arranged by banks in Hong Kong plunged from a high of US$17 billion in the first half of 1997 to a mere US$2.1 billion in the first half of 1998, having previously accelerated from US$14.6 billion in 1995 to US$19.3 billion in 1996.[7]

Notwithstanding the volatility of portfolio flows and capital borrowing, FDI flows into China have emerged basically unscathed from the Asian financial crisis; indeed, they have exhibited a remarkable degree of resilience. This is certainly the case for global FDI inflows, and seems also to be the case for Hong Kong and Taiwan, even if the trends with respect to the two small Chinese entities are not fully endorsed by official Chinese statistics.

Specifically, total cumulative FDI intake by China, in terms of both approved FDI (contractually pledged value of investment) and utilized FDI flows (realized intake), showed a consistent growth trend in 1998 that was virtually as robust as that experienced in 1997 (Figure 7.1). For the whole of 1998, both cumulative FDI approval and actual FDI flows were still marginally higher than those recorded for 1997. Similarly, monthly fluctuations in China's total FDI intake throughout 1998 did not reveal any noticeably adverse impact of the Asian crisis in relation to observed trends since January

Table 7.1 Shares of Hong Kong, Taiwan, and Rest of the World in the Realized FDI Intake by the Mainland of China, 1987–1998

	China FDI intake		Hong Kong			Taiwan			Rest of the world		
Year	**Total (US$ million**	**Yearly change (%)**	**Share (US$ million**	**%**	**Yearly change (%)**	**Share (US$ million**	**%**	**Yearly change (%)**	**Share (US$ million**	**%**	**Yearly change (%)**
1987	2,313.53		1,587.94	68.6					725.59	31.4	
1988	3,193.68	38.0	2,067.60	64.7	30.2				1,126.08	35.3	55.2
1989	3,392.57	6.2	2,036.90	60.0	–1.5				1,355.67	40.0	20.4
1990	3,487.11	2.8	1,880.00	53.9	–7.7	224.26	6.4		1,382.85	39.7	2.0
1991	4,366.34	25.2	2,405.25	55.1	27.9	469.89	10.8	109.5	1,491.20	34.2	7.8
1992	11,007.51	152.1	7,507.07	68.2	212.1	1,050.50	9.5	123.6	2,449.94	22.3	64.3
1993	27,514.95	150.0	17,274.75	62.8	130.1	3,138.59	11.4	198.8	7,101.61	25.8	189.9
1994	33,766.50	22.7	19,665.44	58.2	13.8	3,391.04	10.0	8.0	10,710.02	31.7	50.8
1995	37,520.53	11.1	20,060.37	53.5	2.0	3,161.55	8.4	–6.8	14,298.61	38.1	33.5
1996	42,350.00	12.9	20,677.32	48.8	3.1	3,474.84	8.2	9.9	18,197.84	43.0	27.3
1997	45,278.00	6.9	20,630.00	45.6	–0.2	3,290.00	7.3	–5.3	21,358.00	47.2	17.4
1998	45,582.00	0.7	18,508.00	40.6	–10.3	2,915.00	6.4	–11.4	24,159.00	53.0	13.1

Notes: The 1997 share for Taiwan was obtained by applying the 1997/1996 rate of increase of the broader category to the 1996 figure.

Sources: MOFTEC—*ACFERT*, various issues; for 1998, CSICSC—*CMS*, various issues.

1996 (Figure 7.2). It is not until 1999 that China's FDI intake, in terms of both pledged value and actual flows, began to decline noticeably.[8]

As for FDI inflows from Hong Kong and Taiwan alone, the 1998 quarterly, official Chinese statistics so far available suggest some slowdown, albeit marginal, compared with trends in both overall FDI intake in 1998 and FDI inflows in 1997 (Figure 7.1). Cumulative FDI approval was down by 4.2% for the first quarter of 1998 and down 8% for the second quarter. Actual FDI flows recorded an impressive 15% increase for the first quarter, but by June 1998 the cumulative gains had fallen by 11% compared with the record of the previous year. The decline continued through the fourth quarter, but the total reduction for Hong Kong and Taiwan combined for the whole of 1998 amounted to just around 10%.

While the implications of such random fluctuations remain ambiguous, one important factor, hitherto concealed, is likely to have a significant impact on any interpretation of the possible effect of the regional financial turmoil on

Figure 7.1 Monthly Cumulative FDI Inflows into China and the Quarterly Share of Hong Kong, 1996–1998 (US$100 million)

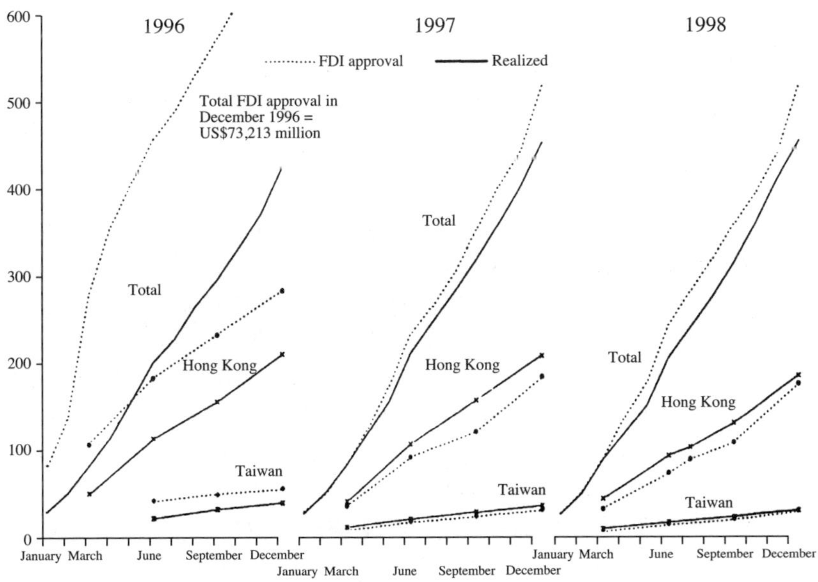

Sources: CSICSC—*CMS*; and HKTDC, various issues.

Figure 7.2 Monthly Fluctuations in China's FDI Intake, 1996–1998 (US$100 million)

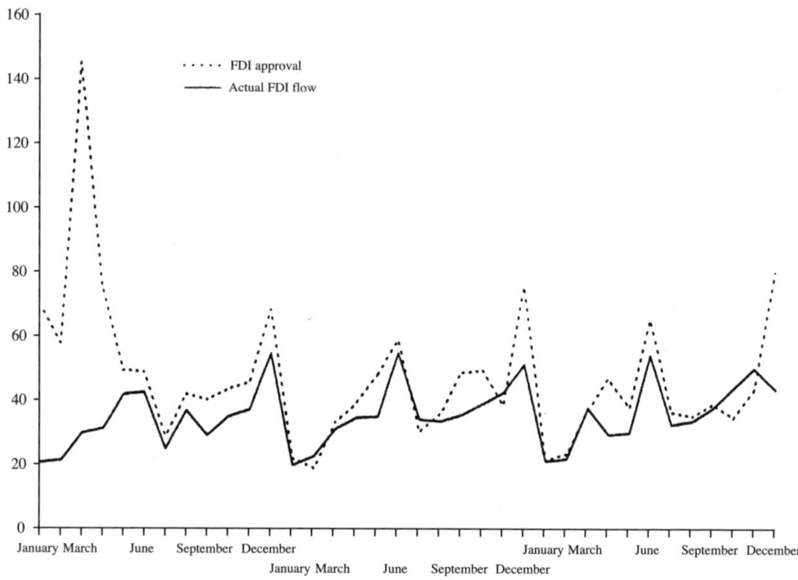

Sources: As Figure 7.1.

FDI flows within Greater China. This critical factor relates to such unlikely FDI suppliers as Bermuda, the Cayman Islands, the Virgin Islands, and even Samoa in the remote South Pacific. In 1997, the year in which Hong Kong was returned to China, total utilized FDI flows into mainland China from the Virgin Islands alone increased dramatically by more than threefold to half that of Taiwan, or nearly one-tenth of that of Hong Kong. Undoubtedly, the sources of such inflows were mostly, if not wholly, Hong Kong and Taiwanese investors in disguise (but also many mainland-backed Chinese enterprises based in Hong Kong). For various reasons, these investors wanted to protect their anonymity by reregistering in the Caribbean islands. Their motivation was not, however, that which drove the earlier nominal removal from Hong Kong to Bermuda of Jardine Matheson, namely, the fear of possible political reprisals after the reversion of Hong Kong to Chinese sovereignty.

Specifically, if these "prodigy" shares were restored to the Hong Kong or Taiwanese account, their combined contribution to China's utilized FDI intake in 1997 (as reflected in Figure 7.1) would undoubtedly rise sharply and substantially surpass their comparable share for 1996. A similar conclusion is likely to apply to the potential bona fide contributions of Hong Kong and Taiwan investors to China's FDI intake in 1998, accelerated increases in China's FDI approval for investors from the Caribbean islands tending to compensate for the reductions in officially recorded FDI approval for Hong Kong and Taiwan in recent years.

In 1997, for the first time, the value of China's FDI approval by both Hong Kong and Taiwan was notably lower than their utilized FDI flows into China (Figure 7.1). There is little doubt that this signalled a continuing replacement by the Caribbean islands and many other similar puppet investors. Note, in particular, that compared with the lacklustre trends in FDI approval for Hong Kong and Taiwan, global FDI inflows into China continued to accelerate impressively throughout both 1997 and 1998 (Figure 7.1), although the absence of separate FDI approval statistics from China for the Caribbean islands for 1997 still makes it difficult to estimate the likely size of the true shares of Hong Kong and Taiwan investors in total realized FDI flows into China in 1998.

Overall, there seems little reason to suggest that FDI flows into China have been adversely affected by the Asian crisis to any significant extent compared with portfolio investment flows. The asymmetry is not wholly inspiring, because portfolio flows are vulnerable to stock market volatility, interest rate regimes, credit crunches, and the risk of foreign exchange fluctuations, particularly in the wake of increased global economic integration and interaction. FDI, however, represents long-term fixed commitments that require prudent cash flow planning to avoid the danger of liquidity traps, bankruptcy, and capital losses. Nonetheless, in the context of the Asian financial crisis as it has affected the Greater China triangle, the difference between portfolio and FDI flows cannot be explained by such simple textbook reasoning.

Several factors explain the relative resilience of the observed FDI flows within Greater China amid the regional financial turmoil. They offer a diversity of perspectives, but taken together, are all related to the fact that most FDI flows from Hong Kong and Taiwan to China are, directly or indirectly, closely associated with export processing, as in the case of the power generation project established by the Cheung Kong Group in Shantou or the Hopewell highway project linking Guangzhou and Hong Kong. They all underpin the rapid development of the highly export-oriented industries dominated by outside investors in the region.[9]

The first and most important factor is that both the United States and Western European countries—the single most important export markets for China, Hong Kong, and Taiwan taken together—were not seriously drawn into the Asian financial whirlpool, except for difficulties associated with reduced import demand from affected Asian countries (members of the Association of Southeast Asian Nations [ASEAN] and the Republic of Korea, in particular). This helped guarantee a stable and continuous stream of export earnings for China-based Hong Kong and Taiwan exporters who were also investors.

Second, the continuous, albeit erratic, weakening in 1998 of the Japanese yen against the US dollar (to which both the Hong Kong dollar, officially, and the renminbi, unofficially, are pegged) helped to enhance cost savings for Hong Kong and Taiwanese investors in mainland China, as they all rely heavily on Japan for imports of equipment and machinery, as well as for industrial materials and semi-manufactures for export processing. The savings have come in tandem with reduced credit costs from the yen depreciation for financing their imports, as well as their FDI ventures at large. Indeed, in conjunction with the massive import of intermediate goods from Japan, a substantial proportion of FDI flows from Hong Kong and Taiwan into China are financed by Japanese banks based in Hong Kong (as testified by personal communication from a former Japanese consul general based in Hong Kong, who said that more than half of Hong Kong's FDI in China was so financed).

Third, in the interests of promoting exports and mitigating increased pressures for a devaluation of the renminbi, mainland Chinese banks had begun, exceptionally, to grant renminbi credits to foreign-invested enterprises by Hong Kong and Taiwanese investors during the crisis. This helped to compensate for fund shortages associated with the severe credit crunch that accompanied the efforts of the Hong Kong government to defend the US dollar peg (mainland-backed Chinese banks based in Hong Kong were also fearful of a renminbi devaluation, and thus preferred to hold US dollars rather than to lend to Hong Kong investors). Similarly, ad hoc increases in value-added tax rebates for a wide range of export commodities were decreed both to promote export incentives and enhance the liquidity of foreign-invested enterprises (FIEs). The effect of a 1% increase in value-added tax rebates is estimated to be comparable to a 1% reduction in the export costs for general merchandise trade, and hence tantamount to a devaluation of the renminbi against the US dollar (*TKP*, 24 June 1998).

Fourth, from the perspective of China's FDI intake, it is fortunate that the Asian financial crisis was preceded by the Chinese government's restoration in mid-1997 of the customs duties exemption for imports by FIEs of the equipment, machinery, and industrial materials needed for export processing. Note that the 1996 suspension of this exemption may have contributed to the sharp reduction of FDI approval in early 1997, in addition to the observed nominal shift in favour of the Caribbean islands. However, by December 1997, FDI approval for Hong Kong investors, in value terms, had already been restored to the June 1996 level when the retraction was announced (Figure 7.1). This, as well as the contributions made by Hong Kong and Taiwanese investors in disguise should have helped to sustain the actual FDI inflow in 1998.

Another important policy initiative the Chinese government took in the wake of the Asian financial crisis may not fall within the purview of promoting export-oriented FDI inflows, but it seems to have averted the possible rediversion of FDI flows from China towards the hard-hit Southeast Asian countries (which had become much more attractive to foreign investors following massive devaluations of their currencies). This relates to the deliberate attempt to open up industrial and service sectors hitherto closed to foreign investment. It is still too early to estimate to what extent FIEs, especially large transnational corporations, have already taken advantage of the new FDI regime. However, given that Hong Kong and Taiwanese investors have been anxious to move into retailing and other service undertakings in China, and that acquisitions of and mergers with Chinese state-owned enterprises have become quite popular in recent years as a way for transnational corporations to gain a foothold in the huge import-substitution investment markets there, this is likely to become a crucial means of enhancing and stabilizing the growth of future FDI flows into China.

From a microeconomic perspective, and to understand the likely trends in Chinese FDI intake in the context of the Asian crisis, distinguishing between replacement and new investments in terms of FDI intake may be useful. For most of the twenty years that China has courted FDI, the value of realized FDI has moved closely in tandem with FDI approval in terms of investment contractually pledged. The implications are clear. After the initial period of any accelerated FDI expansion, subsequent FDI approval will, for the most part, become replacement investment needed to sustain existing undertakings, plus new investment for marginal capacity expansion to cope with secular growth in overseas markets. In short, aside from cyclical fluctuations, China's FDI inflows from Hong Kong, Taiwan, and the world at large will likely sustain their long-term pattern of growth in the years to come.

Impact on trade flows within Greater China

By virtue of the particular pattern of economic integration among mainland China, Hong Kong, and Taiwan, trade flows within Greater China are overwhelmingly dominated by export processing. Thus, outward processing goods consistently make up around half of Hong Kong's total exports to mainland China (Table 7.2). Within the category of materials to be processed for export flowing from Hong Kong into China, the share of re-exports (goods imported from overseas without undergoing any minimal processing in Hong Kong) accelerated from 58% in 1989 to a startling high of more than 80% in 1998. The corresponding share of domestic exports meanwhile fell to a mere 19%, including many that could barely fulfil the country of origin's requirements for exports to be classified as such.

Hong Kong's imports from China are even more heavily dominated by the shipment of processed export commodities and, by 1998, accounted for more than 80% of its total imports (Table 7.2). At the same time, processed goods for export (outward processing goods) imported on behalf of Hong Kong investors based in China constituted nearly 90% of Hong Kong's re-exports of all goods of "Chinese origin" to all countries other than mainland China, with an estimated export markup ranging from 18% to 24% for different years.[10] Given that Hong Kong's total re-exports of Chinese origin (comprising both outward processing goods and non-outward processing goods) are generally 11% to 14% higher than its total imports (of which only around 20% are non-outward processing goods) from China, it seems certain that virtually all outward processing goods flowing from China to Hong Kong are re-exported to third countries, especially the United States and Western European countries. Indeed, the United States alone has consistently taken up more than 40% of Hong Kong's re-exports of Chinese origin of these kinds of export commodities.[11]

By contrast, about 50% of Hong Kong's total exports to China constitute commodities other than goods bound for export processing in mainland China. That is, Hong Kong not only serves as a universal agency for China's processing trade, but also represents an important sourcing venue for end-users in China of imports of equipment and machinery, vehicles, computer software, CD-ROMs, and the like from the West.

Table 7.2 Processing Trade in Hong Kong-China Economic Relations, 1989–1998

	HK exports to China (HK$ million)					HK imports from China (HK$ million)					
		Share of OP goods		Share in OP goods (%)			Share of OP goods		HK re-exports of OP goods of Chinese origin		Implicit value-added
	Total	Value	Percentage (2)/(1)	Domestic exports	Re-exports	Total	Value	Percentage (7)/(6)	Value	Share in total re-exports (%)	proportion (%) [(7)–(2)] /(7)
Year	(1)	(2)	(3)	(4)	(5)	(6)	(7)	(8)	(9)	(10)	(11)
1989	146,764	76,868	52.4	41.58	58.40	196,676	113,581	57.8	–	–	32.32
1990	158,378	91,914	58.0	39.62	60.78	236,134	145,103	61.5	–	–	36.7
1991	207,722	113,931	54.9	35.43	64.57	293,356	187,384	63.9	221,450	74.1	39.2
1992	274,061	141,639	51.7	31.26	68.74	354,348	254,013	71.7	299,833	78.3	44.2
1993	337,928	160,678	47.4	23.09	71.59	402,161	295,203	73.4	364,536	80.8	45.7
1994	383,844	181,179	47.2	23.16	76.84	470,876	354,912	75.4	422,544	82.0	49.0
1995	444,108	217,613	49.0	20.17	79.83	537,052	399,567	74.4	492,461	82.2	45.5
1996	474,038	222,324	46.9	19.38	80.62	566,821	452,890	79.9	552,822	86.0	50.9
1997	503,881	244,886	48.6	19.22	80.78	604,855	491,142	81.2	595,511	88.4	50.1
1998(Q1)	109,806	48,095	43.8	18.23	81.77	126,403	101,628	80.4	126,082	87.8	52.7
1998(Q2)	125,857	61,106	48.6	20.00	80.00	147,212	120,821	82.1	133,292	84.5	49.4
1998(Q3)	112,261	56,355	50.2	19.42	80.58	157,700	131,364	83.2	155,327	88.7	57.1

Notes: OP stands for outward processing; Q for quarter; and "–" denotes "statistics not available". Outward processing statistics are not available prior to 1989, as HKGCSD did not start to compile such statistics until that year.

Sources: HKGCSD—*HKADS*, various issues.

Overall, the economic significance of Hong Kong to China in terms of entrepôt trade is summed up in the fact that around 40% of the mainland's foreign trade is currently handled via Hong Kong, excluding the trans-shipment of goods to and from the mainland, which has also become an increasingly important service trade for Hong Kong. More importantly, China's export processing trade, which now accounts for more than 50% of China's total external trade, is virtually all channelled through Hong Kong.

Two additional points should be considered in assessing the potential impact of the Asian financial crisis on trade flows within Greater China. First, to the extent that under the third country rule adopted by Taiwan FDI, flows and exports from the island to mainland China for processing are channelled through Hong Kong, the outward processing goods flowing from Hong Kong to China, as shown in Table 7.2, clearly also include Taiwanese contributions. Similarly, barring direct navigational links between Taiwan and mainland China, the outward processing goods flowing from China to Hong Kong also cover imports made on behalf of Taiwanese exporter investors.

Second, the statistics in Table 7.2 may not reflect the full magnitude of outward processing trade flows within Greater China. Thus, with FDI intake from Hong Kong and Taiwan being increasingly directed northward since the early 1990s,[12] some processed goods must have also been directly exported through Shanghai and other major ports in north China to, for example, Japan and the United States. To the extent that this occurred, the estimated, implicit value added involving the export processing trade for Hong Kong may understate its true magnitude (Table 7.2). Nonetheless, the estimated values for more recent years are generally in accord with the frequent official Chinese claims that imported input materials and components make up around 50% of the value of the Chinese processing trade. This seems to provide sufficient incentives for both Hong Kong and Taiwanese investors, as well as their Chinese collaborators, to sustain and further develop the processing trade.

It is difficult to gauge exactly the possible impact of the Asian financial crisis on trade flows among Hong Kong, Taiwan, and mainland China. For one thing, the crisis did not really begin to seriously affect relationships within Greater China until mid-1998. Any assessment of the possible long-term implications of the crisis on trade flows within Greater China must therefore be regarded as preliminary. In any case, the complexity of the problems involved simply does not permit definitive conclusions to be drawn at this stage.

One important question is whether the massive devaluation of Southeast Asian currencies after July 1997 really eroded the price competitiveness of Greater China's labour-intensive export processing trade, and thereby broke the flying geese pattern of industrialization in Asia.[13] It would be premature to answer affirmatively. For example, the extent to which Greater China's exports to third countries, notably the United States and European Union (EU) countries, overlap, and thus compete directly with its Southeast Asian neighbours, is not clear. Dai Xianglong, the governor of China's central bank, estimated that the overlap was around 15% of China's total exports to the United States, and viewed this as a reason for not seeking to maintain export competitiveness by devaluing China's currency. That figure may, of course, also translate into a sizeable margin in China's total exports, and bear significantly on Hong Kong's re-export earnings, especially in the wake of enhanced Asian competition.

However, any increased export price benefits for Southeast Asian countries deriving from their currency devaluation may be offset by resultant increases in the cost of imports needed for export processing. The reality is that as in China, most Southeast Asian export producers rely heavily on imported inputs.

More importantly, export producers in Indonesia, Malaysia, and Thailand—central actors in the regional financial turmoil—suffered enormously under the impact of high interest rates and an especially severe credit crunch that resulted from the International Monetary Fund's severe prescription for restoring monetary and fiscal order. Many export factories were forced to close down altogether. By contrast, in Hong Kong, while increased financial illiquidity resulting from the government's massive efforts to defend the US dollar peg may have made it difficult to do business there, the disarray appears to have had only a marginal impact on the Chinese hinterland through its effect on the export processing undertakings of Hong Kong investors.

In fact, as part of the mainland authority's policy to prevent potential export problems, Hong Kong and Taiwanese exporter investors based in mainland China benefited from the rare privilege of obtaining renminbi advances from domestic Chinese banks, in addition to increased value-added tax rebates for exports. Such privileges are, of course, not unrelated to the unusual circumstances prevalent in China in 1998 of declining interest rates coupled with negative inflation. Clearly, because of its capital account control, mainland China was largely spared the contagion of the Southeast Asian financial crisis, thereby giving the Chinese government the luxury of being able to pursue its own, independent, export promotion policy.

Nonetheless, if despite the Asian financial crisis, trade flows within Greater China generally succeeded in maintaining their established course, the single most important contributory factor was the economic sustainability of the final export destinations, that is, the United States and EU countries. The outward processing trade statistics provided by the Hong Kong government (Table 7.2) do not provide country breakdowns in terms of re-exports, but the major proportion of outward processing goods flowing from China to Hong Kong are undoubtedly destined for the North American and Western European markets.

An alternative approach is to distinguish between exports and imports by domestic enterprises (non-FIEs) and FIEs. The latter clearly represent the thousands of US- and EU-bound Hong Kong and Taiwan export producers. Thus, amid declining overall growth in Chinese exports, FIE exports performed remarkably well, in contrast to sharp declines suffered by non-FIEs in 1998 (Figure 7.3). By December 1998, when the overall growth rate of China's exports had fallen to a mere 0.5% from a high of 20.9% a year earlier, FIEs' exports were still increasing by 8%, compared with 22% for 1997. By contrast, the absolute level of cumulative exports by non-FIEs had declined by nearly 5% in 1998.

The background to this divergent export performance by FIEs and non-FIEs lay in the continuous growth of exports to the United States and EU, side by side with the declining or negative growth of exports to East and Southeast Asia as a result of sharply reduced import demand caused by the regional financial upheaval. This drained any foreign exchange reserves held by all these countries, except Japan.

Recent Chinese customs statistics confirm that 85% of the total net increases in exports for the first three-quarters of 1998 derived from the processing trade (*TKP*, 13 October 1998). Exports to the United States and EU increased for the same period, year-on-year, by 16.5% and 22%, respectively, while those to Korea, ASEAN countries, and Japan fell, respectively, by 32%, 16%, and 6.5%.[14] Note also that Chinese exports to Asian countries essentially consist of resource-based products, such as mineral fuel, iron and steel, and cotton, all of which witnessed substantial absolute declines in exports in the first half of 1998.

Figure 7.3 Monthly, Year-to-Date Changes in Cumulative Exports (X) and Imports (M) by Non-Foreign- and Foreign-Invested Enterprises (FIEs) in China, 1996–1998 (%)

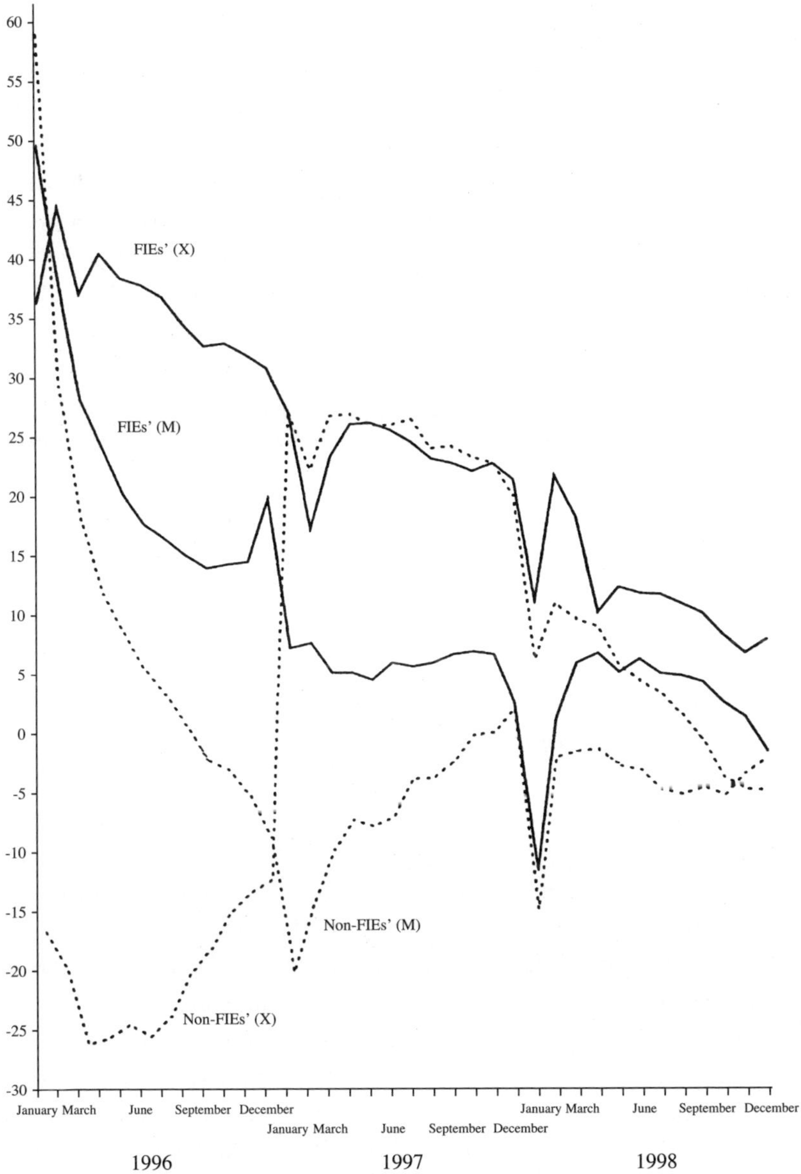

Sources: CSICSC—*CMS*, various issues.

Government policies, economic consequences, and longer-term implications

The governments of Hong Kong and mainland China shared one common feature in terms of their policy response to the Asian financial crisis. As noted earlier, both governments vigorously sought to maintain the existing exchange rate of their respective currencies in relation to the US dollar. In mainland China, under the managed float regime, the renminbi rate has consistently remained at around 8.27 yuan to the dollar. This has been so despite frequent speculation that China would be forced to devalue. In Hong Kong, the US dollar peg at HK$7.8 (intact since October 1983) also successfully withstood several massive currency attacks amid the escalating Asian crisis.[15]

However, the shared desire to defend their currencies concealed widely divergent economic underpinnings in Hong Kong and mainland China. Moreover, the implications of defending their currencies were also quite different. We will examine each case in turn to assess the economic implications and relative merits of the currency defence, especially as they relate to capital and trade flows between Hong Kong and China from a longer-term perspective. We will also relate to the situation in Taiwan, in which after an absolute defence, the government was forced to devalue the new Taiwan dollar in late 1997.

In China, first, the inconvertibility of the capital account eliminated the fear of capital flight out of the country and rendered inoperative the associated need to defend the value of the renminbi. Attempts by individual Chinese exporting and importing enterprises to evade official foreign exchange control may have appeared to proliferate amid widespread fears since early 1998 of a renminbi devaluation, but the Chinese government was able to use familiar administrative fiats to deal relatively easily with any such instances.[16]

Second, a renminbi devaluation would almost inevitably trigger another round of competitive currency devaluations by the hard-hit ASEAN countries, which believed, rightly or wrongly, that the 1994 Chinese devaluation had severely undermined their export competitiveness and contributed to their current misfortune. From the Chinese perspective, therefore, any export price benefits to be derived from a renminbi devaluation in this context might be wholly offset by an emulative response by ASEAN. This is quite separate from the questionable potential economic benefits of a renminbi devaluation as discussed earlier.

Third were the potential implications of a renminbi devaluation for Sino-Japanese economic relations. For China, as for ASEAN countries, Japan is the single most important trading partner in the entire Asia-Pacific region. As China's largest trade partner, in 1997 Japan accounted for 17% of China's global exports and nearly 20% of China's total imports. This compares with a mere 3.6% and 5.3%, respectively, for the "ASEAN Four" combined (Indonesia, Malaysia, the Philippines, and Thailand), or 6% and 8.4%, respectively, if Singapore is included. A renminbi devaluation would merely have raised the cost of imports from Japan for domestic end-user industries that depended on Japan for supplies of advanced equipment and machinery, and thus for the much needed technology transfer for industrial upgrading. Equally important, China's vast export processing trade also relies heavily on Japan for input supplies, so that any export price advantage from a renminbi devaluation might have been offset by increased import costs.

It was only when the free fall of the Japanese yen against the US dollar to around 145 yen in June 1998 threatened effectively to tilt the balance at the expense of Chinese exports to Japan that the Chinese authorities reconsidered their persistent pledge to uphold the external value of the renminbi. Fortunately, the unrestrained yen depreciation was eventually arrested before it could make the Asian crisis even worse.

Consideration of how the Chinese economy fared during the Asian crisis provides a useful context for assessing the longer-term implications for trade and investment flows within Greater China. The observed slowdown in China's export growth in 1998 was clearly more a matter of reduced import capabilities in East and Southeast Asian countries than a relative appreciation of the Chinese currency. Indeed, the reduction resembled the drastic curtailment in US cotton exports to these countries since early 1998. Nonetheless, the Chinese government evidently saw the slowdown as impinging on its much celebrated target of 8% GDP growth in 1998, given estimates that between 1992 and 1997, net export earnings had contributed to about 16% of GDP growth.[17]

The GDP target was of paramount importance to the Chinese leadership, as it was closely bound up with employment generation and other crucial macroeconomic variables. According to a high-level Chinese estimate, a GDP growth of 1% would help to create 1.25 million jobs in the non-farm sector (*TKP*, 4 August 1998). The difficulties of achieving this target growth were also compounded by the great Yangtze flood in mid-1998.

The remedial policy measures the Chinese government adopted included the following:

- Abolishing, in January 1998, the conventional bank loan quotas imposed by the People's Bank of China in order to extend fully-fledged lending autonomy to the commercial banks.
- Reducing the legal reserve ratio requirements from 13% to 8% in late March 1998, coupled with reforming the reserve system to enable the commercial banks to use their fiscal reserves, held by the Ministry of Finance, to fulfil the new, reduced reserve requirements. With the new bank deposits as estimated for 1998, this would have helped to enhance the commercial banks' total lending capacity by a massive US$18.5 billion.
- Reducing the central bank's interest rate in March, July, and December 1998, thereby enabling all industrial and commercial borrowers to save at least US$29 billion in interest cost payments from the five successive interest rate curtailments between 1996 and July 1998.
- Increasing by US$4.5 billion the amount to be extended by the state banks as fixed asset investment loans under the national guidelines for investments, as decreed by the central bank in April 1998.
- Resuming open market operations for repurchasing treasury bonds by more than US$6 billion in May 1998.
- Issuing treasury bonds totalling some US$33 billion in May 1998 to enhance the state banks' capital injection to the Basel capital adequacy ratio of 8%.
- Issuing treasury bonds amounting to US$12 billion in August 1998 to boost infrastructure investments, to be synchronized with bank loans of a similar amount for complementary projects.

The various monetary and financial policy measures may or may not have been directly targeted at compensating for the export earnings losses incurred.[18] However, taken together, they already represented an increase in financial liquidity of more than the national budget expenditure of US$69.5 billion for 1998. The Chinese vice minister of finance estimated that the additional infrastructure investment expenditure alone would, via its income multiplier effect, help to raise the GDP growth rate by 2.5–3% (*TKP*, 19 November 1998). Together with the strictly imposed capital account control, the reflationary policy measures effectively protected China from becoming the next financial domino in the Asian crisis. The realized GDP growth rate for 1998 is now officially confirmed to have been 7.8%, only slightly lower than the original target of 8%.

It is against this background of continuous economic prosperity and stability that FDI has continued to pour into China at the expense of Southeast Asian countries (where, in the mind of foreign investors, potential political and economic instability seems to have outweighed the prospects for improved profitability arising from currency devaluation). It is apparent that throughout 1998, total FDI inflows into China showed little sign of abatement (Figure 7.1), although admittedly large transnational corporations have increasingly played a key role in sustaining overall FDI inflows into China.

Against this background, let us look at the Achilles' heel of Hong Kong during the context of the Asian financial crisis. By the end of 1997, Hong Kong was endowed with foreign exchange reserves to the tune of some US$92.8 billion, third only to Japan (US$220.8 billion) and China (US$139.9 billion). It had hardly any external debt or any serious balance of payments deficit. The government's budget was, as usual, in solid balance, and the economy had been enjoying robust GDP growth of around 5–6% per year for a number of years. Clearly, Hong Kong was dragged into the regional financial meltdown by virtue of being the world's most open economy.

Specifically, in the absence of any form of capital account control, the Hong Kong dollar became a prime destination of international hedge funds for speculative attacks, following the predators' spree through Indonesia, Korea, Malaysia, and Thailand. A surrender on the part of Hong Kong government to allow for a free fall of the Hong Kong dollar would obviously have prompted massive capital flight, as under such circumstances portfolio flows normally do not care about economic fundamentals. However, the decision by the Hong Kong Monetary Authority to put up a massive defence for its US dollar peg sent the Hong Kong economy reeling.

Under the severe credit crunch and high interest rate pressures, both stock market and asset prices plummeted by 50–60% in 1997–98. While mainland China was confidently looking toward meeting its 8% GDP target for 1998, by late November Hong Kong's GDP growth had already been forecasted to be a negative 5% for 1998 (confirmed to be -5.1% in March 1999), with the unemployment rate reaching a twenty-five-year high of 6% by February 1999.

The Hong Kong government adopted a number of significant financial measures to cope with the economic meltdown. These include the unprecedented use of the Exchange Fund's money in August 1998 to purchase Hong Kong stocks to prop up the stock market and restore investors' confidence. The stake was later officially made known to be worth around US$15 billion, making the Hong Kong government by far the largest investor of its kind in the world, but nonetheless, the prestigious Heritage Foundation was poised to downgrade the status of Hong Kong as the freest economy in the world for 1999.[19]

Equally significant was the Hong Kong Monetary Authority's September 1998 package to directly fend off international currency speculators. The rescue measure had two main features. The first was to greatly reinforce the Currency Board's discipline by committing the government to convert the Hong Kong dollars held by all licenced banks in their clearing accounts with the Exchange Fund (rather than just the legal tender in circulation) into US dollars at the fixed exchange rate of HK$7.50 to the US dollar, which was even higher than the official benchmark of HK$7.80 for cash arbitrage. The second was to greatly enhance the financial liquidity of the entire banking system by replacing the restrictive "liquidity adjustment facility" with a "discount window", whereby the banks could repeatedly borrow from the authority with their holdings of Exchange Fund bills and notes as collateral to cope with any drastic overnight demand for liquidity.[20]

Clearly, the new measures were backed by the government's sizeable foreign exchange reserves. Prior to the stock market buy-up by the government in August 1998, reserves had stood at around US$96.5 billion, or quadruple the entire monetary base of US$23 billion. That position was eroded by no more than 16% by the massive stock market intervention.

Subsequent to the launching of the Hong Kong Monetary Authority's package, the prime lending rate of the Hong Kong Association of Banks declined from a high of 10% in October 1998 to 9.25% in early December 1998. As a result, the gap with the comparable US interest rate narrowed from 3% to 2.5%, although clearly the interest rate arbitrage for the US dollar peg was still very much in operation. In essence, however, the interest rate reductions in Hong Kong seem to have been prompted by the similar move by the Federal Reserve Bank, and perhaps more so by the withdrawal of the international hedge funds following their collapse in Brazil, Russia, and elsewhere, than by the enhanced financial manoeuverability in Hong Kong arising from the authority's bold Currency Board reform measures adopted earlier in September. Similarly, both the stock market and the property market in Hong Kong rebounded quite remarkably, as elsewhere in Southeast Asian countries, which have, in addition, also seen their currencies recover substantial ground against the US dollar.

By the third quarter of 1999, the real economic sectors in Hong Kong also began to show real signs of recovery. GDP growth reverted to a rather impressive 2.9% for the whole of 1999, and is now forecasted to be in the range of 8–9% for 2000.

Taiwan's story is quite different from that of both Hong Kong and mainland China. The island is not as restrictive as the mainland in terms of capital account control, but it nonetheless lags far behind Hong Kong in financial liberalization. Unlike Hong Kong, access by foreign investors to the Taiwanese capital market is still quite strictly regulated. By July 1997, foreign capital contributed only around US$6 billion to Taiwan's stock market. The subsequent capital flight of some US$4.86 billion towards the end of 1997 was therefore relatively limited in scale, causing the Taiwan Weighted Index to fall by a mere 0.4% during the year, compared with the 42–75% drops (in US dollar terms) registered by all other Asian markets.[21]

The Taiwanese economy was also strongly underpinned by solid economic fundamentals. For example, its foreign exchange reserves stood at around US$90 billion by June 1997, trailing closely behind Hong Kong's. This is considerably more than triple the size of its external debt, while the reverse is generally the case with Korea and the ASEAN Four (Table 7.3).

The favourable macroeconomic setting clearly enabled the Central Bank of China in Taiwan to defend the new Taiwan dollar against speculative assaults following the eruption of the financial turmoil in July 1997, and eventually to leave it entirely to the foreign exchange market to find the equilibrium rate. By early January 1998, it had settled at NT$34.5 to the US dollar, down only 19%, compared with the precipitous fall of the Indonesian rupiah by 70%, the Thai baht by 55%, the Korean won by 50%, and the Malaysia ringgit by 42%.

Compared with the high price of US$15 billion paid by the Hong Kong Monetary Authority to salvage the stock market in August 1998, the opportunity costs for the central bank in Taiwan to dispose of its foreign reserves (US$7 billion out of a total holding of some US$90 billion in July 1997) to defend the new Taiwan dollar were minimal. This is especially true when set against Taiwan's GDP growth of 4.6% in 1998 (down from 6.7% in 1997), compared with a negative growth of 5.1% for Hong Kong (down from a positive 5.3% in 1997), and a positive growth of 7.8% for mainland China (down from 8.8% in 1997).

To summarize, the remarkable success of the Taiwanese authorities in shielding the island's economy from the contagion of the Southeast Asian financial epidemic comprised the following basic elements: a workable policy endowed with adequate foreign exchange reserves and a continuous current account surplus to ward off currency attacks; a cautious approach to capital account liberalization that helped to contain the international hedge funds; and, perhaps most importantly, the courage of the Taiwanese authorities in eventually floating the new Taiwan dollar after the initial abortive attempt to defend it in late 1997. The Taiwanese approach therefore appeared to blend the relative merits of Chinese capital account control with elements of trade and financial liberalization as adopted by Hong Kong, without, however, being painfully trapped, like Hong Kong, by the Achilles' heel of defending the US dollar peg system.

An important question is how the divergent policy approaches adopted by the three Chinese economic entities in coping with the impact of the Asian crisis may bear on longer-term trends in capital and trade flows within Greater China. The answer hinges essentially on three major factors, all of which are basically external to the parties concerned.

By far the most fundamental factor is the sustainability of the US and EU markets, which are the most important outlets for exports from Greater China. Undoubtedly, these export markets represent the ultimate *raison d'être* for the well-established pattern of FDI and trade flows from Hong Kong and Taiwan to mainland China for export processing since the 1980s. However, this regional framework of specialization is unlikely to be adversely affected by the Asian financial crisis to any substantial extent in the foreseeable future. This is to ignore Soros's apocalyptic scenario, in which a seemingly inevitable slowdown in economic growth in the United States from 1999 on would have eroded its capacity to tolerate the huge trade deficits, and hence undermined the global system of free trade.[22]

For Hong Kong, despite its parlous situation, the latest government statistics have confirmed that for 1998 as a whole, total exports of goods were curtailed by a relatively small margin of 4.3% in real terms, consisting of a 7.9% fall in domestic exports and a 3.7% fall in re-exports.[23] The president of

Table 7.3 External and Internal Balances of Korea, Taiwan, and the ASEAN Four, 1996–1997

Category	Taiwan	Korea	Thailand	Malaysia	Indonesia	Philippines
1. Current account balance (US$ billion)						
1990–94 average	9.1	–3.3	–7.1	–3.0	–3.0	–2.1
1995	5.5	–8.3	–16.3	–7.4	–7.0	–2.0
1996	11.0	–23.1	–14.7	–3.6	–7.0	–4.8
2. Foreign reserves, Jan–June 1997 (US$ billion)	90.0	34.1	31.4	26.6	20.3	9.8
3. External debt, Jan–June 1997 (US$ billion)	25.2	116.8	92.9	45.2	113.6	44.8
4. (2)–(3)	64.8	–82.7	–61.5	–18.6	–93.3	–35.0
5. Domestic savings 1990–96 (% of GDP)	28.0	35.0	34.2	32.1	28.9	18.8
6. Fixed capital formation 1990–96 (% of GDP)	22.6	36.7	40.4	38.3	27.4	22.5
7. (5)–(6)	5.4	–1.7	–6.2	–6.2	1.5	–3.7

Sources: Chen, Yi-Chi, "Country report on Taiwan." In Kar-Yiu Wong (ed.), *The Asian Crisis: What Has Happened and Why*, Seattle, Washington: University of Washington, 1998, http://weber.u.washington.edu/~karyiu/Asia/index.htm.

the Hong Kong Exporters Association was, however, reluctant to accept this as an indication of Hong Kong's deteriorating export performance, arguing that at least Hong Kong toy manufacturers based on the mainland, whose exports were channelled directly through the Chinese ports (rather than Hong Kong) actually showed a growth of 6% for the first nine months of 1998. These figures seem to be substantiated by official Shanghai statistics for the first ten months of 1998, which also indicated that the share of exports by FIEs increased to a remarkable 47% of the municipality's total exports of US$13.77 billion, and its total exports to the United States and EU grew by more than 20% during the same period, as against a drastic decline of 7.1% to US$6.132 billion for other Asian countries (*TKP*, 6 December 1998).[24]

The situation with Taiwan seemed to have been somewhat different. Unlike Hong Kong, Taiwan, which represents a more complete, independent economic structure, is not entirely dependent on mainland China for export processing. The continuous exodus to mainland China of its sunset industries in the past ten years or so has served to precipitate an industrial upgrading in the island. By the late 1990s, capital- and technology-intensive products (electronic components, equipment, chemicals, and other industrial materials) have made up more than 40% of Taiwan's total exports, increasingly squeezing the share of traditional labour-intensive products.

At the same time, however, coupled with Taiwan's increased FDI flows to ASEAN, the island has also become substantially dependent on these countries for its exports, to the tune of around 50% by 1998, compared with only 25% in 1996. As a result, the financial crisis severely affected Taiwan's exports. For the first eleven months of 1998, the island's exports to Indonesia, Malaysia, the Philippines, Singapore, and Thailand fell by a hefty 30% to around US$9.63 billion, compared with a more modest fall in shipments to Japan by 21.3% and to Hong Kong by only 11.9% (*SCMP,* 9 December 1998).

Under such circumstances, the longer-term questions are clearly whether Taiwan would really further substitute mainland China for ASEAN as a target of FDI outflow. Such a move would almost certainly compromise its politically inspired South-oriented strategy for avoiding any significant economic dependence on the mainland. Given that probably only secular, marginal growth of exports can be expected to both US and EU markets, a breakthrough in this regard may only come around with a turnabout in China's FDI strategy to allow for greater import-substitution foreign investment in place of export-oriented FDI. Undoubtedly, both Hong Kong and Taiwan investors have long been poised to cash in on such a prospect.

The second important factor that might affect capital and trade flows within Greater China in the near future is the pace at which potential rivals in Southeast Asia may emerge from their difficulties to reactivate their economic and export activities. There are two aspects to the implications of an early recovery. The first is that it will help to enhance demand for Greater China's exports. For Hong Kong and mainland China, this may not be essential given the small share of ASEAN in China's external trade. However, for Taiwan, it definitely is important. A speedy Southeast Asian economic recovery may well help Taiwan to generate additional export earnings for possible recycling as FDI for Chinese investment markets. Perhaps even more importantly, the second implication is that an early ASEAN recovery, especially in terms of a re-appreciation of the various currencies, may help to mitigate the countries' potential export competitiveness against Greater China exporters.

In this context, the early recovery of ASEAN economies in terms of not only the foreign exchange rate, but also the stock market and asset price seems indeed to point to the very essence of the original 1997 financial disaster: it appeared, after all, to be essentially a matter of "psychic mobility", unjustified by economic reality, and hence the rapid recovery of the various financial indicators.[25] If this view is correct, then regional economic cooperation may soon resume its pre-crisis pattern of specialization, capital, and trade flows, especially with respect to North America and Europe.

The third important factor for a sustainable early recovery from the Asian crisis for Greater China and Asia as a whole is clearly whether a new global financial order can be put in place. As Harvard economist Dani Rodrik remarked, it is simply inept to subject the policy of any government to "what 20 or 30 foreign-exchange dealers in London, New York and Frankfurt think" (*New York Times,* 4 September 1998). In fact, the consensus that arose from the 1998 annual meeting of the World Bank and the International Monetary Fund was that a new global system of financial regulation should be put in place to counter international hedge funds, in particular.

Prospects for further economic cooperation within Greater China

In the wake of the Asian economic crisis, how can the three Chinese entities cooperate with each other, formally or informally, to promote Greater China as a regional economic entity in the global context of economic integration? Any realistic solutions must be sought against the broader Chinese economic background, which sets the overall parameters for the existing mode of capital and trade flows within Greater China. There are two main aspects to this.

The first is that, astonishing as the pace has been at which mainland China has been drawn into the worldwide process of globalization during the past two decades or so, the vast Chinese economy can at best be described as half-reformed and half-opened. We can view it as being divided into two disparate entities to form a system of two economies within one country. Specifically, a highly protected, strictly import-substitution industrial system co-exists with a widely open, export-oriented sector catering to foreign investment and export drives.[26] Clearly, Hong Kong is now fully, and Taiwan increasingly, integrated with the new economic system along the Chinese coastal belt, which has in turn become part of the integrated global system of free trade.

The second aspect is that the two-economy dichotomy not only implies absolute denial of a strategy of full integration of the real economic sector with outside economies, but, by extension, also precludes capital account convertibility (as is indeed the case), so as not to deprive the protected priority industry sector of necessary investment funds. The chief objective of the open, export-oriented sector has been to use FIEs to help generate sufficient foreign exchange earnings to finance investment in the industrialization programme.

The foregoing illustration of the Chinese strategy may overlook some crucial elements, for example, the extent to which China has welcomed selective "intrusion" by transnational corporations with favoured high technology into the closed industrial system. In addition, China has shown clear signs of relaxing its policy with respect to the lesser industrial and services sectors, retail trade in particular, to allow for investments from Hong Kong and Taiwan. However, there is little doubt that the current account convertibility, in effect since December 1996, is essentially meant to be for the open export processing sector principally involving Hong Kong and Taiwanese investment.

The World Trade Organization ranks Hong Kong as the seventh largest trader in the world. Hong Kong derives virtually all its trading opportunities—of which the processing trade is predominant—from mainland China. China itself ranks 10th as an exporter and 12th as an importer, while Taiwan is 14th for exports and imports combined. Taken together, the Chinese entities have amassed a foreign exchange reserve of some US$300 billion, around 25% higher than that of the long-established trading giant, Japan.

This may be seen as a matter of Confucian frugality and prudence or, in the case of Hong Kong, the legacy of British conservatism in hedging against eventual political uncertainty surrounding the handover of Hong Kong, and for Taiwan, perceived political imperatives for ensuring the island's security in relation to the mainland. Whatever the imponderables may be, the stakes could turn out to be enormous for any drastic departure from the proven exchange rate regimes adopted by all three Chinese entities, which are all basically tied one way or the other to the US dollar.

In more practical terms, given the basic Chinese policy orientation and the fundamental economic rationale underlying capital account control, restricting currency convertibility to the processing trade at a fixed rate to the US dollar, there seems little room left for Hong Kong or Taiwanese authorities to engage in an independent exchange rate policy, because of their heavy dependence on the mainland for FDI outflows for export processing activities. For example, a de-pegging of the Hong Kong dollar from the US dollar would almost surely result in a devaluation, and in the absence of a simultaneous move on the part of mainland China, would inevitably result in increases in new FDI costs on the mainland. However, the processing trade, which caters to Western export markets, may not be affected, to the extent that imported materials for processing and the exported commodities are both priced in foreign currency.

More seriously, perhaps, a devaluation of the Hong Kong dollar or new Taiwan dollar would only help to thwart the emerging access, long fought for by investors from Hong Kong and Taiwan, to the domestic mainland market. The devaluation of the new Taiwan dollar in late 1997 is a good case in point, in that, as a result, many consumer goods industries of Taiwanese origin operating on the mainland, especially food processing, which relies extensively on Japan and Taiwan for imports of spices and packaging materials, had to immediately suspend their production because of their inability to withstand price competition from domestic producers.

Thus, to enhance stability in the processing trade and to facilitate further economic integration, a Bretton Woods type of agreement among Hong Kong, Taiwan, and mainland China, tacit or otherwise, would seem to be desirable. Whether this should develop further to a formal monetary integration in the direction of, say, a yuan bloc, following full convertibility of the renminbi by 2020 or before (China's pledge to Asia-Pacific Economic Cooperation in 1997), is, of course, a matter for conjecture.

A more sustainable form of economic cooperation within Greater China should be sought in the real sectors against the background of increased economic interaction between the three Chinese entities during the past two decades or so. To recapitulate, for Hong Kong, conventional labour-intensive, export-oriented manufacturing activities have almost wholly relocated to mainland China. The process has not, however, resulted in any degree of technological upgrading for the remaining, dwindling number of factories in Hong

Kong. In addition, the sunset industries that were removed to the mainland have not received any policy impetus from mainland authorities for technological innovations. Rather, the enormous pressures for generating employment on the mainland have tended to postpone indefinitely the application of any capital-intensive, labour-saving production techniques to these industries.

It was not until after the 1997 handover that the new Hong Kong government looked for ways to cooperate with the mainland in developing new technology and high value added industries to create a new industrial profile for the Special Administrative Region (SAR).[27] While new and practical technological frontiers may eventually be identified and new marketable products with high value added created, the new initiatives represent, nonetheless, a lag of more than ten years behind Korea, Singapore, and Taiwan, which have all gained strong footholds in the global market in electronics and computers. The new approach adopted by the Hong Kong government is, therefore, not entirely uncontroversial. Apart from relative abundance in capital supply and perhaps some comparative advantage in accessing global technological and market information, it seems questionable that, in the long run, mainland collaborators will have to continue to depend on the SAR for such new ventures. Against this background, many major Hong Kong industrialists prefer, rather, to see Hong Kong developed into a fully-fledged Manhattan for the whole of China.

Taiwan appears to be quite different from Hong Kong with respect to industrial cooperation with the mainland. While similar to the Hong Kong exodus in which a wide range of labour-intensive light manufactures (garments, toys, games and sport requisites, clocks and watches, metal products, plastic articles, and so on) have been removed to the mainland, the vacuum has been rapidly filled by the high valued added new industries alluded to earlier. This is a clear case of regional specialization within the Greater China context. More importantly, the relocating of the sunset industries to the mainland has also been increasingly accompanied by larger upstream industries from Taiwan, and increasingly matched by the necessary input supplies from mainland sources as well to substitute for imports from Japan and elsewhere.

The upshot is that the export processing industry on the mainland involving Hong Kong and Taiwanese investors is now basically divided into two different sectors. The first, lower-tier sector (comprising conventional export processing lines) relies essentially on input supplies from Taiwan and mainland sources. The second, higher-tier sector (which includes food products, pharmaceuticals, metal processing, machine parts and components, and the like), continues to derive its input supplies from overseas, principally from Japan. This clearly reflects increased sophistication in regional economic specialization in East Asia, and there is little doubt that the evolving pattern of regional cooperation will transcend the Asian financial crisis to become even more firmly established in the twenty-first century.

In retrospect, economic cooperation within Greater China as it has evolved over the past two decades was single-handedly triggered by China's drastic policy reorientation in 1978–79 in favour of reintegrating China with the global economy. It was also greatly facilitated by the equally unexpected political relaxation in Taiwan in 1987 that allowed Taiwanese residents to visit China, and eventually to invest on the mainland. Viewed this way, two crucial factors may eventually trigger another significant breakthrough to bring the Chinese economy fully into the aegis of globalization. The first is the Taiwanese authorities' possible abandonment of the third country rule, coupled with full liberalization of FDI and trade flows across the Taiwan Strait.

The second crucial factor relates to the admission of China into the World Trade Organization, with all the ensuing implications for trade and investment liberalization in relation to the highly protected Chinese industrial system. Given the increased size of the Chinese economy, this might help to alter the global context of FDI and trade flows in the longer term, and both Hong Kong and Taiwan would clearly be the first to be fully integrated with the entire Chinese economic system to ensure an even more stable and sustained economic relationship.

Given also the current Chinese economic relationships with the outside world, admission into the World Trade Organization is likely to further enhance China's integration with the advanced, industrial West, rather than to affect its relationship with its Southeast Asian neighbours. Neither is this to say, however, that growing Chinese economic power will eventually marginalize the importance of Southeast Asian countries. A more likely scenario is that as China gradually becomes an industrial powerhouse in Asia, it will fuel growth and industrialization, and join Japan to become a crucial supplier of the bulk of industrial producer goods to their Asian neighbours. Moreover, the huge and highly diversified Chinese economy promises to provide sufficient market niches for the highly export-oriented ASEAN countries to diversify their overseas markets. This will all help to create a more integrated Asia-Pacific economic setting, with enhanced and sustainable economic stability for all countries concerned.

8

Financial Restructuring for Economic Recovery in China and the Hong Kong SAR*

China and the Hong Kong Special Administrative Region (HKSAR) are two disparate economic entities, but ones that have been linked through increased capital and trade flows over the past fifteen years or so. They form an economic nexus that, upon closer scrutiny, defies any textbook definition of regional economic integration. There are several aspects to this particular regional system of economic linkages that are important to our understanding of how the Chinese governments in Beijing and Hong Kong have responded differently to the Asian financial crisis.

First, under the "one country, two systems" blueprint (adopted for Hong Kong's reversion to Chinese sovereignty on 1 July 1997), the Hong Kong currency, inherited from the colonial past, has remained fully convertible. This is clearly the single most important political provision for keeping the SAR intact as a separate economic system. However, as the Chinese renminbi is not convertible for capital account transactions (the current account made convertible as recently as December 1996), international currency speculators directed their attacks with full force on the Hong Kong dollar in 1997/1998, amidst the unfolding Asian financial turmoil.

Second, foreign direct investment from Hong Kong (which makes up around two-thirds of China's global FDI stock) represents, for the most part, a "complete migration" of manufacturing plants from the SAR to the Chinese hinterland. Moreover, under the persistent Chinese policy dictate that foreign

---

* Reprinted from "Financial restructuring for economic recovery in China and Hong Kong", in Fu-chen Lo and T. Palanivel (eds.), *Financial Restructuring and Economic Perspectives in East Asia,* Tokyo: United Nations University Institute of Advanced Studies, 2000, pp. 127–44.

investors should "balance their own foreign exchange requirements", Hong Kong FDI in China almost entirely caters to the export market rather than the Chinese domestic market. The Chinese FDI strategy represents clearly an ambitious "leapfrog to export-oriented foreign investment". It stands therefore in sharp contrast to FDI undertaken by large multinational corporations from Japan in Southeast Asia or, for that matter, from the United States and European Union in China. This has essentially been for import substitution, and constitutes a system of vertical industrial integration, with the FDI host and recipient countries "splicing up the value chain". Under such circumstances, the Chinese hinterland as a production base, to the extent that it has been spared from the Asian financial meltdown, has actually provided a safe haven for Hong Kong export manufacturers.[1]

Third, with few exceptions, Hong Kong manufacturers based in China are all engaged in export processing. The overwhelming proportion of inputs are supplied from outside through Hong Kong, and the processed products shipped back to the SAR for exports to overseas markets, the United States and Western Europe in particular. Export orders or letters of credit from overseas buyers are normally received by the parent company or affiliated firm in Hong Kong, not through the mainland Chinese banking system, while foreign exchange outlays on imported materials and on the necessary processing machines and equipment are also incurred outside of China. This particular mode of operation implies specifically that both foreign exchange receipts and expenditure made on the part of Hong Kong investors in China are basically shielded from the volatility of the renminbi. It thus clearly flies in the face of international currency speculators who believe that a yuan devaluation would inevitably call for the de-pegging (i.e., devaluation) of the Hong Kong dollar from the US dollar.[2]

Viewed this way, the repeated speculative attacks on the Hong Kong dollar since the Asian currency crisis erupted in Thailand in July 1997 seem to be essentially a matter of international hedge funds exploiting some popularly mistaken, gross perception that the value of the Hong Kong currency is invariably bound up with the Chinese renminbi, as a result of the SAR's synergistic economic relationships with the mainland.

Whatever the underlying factors, the HKSAR economy was almost brought to its knees by frequent speculative currency attacks in 1998 (the GDP was down by 5.1% compared with a 5.3% growth in 1997), while the Chinese hinterland has basically remained unscathed (GDP still recording an impressive 7.8% growth in 1998).

How did the SAR government cope with the Asian financial contagion and would there have been better alternatives? This raises a number of linked questions: Would the present policy approach bring about an early economic recovery? Could it prevent similar crises in the future? Can China continue to be wholly insulated from similar regional financial disruption? What preventive policy measures have been taken in China? Would they be effective? What would the long-term implications be for the country's economic growth? The remaining sections of this chapter address these questions and highlight the major problems involved.

Hong Kong

There is no doubt that Hong Kong was drawn by default into the Asian financial turmoil. Unlike most of the Southeast Asian financial "dominos", Hong Kong, prior to the crisis, enjoyed both solid internal and external balances, and was indeed endowed with a very substantial foreign exchange reserve (US$92.8 billion), next only to the Chinese mainland (US$139.9 billion) and Japan (US$220.8 billion), the world's largest foreign reserves holder.[3] Moreover, Hong Kong also has one of the best managed financial systems in Asia. For example, the capital adequacy ratio for the entire banking system still stood at 17% (the world's highest) in October 1998, more than double the standard requirement (8%) of the Basel agreement (*TKP*, 28 November 1998). There were of course signs of increased asset inflation as a result of continuous capital inflows from both China and Southeast Asia to take advantage of the brisk economic prospects offered in Hong Kong. However, the latent property bubble in Hong Kong was probably no more serious than elsewhere in Southeast Asia, relative to the particular economic and financial strengths of the SAR just discussed.

This strong background had certainly greatly helped to enhance the SAR government's resolve to fend off any speculative currency attack. More importantly, the repeated pledge by the Chinese government to throw its weight behind Hong Kong with its massive foreign reserves for defending the SAR's US dollar peg had also greatly boosted the confidence of the Hong Kong Monetary Authority. No sooner was the Chinese pledge first made in late July

1997 than it already became quite clear that a most defensive China-HKSAR alliance was formed for the ferocious currency battle.

The upshot is familiar to many, but it should be briefly rehearsed as a background for reflecting on the relative merits of the government's policy towards the crisis. This involved a dramatic interbank liquidity squeeze, a pervasive credit crunch, enormous interest rate pressures, plummeting property and equity markets, widespread business failures, forced salary and wage cuts, rising unemployment and, not least, increased labour militancy which rendered the traditional automatic wage-price readjustment mechanism in Hong Kong increasingly inoperative, thus threatening an early economic recovery. Rigorous remedial policy measures were taken by the SAR government in early summer 1998, when it was first revealed that Hong Kong's GDP registered a decline by 2.0% for the first quarter (later confirmed to be 2.6%, the first negative growth in more than two decades). The remedial measures included the suspension of government land sales (the major source of budget revenue), and the tacit abandonment of the ambitious housing provision target (85,000 units per year), with a view to stabilizing the property market; tax rebates

Figure 8.1 Trends of GDP and Other Major Economic Indicators in Hong Kong, 1991–1998 (%)

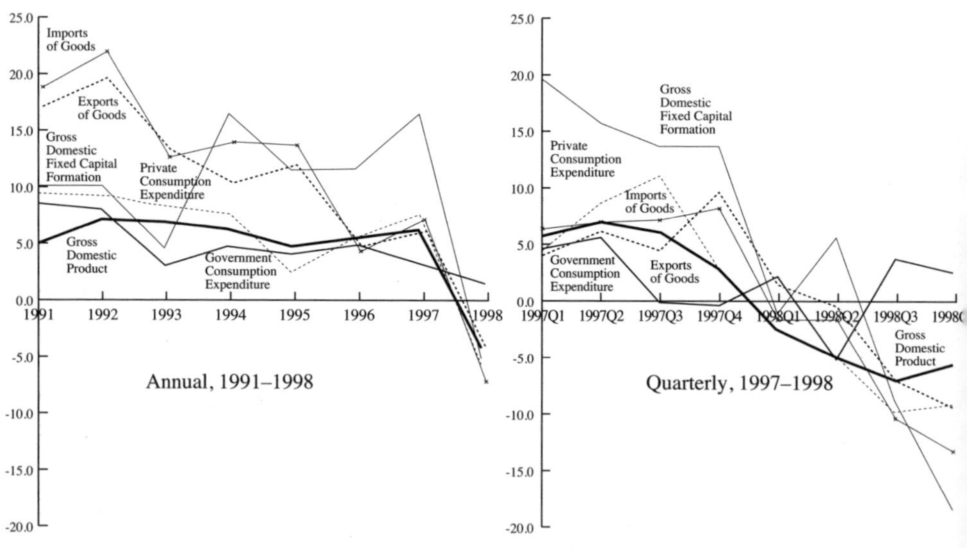

Sources: HKGCSD—*EGDP*, various issues.

and tax reductions for boosting consumer confidence; voluntary salary freeze for senior government officials as an appeal to workers for wage restraint; and, more importantly, the early launching of a number of large infrastructure projects, in conjunction with an emerging deficit spending framework, for the explicit purpose of mitigating unemployment pressures (i.e., first ever Keynesian economics adopted in Hong Kong).[4] Nonetheless, these measures have proved to be largely ineffective, with major economic indicators continuing to deteriorate throughout 1998 (see Figure 8.1).

It is obvious that the continuous economic downturn in Hong Kong under the impact of the Asian crisis precipitated further speculative attacks on the Hong Kong dollar in the summer of 1998, converging subsequently into the full-scale onslaught and the preemptive intrusion by the HKSAR government into the stock market in August 1998. Specifically, in what the financial secretary, Donald Tsang, later dubbed as a "double play", international hedge funds, which had accumulated huge short positions in the Hang Seng Index futures market, dumped around US$4 billion equivalent of Hong Kong dollars (which were allegedly purposefully raised through international financial institutions in the Hong Kong dollar debt market in Hong Kong since February) in the spot market, aiming to push up local interest rates, while shorting in the US dollar forward and the equity markets in order to push down the Hang Seng futures index.[5]

In response, the Hong Kong Monetary Authority moved swiftly with the Exchange Fund money to acquire 33 leading corporate shares to forestall the total collapse of the stock market. The stake involved amounted to a massive US$15.2 billion, i.e., around 16% of the SAR's total foreign reserves. In the words of the financial secretary, the unprecedented and indeed highly controversial move should not be seen as an intervention of the stock market per se. But rather, it was an absolutely unavoidable fiat for upholding the integrity of the paramount US dollar-linked exchange rate regime. While the argument appears persuasive, the question is, of course, for how many more rounds the Exchange Fund, sizeable as it may be, would possibly be able to wrangle with, say, George Soros.

Mindful of the potential risks involved, the HKMA came up with a bold initiative in early September 1998, for revamping the established currency board, in order to help enhance both confidence in the Hong Kong dollar and financial liquidity in the entire banking system for confronting potential future currency attacks. Essentially, the new initiative stipulates, first of all, that henceforth all

Exchange Fund papers will only be issued against the inflow of new funds. This makes the entire monetary base fully backed by foreign reserves.[6] The other provision is to commit the Hong Kong government to a new "convertibility undertaking", whereby all licenced banks in Hong Kong are allowed to convert the Hong Kong dollars held with the Exchange Fund into US dollars at the fixed exchange rate of HK$7.50 to the US dollar. Note that previously the conversion was restricted to the "legal tender in circulation", and in fact at the less favourable official benchmark of HK$7.80 for cash arbitrage. Another critical measure is to establish a "discount window" in place of the restrictive "liquidity adjustment facility", whereby the banks may borrow, whenever deemed necessary, from the HKMA against their holdings of Exchange Fund bills and notes as collateral. This greatly helps the banks to cope with any drastic overnight demand for liquidity.

The new policy measures did indeed result in the prime lending rate in Hong Kong declining successively for six or seven rounds, from the high of 10% in October 1998 down to 8.5% in late April 1999 (*TKP*, 1 May 1999). This helped to substantially narrow the gap with the US dollar interest rate, and thus mitigate the "interest rate arbitrage" for keeping intact the US dollar peg. Nonetheless, the interest rate reductions in Hong Kong seem to have also been prompted by similar moves by the US Federal Reserve Bank and, perhaps even more importantly, by the withdrawal of the international hedge funds following their debacle in Russia, Brazil and elsewhere in summer 1998.

With hindsight, however, the question which should be raised is whether the massive defence of the US dollar peg was really worthwhile. Several points may be made.

First, the major reason for upholding the HK$7.8 per US dollar linked system is to forestall a massive capital flight from Hong Kong. But, unfortunately, the defence, which greatly pushed up local interest rates, did not help to recall capital inflows. Due to the high risk of holding the local currency, there was a frenzied attempt made by local residents to convert the Hong Kong dollar into US dollar. Between September 1997 and August 1998, US dollar deposits in Hong Kong jumped by 34%, compared with a marginal increase of 2.1% for Hong Kong dollar deposits (*HSEM,* 1998). This is clearly the case of a "double loss" scenario, with exorbitant interest rates impairing both consumption and investment confidence without replenishing capital inflows to help reinvigorate the economy.

Second, judging by the pace with which in the past few months foreign capital returned to the devastated Southeast Asian countries and South Korea, and their stock markets and foreign exchange rates regained the lost ground, there seems to be no reason to suggest that, had the Hong Kong dollar been devalued, say, following Singapore and Taiwan in late 1997, the SAR economy would not have been able to recover at an even earlier stage and in a more rigorous style. This is especially so in the light of Hong Kong's relative economic strengths, sound banking and financial institutional setting, strong fiscal and monetary disciplines, and indeed, the continuous robustness of the Chinese hinterland.

Third, it remains of course a matter of judgment as to the nature of the recent massive portfolio capital influx which have, on 4 May 1999, helped to greatly boost the Hang Seng Index in Hong Kong to the post-crisis high of 13,559.69 (only 18% short of the historical high of 16,673 obtained in August 1997).[7] Joseph Yam, chief executive of HKMA, sees it generally as bona fide investments rather than speculative cash influx,[8] in the wake of the Dow Jones corporate shares showing increased signs of being overbought. Yam also believes that "the credit contraction will no longer continue (in 1999)" (*SCMP*, 5 May 1999), in light of surging bank deposits outstripping increases in bank lending.

Fourth, a Hong Kong dollar devaluation in response to the Asian crisis should not necessarily affect the SAR economy adversely in the context of the Hong Kong-China economic synergy, to the extent that it basically would not curtail Hong Kong's foreign exchange earnings from export processing based in the Chinese mainland; given of course that the export markets remain intact. This separate assumption did not quite hold unfortunately for both the HKSAR and China, but what happened was essentially a result of greatly impaired import capabilities in the Southeast Asian countries, South Korea, and Japan, under the impact of the Asian economic meltdown (see Chapter 6).

Fifth, the major, and perhaps the only drawback of a Hong Kong dollar devaluation for the SAR is increased FDI costs in the Chinese mainland, assuming that the Chinese yuan would not depreciate in tandem. However, this should also be weighed against the reduced FDI flows to China that occurred in 1998, as a result of severe credit crunch and high interest rate pressures imposed on Hong Kong investors by the massive defence of the HK-US dollar peg. From the perspective of the Chinese government, however, a Hong Kong dollar devaluation was clearly undesirable, as it would curtail FDI intake from

Hong Kong, given the overwhelming importance of the SAR in this respect, quite apart from the political implications for China relative to the newly born HKSAR. Note that Hong Kong, via FDI flows, makes up annually around 15% of total fixed assets investment made in the Chinese mainland and an even much more significant share in China's exports and manufacturing employment.[9] It seems therefore quite likely that a delinking of the Hong Kong dollar from the US dollar would call for a concomitant renminbi devaluation, rather than the other way round.

Sixth, irrespective of the potential impact of a Hong Kong dollar devaluation or otherwise, the SAR's FDI flows to China probably hinge more on the availability of Japanese funds than anything else. This is because Hong Kong's investments in China are closely tied in with Japanese supplies of input materials, as well as machine and equipment needed for export processing, and are therefore most heavily dependent on financing from Japanese banks based in Hong Kong.[10] Unfortunately, this particular source of funds had been substantially withdrawn in the wake of the Asian crisis, although the withdrawal is essentially a result of domestic difficulties in Japan (cf. *TKP*, 15 June 1999.)

Taken together, a devaluation of the Hong Kong dollar at an early stage of the Asian financial contagion might not necessarily appear to be a less viable alternative to the massive defence by the HKMA of the US dollar-peg system. An early devaluation by floating the Hong Kong dollar, or a re-pegging to, say, a basket of hard currencies, coupled with an early revamping of the currency board along the lines as was later done in September 1998, could prove to be helpful in mitigating speculative currency attacks. The potential costs involved in terms of the economic consequences of capital flight might not necessarily be more substantial than what the present approach has imposed upon the SAR economy since early 1998.

A strong reservation about a Hong Kong dollar devaluation is that, as with the widespread fear for a renminbi devaluation, it might trigger another round of competitive currency devaluation in ASEAN countries. However, judging by the pace at which in recent months all major Southeast Asian currencies have re-appreciated against the US dollar, the original catastrophic devaluation in late 1997 had clearly greatly overshot the economic reality, as a matter of unwarranted financial contagion and "herd behaviour" on the part of investors,[11] leaving thus hardly any room for further deterioration.

China

Mainland China was clearly much less vulnerable to the Asian financial contagion, primarily for the simple reason that the Chinese currency is not convertible for capital account transactions. In addition, foreign capital inflows are dominated by FDI, and even capital borrowing (for indirect investment) is skewed towards medium and longterm debt, unlike most countries engulfed in the Asian crisis where such borrowings are essentially short-term in nature. Moreover, China has been running an increased trade surplus for most of the 1990s, and by 1997/1998 the country has accumulated an impressive foreign reserve to the tune of US$140 billion. Unlike most Southeast Asian countries and South Korea, China therefore need not depend on capital inflows to finance any trade deficit.

By contrast with other Asian countries, China also enjoyed favourable internal balance. The major economic problems encountered domestically by the Chinese government in the past couple of years have been negative inflation and reduced consumption incentives rather than inflation, overheating consumption and investment expenditure.

The impact of the Asian crisis on the Chinese economy is indeed quite marginal, limited essentially to FDI intake and exports. Both experienced a near-zero growth in 1998. The relative slowdown in FDI intake from Hong Kong, as discussed in Chapter 7, was offset by remarkable increases in FDI inflows from the United States and European Union countries, which continue to place confidence in the huge Chinese market, especially in the wake of the country's imminent accession to the WTO.

Similarly, severe reductions in exports to ASEAN countries, South Korea, and Japan as a result of their greatly impaired import capabilities, were overcompensated by increases in exports to the United States, Western Europe and elsewhere, to result in an increase, albeit a marginal one, in total exports from US$182.7 billion in 1997 to US$183.76 in 1998 (see Figure 8.2).

Clearly, the problems associated with sluggish FDI intake and export performance were, nonetheless, aggravated by reduced consumption expenditure (for reason of an entirely domestic origin) that prevailed despite negative inflation (for two years down the track now) and six or seven rounds of official interest rates trimming since 1996, (i.e., prior to the eruption of the Asian crisis). As a result, the Chinese government had to resort to renewed prime—pumping deficit spending on large infrastructure projects to prop up investment

Figure 8.2 Value of China's Exports and Monthly Year-to-Year Changes by Major Regions and Trading Partners, 1997–1998 (US$ million and %)

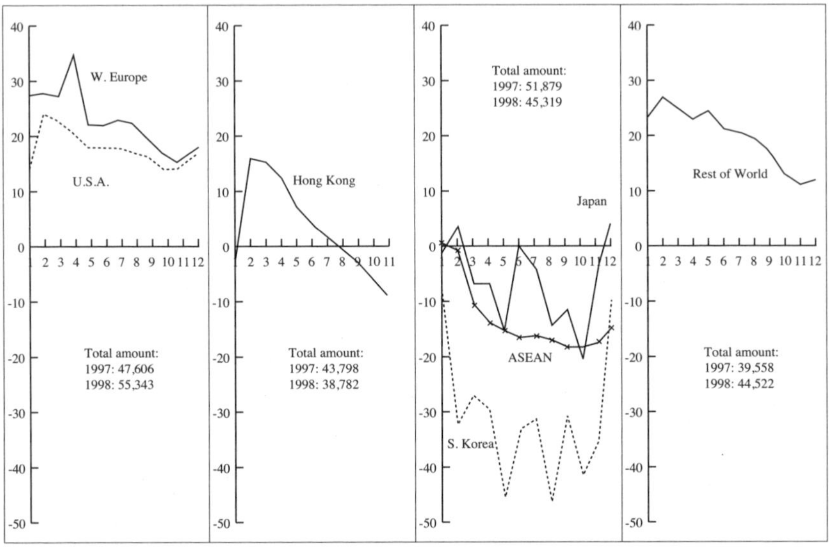

Sources: CSICSC—*CLS*, various issues.

expenditure, in a desperate effort to realize the much celebrated GDP growth target of 8% for 1998, which was originally set in early 1998 in oblivion of the potential impact of the emerging Asian crisis. The upshot is most remarkable: an impressive 7.8% GDP growth in 1998, making China one of the top performers at the global scale. The country has therefore emerged basically unscathed from the Asian crisis.

Nonetheless, the Chinese government is clearly mindful of the wide-ranging implications of the Asian crisis as it may bear on the longer-term economic performance and development of the country. The reason is obvious: the remarkable resemblance China bears to most of the devastated Southeast Asian countries and South Korea, in terms of all the hallmarks of an ailing banking and financial system. Briefly, these include the seriously declining capital adequacy ratio of the major banks owned by the state, continuous rapid buildup of bank credits and non-performing loans, and grossly inadequate loan loss reserves in the entire banking system.

It is difficult to come to grips with the exact magnitude of the non-performing loans incurred by the entire Chinese banking system. According to some

Western estimates, the ratio ranges from 25% to 40% of total loan portfolios (*SCMP*, 10 April 1999). Dai Xianglong, the Governor of the People's Bank of China, put it, however, at less than 10%, with merely 2.9% classified as bad debts by the end of 1998 (*ibid*.). If one considers that the Chinese method of classifying non-performing loans is much more lenient than prevalent Western standards, it seems quite likely that China's banks taken as a whole, which control almost half of the assets of the entire financial system, are approaching, if not already have crossed, the 15% threshold of non-performing loans (net of loss provisions) which is internationally considered as likely to initiate a systemic financial distress.

What practical measures has the Chinese government taken to cope with the immediate impact of the Asian financial crisis, and redress, in particular, the country's ailing financial structure? Interestingly, the financial restructuring that has taken place in China in 1998/1999 seems to be largely independent of the short-term impact of the crisis, setting aside the particular effort made to compensate for the decline in FDI inflows and export growth, as it may bear on the government's imperative of achieving the 8% GDP growth target in 1998. Briefly, the short-term measures included concessionary renminbi credits to export joint ventures with Hong Kong and Taiwan investors who were trapped by the liquidity squeeze in their home base; as well as renewed increases in VAT rebates for a wide range of export commodities to enhance international competitiveness, as in effect the rebate is tantamount to a renminbi devaluation against the US dollar.[12] This appears to be quite significant as net export earnings are estimated by a State Statistical Bureau analyst to be contributing to around 16% of GDP growth between 1992 and 1997, as compared to the 44.3% and 39.9% contributions by consumption and investment expenditure respectively.[13]

Another important financial measure was the issuance in August 1998 of treasury bonds amounting to RMB100 billion yuan (US$12 billion) for the ad hoc purpose of boosting infrastructure investments. This was aimed at arresting the GDP decline and was strongly prompted by the enormous losses incurred with the disastrous Yangtze River floods in the summer of 1998. The Chinese vice minister of finance estimated that this would call for a complementary bank loan expansion of a similar amount and would, via the income multiplier effect, help to raise the GDP growth rate by 2.5–3%, although with the anticipated lag the major proportion of the gains could not be realized until the early part of 1999 (*TKP*, 19 November 1998).

As for the measures for overhauling the ailing financial system, these generally fall within two broad categories: (1) to recapitalize the major state-owned banks as a prerequisite for commercializsation, and (2) to reorganize the entire financial and banking system, coupled with the introduction of new banking regulations and practice for enhancing commercialization and banking efficiency. The reform measures generally date back to a major blueprint formulated in 1993, but they have been most rigorously implemented only after the November 1997 National Financial Work Conference convened by the State Council in Beijing in the wake of the unfolding Asian financial crisis.

Recapitalization of the four major state-owned banks which, for historical reasons have been increasingly loaded with insurmountable non-performing loans, is clearly of critical importance, as a first step for converting them into commercially selfsustainable independent economic entities. The single most important measure taken by the government in 1998 is the issuance in late May of treasury bonds, totalling RMB270 billion yuan (US$32.65 billion), for the ad hoc purpose of injecting sufficient funds into the four major state commercial banks to meet the Basel standard of capital adequacy ratio of 8%.[14] Earlier on, in late March 1998, the banks' "fiscal reserves" held with the Ministry of Finance were converted back into their own reserves to fulfil the legal reserve requirements, which were then reduced from 13% to 8%, with a view to enhancing their lending capacity. At the same time, an increased amount of funds, totalling RMB40 billion yuan (US$4.84 billion) in 1998, was also allocated by the central government to finance write-off of bad debts incurred by state enterprises, which account for the ultimate source of the banks' deteriorating financial health.[15]

However, what is regarded by Dai Xianglong, the Governor of the People's Bank, as truly the first major breakthrough in financial reform in China is the establishment in 1998 of the nine major regional branches of the People's Bank—the central bank of China. The reorganization is clearly patterned after the US Federal Reserve system which has 12 regional branches.[16] By 31 December 1998, all nine regional banks (based in Tianjin, Shenyang, Shanghai, Nanjing, Jinan, Wuhan, Guangzhou, Chengdu, and Xi'an) were firmly established to replace the 32 provincial-level branches. The reorganization has effectively ended the conventional system of dual leadership whereby the provincial branches were presumably subject to control by both the People's Bank in Beijing and the provincial administration, but were nonetheless effectively under the command of the provincial governors in terms of important personnel appointments and bank lending decisions. The old system clearly helped to breed nepotism, crony capitalism and corruption, as was similarly observed in Indonesia and South Korea, and as an important source for the accelerated accumulation of non-performing loans and bad debt.

Unlike the provincial branches, the new trans-provincial branches do not enjoy "natural jurisdiction" over the broad regions under their purview, which are each largely demarcated as an economic rather than administrative region. Rather, they are placed under the vertical control of the Central Bank, and act on its behalf essentially to implement national monetary policy with regards to legal reserve requirements, rediscounting, interest rate readjustment, and cash management; as well as to manage foreign exchange, external debt, and balance of payments within the region.[17]

Another important aspect of the drastic reorganization is that the regional branches will no longer be responsible for non-bank businesses, in particular, both insurance and securities transactions. In fact, parallel to the creation of the nine regional branches, the first Chinese securities law was promulgated, on 29 December 1998, to pave the way for independent development of the capital markets under the watchdog—the National Securities Supervisory Authority in the State Council. The longer-term objective is clearly to provide a fully-fledged alternative system to the established banking monopolies for investment financing. This is of paramount importance as, in China, and to a lesser extent also in Korea, Indonesia, and Thailand, "the lack of well-developed capital markets made it possible for bank loans to be systemically under-priced over the longer run, encouraging excess borrowing and capital formation on the part of companies with preferred access to credit—state-owned firms in China, the *chaebol* in Korea, those well connected to the government in Indonesia and Thailand—while leaving the rest of the economy starved for funds".[18]

Another important step taken for reforming the banking system include the abolition in January 1998 of the conventional mandatory bank loan quotas imposed by the People's Bank of China. The state commercial banks are now basically free in making their lending decisions subject to the Central Bank's regulation on the basis of asset-to-liability ratios. At the same time, a more stringent system of classifying nonperforming loans has been adopted based on the standards of the US and other advanced Western countries (*TKP*, 4 November 1998).

Lately, in April 1999, a financial assets management corporation, named Cinda, was created under the Construction Bank of China—a first ever in China for tackling bad debts through mergers, acquisitions and securitization—an approach which is also patterned after Western experience of the early 1990s, and is entirely consistent with China's overall market-oriented reform programme.

However, the most important measure taken by far in this respect is the central government's hard decision made in early October 1998 not to bailout Guangdong International Trust and Investment Corporation—the largest national *itic* in China, second only to the internationally well-known CITIC. GITIC, the flagship fund-raising vehicle of the Guangdong provincial government, was declared bankrupt in October 1998 with an estimated financial obligation of RMB38.77 billion yuan (*SCMP*, 4 May 1999) and an external debt of US$203 billion.[19] Several major Hong Kong banks involved were forced to drastically alter their balance sheets with 100% bad debt provisions. In the words of the chief executive of the Bank of China Group in Hong Kong, the central government's decision "marks the first step towards the establishment of a mature mainland financial system, (by abolishing) the customary practices of Chinese enterprise (of relying on their state background and an acceptance that they would never be closed down)" (*SCMP*, 7 May 1999).

There is no doubt that the Chinese government has been earnestly pursuing a systemic redress of the country's financial system since the Asian crisis, to avoid possible future bank crisis in the context of an emerging market-based economic system. The reform measures taken in China generally parallel the call for banking and financial reforms in some Southeast Asian countries devastated by the Asian crisis. But fortunately, financial restructuring in China can take place on a real economic base that has basically remained unscathed by the crisis. This clearly also helps to provide breathing space for the necessary reform of state-owned enterprises, which have continued to incur large losses to add to the already insurmountable non-performing loans and bad debts of the banking system. Without a synchronized resolution of the SOEs' losses, any further substantial capital injection by the government to rescue the insolvent Chinese banking system would, with the implied increases in fiscal costs, only help to increasingly slow down overall economic growth, and thus precipitate unemployment pressures.[20] It remains to be seen, whether Premier Zhu Rongji's celebrated programme for effectively turning around the major SOEs by the end of year 2000 will prove to be workable. But, meanwhile, the Chinese government will clearly continue to be confronted with the enormous predicament of how to skilfully phase-in the required recapitalization to make the major state-owned commercial banks at least temporary commercially viable.

Looking ahead

In his 1999/2000 budget speech delivered on 3 March 1999, the HKSAR Financial Secretary Donald Tsang forecast a GDP growth of only 0.5% for 1999. The dire forecast clearly underpins the impressive policy measures he has proposed to eventually bring the SAR economy back on track. The measures include, above all, an immediate tax rebate of 10% of the total paid for fiscal 1997/1998 for both businesses and households. This is clearly intended to boost both consumption and investment expenditure. In addition, negotiation is under way with the Disneyland Company for putting up a second theme park in Asia in Hong Kong, next to Tokyo. Similar projects include the construction of a fisherman's wharf in Aberdeen (the familiar tourist favourite on Hong Kong Island), patterned after San Francisco's popular tourist spot; as well as the development of a "cyber-port" worth HK$13 billion (US$1.67 billion) to provide high-technology information services to businesses and the financial sector in Hong Kong and the region. These have all come on top of the earmarked budget expenditure of HK$230 billion (US$29.49 billion) given in the previous year's budget for large-scale infrastructure and public housing projects four years down the track.

Whether these long-term projects would be able to help restore private investment confidence or eventually compensate for the declined private investment expenditure should remain a separate issue. What seems to be quite clear is that the SAR has become far too expensive as a tourist and regional financial services centre, as a result of the relative appreciation of the Hong Kong dollar, not to mention with the cloud of global financial uncertainty still hanging over the SAR. Even with the recent financial euphoria that overwhelmed the local equity market, the chief executive of the HKMA, Joseph Yam, optimistic as he has been, is still mindful of a possible regroup of international hedge funds to renew their attack on the Hong Kong currency. Thus, for good reasons, Yam remains adamant that an international solution must be sought for a new global financial order to ensure regional stability. This is clearly of utmost importance to such an entirely open, small economy as the Hong Kong SAR.

In this context, the only spot that offers a ray of hope and comfort is the "China connection". As long as the home base for Hong Kong's export processing remains intact and the North American and West European markets remain resilient with their import demand, there should be no grounds for any apocalyptic conjecture to prevail. This, of course, goes for China as well, given that a major proportion of her exports are channelled through Hong Kong to similar overseas destinations.

However, to the extent that both the renminbi and the Hong Kong dollar have become overvalued relative to most of the devalued Southeast Asian currencies against the US dollar, and to the extent that the J-curve seems to have increasingly taken effect with respect to the competing Southeast Asian exporters,[21] pressures for a devaluation of both the renminbi and the Hong Kong dollar will inevitably continue to build up. As a matter of fact, in an effort to maintain its threatened export competitiveness, the Chinese government has already, since mid-1998, raised the export VAT rebate rates several times across a wide range of export commodities which are essentially destined for the North American and West European markets, as well as Southeast and East Asian countries. By early 1999, it appears that the full VAT rate of 17% would be very soon exhausted. And this indeed did not help to arrest the accelerated decline in Chinese exports through the early months of 1999.[22]

In a way, the predicament presently faced by the Chinese government seems to be quite similar to the deteriorating export competitiveness plaguing some of the Southeast Asian countries, as a result of the substantial devaluation of the Chinese yuan in January 1994. Professor Lawrence Klein has estimated ASEAN's export losses in that context to be around 20%, and he sees it as a factor underlying the eruption of the Southeast Asian financial crisis in 1997.[23]

One of the reasons frequently given by the Chinese government for not wanting to devalue the yuan amidst the massive devaluation of Southeast Asian currencies and the Korean won in 1997/1998 is the self-imposed obligation to help maintain regional stability, as a renminbi devaluation might well trigger another round of competitive devaluation by ASEAN countries. This might or might not be the case; we really do not know for sure. But now that the dust of the Asian financial upheaval has largely settled and most of the countries involved are well on the path to economic recovery, the question is whether it would be more opportune for China to adopt a more flexible exchange rate regime. Jeffrey Sachs, for example, advocates "a downward adjustment [of the yuan] of 'a few percentage points' to counter the impact of the region-wide devaluation which have hurt mainland exports", and is confident that "a gradual devaluation of the yuan [would help to ease] the pressures within the mainland economy" and that "this could be achieved with relatively little pain for Hong Kong or the region". Sachs made these points at the Credit Suisse First Boston's Asian Investment Conference held in Hong Kong on 24 March 1999 (*SCMP*, 25 March 1999).

Over the longer run, the most crucial question remains whether the Chinese government would be able to effectively sustain the present pattern and pace of restructuring the entire financial and banking system, hopefully without—in the face of the formidable requirements for bank recapitalization—impairing the country's good record of economic growth. The restructuring appears indeed to be all the more imperative and urgent, given China's imminent accession to WTO, which clearly will herald a new era of banking and financial opening to the outside world. Judging by the terms imposed by the US on China (during the Sino-American negotiations in Washington in April 1999), requiring China to entirely lift ownership control and geographic restrictions for foreign banking interests and insurance business in three to five years,[24] it seems quite clear that failing a timely restructuring and strengthening of the country's financial system, China would inevitably be swiftly colonized by various Western banking and financial institutions. This explains clearly why Premier Zhu Rongji returned from Washington to Beijing in April resolute not to yield to US demand in this particularly sensitive sphere.

9

The "China Factor" vs. the "US Dollar Peg" in the Success Story of Hong Kong*

The Hong Kong dollar was pegged to the US dollar at the rate of HK$7.8 in October 1983. Not long afterwards, commencing in April 1984, China made a decisive move to court more foreign investment by opening fourteen cities along the eastern seaboard.[1] Launched with entirely different objectives, these two important policy measures have nevertheless jointly and profoundly affected the performance of the Hong Kong economy over the past two decades.

The dollar peg, aimed at stabilizing the Hong Kong currency following the severe loss of investor confidence resulting from the deadlock in the Sino-British negotiations over the future of Hong Kong,[2] immediately deprived the Hong Kong government of monetary policy flexibility in countering cyclical economic movement, and actually contributed to increased economic instability. However, export manufacturers were permitted to relocate to the Chinese hinterland to take advantage of the open-door policy, and thereby avoid the pressures of spiralling wage and land costs. The manufacturers were able to remain competitive, which was crucial to a small, entirely open economy as Hong Kong's, and the integrity of the peg was upheld.

The goal of this article is to study the interplay between the so-called "China factor" and the dollar peg in Hong Kong in the run up to the 1997 handover, through the Asian financial crisis and beyond. The first sections describe the general changes in the economy following the adoption of the peg, and the factors precipitating the complete migration of Hong Kong's manufacturing

* Reprinted from "The interplay of the 'China factor' and US dollar peg in the Hong Kong Economy" (coauthored with Raymond Ng), *The China Quarterly* (*CQ*), No. 170 (June 2002), pp. 105–30.

industries across the border to China. This is followed by a detailed analysis of how the manufacturers' exodus helped to expand the economic base of Hong Kong's export industries on the one hand, while keeping Hong Kong's exports internationally competitive on the other, despite a bout of accelerated domestic inflation caused by the peg before 1997/1998. The analysis extends to the present, examining how the peg has fuelled deflation but the "China factor" may have helped mitigate it.

Important questions are raised about the peg in light of the disastrous consequences of the Asian financial crisis for some Asian economies, and about the concomitant search for a more viable exchange rate regime. The article concludes that despite the increased integration of the Hong Kong and mainland China economies, the likelihood of the Hong Kong dollar being de-pegged from the US dollar and re-pegged to the Chinese currency is yet remote.

Economic instability under the US dollar peg

The major features of the US dollar peg as adopted in Hong Kong are familiar, but they will be briefly outlined to provide a proper framework for understanding the subsequent economic changes in Hong Kong. In essence, the dollar peg resembles the currency board arrangement. It is a "hard currency" system which requires the issuing of the domestic currency to be fully supported by the holding of US dollar reserves. Whilst the rate of HK$7.8 per US dollar has been fixed for the issuing and redemption of the Hong Kong currency, the exchange rate of the Hong Kong dollar is nevertheless freely determined in the foreign exchange market. The desired exchange rate stability is to be maintained through a self-restoring mechanism in the form of cash and interest rate arbitrage.[3] The primary and only monetary policy objective is to help stabilize any exchange rate fluctuations. A country operating such a currency board should normally enjoy a lower and more stable inflation rate, as a result of the more prudent monetary and fiscal disciplines imposed by the system.

A stable exchange rate is indeed considered crucial for Hong Kong, a small and entirely open economy serving as an international financial centre. The major drawback, however, is that the government is effectively deprived of any autonomous control over money supply. It is therefore not in a position to run any counter-cyclical policy. Hong Kong's money supply is ultimately dependent on its international balance of payments position. In addition, its interest rate must closely follow that of the US, otherwise interest rate arbitrage would set in and lead to exchange rate volatility. A tight money supply and the high interest rates that may ensue could stimulate capital inflow and cause the money supply to increase. Initially, they would perhaps help to contain inflation by easing demand pressure. Thus, under such a currency board system, macroeconomic stability can only be restored by way of internal wage and price readjustments.

The US dollar peg has meant that Hong Kong has been subservient to cycles in the US economy. This was exactly the case in the late 1980s and early 1990s (see Figure 9.1). At that time, Hong Kong had high inflation coupled with strong GDP growth recovery after the 1989 trough. As interest rates in Hong Kong had to be kept in line with those in the US to keep the dollar peg intact, the overheated demand could not be contained by adjusting prevailing interest rates upwards. The result was continuous overheating and persistent inflationary pressure, with real interest rates approaching zero for most of the years after the US dollar peg was adopted, until the trend was abruptly ended by the Asian financial crisis.

It is difficult to distinguish exactly the sources of increased macroeconomic instability in Hong Kong as observed from the late 1980s onwards. As shown in Table 9.1, however, Hong Kong's balance of payments had recorded quite impressive surpluses until the mid-1990s after the US dollar peg was adopted in 1983. This, coupled with increased capital inflow in the form of foreign direct investment (FDI) and portfolio capital taking advantage of the robust economic growth in Hong Kong, seems to have led to remarkable increases in the territory's money supply. Thus, the different measures of money supply (in Table 9.1) all show rate of increases substantially higher than the GDP growth rate, resulting in persistent inflation since the mid-1980s (Figure 9.1).

Theoretically, macroeconomic stability for a country operating under a pegged exchange rate system may be restored automatically through balance of payments readjustment. That is, if a country experiences an economic boom fuelled externally by a balance of payment surplus, prices will adjust upward, with the exchange rate and interest rate being fixed. Higher prices should, however, weaken the economy's price competitiveness, thus discouraging exports and stimulating imports. This will in turn reduce demand pressure, and the deteriorating trade balance will offset the initial expansion in money supply. However, as both the exchange and interest rates are not allowed to adjust, price readjustments to restore macroeconomic stability are bound to be

Table 9.1 Balance of Payments, Money Supply and Inflation in Hong Kong under the US Dollar Peg System, 1983–2000 (HK$ million)

	Balance of payments	M1	Annual change (%)	M2	Annual change (%)	M3	Annual change (%)	Inflation rate (%)
1983	2,179	30,896	–	257,685	–	311,146	–	–
1984	19,078	36,791	19.08	314,081	21.89	388,301	24.80	8.10
1985	25,636	45,266	23.04	390,239	24.25	457,803	17.90	3.20
1986	26,573	56,094	23.92	518,131	32.77	582,208	27.17	2.80
1987	37,993	81,902	46.01	677,042	30.67	743,353	27.68	5.50
1988	40,071	88,834	8.46	824,648	21.80	893,342	20.18	7.50
1989	60,264	94,858	6.78	988,836	19.91	1,060,207	18.68	10.10
1990	49,303	107,509	13.34	1,210,050	22.37	1,288,028	21.49	9.80
1991	44,117	128,497	19.52	1,371,029	13.30	1,435,743	11.47	12.00
1992	41,601	155,557	21.06	1,518,777	10.78	1,574,265	9.65	9.40
1993	63,123	187,608	20.60	1,764,416	16.17	1,823,108	15.81	8.50
1994	12,187	185,334	–1.21	1,992,351	12.92	2,070,831	13.59	8.10
1995	–46,821	190,471	2.77	2,282,849	14.58	2,363,963	14.16	8.70
1996	–16,682	217,460	14.17	2,532,236	10.92	2,611,636	10.48	6.00
1997	–45,613	208,093	–4.31	2,742,993	8.32	2,825,609	8.19	5.70
1998	13,884	197,666	–5.01	3,066,089	11.78	3,122,345	10.50	2.55
1999	66,295	225,156	13.91	3,313,534	8.07	3,361,805	7.67	–3.25

Table 9.1 (to be continued)

Table 9.1 (continued)

	Balance of payments	**M1**	**Annual change (%)**	**M2**	**Annual change (%)**	**M3**	**Annual change (%)**	**Inflation rate (%)**
2000	59,978	243,847	8.30	3,605,213	8.80	3,648,473	8.53	–3.00
1986–90	42,841	85,839	19.70	843,741	25.51	913,428	23.04	7.14
1991–95	22,841	169,493	12.55	1,785,884	13.55	1,853,582	12.93	9.34
1996–00	15,572	218,444	5.41	3,052,013	9.58	3,133,974	9.07	1.60

Notes: (1) The balance of payments covers only visible and invisible trade. HKGCSD did not attempt to compile capital account figures until the late 1990s. As a major international financial centre that is free from any kind of foreign exchange or capital account control, it is extremely difficult and costly for the government to keep track of the voluminous and volatile portfolio capital flowing into and out of Hong Kong. (2) Money supply M1 is defined as the sum of legal tender notes and coins held by the public plus customers' demand deposits placed with licenced banks. M2 refers to the sum of M1 plus customers' savings and time deposits with licenced banks, plus negotiable certificates of deposits (NCDs) issued by licenced banks held by non-authorized institutions; and M3 the sum of M2 plus customers' deposits with restricted licenced banks (RLBs) and deposit-taking companies (DTCs) plus NCDs issued by RLBs and DTCs held by non-authorized institutions.

Sources: HKGCSD—*HKADS*, various issues.

Figure 9.1 Major Indicators of Economic Instability in Hong Kong in Relation to the Economic Cycles in the United States, 1981–2000 (%)

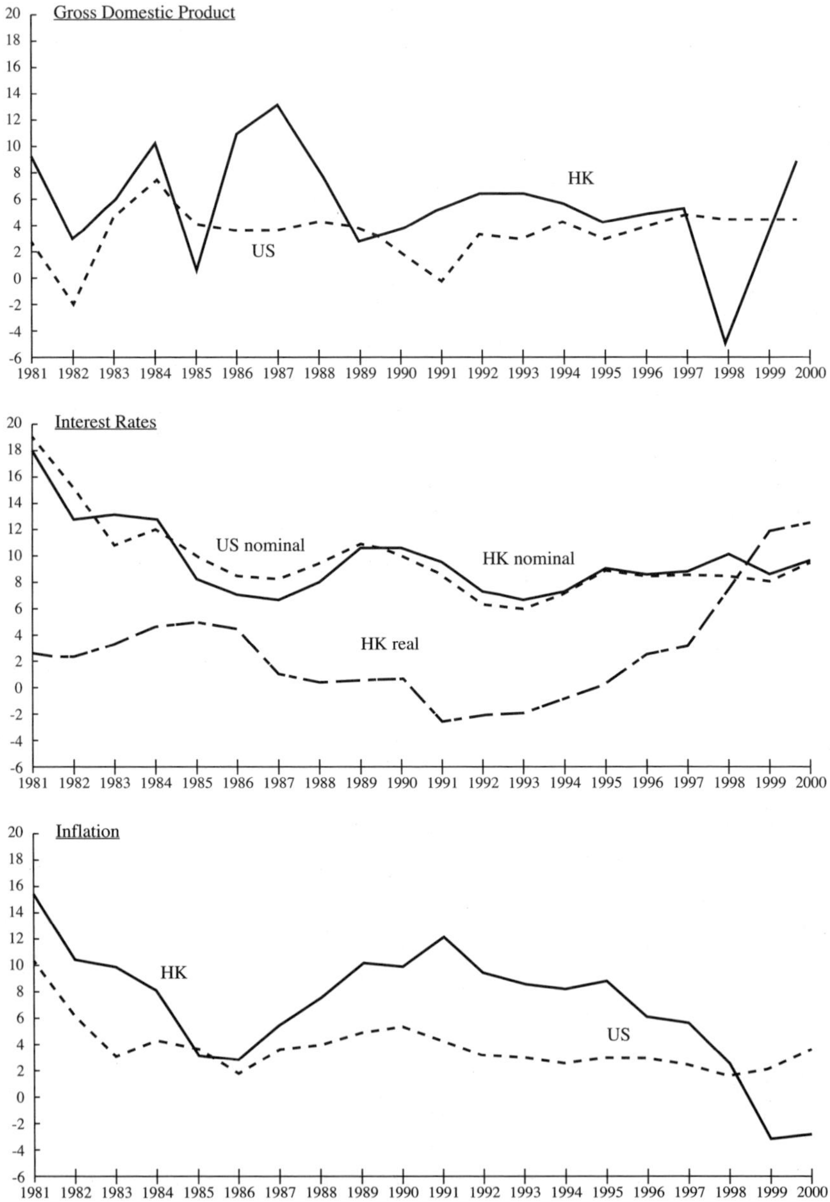

Notes: Hong Kong's real interest rate is given as prime lending rate minus inflation.

Sources: HKGCSD—*HKADS*, various issues; and IMF—*IFSYB*, various issues.

more volatile and prolonged than would otherwise be expected under a floating exchange rate regime, under which the interest and exchange rates may readjust freely alongside any price movements to help moderate any inflationary pressures. A pegged exchange rate regime therefore does not guarantee economic stability. More importantly, inflation can be expectation-augmented, generating its own self-fulfilling momentum.

Necessary to the understanding of the high inflation in Hong Kong during the late 1980s and early 1990s are asset price inflation and the wage-price spiral. Both aspects are clearly reflected in the statistics shown in Figure 9.2.

In the 1986–90 and 1991–95 periods, average annual prices for domestic properties increased by a startling 18.44% and 21.01% respectively. Retail properties and office spaces recorded similar phenomenal gains. It was not until the summer of 1994, when property market speculation had run out of control, that the government resorted to the unusual administrative fiat of drastically restricting bank lending by imposing a ceiling on property mortgage loans.[4] Property prices did, as a result, decline quite remarkably. Real interest rates remained persistently negative (see Figure 9.1), however, and the downturn was short-lived, lasting for not more than two years. Shortly before Hong Kong was to take the full impact of the Asian financial crisis in 1998, property prices, especially housing properties, recorded yet another all-time high in 1997 (see Figure 9.2).

Persistent negative real interest rates had clearly provided a strong incentive to the public to invest in real property assets rather than interest-bearing financial assets. In land scarce Hong Kong, real estate investment has long been regarded as an effective hedge against inflation. Worse still, not only end-users, but corporate and casual investors all joined in the property-shopping spree, pushing property prices to astronomical levels. In the end, the positive "wealth effect" helped to fuel domestic demand and inflation further.

There is yet another important dimension to Hong Kong's asset price bubble in the 1990s. With the expectation that asset prices would continue to rise in tandem with high inflation, international investors also rushed into Hong Kong's property market, anticipating substantially higher rates of return than those promised by their home countries. Most importantly, they all assumed that the US dollar peg regime, in combination with the government's huge foreign exchange reserves and the absence of any fiscal deficits and external debt, would guarantee that the accumulated HK dollar assets could be easily disposed of and converted into foreign currency with virtually zero exchange

Figure 9.2 Wage Inflation and Property Prices in Hong Kong, 1980–2000 (1980 = 100)

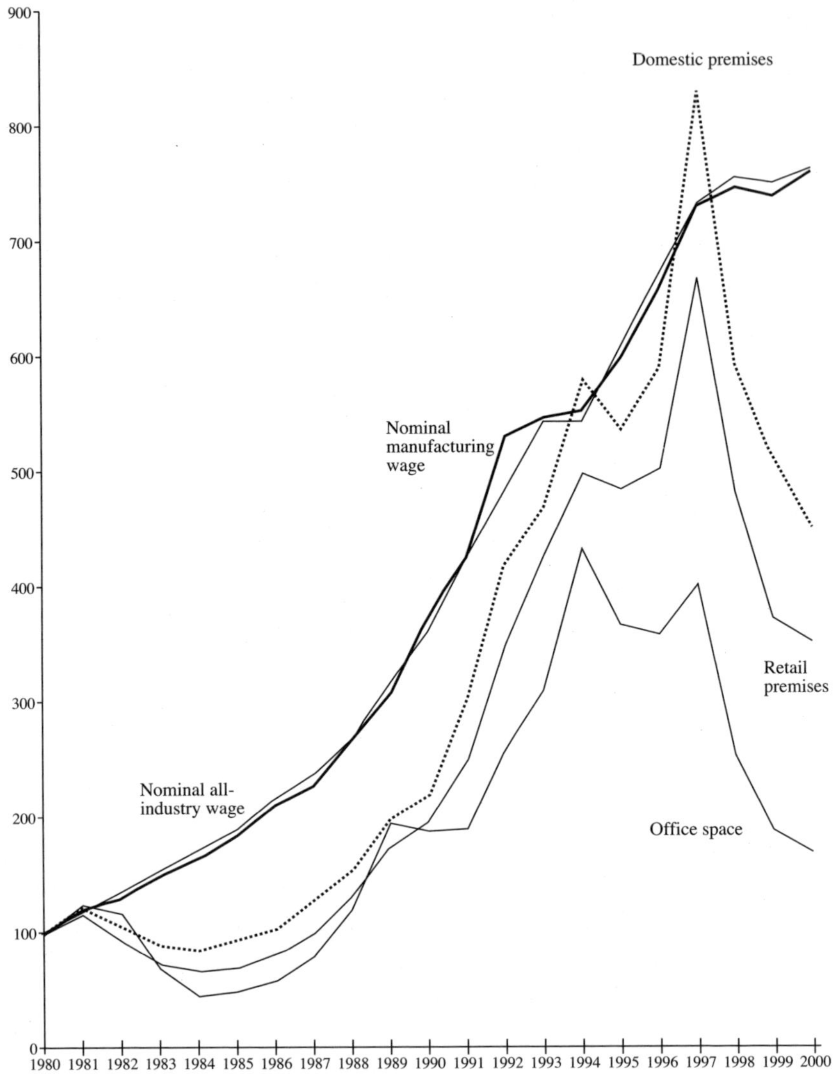

Sources: HKGCSD—*HKADS* and —*HKMDS*, various issues.

risk. This helped to boost considerably the risk-adjusted rate of return for overseas investors.

High inflation and hence high costs of living caused wages to spiral. Thus, as revealed in Figure 9.2, the nominal wage for all industries in Hong Kong rose by an annual average rate of 13.71% between 1986 and 1990 and 11.18% between 1991 and 1995, that is, by an annual average rate of 12.4% for the whole decade from 1986 to 1995. Wages in the manufacturing industry alone increased annually by 12.7%. The most rapid annual increases occurred between 1988 and 1992, at 18.4%. This period corresponds exactly to when most of Hong Kong’s manufacturing industry relocated to China.

Industrial relocation and restructuring

There is no doubt that the pull factors, namely the cheap labour and low land costs offered on the other side of the border, would already have been sufficiently attractive for Hong Kong manufacturers to relocate there. The push factors, specifically the high wages and land rental volatility, as conditioned by the US dollar peg, also strongly accelerated investors’ exodus to China. By the mid-1990s, virtually all Hong Kong manufacturers had migrated to China. Employment in the territory’s manufacturing industry declined from a high of nearly one million in the mid-1980s to less than a quarter of that by 1996/1997. Apart from the employment figures, another measure of the relocation impact on Hong Kong is the capital outflow in the form of FDI across the border, to the Pearl River Delta in particular.[5] Hitherto, such capital would probably have remained in Hong Kong. Figure 9.3 shows the trends and fluctuations in FDI from Hong Kong to China between 1986 and 1998 in relation to changes in Hong Kong’s inflation and nominal wage rates.

Apart from the dramatic upswing in 1992/1993 prompted by the so-called “Deng Xiaoping whirlwind” (see note 1), FDI by Hong Kong investors in China in terms of both total value pledged (contracted) and realized generally moved in tandem with changes in nominal wage rates or inflation in general.

The findings basically support the point made that insurmountable inflation and wage price pressure arising from the US dollar peg system drove Hong Kong manufacturers to relocate their plants to China beginning in the mid-1980s. This, together with the simple fact that virtually all the output is shipped back to Hong Kong for export to Western markets, attests to the nature of the relocation, which is very different from the import-substitution FDI made by overseas investors in the Chinese interior or further north aimed at the huge Chinese domestic market.

Figure 9.3 Indices of FDI Flow from Hong Kong to China in Relation to Changes in Inflation and Nominal Wage Rates in Hong Kong, 1986–2000 (1986 = 100)

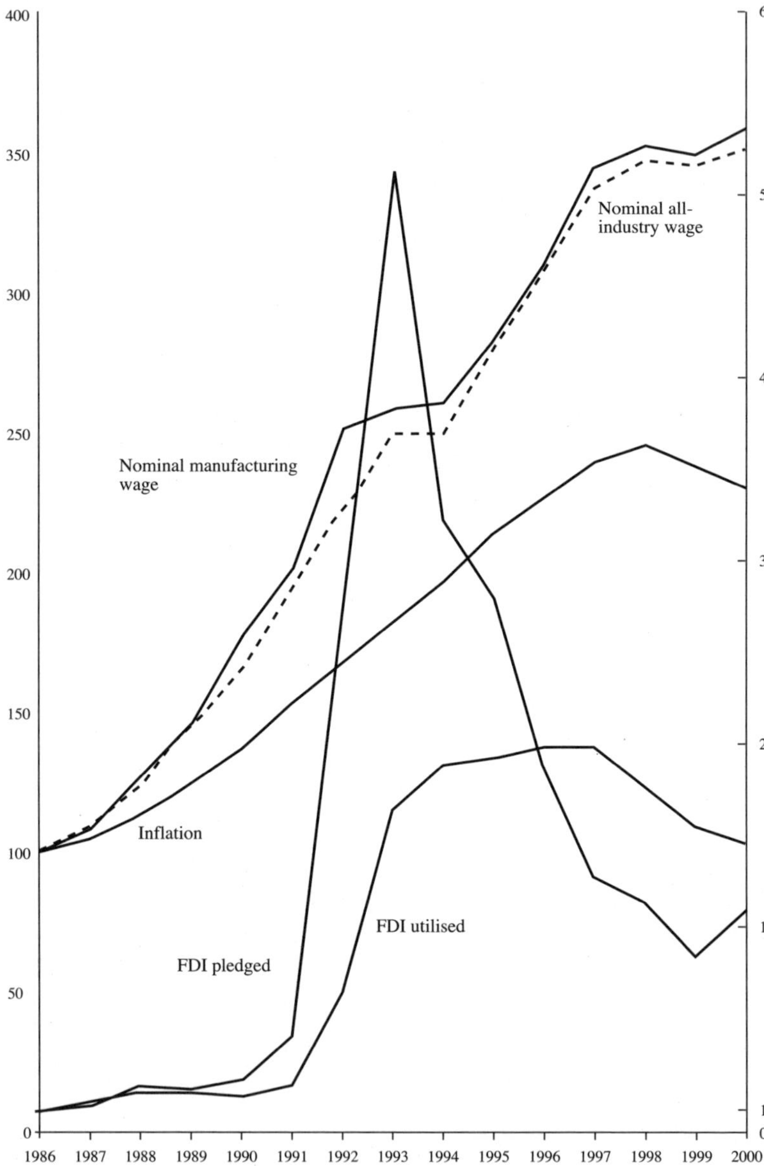

Sources: MOFTEC—*ACFERT*, various issues; and HKGCSD—*HKADS*, various issues.

By 1998, FDI from Hong Kong accumulated to a total stock of some US$140 billion, accounting for more than 52% of total Chinese FDI intake between 1979 and 1998. More strikingly, according to some rough calculations, Hong Kong-invested firms in 1998 employed more than five million Chinese workers in Guangdong Province alone.[6] This is more than five times the size of Hong Kong's manufacturing employment in 1985/1986.

The massive relocation of Hong Kong's manufacturing industry to China underpins the drastic restructuring of the economy as a whole over the past decade or so. Consistent with the decline in manufacturing employment, the relative contribution of the manufacturing sector to Hong Kong's GDP fell from 22.1% in 1985 to only 6.2% in 1998. Meanwhile, the service sector share rose rapidly from 69.6% to 84.7% over the same period.[7] Such a dramatic and complete shift within a span of less than fifteen years is probably unparalleled in world economic history.

Even more remarkably, from 1985/1986 to 1996/1997, despite the massive manufacturing exodus to China, Hong Kong's GDP grew at an average annual rate of 5.7%, while labour supply increased only at an annual rate of 1.7% over the same period.[8] That is to say, the accelerated industrial relocation not only resulted in low unemployment in Hong Kong, but in fact, by virtue of the drastic concomitant expansion of the service sector, there was a labour supply shortage prior to the outbreak of the Asian financial crisis. This constraint on GDP growth could only be resolved in part by the government's yielding, quite reluctantly for obvious political reasons, to employers' lobby for labour imports, and through the acceleration of technological upgrading.

Hong Kong and Guangdong have a simple symbiotic relationship. The export manufacturing capacity, now based almost completely in Guangdong, requires a continuous flow of complementary inputs from the service sector. The container port facilities, air, rail and road transportation between China and Hong Kong, as well as the banking, finance, insurance and telecommunications sectors all help to generate employment and income in Hong Kong. Less obvious but even more crucial to the entire dynamic of the economic restructuring in Hong Kong has been the rare versatility of Hong Kong's human capital. The pace with which manufacturing workers adjusted their training and skills to suit the needs of the increasingly capital-intensive and technology-based service sector was also unparalleled in modern economic history. With some minor qualifications, structural unemployment was virtually unknown in Hong Kong amidst the great economic upheaval associated with the drastic industrial restructuring that took place.

Trade reorientation and expansion

For conceptual clarity, an important statistical point is necessary to facilitate further discussion. That is, with the massive manufacturing relocation to China, Hong Kong's "domestic" exports have been statistically reduced to a minimum. Official Hong Kong statistics treat exports originating from Hong Kong-invested manufacturing plants in China as a special category of re-exports of Chinese origin (rather than Hong Kong's own domestic exports), alongside re-exports of truly Chinese origin. Given the fact that the bulk of export processing by Hong Kong-invested firms in China does not normally involve any intermediate processing in Hong Kong of raw import supplies from overseas, it is apparent why Hong Kong has rapidly converted from an export manufacturing centre to a global entrepôt port within only about a decade. Adding to this unusual development is of course the ongoing attempts by the mainland Chinese themselves, both exporters and importers, to take advantage of Hong Kong's worldwide network of marketing and merchandise sourcing (as well as the efficient port and shipping facilities, and excellent banking, insurance and telecommunications services). Against this backdrop, the standard trade statistics indicate that the share of domestic exports in Hong Kong's total exports declined steadily from 73.4% in 1979 to a low of 14% by 1997, while the share of re-exports simultaneously rose.[9]

For the purposes of this article, it is necessary to treat "re-exports" of goods manufactured in China by Hong Kong manufacturers and exporters as domestic exports, as with goods produced internally in Hong Kong for export to overseas markets other than China. Obviously, in practice, it is difficult statistically to distinguish this special category of imports from China from China's total exports to Hong Kong. The reason for this is simple: most Hong Kong investors in China are involved in joint ventures with Chinese partners with both equity share and scale of production varying from firm to firm. Given the large number of Hong Kong-invested firms in China, it is extremely difficult to isolate accurately in aggregate terms the export share attributable to the Hong Kong investors.[10]

Fortunately, since 1989, the Hong Kong government has published a quarterly set of trade statistics relating specifically to what is officially referred to as "outward processing" (OP) export flows to China and the corresponding "outward processing" import flows from China with breakdowns for major export commodity categories. Statistics for re-exports to countries other than China are also included, although unfortunately, no further breakdowns are available for market distribution by country. The government statistics are based on regular sampling surveys conducted of Hong Kong firms in conjunction with custom import and export statistics. They should therefore be interpreted with care. A rough examination of the "processing" margin (value of OP import flows minus OP export flows as a percentage of total OP import flows) across the different commodity groups reveals, however, a pattern and margin of earnings generally consistent with information given by Hong Kong manufacturers and exporters. This is also true for the OP re-export margin.[11]

Without a better alternative, the given OP-type of exports (or rather, re-exports by custom statistics) may therefore be added to the truly "domestic" exports of Hong Kong, for the purposes of examining how Hong Kong's export capacity in total may have been expanded with the complete migration of its export manufacturing industry to China over the past fifteen years. The vertical distance (TEC minus PDX in Figure 9.4) between the estimated trend line of domestic exports and the realized total export volume (comprising both domestic exports and what may be called Hong Kong's domestic-exports-in-disguise in the form of OP re-exports) shows that, being entirely released of the severe land and labour supply constraints, Hong Kong export manufacturers have indeed been able to expand their export capacity very substantially in the 1990s.[12] This estimated capacity expansion also appears to be roughly consistent with the increases in employment from some one million workers in 1985/1986 in Hong Kong to over five million by 1997/1998 across the border in Guangdong Province. Of course, if the bulk of re-exports of truly Chinese origin is also to be considered, the real total export capacity in Hong Kong is much larger than implied here.

A major question that arises is how the US dollar peg is related to the continuous export expansion in Hong Kong. This can be examined in the context of Figure 9.5, which gives different measures of the Hong Kong dollar/US dollar real exchange rate, deflated by nominal wage price, consumer price, export price and the GDP deflator. Several points can be made. First, during the period 1983–97, the real exchange rate as deflated by export price (Xp) remained quite stable. Secondly, by contrast, each of the other three measures indicates consistent appreciation against the US dollar. Specifically, measured

Figure 9.4 Trends in Realized (R) and Projected (P) Domestic Exports (DX), "Outward Processing" Type of Exports (OPX), and Estimated Total Exports Capacity (TEC) of Hong Kong, 1981–2000 (1981 = 100)

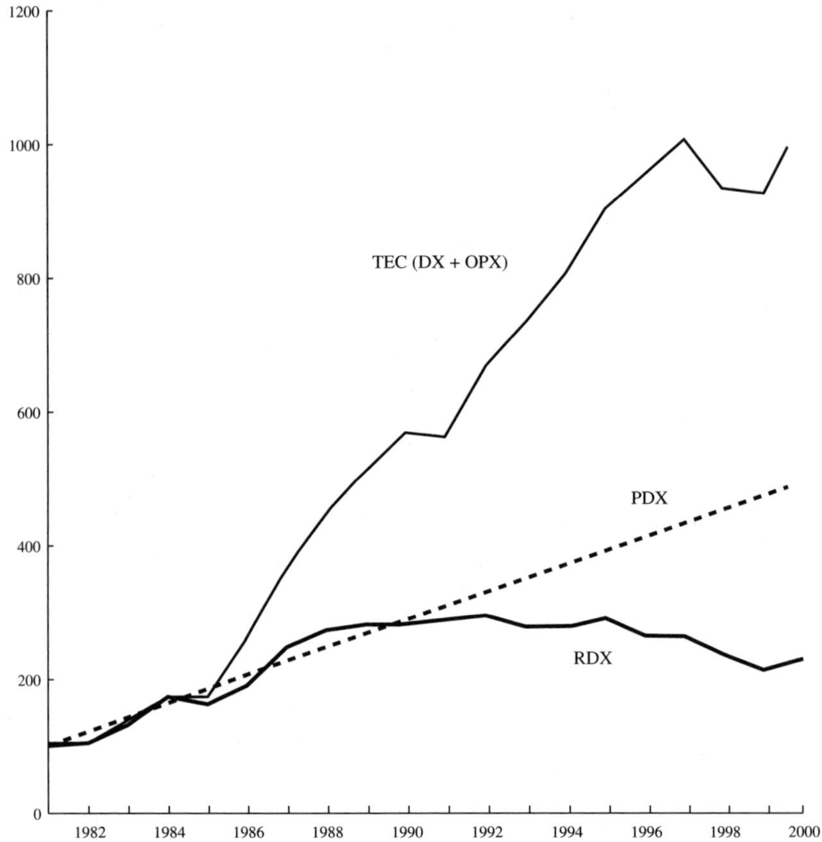

Notes: (1) The projected trend line (PDX) is derived from a simple linear regression equation fitted with the RDX values of 1978–88. (2) OPX refers to exports from export processing conducted by Hong Kong's manufacturers in the Chinese mainland. Official Hong Kong statistics for OPX are available from 1991 only, although such exports began to take place in the early or mid-1980s. To complete the series, a similar time trend is thus fitted with the available 1991–2000 data to provide the OPX figures for the years prior to 1991. Note also that the OPX figures (TEC–RFX) do not include "outward processing" export flows to mainland China (i.e., intermediate goods destined for export processing).

Sources: HKGCSD—*HKADS*, various issues.

against the benchmark of 1983, the real exchange rates based on the deflators for GDP, consumer price (Cp), and nominal wage (Wm), actually appreciated substantially by 41%, 38% and 60% respectively by 1999. Thirdly, the divergent trends in Hong Kong dollar's real exchange rate between the export-price deflator on the one hand, and the three other measures on the other, reflect the fact that inflation in Hong Kong's non-traded goods sector was much more pronounced as a result of the US dollar peg regime, though the territory was able to maintain its overall export price competitiveness vis-à-vis Western markets, the US in particular.

The basic economic implications are clear: without the opportunity to relocate to the Chinese hinterland for substantial cost savings, Hong Kong's manufacturers would probably have not been able to withstand the insurmountable wage price and land cost pressures arising from the government's highly defensive protection of the US dollar peg. Put differently, the success story of Hong Kong up to the onset of the Asian financial crisis is intimately bound up with China's decisive move to open up its frontier to the outside world.

Nevertheless, with the US dollar weakening against the Japanese yen for most of the period after 1983, the Hong Kong dollar was correspondingly depreciating against the yen as well. The result was that Hong Kong's exports to Japan grew even faster than those to the US, at least up to the crisis years, as shown in Figure 9.6. This can be viewed as a "double benefit" wrought from both export cost savings arising from the manufacturing sector's relocation to China and the depreciation of the Hong Kong dollar against the yen. Without doubt, the cost-saving factor was dominant.

China in the SAR's financial crisis

The impact of the Asian financial crisis was mentioned above. Notice should be taken of the sharply contrasting movement of the major economic indicators in Hong Kong before and after 1998: high GDP growth, high inflation and negative real interest rates prior to 1998, versus negative GDP growth, severe deflation and remarkable increases in real interest rates after 1998 (see Figure 9.7). And to add to the near-perfect symmetry, the continuous expansion of exports in Hong Kong was abruptly brought to an end by the Asian crisis in early 1998, to turn into absolute decline for six quarters consecutively before any real signs of recovery appeared at the end of 1999 (see Figure 9.7). How has the "China factor" fared in this extreme economic volatility in relation to

Figure 9.5 The Real Exchange Rate of the Hong Kong dollar against the US dollar as Deflated by the Export Price (Xp), Consumer Price (Cp), Manufacturing Wage (Wm), and GDP Growth (HK$/US$), 1978–2000

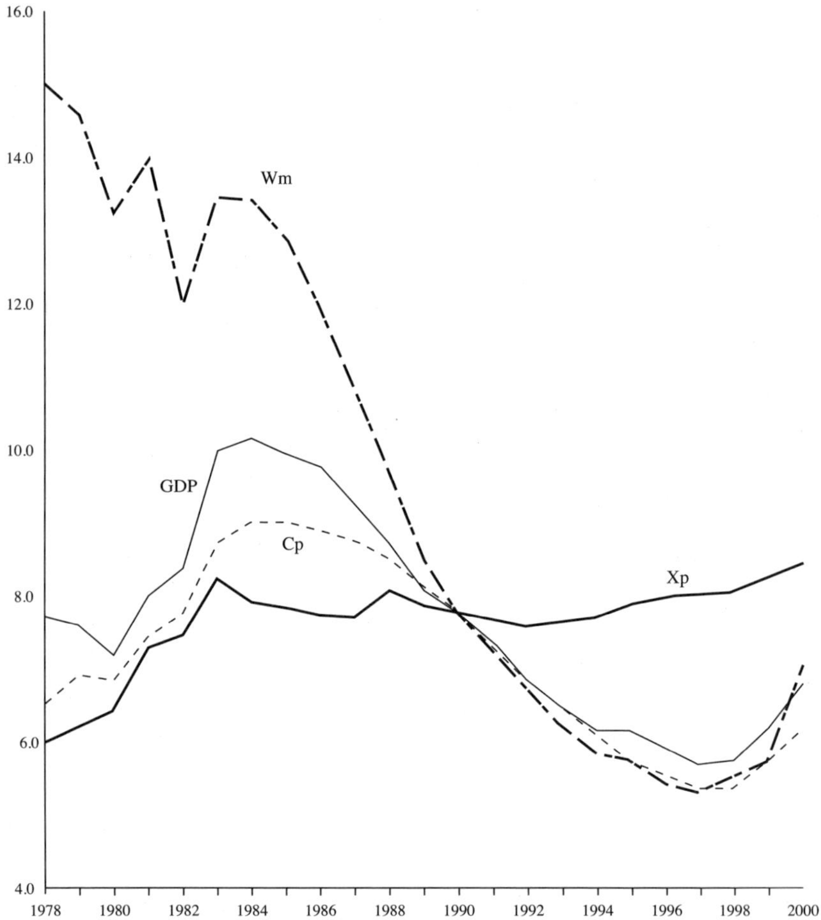

Notes: The different deflated exchange rate measures are obtained by applying the relevant price ratio (US price index to Hong Kong price index) to Hong Kong's nominal exchange rate. The year 1990 is taken as a benchmark (HK$/US$ = 7.8) for gauging the trend of changes.

Sources: HKGCSD—*HKADS*, various issues; and IMF—*IFSYB*, various issues.

Figure 9.6 Trends in Hong Kong's Total Exports to the United States and Japan in Relation to the Respective Real Exchange Rates of the Hong Kong dollar, 1981–2000 (1990 = 100)

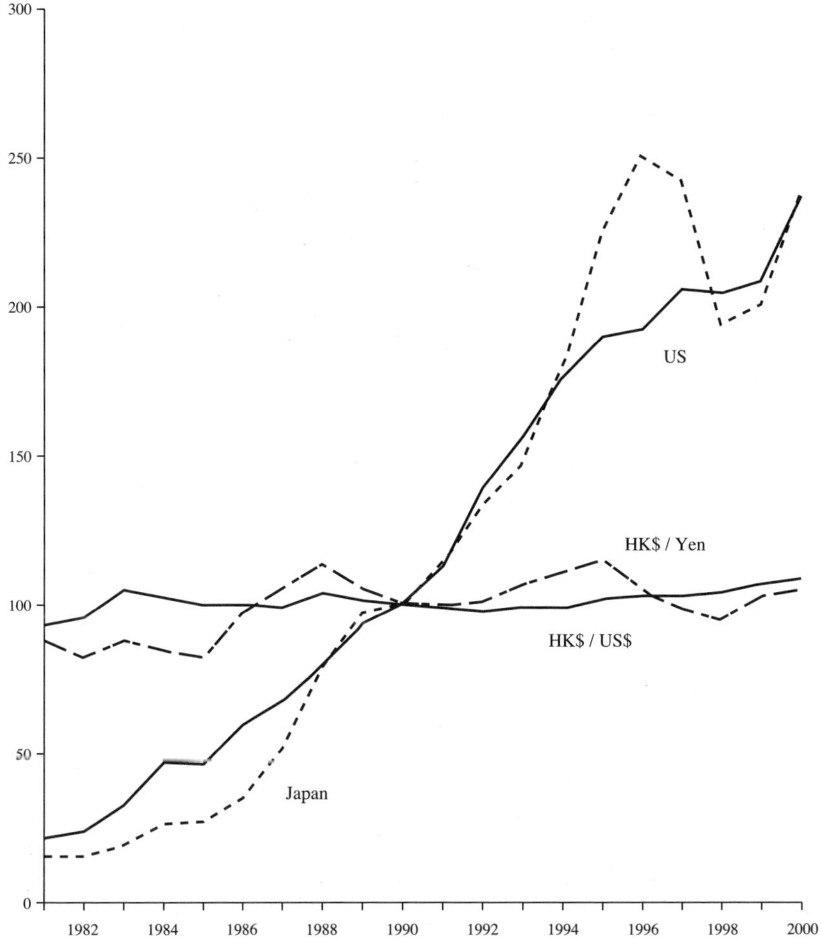

Notes: (1) Total exports comprise domestic exports, re-exports of Chinese origin, and "outward processing" type of exports (see Figure 9.4 for explanation). (2) The HK$/Yen line is similarly obtained as explained in Figure 9.5 with respect to the real HK$/US$ exchange rate.

Sources: HKGCSD—*HKADS*, various issues; and IMF—*IFSYB*, various issues.

Figure 9.7 Quarterly Trends in Gross Domestic Product (GDP), Gross Domestic Capital Formation (K), Private Consumption Expenditure (C), Government Expenditure (G), Imports (M) and Exports (X) of Goods in Hong Kong under the Impact of the Asian Financial Crisis, 1997 to Fourth Quarter, 2000 (year-on-year percentage change)

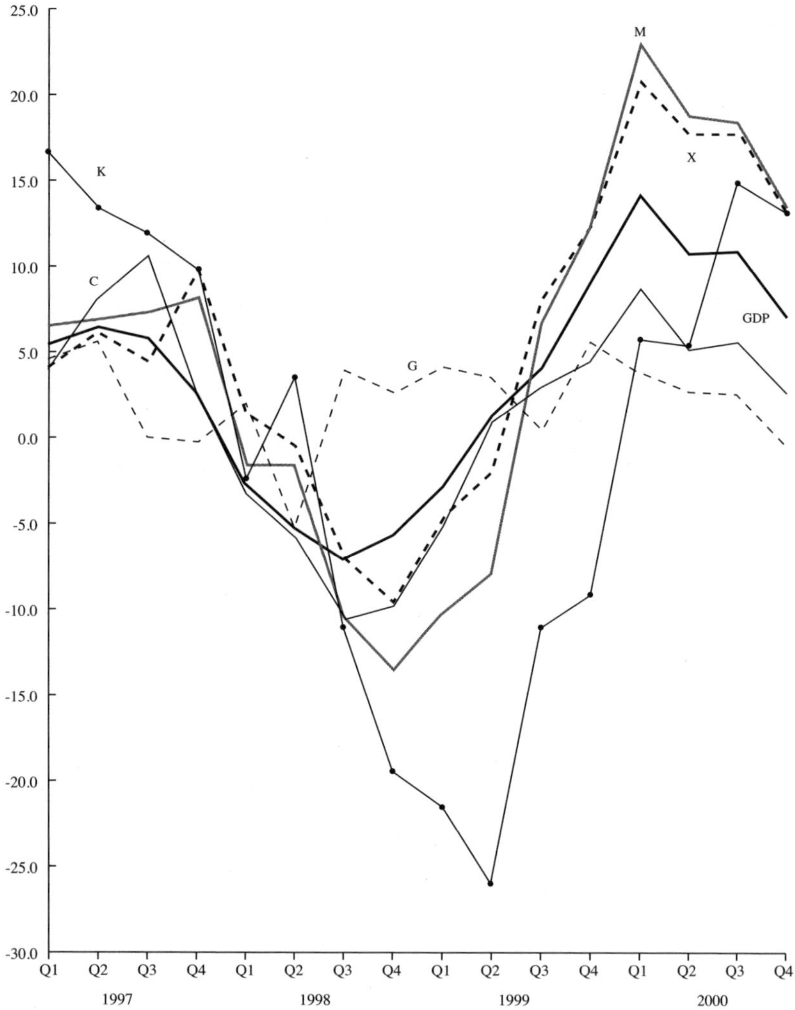

Sources: HKGCSD—*HKADS*, various issues.

the role of the US dollar peg? To address the issue, some background is necessary on why Hong Kong bore the full impact of the Asian crisis.[13]

It must be noted that the tough monetary policy measures, taken by the Hong Kong government at the peak of the financial crisis to defend the Hong Kong dollar against international hedge funds speculating for a forced devaluation, sent nominal interest rates skyrocketing. The persistent threat of an interest rate rise in the US aimed at preventing its buoyant economy from overheating also prompted the Hong Kong authorities to keep local interest rates at a consistently high level, in order to maintain the US dollar peg. This resulted in the bursting of the asset price bubble virtually overnight (Figure 9.2). Average property values halved within months, consumer confidence plummeted and spending virtually halted, causing widespread business closures and unemployment, and highly depressed investment expenditure under high interest-cost pressures, both locally as well as in China by way of reduced FDI outflow to the mainland. Compounding the difficulty, wages remained relatively high because of strong resistance by trade unionists to any downward movement (Figure 9.2). Earners had come to expect two-digit growth in nominal wages, such as had been given them every year over the past two decades. Reinforced by falling consumer prices, real interest rates were repeatedly raised, reaching historical highs throughout 1998 and 1999, averaging 7.1% and 12.5% respectively.

As it had turned out, Hong Kong's 1998 GDP was curtailed by 5.3% in real terms, gross domestic capital formation by 6.1% and private consumption expenditure by 6.8% (see Figure 9.7). The depression persisted through the summer of 1999. It was not until late 1999 that any revival appeared, fuelled primarily by a strong recovery in exports growth. A positive growth of 2.9% occurred for the whole of 1999. Indeed, among the Asian economies, Hong Kong proved to be the hardest hit not only in terms of scale but also in the duration of the depression. The event was astonishing, especially considering that unlike most of the other financial "dominos", Hong Kong had been endowed with probably the best and most secure banking and financial system in Asia, strong fiscal and monetary discipline, and a huge foreign exchange reserve shortly prior to the crisis.[14]

It therefore seems apparent that the sudden collapse of the Hong Kong economy had a great deal to do with the highly defensive protectionist measures carried out by the Hong Kong Monetary Authority amidst the crisis. Not only did the defence not help to forestall a massive capital flight from Hong

Kong, but it consistently pushed up local interest rates in both nominal and real terms. This is a clear case of "double loss", in which exorbitant interest rates impaired both consumption and investment confidence, and did not induce replenishing capital inflows to help reinvigorate the economy as the perceived scheme of interest rate arbitrage had suggested under the US dollar peg system. With the advantage of hindsight, a legitimate question is whether or not the SAR economy, given its relative strengths and sound financial setting, would have suffered less and recovered at an earlier stage and in a more rigorous style, compared with the other two "little dragons",[15] had the Hong Kong currency been de-pegged from the US dollar (that is, devalued), say, following Singapore and Taiwan in late 1997.

We have addressed this hypothetical question at some length elsewhere.[16] Despite the remarkable economic recovery in most Asian countries affected by the crisis, the region as a whole is still fearful of a possible regrouping of the international hedge funds, now commonly called highly-leveraged institutions (HLIs), for renewed currency attacks.[17] This has at times prompted a renewed aspiration in many Asian countries to find an alternative exchange rate regime.[18] How then should the US dollar peg for Hong Kong be seen in this light? The question clearly cannot be pursued in isolation from the SAR's firmly established "Chinese connection". This can also be more specifically seen from the role China has played in the equation of the great depression in Hong Kong of the past couple of years. Several points emerge.

The first refers to the investment linkage. When Hong Kong was overwhelmed by severe credit crunch as a result of the SAR government's massive defence of the Hong Kong dollar, and when new FDI flows from Hong Kong investors to the Chinese hinterland therefore began to slow down or even decline in 1997/1998 (see Figure 9.3),[19] mainland state banks immediately felt obliged to rescue them by granting the first ever renminbi credits for the purposes of sustaining export processing activities.[20] It is not possible to verify the quantitative significance of such timely liquidity assistance. But the special concessions should perhaps not be seen as just a temporary bailout. Rather they seem to signal an important Chinese policy shift towards closer integration of the hundreds of thousands of export manufacturing enterprises run independently by Hong Kong and Taiwan investors or as joint ventures with various Chinese partners, with the mainland Chinese economy. After all, these enterprises were very much the backbone of the entire Chinese exporting system, being responsible for around half of China's total exports to the outside world and creating hundreds of thousands of jobs for low-skilled workers.

The second factor affecting Hong Kong was the Chinese government's granting of a value-added tax (VAT) rebate to promote exports. The VAT stood at 17% prior to the Asian crisis. The initial rebate was given in mid-1998, when the full force of export competition from Southeast Asian countries, which had their currencies greatly devalued, was being felt in China where the value of the renminbi had been steadfastly upheld. By mid-1999, for a wide range of export commodities that were routed through Hong Kong to major Western markets, the continuous increases in rebate appeared to have exhausted rapidly the full VAT rate of 17%. It is difficult to estimate the extent to which the VAT rebate helped to enhance the international competitiveness of Chinese exports, but according to one authoritative Chinese analyst, a 1% increase in VAT rebate was comparable to a 1% reduction in export costs in China.[21] The rebate, therefore, was tantamount to a renminbi devaluation against the US dollar with respect to its effect in promoting export sales through Hong Kong or elsewhere. It was, however, free from the potentially destabilizing effect of a real renminbi devaluation in relation to the US dollar peg in Hong Kong.

The third point relates to what may be summarized as the "safe haven effect" provided by China to Hong Kong's export manufacturing industry. Specifically, if a distinction is made between Hong Kong's truly domestic exports on the one hand and re-exports on the other—the latter being essentially of China origin in the form of Hong Kong exports-in-disguise—then at least for the initial year of the crisis, 1998, the former was curtailed in real terms, by a rather hefty 7.9%, compared with a marginal decline of only 3.7% for the latter.[22] The discrepancy seems to imply, *ceteris paribus*, that China-based export processing enjoys, by virtue of comparative cost advantage, a greater competitive edge in overseas markets than locally based producers which are subject to wage-price rigidities despite the economic downturn, coupled with the continuous, albeit mitigated, land-cost constraint in Hong Kong.[23] More remarkably, in recent years, an increasing proportion of export manufactures produced in China by Hong Kong entrepreneurs is actually channelled through some major Chinese ports, notably Shanghai, rather than being shipped back to Hong Kong to be re-exported to the West. In 1998, at the peak of the Asian financial crisis, official Shanghai statistics confirmed that total exports made by foreign-invested enterprises based in the municipality (mostly of Hong Kong or Taiwan origin) to the US and the European

Union could still score an impressive growth of 20%, accounting for 47% of the municipality's total exports.[24]

The fourth point is clearly the fact that the strong economic recovery in Hong Kong since the third quarter of 1999 was singularly underpinned by the SAR's most remarkable revival in exports (see Figure 9.7), which is in turn invariably bound up with the spectacular rebound of the mainland's exports since summer 1999. Note that for the first half of 2000, China's total exports recorded a 38% growth over that of the corresponding period in 1999, and the GDP growth for Hong Kong for the year 2000 taken as a whole bounced back strongly to 10.5%, against the backdrop of an extremely impressive 14.3% growth for the first quarter of the year. Unfortunately, with economic growth in the United States—the single largest export market for Hong Kong—beginning to slow down towards the end of year 2000, the SAR has also increasingly felt the pain throughout 2001. Its GDP growth is now generally forecast to be reduced to near zero for 2001.

Another point making Hong Kong unique relates, finally, to the value of renminbi, as it may bear on the stability of the US dollar peg system in Hong Kong, and hence the SAR's export performance. There is no doubt that the renewed pledge made by the Chinese government not to devalue the Chinese currency has greatly helped the Hong Kong dollar fend off repeated speculative attacks amidst the Asian crisis in 1997/1998. There is also little doubt that by not devaluing both the Chinese and Hong Kong SAR currencies, there should have been a certain degree of industrial restructuring, managerial re-strengthening, and improvement in labour discipline and efficiency for enhancing cost savings in order to withstand increased export competition from the devalued Southeast Asian countries and South Korea. Still, there also seems to be no reason to suggest that by not devaluing, the HKSAR's synergistic economic relationship with China in labour-intensive export processing would eventually be broken within the "flying geese" pattern of intra-regional specialization and industrialization, in favour of the other newly industrializing Southeast Asian competitors.[25] It is, of course, an entirely different matter whether any truly practical gains in this regard could have helped mitigate the magnitude of export losses in Hong Kong, and in China as well, such as those incurred in 1998/1999 as a result of weakened international competitiveness.[26] Nevertheless, if anything, Hong Kong seems to have suffered less pain by virtue of its particular connection to China which, as referred to above, was able to "subsidize" indirectly the SAR's export manufacturers based on the mainland through extending urgently needed credit supply and increased VAT rebates at the peak of the Asian financial crisis.

At this juncture, it may reasonably be asked if the US dollar peg is still viable. Should the Hong Kong dollar perhaps rather be pegged to the Chinese yuan? There is no easy answer. What should first of all be asked is why amidst renewed speculative attacks on the Hong Kong dollar during the crisis, was the Hong Kong dollar's value seen to be intricately linked up with that of the renminbi; and why was it believed that a devaluation of the Chinese currency would inevitably force the Hong Kong dollar to devalue in tandem? Were these perceptions based on compelling hard economic facts, or was it simply a matter of international currency speculators exploiting the "psychic mobility" and "herd behaviour" of the masses? Exploration of these ideas can assist in settling the fate of the US dollar peg.

Hanging the US dollar peg in the balance?

It is beyond the scope of this chapter to pursue the question in great depth. Here are a few fundamental points. First, the perception that the fate of the Hong Kong dollar is invariably bound up with the value of the renminbi seems to have missed the most basic, yet peculiar aspect of the China-HKSAR economic synergy in export processing. That is, for the vast number of Hong Kong and Taiwanese export manufacturers based in the mainland, export orders or letters of credit from overseas buyers are normally not channelled through the Chinese banking system. Rather, they are generally intercepted by business affiliates in Hong Kong or Taiwan. Similarly, as a corollary, foreign exchange outlay on input materials, equipment and machinery imported from say, Japan, en route Hong Kong to the Chinese hinterland is also incurred outside China. In other words, both foreign currency income and expenditure made on the part of Hong Kong investors in China are shielded from the volatility of the renminbi.

Secondly, a devaluation of the renminbi without a concomitant devaluation of the Hong Kong dollar would actually help to reduce the costs of investment made by Hong Kong's export manufacturers in China. This relates especially to the costs of supplies from Chinese sources, building materials for plant construction being a good case in point. In the past, such supplies were strictly subject to centralized allocation, but they are now readily available in the Chinese markets at renminbi prices. Managerial and wage costs may also be similarly reduced, to the extent that the outlay is denominated in renminbi, unlike in the past, when payment was generally by joint venture contract and specified in foreign currency, that is, Hong Kong or US dollars.

The third point relates to exports of third-country origin from Hong Kong to end-users in China, that is, goods other than those destined for export processing on behalf of Hong Kong manufacturers. This has consistently made up around half of the SAR's total exports to the Chinese mainland in recent years. Probably more than one-third of China's imports from the US are presently channelled through Hong Kong.[27] The sheer magnitude, therefore, makes it worth pondering the implications of a renminbi devaluation for the Hong Kong dollar. Specifically, if the Hong Kong dollar were to devalue as well, it would probably only impair the import incentives of Hong Kong middlemen, without being able to improve the import capability of Chinese customers.

Another variable that may come into the equation involves import supplies from China in the form of wage foods, basic clothing and other light industrial goods retained for local consumption by the masses in Hong Kong. This variable appears to be crucial, given the size of the Hong Kong population (6.7 million) and, indeed, the virtual monopoly China conventionally enjoys as Hong Kong's food supplier. Nevertheless, upon closer scrutiny, the variable may not actually be that relevant, for the simple reason that Chinese supplies to Hong Kong over many decades have been quoted in Hong Kong dollars or the greenback, rather than in Chinese yuan.[28] There is no reason that Chinese suppliers would be willing to pass on to Hong Kong consumers any price benefits that may arise from a renminbi devaluation, by quoting lower export prices in Hong Kong dollars.

Taken together, there seems to be no tenable economic reason why the Hong Kong dollar should be seen as a fellow traveller of the renminbi. In a way, the reverse may actually be true, given the weight of the "Hong Kong factor" in the Chinese mainland economy. Note that Hong Kong, via FDI flows, makes up around 15% of total fixed asset investment made in the mainland each year and an even more significant share of China's total exports, in addition to the enormous contribution to manufacturing employment.[29] As a Hong Kong dollar devaluation would imply increased FDI costs and hence reduced FDI flows to the mainland, it might as well call for a renminbi devaluation for the Chinese government to mitigate the losses. At any rate, within the present context there hardly exists any compelling economic rationale for the Hong Kong dollar to be de-pegged from the US dollar in favour of a re-pegging to the Chinese currency. As a matter of fact, the Chinese renminbi itself is clearly also de facto pegged to the US dollar under the exchange rate regime of "managed float" adopted in 1994.

Nevertheless, with China's imminent entry into the World Trade Organization (WTO), the situation appears to be increasingly parlous. WTO membership implies, among other things, a significant reorientation from export-oriented FDI towards import-substitution FDI in China. For Hong Kong investors and others, this means, of course, increased access to the huge domestic mainland market. However, to the extent that Hong Kong investors manufacturing products for the internal Chinese market rely on third countries for essential input supplies, this would tend eventually to force the value of the Hong Kong dollar to be more closely tied to that of the Chinese renminbi. A good case in point is the swift devaluation of the Taiwan dollar in late 1997 when the Asian financial crisis erupted. Shortly afterwards, major mainland-based manufacturers of Taiwan origin engaging in food processing (a sector which had been accorded the rare privilege of entering the Chinese market at an early stage, and which relied extensively on Japan and Taiwan for supply of spices and packaging materials) were forced by mounting import bills to suspend production. They were simply unable to withstand the price competition from domestic producers.[30]

Thus, with increased integration among the Hong Kong, Taiwan and mainland economies under the WTO framework, a Bretton-Wood type of agreement among the three Chinese economic entities, tacit or otherwise, may eventually emerge. Whether there ought to be a formal monetary integration, for example a "yuan bloc", following full convertibility of the renminbi by 2020 or before (this was China's pledge to APEC in the "Manila Framework" of 1997), is of course entirely conjectural.

Meanwhile, the Hong Kong dollar will probably continue to be overshadowed by the traumatic experience of defending its peg to the US dollar in 1997/1998, notwithstanding any search launched for an alternative exchange rate regime or a more viable defence mechanism against international currency speculators.

Conclusion

Under the US dollar peg system, the Hong Kong economy seems to have suffered from increased instability, both prior to and amidst the Asian financial crisis, primarily because it had to be subservient to the economic cycles of the US. Thus, it was unfortunate that just when, towards the year 2000, the Hong Kong economy was about to recover from the most severe depression ever experienced in its postwar history, the peg with the US dollar dragged it down. The high interest rates prescribed by the Federal Reserve Bank to cool the increasingly overheating US economy were the exact opposite to what the Hong Kong economy needed.

It is equally unfortunate that just when the American economy was slowing and the economic cycles of Hong Kong and the US were finally beginning to converge, the HKSAR could not escape the full brunt of the drastic curtailment in US import demand (Hong Kong export supply), the curtailment following the September 11 tragedy notwithstanding. It is to be hoped that the two economies will eventually synchronize and together return to sustained growth.

Fortunately, prior to the Asian crisis, the overheating and instability in Hong Kong caused by the peg were mitigated by the timely actions of the Chinese government as it steadily opened further to the outside world. Permitting Hong Kong's export manufacturing industries to relocate in China enabled the industries to escape crippling increases in property values and wages. Similarly, amidst the Asian crisis, China was able to come to the rescue, first by pledging steadfast defence of the Hong Kong dollar under the peg with its huge foreign exchange reserves, and second, by granting real assistance to China-based export manufacturers from Hong Kong in the form of urgently needed credit supply and VAT rebates.

Despite the increased integration of the two economies, it does not seem that the SAR should abandon the US dollar peg in favour of a re-pegging to the Chinese yuan. Actually, the Chinese currency itself is also de facto pegged to the US dollar with the similar objectives of promoting and maximizing export earnings from the US and other major overseas markets. Indeed, the case for the currency of the small and entirely open HKSAR economy to be anchored to the US dollar or a basket of major Western currencies today seems even more pressing.

Perhaps the Hong Kong dollar should be pegged to the US dollar at a more workable rate. With deflation fuelled by the existing dollar peg persisting now for more than three years, influential voices in Hong Kong have recently been calling more frequently for a rethink of the eighteen-year-old peg.[31] However, any re-pegging (equivalent to a devaluation of the Hong Kong currency) must obviously be weighed against the risks of a sudden capital outflow from Hong Kong and the consequent rise in interest rates that would further erode consumer and corporate confidence. In the words of Joseph C. K. Yam, chief executive of the Hong Kong Monetary Authority: "If, heaven forbid, de-pegging were to be carried out in the conditions that we have now, then we might add a third word to uncertainty and instability: catastrophe." [32]

Finally, China's new membership in WTO (as of December 2001), the increased trade and investment liberalization, and expected convertibility of the capital account at some later stage are all likely to have the effect of reducing the differences between the Hong Kong and mainland economies, perhaps laying the ground for an eventual monetary union. Such a prospect, however, still appears to be quite remote. Under the existing US dollar peg, the Hong Kong dollar will inevitably continue to be subject to occasional speculative attack.

10

China and the Prospects for Economic Integration within APEC*

In the last few years, it has been widely argued that the world's centre of gravity for economic activities will inevitably shift from the Atlantic to the Asia-Pacific region in the twenty-first century. This popular perception has clearly been prompted by the spectacular economic growth of China in the past fifteen years, following accelerated domestic reforms and, in particular, her "opening up" to the outside world. There is no doubt that the "China factor" has greatly assisted in sustaining the growth dynamism of the newly industrialized economies in Asia (notably Taiwan and Hong Kong, but also—and increasingly—South Korea). The strength and global importance of the Japanese economy lends further weight to the emerging scenario for the twenty-first century.

There are two dimensions to the rising expectation of the emergence of an "Asia-Pacific era". The first, reflecting a broader consideration, relates to the involvement of the countries of the East Pacific (above all the United States). The second—a narrower consideration—embraces the likelihood of self-sustaining development by Asia-Pacific economies into a fully integrated regional economic entity, with China and Japan as the critical core by virtue of their industrial status and market size.

It has become a foregone conclusion that the perspective of the "Asia-Pacific era" is already imminent. After all, "intra-regional" trade among a number of

---

* Reprinted from "China and the prospects for economic integration within APEC", in Joseph C. H. Chai, Y. Y. Kueh, and Clement A. Tisdell (eds.), *China and the Asia Pacific Economy*, Brisbane (Australia): The University of Queensland Economics Conference Monograph No. 3, 1997; published by New York: Nova Science Publishers, 1997, pp. 29–47.

countries of the Asian Pacific Economic Cooperation (APEC), including the US and other North and South American economies facing the Pacific Ocean already accounted for 47% of total world trade in 1993. In addition, APEC economies are responsible for the overwhelming share of global GNP, with the US and Japan ranking first and second, and mainland China approximating (after Germany) fourth in terms of purchasing power parity (PPP) estimates of GNP made recently by the World Bank.

Against this background, we propose to confine our analysis to "APEC proper", by excluding countries on the American side of the Pacific. We do not, however, assume the view of Premier Mahathir of Malaysia, whose radical concept of the East Asian Economic Caucus (EAEC) excludes Australia and New Zealand, as well as Taiwan and Hong Kong.

Several major issues follow in respect to the economic potential of the "narrower" APEC, or APEC proper, as just defined. It is as well to emphasize that it is not this chapter's intention to examine the domestic growth prospects of individual member countries. Our major task is to address the overall potential for intra-regional trade, as opposed to trade with outside world.

The main focus is, then, on trade and related investment issues. It is clear that China holds the key to many of these issues: after all, while APEC proper constitutes countries with economies which are already open and market-orientated, and whose potential for growth is marginal, the Chinese economy remains in a state of flux. Any relaxation in market access restrictions, in terms of adjustments of tariffs and non-tariff barriers and the removal of impediments to foreign investment, promises to alter substantially the patterns of trade, service, and capital flows within the APEC region, in accordance with fundamental patterns of regional comparative advantage.

We shall therefore focus on China in order to show how, as an emerging economic power, it may help to promote economic integration in the Asia Pacific. In what follows, we first give a brief review of the relative strengths of the Chinese economy in terms of its GNP size, output structure, degree of industrialization and trade volume, relative to that of the various APEC economies. This provides a background for assessing possible future patterns of economic interaction between China and other APEC economies.

In the second section, we examine the changing trends in China's trade within APEC, vis-à-vis trade with countries outside the region since the early 1980s. This serves to reveal the impact of China's economic and trade reforms in the past fifteen years on regional trade, as well as indicate the potential for economic cooperation within APEC in the future.

Section three attempts to identify the major obstacles and constraints inherent in the present Chinese economic system, as well as policies for further economic integration within APEC and with the outside world in general. This provides the necessary basis for assessing the prospects of China as a member of an APEC trading bloc.

The concluding section discusses the basic implications for China of the APEC tariff agenda established under the Bogor Declaration of November 1994, under which the long-term goal of free and open trade and investment in the Asia-Pacific region is to be achieved no later than 2020, or by 2010 for the industrialized economies of APEC.

Underlying the analysis are overlapping, multifaceted and enormously complex problems. For almost every issue raised, in-depth and careful research is needed before any firm statement can be made. To that extent the goals of this chapter are limited: that is, we seek to illustrate the broad contours of the fundamental issues and point to possible outcomes, rather than put forward firm conclusions and proposals. In short, the exercise generates more hypotheses and questions than it does answers.

The relative strength of China and APEC economies

The Chinese economy assumes a leading position within APEC, whether defined as the broader APEC (including the American side of the Pacific) or the narrower APEC (merely embracing the Asian Pacific Rim (APR) economies). There are several aspects to this. The first is the sheer size of China's population and economic power. Adjusted by the PPP-estimate (which gives a multiple of around 6.6 over the official Chinese figure in terms of US dollars, based on the depreciated official renminbi rate), China's absolute GNP has already surpassed that of Japan, and is 11 times larger than that of South Korea—the next largest APR economy. It is also nearly 15 times the size of Australia's GNP in 1993/1994, as revealed in Table 10.1.

Second, with around 48% of her national gross output generated from manufacturing and construction, China is clearly also an industrial giant, standing alongside Japan within APEC. It is evident too that after four decades of forced-draft industrialization under a highly protective trade regime, the country has built up an independent, comprehensive, and largely self-sufficient industrial system characterized by considerable technological sophistication. This is unmatched by any other APR economy except Japan.

Third, by the same PPP measure, per capita GDP in China (US$2,401) was, as of 1993, already substantially higher than that of Indonesia, the Philippines and Thailand, and only 30% below that of Malaysia. Note that the original, unadjusted Chinese per capita GDP (US$360 in 1993) conveys no economic logic. The figure is indeed almost the same as that of the early 1980s, which was obtained by simply converting the official renminbi value into US dollar according to the prevailing official exchange rate. The accelerated renminbi devaluation against the US dollar since the mid-1980s has undoubtedly greatly distorted the comparative Chinese income strength. The reality is, however, that per capita GDP in China has grown, in real terms, by an average of 8.4% per year from 1980 to 1994, based on consistent renminbi reckoning. [1]

In any case, the readjusted figure of US$2,401 for China clearly suggests a per capita GDP level which is substantially above the threshold of subsistence—implying rising consumerism and increased potential for external trade. But it is also clear that substantial income disparity has emerged between coastal and interior Chinese provinces. In Guangdong Province, for example, per capita GDP was probably around US$4,100 in 1994 (by the same PPP-measure), thus trailing behind South Korea by less than half of its level.[2] From this perspective, the prosperous Chinese coastal belt already constitutes a powerful base for economic cooperation with member APEC economies.

Consider next the relative "openness" of the Chinese economy in terms of her external trade volume relative to GNP size. Surprisingly, the trade/GNP ratio given in Table 10.1 suggests that China is currently even more "open" than Japan and is comparable with Australia, even if it still lags far behind such entirely trade-dependent APEC economies as Hong Kong and Singapore. If Guangdong Province and the municipality of Greater Shanghai (another provincial-level unit) are taken as the basis for comparison,[3] their ratios are certainly comparable with those of South Korea, Taiwan and Thailand, which are all heavily export-oriented.

Here again, the real Chinese picture seems to have been highly distorted as a result of the statistical bias associated with the official renminbi exchange rate used for the estimates. The reason is simple. While export and import statistics are normally based on the original US dollar quotation, Chinese GNP figures in US dollar are derived from straightforward conversions from officially reported renminbi values according to the highly depreciated yuan rate

Table 10.1 Major Economic Indicators for China in Comparison with other Major APEC Economies, 1993/1994

	Population (1994)		GNP (1993)		Per Capita GDP (1993)	Output Structure (1993)			Export (1994)		Import (1994)		Trade/ GNP Ratio
	Millions	%	US$ million	%	US$	%			US$ million	%	US$ million	%	%
	(1)	(2)	(3)	(4)	(5)	(6)			(7)	(8)	(9)	(10)	(11)
						A	I	S					
China	1,191.8	68.11	581,110	11.75	361	20	48	33	104,672	9.43	114,564	11.12	37.73
			(3,864,382)	(46.97)	(2,401)								(5.67)
Japan	124.0	7.09	2,996,052	60.59	31,558	3	32	65	360,705	32.49	238,716	23.18	20.01
				(36.41)									
Hong Kong	6.3	0.36	104,730	2.12	19,600	0	17	83	151,399	13.64	161,841	15.71	299.09
				(1.27)									
S. Korea	44.5	2.54	338,060	6.84	7,496	7	43	50	96,013	8.65	102,349	9.94	58.68
				(4.11)									
Taiwan	21.0	1.20	226,240	4.58	10,703	4	37	59	92,833	8.36	85,489	8.30	78.82
				(2.75)									
Singapore	2.9	0.17	55,370	1.12	18,458	0	37	63	96,457	8.69	102,400	9.94	359.14
				(0.67)									
Malaysia	19.5	1.11	60,060	1.21	3,384	16	44	40	58,147	5.24	59,414	5.77	195.74
				(0.73)									
Indonesia	190.7	10.90	136,990	2.77	773	19	39	42	39,487	3.56	35,132	3.41	54.47
				(1.66)									
Philippines	68.6	3.92	54,610	1.10	747	22	33	45	12,124	1.09	22,638	2.20	63.66
				(0.66)									
Thailand	59.4	3.39	120,240	2.43	1,892	10	39	51	45,061	4.06	54,365	5.28	82.69

Table 10.1 (to be continued)

Table 10.1 (continued)

	Population (1994)		GNP (1993)		Per Capita GDP (1993)	Output Structure (1993)			Export (1994)		Import (1994)		Trade/ GNP Ratio
	Millions	%	US$ million	%	US$	%			US$ million	%	US$ million	%	%
	(1)	(2)	(3)	(4)	(5)	(6)			(7)	(8)	(9)	(10)	(11)
						A	I	S					
				(1.46)									
Australia	17.5	1.00	233,109	4.71	14,485	3	29	67	42,723	3.85	43,476	4.22	36.98
				(2.83)									
New Zealand	3.5	0.20	37,956	0.77	10,809	8	25	67	10,430	0.94	9,649	0.94	52.90
				(0.46)									
AP total	1,749.7	100.00	4,944,527	100.00	3,298	5	34	60	1,100,511	100.00	1,030,033	100.00	43.28
			(8,227,799)		(4,690)								(26.01)

Notes: (1) The two bracketed absolute GDP figures for China are obtained by multiplying the given official figures with 6.65. The ratio of 6.65 is obtained by relating the World Bank's PPP (Purchasing-Power-Parity)-based per capita GDP of US$2,460 for 1992 to China's own estimate of US$370 (as converted from renminbi using the official exchange rate). The International Monetary Fund (IMF) has made a similar PPP estimate for China, also for 1992, and come up with a lower per capita GDP of US$1,700 compared with the World Bank's figure cited above. The IMF estimate would give a lower multiple of 4.59 (i.e. US$1,700/US$370), and therefore a lower total GNP of US$2,667,295 million and per capita GDP of US$1,657, but a higher trade/GNP ratio of 8.22. (2) Output figures for the A (agriculture), I (industry) and S (service) sectors are all in gross values rather than in value-added terms. (3) The statistics for population, export and import for Japan, Australia and New Zealand are all 1993 figures.

Sources: (1) All population, GNP/GDP, and trade statistics are from ADB—*KIDAPC* 1995; except those for Japan, Australia and New Zealand, which are given in World Bank, *World Tables* 1995 and UN—*ITSYB* 1994; and the Hong Kong population figure which is from HKG—*HKYB* 1995. (2) All gross output figures are from World Bank, *World Tables* 1995; except those for Taiwan, which are taken from TCEPAD—*TWSDB* 1995. (3) The PPP-estimates are reported in *The Economist*, 15 May 1993 exports (for World Bank's) and *TKP*, 18 May 1993 (for IMF's).

against the US dollar. This has helped grossly to understate Chinese GNP in renminbi denomination.

Thus, if we were instead to apply the PPP-estimates of the World Bank in order to estimate China's GNP, the trade/GNP ratio would probably be reduced from 37.7% to no more than 6% (1993/1994). Or, if the similar, but more conservative IMF estimate were used, the estimated trade ratio would be only around 8.2% in 1993 (see notes to Table 10.1). Ultimately, no unambiguously precise estimate is possible. But it is safe to propose that the relative openness of the Chinese economy is substantially less than the "official" trade/GNP ratio would suggest.[4] The implication is that there still is considerable potential for enhancing trade and investment flows between China and other APEC members.

To sum up, given the size of the Chinese economy, which accounts for nearly 50% of the total GNP of APEC proper by the PPP-estimate (or 12% by the nominal official statistics), there is a prima facie case for believing that China will join Japan to become one of the two pre-eminent forces in the economic integration of the Asia Pacific—and, in the context of APEC, play a much more significant role than the US in the global economy. Against this background, we now consider China's trade relations with member APEC economies since the early 1980s.

Trends in China's trade with APEC economies

The basic question here is whether, as a result of China's domestic reforms and accelerated opening up to the outside world, her trade flows with other APEC economies have been enhanced to any significant extent, vis-à-vis those with other countries outside of the Asia-Pacific region. The widely-held view is that trade among APR countries has increased substantially in the past fifteen years, highlighting strengthened economic integration within APEC proper. This view is further strengthened by the general perception that in addition to the benefits of geographical proximity, APEC proper economies are complementary to each other, by virtue of their great diversity (in terms of GNP size, factor endowment, stage of development, and technological levels).

However, the picture which emerges from the statistical trends shown in Table 10.2 is at best a mixed one. The figures there offer evidence of the changing magnitude of China's trade flows with various APEC proper economies relative to North American (NA) and selected Western European countries (E) for the benchmark years—1980, 1985, 1990 and 1994. A number of points may be made.

First, in support of the general perception, China's merchandise trade (exports plus imports) with APEC countries as a whole did indeed increase from 46% (1980) to 57% (1994) of its global trade. However, such increases seem to have taken place at the expense of ROW (rest of the world) countries (the share falling from 27% to 16.2% between 1980 and 1994), rather than "NA + E" countries (share remaining at 27% from 1980 to 1994, despite a marginal decline to 22% in both 1985 and 1990). To the extent that the ROW share consistently declined after 1980 through the interval benchmarks 1985 and 1990 to 1994, it would appear that a realignment of China's trade links with APEC countries away from such remote ROW trade partners as Africa, Latin America, and Middle Eastern countries has taken place.

Second, however, China's increased trade share with APEC countries seems to have essentially, if not exclusively, derived from the remarkable increases with Hong Kong and Taiwan—and latterly, South Korea. Such trends helped to boost China's combined trade share vis-à-vis the "four little dragons" (including Singapore) from 15% (1980) to 32% (1994).

Third, it is striking that the Chinese trade share with ASEAN (with or without Singapore), has remained virtually the same—a little more than 3%—during the past one and a half decades. It is interesting that this should be so, given the strategic aspiration voiced by both China and Malaysia in the context of APEC negotiations in Bogor with respect to the tariff agenda for the years 2010 and 2020,[5] as well as the continued improvement in political relations between China and ASEAN (whose exports and imports were 25% and 45% larger than those of China in 1994, excluding Singapore).

Fourth and most remarkably, the combined share of Australia and New Zealand in China's external trade fell quite consistently from 3.9% (1980) to a mere 1.9% (1994). This decline took place despite massive efforts by the governments of both countries to boost their trade with China from the early 1980s. Moreover, Australia consistently enjoyed trade surpluses with China after the establishment of diplomatic relations, and was for many years a net recipient of Chinese capital, intended to develop iron ore and aluminium smelting for export back to China. Amongst China's major trading partners, Australia has also had the fewest bilateral trade policy disputes with China.

The Australian and the New Zealand markets are of course too limited in size to exploit any scale economies in trading with China merely in order to sustain their share against the United States, Germany, Britain, France or Japan—all of whom can offer China much more advanced technology exports, as well as a larger export market.

These broad contours of change in China's trade relations clearly suggest that if economic integration within APEC is to be the main reference point, such integration has essentially taken place within what is popularly known as the "Greater China economic growth triangle", comprising the Chinese mainland, Taiwan, Hong Kong and Macau. But in this context too, the nature of economic integration, as shown by the statistical evidence in Table 10.2 and discussed above, should be interpreted with care.

Indeed, careful examination of the export and import statistics in Table 10.2 reveals that the increases in China's trade share with Hong Kong reflect changes in both exports and imports, with the latter perhaps assuming greater weight in the long run. This apparent paradox is easily resolved.

Increases in China's exports and imports vis-à-vis Hong Kong derive from two different sources. The first is trade related to so-called "outward processing" (OP) activities, commissioned by Hong Kong-based manufacturers from enterprises based in China. The latter include both the tens of thousands of joint ventures of Hong Kong origin, as well as a large number set up by local Chinese producers. While OP has become a familiar phenomenon in South China, it may still be a surprise to anyone unfamiliar with the scale and intensity of the economic synergy that the magnitude of associated Hong Kong exports (of raw materials, semi-manufactures, and machine and equipment) to and imports (essentially processed goods) from China should have reached such spectacular levels. According to official estimates by the Hong Kong government, in 1994, OP-related goods flowing from China accounted for 76% of Hong Kong's total imports from China, while goods outward bound for China within the same OP context constituted 69% of Hong Kong's domestic exports and 43% of total re-exports to China.[6]

Since 1987, Taiwan's trade relations with mainland China have followed the same pattern as Hong Kong's, except that most of the island's exports to and imports from the mainland have had, for well-known political reasons, to be channelled through Hong Kong. Figure 10.1 shows that, after the adoption of a new political reorientation towards mainland China in 1987 (allowing "indirect" personal and business contacts with mainland counterparts through third parties), Taiwan's trade with Hong Kong soared dramatically. There is no doubt that the overwhelming proportion of Taiwan's exports to and imports

Table 10.2 China's Trade with APEC Proper (AP), North America (NA) and Major European Countries (E), and with the Rest of the World (ROW), 1980–1994

	Export								Import								Export + Import			
	1980		1985		1990		1994		1980		1985		1990		1994		1980	1985	1990	1994
	US$m	%	US$m	%	US$m	%	US$m	%	US$m	%	US$m	%	US$m	%	US$m	%	%	%	%	%
World	18,139	100.0	27,329	100.0	62,876	100.0	120,822	100.0	19,505	100.0	42,534	100.0	53,915	100.0	115,629	100.0	100.0	100.0	100.0	100.0
AP	9,831	54.2	16,257	59.5	41,492	66.0	68,517	56.7	7,613	39.0	22,354	52.6	29,226	54.2	66,803	57.8	46.3	55.3	60.6	57.2
NA&E	3,087	17.0	4,195	15.3	10,010	15.9	33,012	27.3	7,084	36.3	11,171	26.3	15,199	28.2	29,722	25.7	27.0	22.0	21.6	26.5
ROW	5,221	28.8	6,877	25.2	11,374	18.1	19,293	16.0	4,808	24.7	9,009	21.2	9,490	17.6	19,104	16.5	26.6	22.7	17.9	16.2
Japan	4,032	22.2	6,091	22.3	9,210	14.6	21,490	17.8	5,169	26.5	15,178	35.7	7,656	14.2	26,319	22.8	24.4	30.4	14.4	20.2
S. Korea					433	0.7	4,376	3.6					236	0.4	7,318	6.3			0.6	4.9
Taiwan					320	0.5	2,242	1.9					2,254	4.2	14,084	12.2			2.2	6.9
Hong Kong	4,353	24.0	7,148	26.2	27,163	43.2	32,365	26.8	570	2.9	4,762	11.2	14,565	27.0	9,488	8.2	13.1	17.0	35.7	17.7
Singapore	421	2.3	2,063	7.5	2,016	3.2	2,563	2.1	190	1.0	241	0.6	849	1.6	2,481	2.1	1.6	3.3	2.5	2.1
Malaysia	180	1.0	186	0.7	370	0.6	1,118	0.9	240	1.2	198	0.5	852	1.6	1,623	1.4	1.1	0.5	1.0	1.2
Thailand	312	1.7	116	0.4	854	1.4	1,159	1.0	140	0.7	263	0.6	386	0.7	864	0.7	1.2	0.5	1.1	0.9
Indonesia	21	0.1	124	0.5	401	0.6	1,052	0.9	14	0.1	330	0.8	849	1.6	1,589	1.4	0.1	0.6	1.1	1.1
Philippines	258	1.4	314	1.1	205	0.3	476	0.4	70	0.4	97	0.2	90	0.2	272	0.2	0.9	0.6	0.3	0.3
Australia	224	1.2	183	0.7	468	0.7	1,488	1.2	1,063	5.4	1,124	2.6	1,361	2.5	2,448	2.1	3.4	1.9	1.6	1.7

Table 10.2 (to be continued)

Table 10.2 (continued)

	Export								Import								Export + Import			
	1980		1985		1990		1994		1980		1985		1990		1994		1980	1985	1990	1994
	US$m	%	US$m	%	US$m	%	US$m	%	US$m	%	US$m	%	US$m	%	US$m	%	%	%	%	%
New Zealand	30	0.2	32	0.1	52	0.1	138	0.2	157	0.8	161	0.4	128	0.2	317	0.3	0.5	0.3	0.2	0.2
4 DRAGONS	4,774	26.3	9,211	33.7	29,932	47.6	41,546	34.4	760.0	3.9	5,003	11.8	17,904	33.2	33,371	28.9	14.7	20.3	41.0	31.7
SK & TWN	0	0.0	0	0.0	753	1.2	6,618	5.5	0	0.0	0	0.0	2,490	4.6	21,402	18.5			2.8	11.9
HK & SING	4,774	26.3	9,211	33.7	29,179	46.4	34,928	28.9	760.0	3.9	5,003	11.8	15,414	28.6	11,969	10.4	14.7	20.3	38.2	19.8
ASEAN (expt SING)	771	4.3	740	2.7	1,830	2.9	3,805	3.1	464.0	2.4	888	2.1	2,177	4.0	4,348	3.8	3.3	2.3	3.4	3.4
AUS & NZ	254	1.4	215	0.8	520	0.8	1,676	1.4	1,220.0	6.3	1,285	3.0	1,489	2.8	2,765	2.4	3.9	2.1	1.7	1.9

Notes: AP covers the individual countries/region as listed, NA—United States and Canada, and E—United Kingdom, Germany, France and Italy.

Sources: IMF—*DTSYB*, various years.

from Hong Kong during this period, as may be measured by the discrepancy between the actual and predicted values shown in Figure 10.1, has been bound for or has originated from the mainland. To the extent that these flows officially constitute trade with Hong Kong, the estimated Taiwanese shares of exports to and imports from the mainland may already have been subsumed in Hong Kong's trade statistics with China.[7]

The share of South Korea in China's export and import trade also increased sharply following the establishment of diplomatic relations in 1992 (see Table 10.2). The major difference between Taiwan and South Korea in this respect is that the latter engages in direct trade with China and possesses no major political leverage for restricting imports from China, as Taiwan does. As a result, its positive trade balance appears to be less impressive than that of Taiwan.

Given the pre-eminence of outward processing-related trade, it is a matter of debate whether increased trade flows between China and Hong Kong/Taiwan/South Korea really do indicate enhanced economic integration within Greater China, or, more generally, Northeast Asia.

Before we consider this further, let us look at the second source of the increases of Hong Kong's share in China's external trade. This involves the accelerated increases in re-exports, both to and from China (in the latter case, especially to the United States).

According to our recent estimates made in a different context, the share of Hong Kong's total imports from China subsequently re-exported to the US increased from 4.86% (1979) to 41.6% (1994)—an average growth of 12.8% per annum in absolute terms. While the re-export value comprises a substantial proportion of OP-related imports from China and should therefore be counted more as Hong Kong's than China's exports to the US, it remains astonishing that Hong Kong's exports to China comprised goods of US origin which accounted for an average of 51% of the total during 1990–94 (and which, as a share of total US exports to China, increased from a negligible 1.6% in 1980 to a remarkable 29.6% in 1994).[8]

In other words, nearly one-third of total US exports to China are now channelled through Hong Kong. Nor is there any reason why European exports to China should not have followed the same pattern in the last fifteen years in order to take advantage of the trading facilities offered by Hong Kong in respect to sourcing, marketing, telecommunications, shipping, banking, financing, insurance, and so on.

Figure 10.1 Taiwan's Trade with Hong Kong and the Chinese Mainland, 1975–1994 (US$ million)

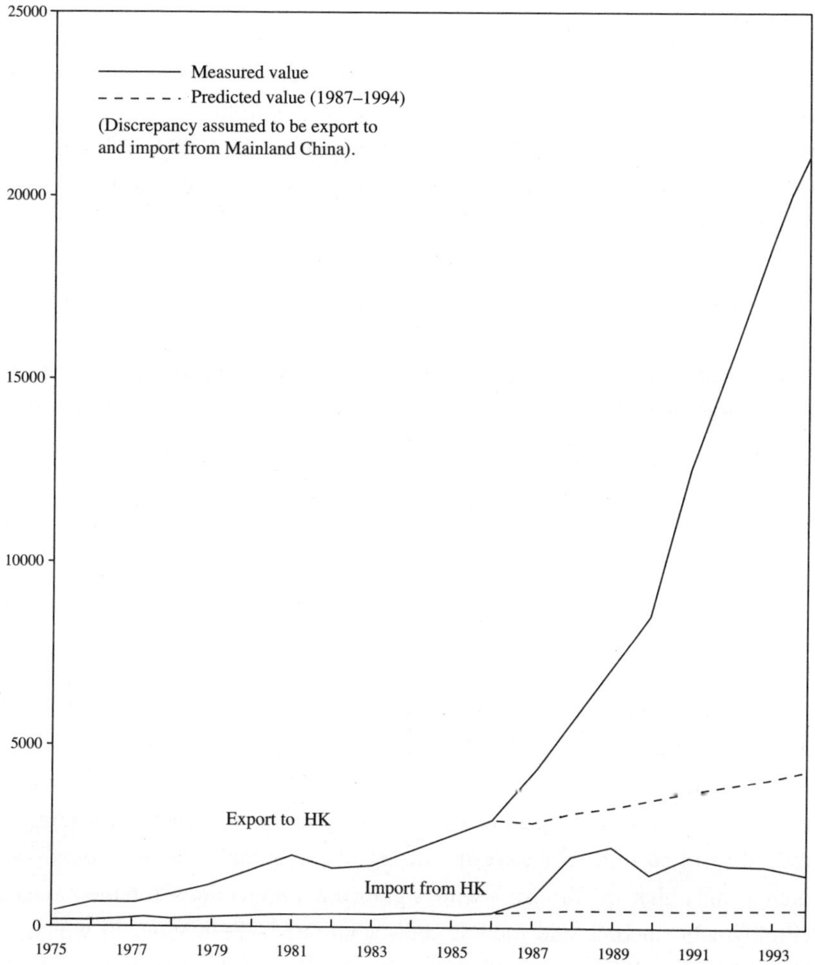

Notes: The predicted values are derived from a linear time trend fitted with the 1975–86 data.

Sources: TCEPAD—*TSDB* 1995.

But in accordance with the United States' statistical reporting convention that indirect exports to China count as exports to the immediate importing destination (in this case Hong Kong), the figures in Table 11.2 clearly understate China's trade shares with the "NA+E" countries. If the Hong Kong connection, as described above, is taken into account, the corresponding AP share must be substantially readjusted downwards in favour of the "NA+E" share. That is, since the mid-1980s, China's trade with "NA+E" may have grown even more rapidly than with AP countries as a whole, at the expense of ROW countries.

Implications for economic integration with APEC proper

The foregoing discussion suggests that the most visible process of economic integration among APEC countries has taken place within the Greater China growth triangle. The accelerated increases in trade flows between mainland China, Hong Kong, and Taiwan have also been accompanied or preceded by impressive direct investment made by Hong Kong and Taiwanese investors in the Chinese mainland.[9] While this bears all the hallmarks of increased economic interaction among the three Greater China economic entities, the nature and intensity of the perceived integration demands careful interpretation. Several points may be made in respect to these findings:

The first is that massive OP-related trade flows have been associated with direct investment from Hong Kong and Taiwan in mainland China, which has reflected no more than the massive relocation of Hong Kong and Taiwanese manufacturing activities to the vast Chinese hinterland. Such relocation has indeed resulted in a radical restructuring of the Hong Kong economy—and increasingly that of Taiwan—with significant implications for their output, employment, income and income redistribution.[10] The manner in which the Hong Kong and Taiwan economies have readjusted through increased economic interaction with the Chinese mainland is a clear case of economic integration. The impact on both of these small open economies has also predictably been much more effective and intensive than the impact of such integration on the vast mainland economy.

Second, however, by virtue of China's policy towards foreign direct investment (FDI) in China, the effect of the relocation of both Hong Kong and Taiwanese manufacturing activities onto the Chinese hinterland has inevitably been quite limited. It is well known that unlike the experience of many industrializing Asian countries, the Chinese government's FDI policy has leapfrogged from import substitution to export-orientated foreign investment. This inherently denies "national treatment" to foreign investment, while requiring foreign investors (of Chinese policy practices) to "balance their own foreign exchange requirements" by generating as much foreign currency earning as possible from their joint venture exports to the outside world.

The upshot has been the emergence of a "one country, two economies" system, under which a highly protective industrial system receives high priority in the national development and investment strategy, but coexists with a widely open sector catering to foreign investment and export drives.[11] Moreover, the chief mission of the latter has mainly been to use joint ventures with foreign investors to help generate sufficient foreign exchange earnings to finance investment in the forced-draft industrialization programme. Viewed this way, the "two economy" dichotomy implies an absolute denial of a strategy of full integration with outside economies.

Third, China's open-door strategy for courting foreign investment has nonetheless helped in a most impressive manner to establish a new, sui generis economic system along the Chinese coastal belt. This system has become increasingly and comprehensively integrated with the outside world, and has simultaneously assumed great economic importance in the national context. This is reflected not only in the growing importance of outward processing trade flows involving Hong Kong and Taiwan, but more importantly, in the fact that FDI in China now constitutes about 20% of annual domestic fixed capital formation, with Sino foreign joint venture exports accounting for around 40% of national exports. In this respect, therefore, the "open economy" sector of China has become fully integrated with the outside world.

The fourth point relates more specifically to the role of the Greater China growth triangle as a source of foreign exchange for the Chinese mainland. Its interaction with Hong Kong and Taiwan, both of whom have traditionally enjoyed huge trade surpluses with the US, has decisively helped to transfer the surplus to mainland China by way of investment and export processing. In other words, economic synergies have enabled both Hong Kong and Taiwan to export their bilateral trade deficits with the US to the mainland. Put differently, mainland China has been able increasingly to resort to the traditional export markets of Hong Kong (latterly, Taiwan's too) to finance its trade deficits with the United States, Western Europe, and Japan.

Table 10.3 sets out China's balance of payments vis-à-vis Hong Kong and the outside world. Between 1979 and 1993, in every year except one, China incurred a bilateral trade deficit with the US. The combined total of US$23 billion for the period was, however, easily offset by its accumulated trade surplus of US$142 billion with Hong Kong. Indeed, that same surplus was more than two times greater than China's combined deficit with the United States and Japan.

In short, China's total export earnings from Hong Kong alone, net of the corresponding import expenditure, have been more than sufficient to finance China's net import bills incurred with the United States and Japan, and even the world at large, for the entire period of 1979–93. Even if the outward processing (*sanlai yibu*) component is omitted from China's exports to Hong Kong, its trade surplus with Hong Kong is still more than sufficient to offset the country's combined deficits with the US and Japan for the whole period of 1989–93. This unequivocally highlights the pivotal importance of Hong Kong in both Sino-American and Sino-Japanese trade relations, or indeed, in the entire Chinese foreign trade system.[12]

This specific dimension of economic integration explains the accelerated growth of China's trade relations with APEC proper and with our aggregate category of "NA and E" countries, at the expense of ASEAN, and Australia and New Zealand.

Disregarding the economies of Australia and New Zealand, which are both small and remote, ASEAN countries would appear to assume a competitive, not complementary, position vis-à-vis the Chinese economy, in terms of export drive. This would explain ASEAN's stagnating or shrinking relative trade volume with China, with economic integration with their northern neighbour remaining a distant prospect. The reality is that individual ASEAN countries have increasingly felt the full weight of Chinese export competition in the past decade or so.[13]

A few words about Sino-Japanese economic relations are in order in this respect.

Unlike its ASEAN counterparts, Japan has played a role for China which has been very similar to that of the United States: first, as a supplier of industrial producer goods needed to feed China's massive industrialization programme; second, as an increasingly important export market for China. A very substantial proportion of Japanese exports to China has been channelled through Hong Kong. However, unlike the Hong Kong and Taiwan models,

Table 10.3 China's Trade Balance with Major Trading Partners, 1979–1994 (US$ 100 million)

Year	All Countries	USA	Japan	Hong Kong		Ratio 1	Ratio 2	Ratio 3
				Gross of *Sanlai yibu*	Net of *Sanlai yibu*			
	(1)	(2)	(3)	(4)	(5)	(4)/(1)	(4)/(2)	(4)/[(2)+(3)]
1979	–20.10	–12.62	–11.80	33.33	–	1.66	2.64	1.36
1980	–19.00	–28.48	–11.37	40.34	–	2.12	1.42	1.01
1981	–0.10	–31.49	–13.95	40.33	–	403.30	1.28	0.89
1982	30.30	–25.23	9.07	38.67	–	–	1.53	2.39
1983	8.40	–10.45	–9.83	41.05	–	–	3.93	2.02
1984	–12.70	–16.05	–30.86	39.60	–	3.12	2.47	0.84
1985	–149.00	–27.51	–89.26	24.07	–	0.16	0.87	0.21
1986	–119.60	–20.85	–76.59	41.75	–	0.35	2.00	0.43
1987	–37.80	–17.94	–36.76	53.41	–	1.41	2.98	0.98
1988	–77.60	–32.86	–31.41	62.93	–	0.81	1.92	0.98
1989	–66.00	–34.54	–21.39	93.76	46.69	1.42	2.71	1.68
1990	87.40	–14.09	14.23	123.96	55.67	–	8.80	–
1991	80.50	–18.49	1.88	146.74	39.36	–	7.94	8.83
1992	43.50	–3.07	–20.04	169.79	24.61	–	55.31	7.35
1993	–121.90	–12.13	–74.74	241.95	115.91	1.98	19.95	2.79
1994	53.46	74.91	–47.48	229.08	–	–	–	–8.35
Total	–320.24	–230.89	–450.30	1,420.76	282.24	4.44	6.15	2.09

Table 10.3 (to be continued)

Table 10.3 (continued)

Year	All Countries	USA	Japan	Hong Kong		Ratio 1	Ratio 2	Ratio 3
				Gross of *Sanlai yibu*	Net of *Sanlai yibu*			
	(1)	(2)	(3)	(4)	(5)	(4)/(1)	(4)/(2)	(4)/[(2)+(3)]
Average								
1979–85	–23.17	–21.69	–22.57	36.77	–	1.59	1.70	0.83
1986–94	–17.56	–8.78	–32.48	129.26	56.45	7.36	14.72	3.13
1979–94	–20.02	–14.43	–28.14	88.80	56.45	4.44	6.15	2.09

Notes: Figures for 1981–83 are converted from RMB yuan to US dollar by using the official annual average exchange rates. The two 1993 figures for trade balance with HK are tentative estimates, and could be very problematic. The reasons are as follow: the year 1993 saw curiously both Chinese exports (US$22.1 billion) to and imports (US$10.5 billion) from HK being drastically curtailed from the previous year's high of US$37.5 billion and 20.5 billion respectively. A likely explanation for the precipitous drop is that the 1993 figures do not include the *sanlai yibu* components with HK. This is because HK government's statistics show that both outward processing (*sanlai yibu*) consignments (US$20.7 billion) to China and *sanlai yibu* imports (US$38.2 billion) from China in 1993 (as given in Table 10.1, Panels A and B) are themselves very substantially larger than the given Chinese total exports to and imports from HK. Thus, barring any other better explanation, we simply regard the original Chinese export and import figures as net of the *sanlai yibu* component. This results therefore in the trade balance with HK of US$11.6 billion for 1993 as given for the net series. This figure is of course not directly comparable to those for 1989–92 (which are derived from HK government statistics) and seems to be biased upward. For the 1993 trade balance (with HK) figure, we have in turn added Hong Kong's "outward processing"-related exports and imports to the original Chinese figures to derive the trade balance gross of the *sanlai yibu* components. In the estimates, HK's *sanlai yibu* import figure of US$38.2 billion is adjusted downward by 10% and the comparable export figure adjusted upward by 5% to account for the possible FOB/CIF discrepancy. This gives therefore the trade balance figure of US$24.195 billion for 1993.

Sources: *ZGTJNJ*, various issues.

re-exports of Japanese origin seem to have been more closely related to Hong Kong and Taiwanese FDI in China (in the form of industrial inputs, transport equipment, and machinery) than to Japanese FDI itself.[14]

It is interesting that the Japanese have contributed a much smaller share of FDI in China than Hong Kong, and have lagged behind Taiwan since the early 1990s. This has been widely interpreted as signalling a lack of Japanese interest in effecting technology transfer to China. No doubt there is an element of truth in this. However, a more potent consideration is, in our view, that the Japanese have simply not recognized an urgent need to expand their share in the Chinese FDI market, because of their involvement, albeit indirect, as suppliers to Hong Kong and Taiwan investors of the bulk of the necessary industrial inputs to back up their FDI in China. We would argue that this indirect involvement represents a more rational economic strategy, given widespread Japanese concern that the FDI market in China is still full of uncertainties associated with an undeveloped legal framework, bureaucratic complications, inadequate patent protection and, above all, pervasive restrictions to domestic market access.

From the Japanese perspective, it may well be more worthwhile to pay the tens of thousands of small "rent-seeking" firms from Hong Kong and Taiwan to expand their commodity export share in the Chinese market, rather than to become personally involved in establishing small export processing plants in China in pursuit of the last margins of earnings from "second-round" exports to the third countries.

Conclusion: Prospects for the APEC tariff agenda

The main issues arising from the Bogor Declaration (1994) address the tariff agenda for the year 2020 more than for 2010. There is no doubt that the advanced industrialized APEC member economies would be able to meet the 2010 free trade and investment requirements with relative ease. But for the developing APEC economies (with the notable exceptions of Hong Kong and Singapore), reconciliation of tariff concessions could still pose serious problems. China's unweighed average tariff level was 35.9% in 1995. Even following the massive reductions by around 33% following the voluntary offer made by President Jiang Zemin at the APEC summit (Osaka, November 1995), it remains at 22–23%. This is much higher than the average of 8–13% for other major developing APEC economies, let alone the 3–4% for advanced countries. Thailand is the only country within APEC which has a higher average tariff level than China (39.6% in 1993).[15]

It is difficult to predict when China will effect a further adjustment of tariff rates in line with those of other APEC countries. The target set in the 9th Five-Year Plan (1996–2000) is to reduce the average level to 13% by year 2000. Even if fulfilled, this would still be higher than the average for major developing APEC economies. Whether in such circumstances it would then be possible for China to further accelerate the process of tariff reduction in pursuit of the long-term Bogor target of zero tariffs by 2020 is a matter for conjecture. Both China and Malaysia made it clear in Bogor that while they agreed in principle with the declaration, they did not wish to be bound by it officially.

In any case, from the present perspective, any accelerated tariff reductions undertaken by China could prove to be detrimental to many key branches of her infant industries, including electronics, chemicals, pharmaceuticals and—above all—the car industry. This is what is at stake in the prolonged Chinese negotiations with the United States for an early entry into GATT/IWTO.[16]

Malaysia's reservations over the Bogor Declaration for an entirely free trade and investment regime by 2020 clearly reflect similar aspirations and concerns. Likewise, there is no apparent reason why the policies of other major Asian APEC members, such as Indonesia and Thailand, should not be driven by similar considerations.

In a sense, the WTO predicament the Chinese faces is compounded by their ambitious pursuit of foreign capital inflows. Exemptions of import duties for imports of raw materials, semi-manufactures, machine and equipment, for joint venture investments are still widely applied. In the framework of "one country, two economies" (see above), nominal import tariffs may have to be kept at a relatively high level to compensate for concessions made to foreign investors, and to protect sizeable import substitution and inward-orientated priority sectors. This basic policy orientation may obviously continue to hinder the major dismantling of the Chinese tariff system.

Nonetheless, the more fundamental issue raised is whether, in the light of the Bogor target for APEC to become a free trade and investment region by 2020, the Chinese economy will become more closely integrated with the advanced APEC economies (Japan and the United States) and Western Europe, or with ASEAN and Australia. This is clearly not a zero-sum game situation, and it deserves careful consideration.

First, what is certain is that for many years to come, China will continue to trade with Japan and the highly industrialized Western countries to a much greater extent, in terms of bilateral flows of goods, investment and services, than with the countries of APEC proper. This trend will intensify, as the huge Chinese industrial system becomes increasingly mature and diversified.

Second, the South China growth triangle (comprising Hong Kong, Taiwan, and Guangdong Province) is likely for many years to remain the driving force behind Chinese re-export and export processing activities, generating the necessary foreign hard currencies for financing the country's industrialization programme. Shanghai apart, this will also remain the Greater China window for attracting foreign capital and investment in China in the foreseeable future.

Third, early admission of China into WTO is likely merely to further enhance China's integration with the advanced industrialized West, or with northern APEC, than to affect its relations with countries of southern APEC proper. It is self-evident that any further concessions which China may make in order to facilitate GATT/IWTO membership, whether in relation to tariff and non-tariff barriers, investment impediments, or market restrictions to such service sectors as banking, insurance, telecommunication and transportation, will attract more complementary goods and capital inflows from the North rather than from the South.

Southern APEC members, especially ASEAN countries are—by virtue of their factor endowments and the stage of development each has reached—in basic competition with China for a share in the export markets of major Western countries as well as for foreign investment. It is likely that they will lose out as China's influence expands further.

However, such arguments are not intended to imply that growing Chinese economic power will marginalize the importance of southern APEC member economies. A more likely scenario is that as China gradually becomes an industrial powerhouse of Asia, it will fuel growth and industrialization within APEC proper, joining Japan to become a crucial source of supplying the bulk of industrial producer goods to her Asian neighbours. Moreover, the huge and highly diversified Chinese economy promises to provide sufficient market niches for the highly export-orientated ASEAN countries to diversify their overseas markets. It is not too much to hope that such developments will eventually help to make the APEC agenda for a free trading bloc a reality.

In the context of the massive export drive of all export-orientated members of APEC proper, China currently represents the very tail of the "flying geese" formation by reason of its comparative advantage in labour-intensive manufactures exports. However, the Asia-Pacific region must anticipate the time when the emerging industrial giant will join Japan as the dragon head of economic growth in the region. With or without the creation of a trading bloc under APEC, the economic centre of gravity of the world will then have shifted to the Asia-Pacific region.

11
China's New Industries and Regional Economic Realignment in the Asia Pacific*

Purpose and scope of the study: A WTO perspective

The main purpose of this study is to examine the pace and pattern of development of China's new industries, as they may bear on the regional production networks in East Asia. Two new industries are selected for the study. First is the electronics and information technology (IT) industry, and second is the automobile industry. Both industries are considered new, and have experienced accelerated application of new technologies supplied from abroad, which until the late 1980s were almost totally alien to the Chinese industrial system.

The other major characteristic is that these new industries cater substantially to an entirely new spectrum of clientele. Thus, while just a few years ago, saloon cars were still far beyond the dreams of private individuals, they now have rapidly entered the realm of possibility for hundreds of thousands of urban households, similar to the case of coloured televisions, video recorders, and refrigerators from the mid-1980s onwards, and air conditioners since the early 1990s.

The two new industries are selected for study mainly because they seem poised to significantly affect the industrial setting of the neighbouring East

---

* Reprinted with minor adaptation from Ponciano Intal, Jr. Marissa Garcia and Miguel Roberto Borromeo (eds.), *Production Networks, Industrial Adjustment, Institutions and Policies and Regional Cooperation—Country Cases and Regional Paper,* Manila: De La Salle University-Angelo King Institute for Economics and Business Studies, 2009 (a project funded by the International Development Research Centre of Canada, see http://www.dlsu.edu.ph/research/centres/aki/-pdf/-concludedprojects/-countrycases/kueh/.pdf).

Asian economies in the years to come. Just within a few years of its debut in the late 1980s, the Chinese electronics and IT industry has swiftly established itself as a highly export-oriented undertaking, threatening to erode the global market shares of such star forerunners as Taiwan, South Korea, Malaysia, and Singapore, and in fact, even more remarkably, that of Japan as well. Likewise, there are clear signs that the Chinese automobile industry, by virtue of the enormous advances made in the domestic market in the past several years, is now on the threshold of targeting the export market in Asia and other parts of the world. Hopefully, Thailand—the most important car manufacturing and exporting country in Southeast Asia—will be able to withstand the expected Chinese foray in the future.

This study attempts therefore to trace the development of the two Chinese industries, focusing on the role of FDI and their exports records or export potentials. The relative strengths of the Chinese electronics and IT industry as an exporter will be estimated in detail, specifically vis-à-vis that of neighbouring economies. The estimation applies the familiar revealed comparative advantage (RCA) methodology, and concentrates on the US market, which is the single most important export destination for all East Asian exporters. The analysis will generally cover the period from the mid-1990s to 2004. This will hopefully help to shed some light on the changing competitiveness of the Chinese electronics and IT industry, as it may impinge upon similar industries in other parts of the region. It should also be of great interest to see how the smaller neighbouring economies cope with the impact from China and exploit the niches offered by the emerging new regional production networks. In more positive terms, the question posed is what may possibly become the new pattern of regional economic cooperation, and what may be the practical implications of all such changes for regional trade and investment flows in the foreseeable future.

The analysis of the Chinese automobile industry will largely be confined to the production and sales of passenger cars in China. It will also be kept in relative brevity, given that the industry has yet to start testing the Asia-Pacific waters for exporting its maturing array of vehicles. The two new Chinese industries are to be examined, to a certain extent, as case studies on the regional economic impact of China's accession to the World Trade Organization (WTO) since 2001. There are three aspects to this complex problem.

First is how, under WTO's free trade regime (continuous tariff concessions and import quota reductions), the comparative advantages (or disadvantages) of the Chinese industries, in terms of factor endowment or technological attainment, may come into full play. This is bound to trigger, by virtue of the sheer size of the Chinese economic potentials, a wide-ranging realignment of trade and capital flows, both within East Asia and with respect to the region's external economic relationships.

Second, as a new member of WTO, China is being strongly drawn into the process of globalization, with major transnational corporations repositioning their FDI strategy towards China to take advantage of WTO's regime of investment liberalization and technology transfer. The upshot is likely a continuous migration of labour-intensive manufacturing industries to China, concomitant industrial restructuring or upgrading, as well as increased industrial and labour market dislocations in the affected East Asian economies.

Third is for China to bear the "intrusion" of foreign industrial conglomerates.

The impact, however, may differ from industry to industry, in terms of employment, income, investment, output, and technological development.

The problems involved are therefore multifaceted and complex. We cannot tackle all of them in a single manuscript. What we propose to do is to first look at the salient aspects of changes and development in the two selected Chinese industries. This will provide a basis for examining export performance. Before we proceed, however, an integrated view of the major differences of the two industries should be briefly sketched, so that the comparative analysis and assessment of the two industries may be kept in proper perspective.

First of all, the Chinese electronics and IT industry clearly represents a leap from "import substitution" to "export-oriented" FDI. This is very much in line with the successful Chinese strategy of courting FDI. It is, however, very much at variance with the experience of other Asian industrializing countries, in which FDI normally started with targeting the output at the domestic demand (i.e., to substitute for imports of similar products), before aiming at export markets. By contrast, the Chinese automobile industry is still at the stage of import substitution, catering exclusively to domestic users. It is also strongly dominated by FDI especially with respect to the newborn passenger car industry.

Second, exports of the Chinese electronics and IT industry are essentially a matter of processing trade. Export sales may therefore be generally considered as "pre-guaranteed". This greatly enables foreign investors to earn foreign exchange (by exporting their products) to balance their own hard currency outlay (on imported inputs for processing), as strictly required by the

Chinese government. However, by the very nature of the automobile industry, it is apparently difficult for foreign carmakers to meet this "foreign exchange balance requirement" (as it is commonly known by foreign investors in China). This is in fact considered by Mr Wang Rongjun, the former managing director of the Shanghai Volkswagen joint venture, as a prohibitive factor for many global automobile giants, notably Japanese ones, for investing in China, prior to the country's accession to WTO (personal interview with Mr Wang; see acknowledgements for background information).

Third, under the WTO accord, trading in electronics and IT products is subject to liberalization at a quicker pace than that in vehicles. Based on the Information Technology Agreement (ITA) accepted by China (i.e., upon WTO accession), all IT product quotas were to be abolished immediately. By 2005, the country's import tariffs for all IT products, including semiconductor-manufacturing equipment, are to be slashed from an average of 13.3% to zero from the year 2000 onwards. By contrast, however, car import quotas will not be phased out until 2005, and car import tariffs will still remain at 25% (down from the pre-WTO accession high of 80–100%) by 2006. Obviously, the Chinese automobile industry is considered as more or less an infant industry which has not yet reached the mature stage of its life cycle to be able to compete internationally.

Fourth, given that the electronics and IT is a totally new industry in China implanted from abroad with FDI and foreign technology, the net economic gains accruable may actually be regarded as "absolute" or "perfect" (i.e., without any opportunity costs incurred to the country). Specifically, the foreign-sponsored industry helps to generate employment, train unskilled labour, create income, earn foreign exchange, and upgrade production technology. This is all done in an environment that is inundated with masses of unemployed workers, and in a country which is very much in need of both foreign technological know-how and hard currency to support the modernization drive. The situation in the automobile industry is mixed, however. While FDI helps to ease the country's capital constraint and bring in new foreign car-making technology, it has, nevertheless, threatened to render redundant a great number of existing small and inefficient Chinese automobile manufacturing or assembly plants.[1] The labour displacement and industrial restructuring involved could be quite painful. Moreover, profit expatriation from such import-substitution FDI also implies a potential drain on the country's foreign exchange reserves. However, an expanded and more efficient automobile industry in China, as driven by FDI and advanced Western technology, may help to strengthen many other associated industries and create new jobs as well.

Taken together, however, China's accession to WTO, coupled especially with the signing of the ASEAN 10+1 (China) Free Trade Area agreement in November 2002, is bound to forcefully trigger a process of mutual adaptation among the various relevant East Asian economies. To the extent that all are highly export-oriented and depend at the same time on advanced Western economies for the supply of the necessary technology, the process may result in increased regional specialization, and hence a significant reshuffling of the East Asian production network. Against this background, we now proceed to look at the experience of the Chinese electronics and IT industry and examine how the automobile industry may draw on the experience in the course of its development in the years to come.

China's electronics and IT industry: The domestic scene

A high-tech perspective

High technology industries as defined in China comprise the manufacturing of (1) medical and pharmaceutical products, (2) aircraft and spacecraft, (3) electronic and telecommunications equipment, (4) computers and office equipment, and (5) medical equipment and meters. Categories (3) and (4) come under the scope of this study.

Taken as a whole, the various high-tech industries represent the fastest growing industrial branch in China. As shown in Table 11.1, from 1995 to 2001, the growth rates of their combined gross value of industrial output (GVIO) amounted to an annual average of 24%, compared to only 12% for all manufacturing industries. The share in the national GVIO, at constant 1990 prices, increased markedly from 11% in 1995 to 21% in 2001, or from 8% to 15%, at current prices. High-tech industries have now become the largest industrial branch in China, surpassing metallurgy and machine building to be the pivot of the entire Chinese industrial system.

Several important points emerge from Table 11.1:

First, the value of exports (or "export delivery" at ex-factory prices) of the high-tech industries tended to increase even faster than GVIO from 1995 to 2001, namely at an average of 25% per year, compared to only 13% for the all-industry measure. As a result, their share in total exports for all manufacturing

Table 11.1 The High-Tech Industries in China: Major Measures of Economic Trends and Shares in Combined Total for All Manufacturing Industries, 1995–2001 (100 million yuan and %).

	No. of enterprises	**Employment (person)**	**GVIO (Current prices)**	**GVIO (1990 prices)**	**Value added**	**Sales revenue**	**Profits**	**Exports**
1995	18,834	4,484	4,098	4,713	1,081	3,917	178	1,125
	(4.08)	(6.34)	(8.41)	(11.37)	(8.85)	(8.48)	(14.53)	(14.92)
1996	18,909	4,610	4,909	5,580	1,272	4,497	207	–
	(4.28)	(0.70)	(9.57)	(12.80)	(9.36)	(9.81)	(27.20)	
1997	17,411	4,305	5,972	7,163	1,540	5,618	309	–
	(4.13)	(0.67)	(9.96)	(13.58)	(9.77)	(10.35)	(27.81)	
1998	9,348	3,927	7,111	9,055	1,785	6,580	311	2,042
	(6.25)	(0.27)	(11.92)	(6.75)	(11.70)	(11.96)	(32.50)	(19.45)
1999	9,492	3,845	8,217	10,878	2,107	7,820	432	2,413
	(8.86)	(0.81)	(12.85)	(17.87)	(12.50)	(13.06)	(26.18)	(21.51)
2000	9,758	3,900	10,411	14,111	2,759	10,034	673	3,388
	(6.58)	(0.85)	(13.86)	(19.76)	(14.00)	(13.99)	(24.62)	(23.87)
2001	10,479	3,983	12,263	17,083	3,095	12,015	688	4,282
	(6.68)	(0.88)	(14.53)	(20.80)	(13.87)	(14.96)	(22.04)	(26.96)
Growth % p.a.	– 9.31	– 1.96	20.04	23.94	19.16	20.54	25.27	24.95

Sources: *CSYBHTI* 2002 (for full title of this and other similar sources specific to this chapter, see list of abbreviations, Part 3 of Acronyms and Glossaries).

industries increased from 15% in 1995 to a hefty 26% in 2001. High-tech industries have indeed rapidly replaced the textile industry to be the largest foreign exchange earner for the country a few years ago.

Second, as compared with the increases in total sale revenue, which stood at a relatively high rate of 21% per year in 1995–2001, the higher growth rate of the export value at 25% per year, seems to imply that an increasingly larger share of the marginal output of high-tech industries was being exported rather than sold in the domestic markets.

Third, quite remarkably, the size of employment by the high-tech industries declined over the same period in both absolute terms (from 44.84 million persons in 1995 to 39.83 million in 2001) and relative to total employment by all manufacturing industries combined (share down from more than 6% to less than 1% over the same period).

Fourth and equally interesting is the absolute decline in the number of high-tech enterprises, from some 18830 thousand in 1995 to 10480 thousand in 2001. A higher degree of decline is in fact observed with the total number of enterprises for all manufacturing industries. The upshot is an increased share in this respect for the high-tech enterprises from 4.1% to 6.7% over the same period.[2]

Taken together, the last two points suggest that an overall industrial restructuring has taken place quite strongly in China, in favour of expanding scale economies. In the process, high-tech enterprises have moved towards a higher degree of capital intensity (versus labour intensity) in operation. This has occurred considerably faster than that for the non-high-tech enterprises. However, being a modern industry and latecomer, high-tech enterprises were already operating at a comparatively larger scale by the mid-1990s (average employment of 239 persons per enterprise against 153 for all industries in 1995). This may explain the fact that, as observed in Table 11.1, the decline in the number of enterprises in the high-tech industry (or rather, the process of consolidation and conglomeration through merger and acquisition) appears not to be as pronounced as that for the all-industry measure.

The same sources of statistics also reveal that the fixed assets owned per high-tech enterprise (at original purchase prices) increased by more than twofold from the average of 10.39 million yuan in 1995 to 38.33 million yuan in 2001. Being highly export-oriented, high-tech industries are clearly compelled by global competition to enhance competitiveness by constantly enhancing scale economies and product efficiency. What is said above of the

Table 11.2 The Rising Share of Electronics and Information Technology in Total Output of the High-Tech Industries in China, 1995–2001 (%, based on GVIO at current prices)

	Medical and pharmaceutical products	Aircraft and spacecraft	Electronics and telecom equipment	Computer and office equipment	Medical equipment and meters
1995	23.46	6.56	53.24	8.65	8.09
1996	23.45	5.83	51.01	11.83	7.87
1997	21.14	5.24	53.12	13.35	7.15
1998	19.31	4.55	54.11	15.76	6.28
1999	18.22	4.05	57.31	14.65	5.78
2000	17.11	3.72	57.45	16.11	5.61
2001	16.64	3.83	56.27	17.94	5.32

Sources: *CSYBHTI* 2002.

high-tech industries as a whole certainly applies even more forcefully to the electronics and IT industry, given that the two categories (3) and (4) of high-tech industries referred to have seen the combined output share increasing most impressively, from 62% in 1995 to 74% in 2001, at the expense of the other three categories (see Table 11.2).

Output trend and composition of the industry

The two broad categories of the Chinese electronics and IT industry (i.e., "electronic and telecommunications equipment" and "computers and office equipment") cover a large number of subcategories for their various products. Table 11.3 gives an overview of the production trends and the changing output composition from 1995 to 2001. Several important points may be made.

First, the combined output of the two broad categories increased most remarkably by an average annual rate of 28% in the period under study. The growth of the "computers and office equipment" branch by 35% per year is especially noteworthy. Thus, by the end of 2000, users of computer networks in China had already soared to 22.5 million (from a mere 7,000 in 1995); and earlier that year, Legend, one of the country's electronics giant, had surpassed IBM and Compaq to become the largest PC producer in the Asia-Pacific region.[3]

Second, "household audiovisual equipment" as a branch, which includes coloured TVs, DVDs, VCDs, VCRs, hi-fi stereos and the like, remained a bright point of growth for the industry. Although its GVIO share dropped from 28% in 1995 to 22% in 2001 (Table 11.3), the average annual rate of growth still stood at a high of 24% for the period (as can be estimated from the underlying figures). The continuous high growth has in fact resulted in an enormous glut in China of coloured TVs, among other similar products, to trigger a fierce price competition among major producers in the past couple of years.[4] As a result, by 2002/2003, Chinese coloured TV sets have started to flood overseas markets, prompting the US to eventually introduce sanctions in November 2003 against the four Chinese electronics giants—Changhong, Xiahua, TCL, and Konka—for "dumping".[5]

Third, likewise, for the other two subcategories, "electronic apparatus" and "electronic components", while their combined GVIO share basically remained unchanged from 1995 (at 35%) to 2001 (32%), their absolute output value increased, nonetheless, by an average of 22% per year in 1995–2001. The two subcategories comprise such products as electronic vacuum apparatuses, semiconductor separated parts, integrated circuits (ICs), and various electronic components. Amongst these, output of ICs—dubbed the "food grain" of the electronic industry—grew fastest by 25% per year, again in terms of GVIO at constant prices. However, by 2001, China's ICs production (6,362.88 million physical units) (*CSYB 2003*, pp. 510–3) was at best on par with Thailand's (7,070 million in 2000, or 4,400 million in 2001).[6] In terms of both output and exports, the country lags far behind Malaysia, Korea, Taiwan, and Singapore as well.

Fourth, the largest sector by far in the Chinese electronic and IT industry is the subcategory "telecommunications equipment", which comprises transmission, exchange and terminal equipment. It scored a spectacular growth rate of 35% per year over the period of 1995–2001, and by the end of the period, had already taken up 43% of the GVIO of the "electronic and telecommunications equipment" branch. This amounts to nearly one-third of the GVIO of the entire electronics and IT industry as defined, "computers and office equipment" included. The records reflect clearly the massive efforts made by the Chinese government to build up the national infrastructure for telecommunications at maximum speed. Notice that the annual sales of programme-controlled switchboards in China increased from 11.04 million lines in 1995 to 93.97 million lines in 2001 (*CEIYB 2001/2002*), annual output of telephone

Table 11.3 Output Trends and Composition of the Electronics and IT Industry in China, 1995–2001 (100 million yuan and %)

Items	1995	1996	1997	1998	1999	2000	2001	Growth (% p.a.)
Electronic and telecommunications equipment								
Telecom equipment	27.76	29.94	30.20	32.58	32.21	36.42	42.65	35.21
Radar and peripheral equipment	5.00	1.42	0.95	0.69	0.68	0.63	0.72	–15.20
Broadcast and TV equipment	0.83	0.81	0.55	0.55	0.46	0.58	0.50	5.95
Electronic apparatus	16.04	15.40	13.52	13.10	14.15	15.89	13.04	22.87
Electronic components	18.68	17.84	17.27	17.73	18.28	17.56	17.43	21.22
Household audiovisual	88.24	31.96	33.89	31.83	30.58	24.39	21.86	24.33
Others	3.45	2.63	3.62	3.51	3.61	4.52	3.80	21.47
GVIO (C)	2,181.67	2,504.21	3,172.01	3,847.27	4,708.52	5,981.38	6,900.45	
GVIO (F)	2,598.80	2,945.84	3,982.01	5,158.11	6,619.58	8,482.42	10,286.38	25.77
Computer and office equipment								
Computers	40.11	33.04	29.45	39.45	42.48	40.87	42.65	33.63
Peripheral equipment	51.11	56.08	61.19	47.89	45.53	48.15	47.68	37.24
Office equipment	8.78	10.88	9.37	12.66	12.00	10.99	9.67	38.37
GVIO (C)	354.46	580.94	796.95	1,120.60	1,203.49	1,676.95	2,199.80	
GVIO (F)	484.07	730.77	1,026.29	1,543.59	1,642.36	2,407.18	2,985.00	35.42

Notes: GVIO is given at both fixed (F) 1990 prices and current (C) prices. Figures for percentage shares are based on GVIO (C).

Sources: *CSYBHTI* 2002.

sets from 99.56 million in 1995 to 118.92 million in 2002, and that of mobile phones from 12.13 million sets to 121.46 million sets (*CSYB 2003*, pp. 510–3).

The changes in the output composition of the Chinese electronics and IT industry may yet be looked at from another, simplier perspective. The share of producer electronics has steadily increased from 22% in 1993 to 38% in 1998, and 49% by 2001 at the expense of consumer electronics, for which the share has been curtailed from 44% to 34% and then 26%; the balance being the share of electronic components and apparatuses at 34%, 28%, and 25% respectively (*CIDR 1999*, p. 184 and *CYBDHNTI 2002*, p. 646–8). This underscores the increased importance of the electronics industry in China's attempt to catch up with technological advances in the West, upgrading conventional industries through electromechanical integration, application of computer-added modelling and simulation testing, and by increased adoption of electronically-controlled fuel injection in car manufacturing, for example.[7] Meanwhile, the glut of consumer electronics and their spillover to global markets also clearly imply that increased domestic competition has continuously prompted the industry to improve product quality and enhance technological sophistication, as well as export competitiveness.

FDI and technology transfer

The high-tech industries in China are heavily dominated by foreign direct investment. In 1996, FDI already took up a 26% share in the total fixed assets of the industries. By 2001, the share moved up to 45%. If the electronics and IT industries (as defined to comprise the two major categories of electronic and communication equipment, and computers and office equipment) are taken separately, the FDI share is even more remarkable, standing at 42% in 1996 and 63% in 2001 (*CSYBHTI 2002*, pp. 107 and 223).

Table 11.4 shows more details about the growing size of FDI, in absolute terms as well as relative to total fixed assets accumulated by the Chinese electronics and IT industry in 1996–2001. Several points may be made.

First, FDI has clearly concentrated much more on the manufacturing of "electronic apparatuses and components" (which represents the basic inputs for any electronics assembly industry), rather than consumer electronics (as represented by the "household audiovisual equipment" sector). Note that the FDI contribution to fixed capital stock of the former sector amounted to 14,854 million yuan in 1996. This is only double the size of its contribution to the latter sector. However, by 2001, the comparable FDI contribution in the former sector has increased most remarkably to a total of 88,372 million yuan, representing nearly six times its contribution to the latter.

Second, the increased "scissors differential" as observed implies that foreign investors are able to take advantage of their technological strengths to expand the scale of production for electronics devices and components. However, over the years, domestic producers have also become comparatively better equipped in assembling the final products for consumer electronics. As a matter of fact, since the late 1990s, quite a few Chinese electronics giants, such as Changhong, Konka, Haier, Haixin, TCL, Legend, and Great Wall, have rapidly developed to be national brand names for coloured TVs, VCDs, and personal computers as well, and have indeed begun to erode substantially the market shares of major foreign brands (*CIDR 1999*, p. 189). The same holds for Bird, TCL, and Amoi as Chinese manufacturers of mobile phones. These are all latecomers in the market, but within a few years, they have nonetheless been able to cut deeply into the market shares of Nokia, Motorola, and Sony Ericsson in China, as the author was told by Mr Yenho Tree, managing director for Asia of Centurion Electronics (Shanghai) Ltd. during a personal interview in Shanghai (see acknowledgements for background information).[8]

Third, similar to the "electronic apparatuses and components" sector, the "computers and office equipment" sector is also heavily dominated by FDI in terms of the stock of fixed assets. This is especially true with the subsector "peripheral equipment of computer". Interestingly, the figures in Table 11.4 also reveal that between 1996 and 2000, the FDI share in the "computers" subsector declined quite substantially from 53% in 1996 down to 31% in 1998 and 29% in 2000, before reverting to 58% in 2001; whereas the comparable share in the "peripheral equipment" subsector increased remarkably from 47% in 1996 to 69% in 1998 and further to 85% in 2000, before being curtailed to 71% in 2001. This drastic exchange of the FDI shares between the "computers" and "peripheral equipment" subsectors seems to underscore once again that foreign investors concentrate more on the manufacturing of critical electronic parts and components, with which they control the core technology. Investments in mere assembling plants for final products with lower profit margins are left to domestic Chinese manufacturers, who have become increasingly better equipped and indeed most aggressive in attempting to slice off a share in the value chain of the entire electronics industry (*CIDR 1999*, p. 187).

Table 11.4 The Contribution of FDI to Fixed Assets of China's Electronics and IT Industry, 1996–2001 (million yuan and %)

	1996		1998		2000		2001	
	Stock	**Share**	**Stock**	**Share**	**Stock**	**Share**	**Stock**	**Share**
Electronic & telecom equipment								
Telecom equipment	14,511	61.8	14,022	53.8	14,822	52.4	31,054	63.2
Electronic apparatus & components	14,854	32.4	34,874	52.9	54,774	60.4	88,372	67.0
Household audiovisual equipment	6,292	42.9	9,992	49.8	15,546	58.3	15,621	51.8
Total	36,214	40.6	59,237	50.1	87,276	54.4	138,378	62.6
Computers & office equipment								
Computers	3,231	53.4	1,886	30.8	1,588	29.1	3,785	58.3
Peripheral equipment	1,386	47.7	4,064	69.5	8,546	85.4	9,871	71.4
Office equipment	495	55.3	791	67.1	1,576	77.9	2,756	87.2
Total	5,112	51.9	6,723	51.1	11,710	66.9	16,412	69.9

Notes: The stock figures refer to FDI contributions to total (year-end) fixed assets of the respective categories of the electronics and IT industry.

Sources: *CSYBHT* 2001.

The point made is borne out by information shared by Mr Tree during the interview. Mr Tree enlightened the author with the experience of the three Chinese mobile phone manufacturers referred to above. Bird, for example, started out with simply "pasting" its own brand name onto finished mobile phone sets purchased from outside (which may be dubbed "reversed" original equipment manufacturing (OEM)—a specific term referring to the widespread practice in China and other East Asian industrializing countries being commissioned by importers of advanced Western countries for OEM according to required specifications. The products are then labelled with the brand name of the importing conglomerates rather than that of the manufacturers). This was then followed by the modifying of the phone sets' front covers. However, through aggressive research and development, manufacturers are now able to design their own modules, with the chips and other key components being supplied by other upstream manufacturers. Mr Tree's own company, which is part of the US-based Centurion Wireless Technologies, Inc. supplies 45% of the mobile phone antennae needed by TCL.

A hierarchy of production technology and networking has therefore emerged in the Chinese electronics and IT industry. Accelerated Chinese exports to the world market have led to a marked realignment in the regional production networks in East Asia as well. Before more is said on this point, we should briefly give a more complete quantitative picture of the significant contributions of FDI in this respect.

Table 11.5 reveals that by any significant economic measures used—number of firms and employment, GVIO, investment completed annually, total fixed assets accumulated, sales revenue, and exports—the shares of foreign investors in the Chinese electronics and IT industry have increased remarkably in the past decade or so. The FDI share in Chinese electronics exports is especially noteworthy, rising from 38% in 1993 to a startling high of 79% in 2001. Over half of the industry's GVIO is now accounted for by foreign investors, as compared with just one-fifth in 1993. Most interestingly, while total investments made in the industry have tended to level off in 2001, the share of FDI has nonetheless continued to rise most substantially to 31% in 2001 from 14% a year ago. This seems to suggest that while local producers were being overwhelmed by insurmountable excess capacity and hence attempted to curtail further investment (*CIDR 1999*, pp. 185–6), the highly export-orientated foreign investors (which cater to the more refined global markets) could still see some bright spots overseas. This shows that the industry has indeed

Table 11.5 Share of FDI in China's Electronic Industry by Major Economic Indicators, 1993–2001 (industry total in million yuan and share in %)

	1993		1995		1999		2001	
	total	%	total	%	total	%	total	%
No. of firms (unit)	3,393	12.6	3,502	22.2	2,839	26.0	3,062	28.3
Employees (100 persons)	17,067	6.8	17,002	12.8	–	–	15,664	31.1
GVIO	111,721	21.3	188,084	41.0	467,867	47.3	844,870	54.0
Investment completed	10,827	14.0	14,486	30.2	30,717	10.1	40,310	31.2
Fixed assets	47,865	19.7	119,558	35.2	141,823	38.5	199,932	43.4
Sales revenue	119,283	20.8	178,627	41.1	457,828	47.7	827,483	51.6
Exports	18,942	37.8	62,855	74.5	125,410	73.9	273,320	78.8
Gross profits	4,303	32.1	9,683	64.0	–	–	48,900	51.0

Notes: The FDI shares cover both wholly-foreign-owned enterprises and Sino-foreign (equity and cooperative) joint ventures, and include a large proportion by investors from Hong Kong, Macao, and Taiwan. GVIO refers to gross value of industrial output at current prices. Investments completed include both basis investment and investment in technological innovation for 1995. For 1999, these seem to be lumped into a single category titled "long-term investment". Figures for fixed assets (at original purchase prices) and exports for 1995 are not available. The 1996 figures are used instead.

Sources: *CEIYB*, various years.

become increasingly mature and sophisticated as a result of enhanced domestic competition in China.

The technological implications of foreign investments in China on the electronic and IT industry are multifaceted. We should, first of all, distinguish between at least four layers of the technological hierarchy for ease of explanation. At the top of the ladder stands the design of semiconductors (i.e., more specifically, integrated circuits or chips). This represents the core technology for any electronic industry. Next is the "fabrication" or manufacturing of the chips, which in turn requires design of the most appropriate and cost-saving manufacturing technology. What follows is the design and manufacturing of various apparatuses, devices and electronic components. The technology of assembling the final products, as well as the techniques of assembling itself stands at the bottom of the hierarchy, together with the standards and processes of quality control and management.

As a Chinese expert puts it, citing personal computer manufacturing as a reference, "[The] PC industry is a clear case of global labour division. US manufacturers monopolize the core technology for chips and operating systems, thus reaping the most substantial parts of the profits. Japan, Korea, the Taiwan province, and others, share the second layer of profits from memory and hard disks. China and many other developing countries are left with the meager profits for the assembling and packaging jobs (for the final products)" (*CIDR 2001*, p. 157). This, of course, is a simplified version of the global fragmentation of production and the value chain.

According to Dr Steven S. L. Lee, Taiwan is actually quite advanced in Integrated Circuit (IC) design, and is second only to the US. In many respects, his company's VIA chips, globally applied under the brand name C3, is also popularly known in China as "China chip" (*zhongguo xin*), especially for the variant "Anter" (*Hanteng*), which is widely used for mobile computing and communications equipment. Dr Lee regards the mainland's IC design industry as still lagging behind its Taiwanese counterparts by five to eight years. Nonetheless, he also notes that the mainland's chip manufacturing technology is rapidly catching up with that of Taiwan, Japan, and even the US. The gap between the mainland and Taiwan in this respect has been narrowed down to one to one-and-a-half generations (i.e., just about two years, generally speaking). This has, to a great extent, resulted from the continuous relocation of major Taiwanese foundries to the mainland. The major points of the transcription of the interview are given in Box 1 below to provide further interpretative perspectives for looking at the evolving regional production networks, especially in the context of trade and investment flows.

BOX 1: IC Design and Manufacturing in East Asia

(Interview with Dr Steven S. L. Lee, VIA Technologies Inc.)

About VIA

It is a world-leading IC design house. Its business in China covers CPU, graphics, telecommunications, and system designs. VIA's CPU—dubbed the "China chip"—is characterized as "high-performance with low-power consumption". The chip distinguishes between three variants: the first is globally known as C3, used for desktop personal computers. The second is named Eden, normally applied to industry PCs, "thin clients", and multimedia portable devices—all embedded applications of fanless technology. The third one is popularly known in China as Antar (or *Hanteng* in Chinese), used in mobile computing/telecommunications equipment.

Centre of gravity shifting

The global centre of the industry was in the United States in the 1970s. It shifted to Japan in the 1980s, and subsequently to both South Korea and Taiwan from the 1990s onwards. China is now rapidly emerging as a new centre as well. However, the industry in the Far East emphasizes, generally speaking, more on semiconductor manufacturing rather than IC design. The US is still most advanced in IC design. Taiwan is second only to the US in terms of IC design capability. Japan focuses on high-end IC design, and has increasingly moved away from manufacturing, in favour of outsourcing to Taiwan and mainland China.

Regional specialization

In the IC design industry, Taiwan enjoys a particular capability "unparalleled by any other countries" in extending advanced US technologies to commercial application. The development of SOC (systems-on-chip) is a good case in point, which involves enormous brainpower for integration. Taiwan is also exceptionally strong with both OEM and ODM (see text), done either on the island itself or by manufacturers of Taiwan origin located on the mainland. As a rule, semiconductor design and pilot manufacturing are conducted in Taiwan, but mass production in the mainland, obviously for cost-saving reasons.

South Korea is better equipped for design and manufacturing of electronic devices (as represented by Samsung especially) and manufacturing technology for mobile phones (Samsung and LG). Samsung is in fact famous for surpassing Sony in TFT (thin-film-transistor) technology for manufacturing large display units. The country is also well known for such IT devices as FLASH and DRAM (Dynamic Random Access Memory) used in computers and mobile phones. A particular strength of the country is that, unlike Taiwan, it has been able to develop in many cases its own national brands in IC design and manufacturing.

Singapore is not poised to develop any IC design industry. The country used to be relatively advanced as a high-tech assembly house, for hard disk drives, for example. It focuses now essentially on the semiconductor manufacturing business—all on an OEM basis like Taiwan in the past. Under highly competitive pressures from neighbouring exporting rivals, Singapore hopes to be able to move to high-end IC manufacturing. The situation in Malaysia (hitherto a major OEM-based, IC-manufacturing exporting country) is similar. However, the country is poised to increasingly lose its manufacturing cost advantage to such other ASEAN countries as Vietnam, Indonesia and the Philippines.

The technological gap

The IC design industry in the Chinese mainland lags behind that of the US by 10 to 15 years, and Taiwan by 5 to 10 years (or perhaps less). In terms of IC manufacturing, however, it probably lags behind Taiwan, Japan, and the US by as little as one to one-and-a-half generations only—i.e., two years, or, more generously speaking, not more than four years. This is primarily a result of massive investments from Taiwan in the industry. Taiwanese investors have brought along not only cash capital, but also proven technology, machine, expertise, and professional manpower as well. At present, Taiwan is still more advanced in IC manufacturing technology, especially in the development of processing technology. Mainland Chinese still lack the capability for such development, but they possess enormous technical skills in copying and adopting the inventions.

In this context, an important point should be made about the potential impact of China's entry into WTO and its acceptance of the TRIMs (i.e., the global agreement of Trade-Related Investment Measures) and the TRIPs (Trade-Related Aspects of Intellectual Property Rights). Both agreements preempt any forced technology transfer, mandated offsets, local content requirements, and other similar restrictive measures. Coupled with import tariffs being reduced to zero by 2005 for all IT products, the country has indeed already seen a continuous influx of foreign technologies, as embedded in advanced semiconductor-manufacturing equipment, for example. In such circumstances, it should be clear that Chinese manufacturers would find it increasingly not worthwhile to initiate or engage in any major, costly R&D activities. If proven correct, then the Chinese electronics and IT industry may be expected to be further subjected to Western technological supremacy. Viewed this way, the given global or regional hierarchy of technology would clearly help to perpetuate the existing pattern of regional specialization within East Asian production networks for many years to come.

Nonetheless, in light of the enormous pool of manpower, skilled or unskilled, and an ever enlarging stream of technicians and university-level specialists, China is bound to become a global manufacturing centre for electronics and IT products. We may now proceed to examine how it works and how it may affect the industry in the neighbouring economies.

Electronics and IT as an export industry for China

The coastal bias

The Chinese electronics and IT industry, being overwhelmingly dominated by export-oriented FDI, is marked by two highly outstanding and closely related features. First, the majority of the manufacturing plants are located in the coastal region and, in fact, in two relatively narrowly defined areas: the Pearl River Delta (PRD) and the Yangtze River Delta (YRD). The second feature is that by any measure, the industry is most representative of the export processing trade. We look first at the coastal bias in the regional distribution of the industry.

By year 2000, 55% of the electronics and IT products exported from China originated from the PRD, while YRD (comprising Shanghai and the adjacent parts of Jiangsu and Zhejiang provinces) took up 24% (*CEIIAR 2001*, pp. 186–9). Both Dongguan municipality (just north of Shenzhen which borders

Hong Kong) and Suzhou city in Jiangsu Province (just to the west of Shanghai) have from the late 1990s rapidly emerged to be the global bases of PC manufacturing. Briefly, the global market shares of Dongguan are: 40% for magnetic heads, computer cases, and semi-fabricated products; 30% for copper-plated boards and driver units; 25% for semi-conductor grade capacitors and transformers; 20% for scanners and micro-motors; 16% for keyboards; and 15% for mother boards. Basically, over 95% of components and accessories needed for processing and assembling the computers are available in Dongguan in the PRD (*CIDR 2001*, p. 157). The municipality has indeed already become a major global outsourcing centre for IBM and Compaq (*CEITPERR 2001*, pp. 176–8). IBM has subsequently handed over its manufacturing bases in Japan, Melbourne, and South Korea to the Shenzhen-based Great Wall IT International Inc. Likewise, Intel has also relocated its manufacturing plants in Malaysia and Ireland to Shenzhen as well.[9]

For Suzhou in the YRD, which is globally known for its Singapore-sponsored Industrial Park, the comparable global market share for its computer manufacturing industry is 65% for mouses, 13% for scanners, 10% for mother boards, and 10% for keyboards (*CIDR 2001*, p. 157).

Both Dongguan and Suzhou are well known nationally as the important bases of Taiwanese investment in China. Especially in the aftermath of the disastrous earthquake of 20 September 1999 in Taiwan, many highly capital-and technology-intensive large electronics and IT enterprises relocated their manufacturing plants across the straits to the mainland to avoid further risks, together with a large number of affiliated firms producing components and accessories. Thus, within a year, a complete industrial chain headed by Taiwanese investors emerged swiftly in Suzhou and the neighbouring Kunshan municipality to produce various notebook computers, mobile phones, and digital cameras (*CIDR 2001*, p.157).

Virtually all Chinese semiconductor giants are also located in the YRD region, especially in the Pudong New Zone in Shanghai. These include Huahong Microelectronics (with technology support from Japan's NEC), SMIC (Semiconductor Manufacturing International Corporation; Toshiba technology[10]), and Shanghai Grace Semiconductor Manufacturing (funded jointly by a number of international high-tech conglomerates; Oki electric technology). Similarly, Konka is based in Shenzhen, and Haier in Qingdao (in Shandong Province), the notable exception being Changhong in Sichuan Province.

Exports as a processing trade

The figures in Table 11.6 reveal why the Chinese electronics and IT industry bears all the hallmarks of an export processing trade. Before we comment on the statistical tabulation, a few words are in order about the two different types of export processing. For simplicity, they are respectively referred to as the LL and JL types of export processing. For the LL type, foreign partners supply the whole or parts of raw and supplementary materials, parts arid accessories, packaging materials, and if necessary, machine and equipment as well; the Chinese side processes the "supplies from outside" (*lailiao* in Chinese) according to specified requirements. The finished and properly packaged products are to be delivered to the foreign partners for export on their own account, whereas the Chinese side earns the agreed processing fees. Foreign partners will also be compensated for the costs of supplying the machine and equipment with the processing fees earned. For reason of this element, this type of export processing is also commonly known as "compensation trade".

As for the JL type, the basic difference is that the "imported inputs" (*jinliao*) and exports of the finished or semi-finished products are both for the own account of the Chinese export manufacturers. The processing may or may not involve input of materials and parts from domestic sources.

Table 11.6 The Chinese Electronics and IT industry as an Export Processing Trade, 1995–2001 (US$ 100 million and %)

	JL-type exports	**LL-type, exports**	**JL+LL exports**	**Total E/IT exports**	**(3) / (4)* 100**
	(1)	**(2)**	**(3)**	**(4)**	**(5)**
1995	10,492	3,802	14,294	16,532	86
1996	14,904	4,635	15,538	21,498	91
1997	18,815	5,367	24,183	26,929	89
1998	17,173	5,820	22,993	25,671	89
1999	25,759	9,062	34,821	38,352	91
2000	38,672	10,886	49,558	55,161	89
2001	47,110	11,380	58,490	65,020	90

Notes and sources: *CEITPERR* 2001 for 1995–2000, and *CEIYB* 2002 for 2001. See text for definition of JL and LL types of electronics and IT exports.

Both LL and JL types of export processing are entitled to a rebate of value-added taxes. However, for the imported inputs, a "bonded" system is in place as prescribed by the government, in order to oblige the manufacturers involved to export the final products, although in most cases, the system appears to be merely a matter of bookkeeping (i.e., without involving any real cash deposits with the Chinese custom service) (*CEITPERR 2001*).

Several interesting points may now be made from Table 11.6. First and the most startling point is that at least since 1995, LL and JL types of export processing combined have made up between 86% to 91% of China's total electronics and IT exports. That is to say, "general trade" (as opposed to processing trade), or namely exports of truly Chinese origin, accounted consistently for just around 10%, or at most 14% (as in 1995) over the years.

Second, the value-added margin for export processing (i.e., the ratio of net exports to total imports) seems quite substantial. For the period 1995–2001, it averaged 0.68 for the LL type and 0.63 for the JL type (i.e., for every one US dollar worth of input imported, the net export value earned is 68 cents and 63 cents respectively).

Third, the share of the LL type (which, strictly speaking, is the prototype of export processing) in the combined total of the relevant exports tended to decline over the years, from 30% in 1995 down to 19% in 2001 in favour of the JL type. The decline may have been prompted by the higher value-added margin, albeit a slight one, for the LL type, in that domestic Chinese enterprises have found it increasingly more profitable to conduct export processing on their own account, rather than on behalf of their foreign partners.

The nature of the electronics and IT industry as a processing trade is also clearly reflected in the composition of imports and exports of the industry. Thus, as shown in Table 11.7, electronic apparatuses and devices needed for export processing made up nearly one-third of total imports in 2001 for the industry, as against only 7.63% for exports. The same goes basically for imports and exports of electronic components (i.e., 16% versus 13%). The smaller magnitude of difference for the latter category can obviously be explained by the fact that China imports the key expensive components, while exporting increasingly a large amount of low-grade ones.

By contrast, however, finished electronic or electrical home appliances made up 24% of total exports versus only 8% for imports. And for computers, the shares are respectively 34% for exports (almost all are minicomputers) and 22% for imports (essentially large-and medium-sized advanced computers,

Table 11.7 Imports and Exports of the Chinese Electronics and IT Industry by Major Products, 2000 and 2001 (%)

	Exports 2000	Exports 2001	Imports 2001
Household electronics	21.9	23.88	8.29
Electronic components	15.6	12.88	16.07
Electronic materials	1.2	0.99	2.49
Telecommunications equipment	12.4	14.19	13.55
Computers	31.8	34.28	21.57
Electronic instruments	4.8	4.53	6.31
Electronic apparatus	9.3	7.63	31.05
Broadcast & TV equipment	3.0	1.62	0.67

Sources: *CEITPERR* 2001 for exports and *CEIYB* 2002 for imports.

which the country is not capable of producing). As a matter of fact, China as a global electronics manufacturing centre still depends on Intel processors to make computers and Texas Instruments chips to churn out mobile phones. Such semiconductors are simply still beyond the design and manufacturing capabilities of the country, as one observer noted recently (*SCMP*, 20 March 2004, p. B3).

In absolute terms, total imports of electronic apparatuses and components, plus electronic materials and electronic instruments and equipment, amounted to US$31.05 billion as against only US$17.04 billion for exports in 2000. The imbalance between imports and exports has indeed remained most crucial for integrated circuits—the "food grain" of the electronics industry—as shown below:

Items	1996	1997	1998	1999	2000	2001	2002
Imports (US$ billion)	2.72	3.64	4.78	7.92	13.80	17.00	26.38
Exports (US$ billion)	0.60	0.93	1.15	2.06	2.94	2.63	4.32

In the same vein, the import supply sources and export destinations of the Chinese electronics and IT industry also clearly point to the nature of the industry as an export processing trade. Take again integrated circuits as an example: one-third of China's imports in 2000 came from Japan, a quarter from Taiwan, and the rest from South Korea, the US, Malaysia and Singapore.

As for IC exports, Hong Kong remained the largest outlet, not because of any substantial local demand, but because of its being the most important entrepôt for China.

Table 11.8 shows the major sources of import supply and export destinations for the Chinese electronics and IT industry taken as a whole during 2000–2001. Thus, Hong Kong took up a hefty 26% of total exports as against only 5% as an import source. Obviously it is because Hong Kong is most instrumental in channelling the bulk of China's consumer electronics exports to the US and other major Western countries. Even without considering re-exports from Hong Kong, the US itself still represents the single most important destination of China's electronics exports, taking up a total 21%, as against 14% as an import supplier for Chinese electronics and IT export processing.

Export composition and trend

Rapid and sustained technological upgrading and diversification over the past decade has enabled the Chinese electronics and IT industry to swiftly penetrate the world market with a rather complex array of new export commodities.

Table 11.8 Major Import Sources and Export Destinations for China's Electronics and IT Processing Trade, 2000 and 2001 (%)

	Exports 2000	Exports 2001	Imports 2001
Hong Kong	24	25.60	5.02
United States	23	20.99	13.53
Japan	12	12.60	21.16
The Netherlands	5	4.86	–
Germany	4	4.25	3.75
Singapore	4	3.52	–
South Korea	4	4.10	8.97
Malaysia	–	–	4.85
United Kingdom	3	–	–
Taiwan	2	–	12.57
France	2	–	–
Others	17	24.62	30.15

Sources: *CEITPERR* 2001 and *CEIYB* 2002.

By the early 2000s, capital-intensive and high-technology products such as programme-controlled switchboards and minicomputers have already increasingly dominated the export structure, alongside the large-scale supply of coloured TV sets, DVDs, VCRs, hi-fi stereos and the like. The advancements appear especially impressive when compared against the situation back in the 1980s, when the industry was literally made up of nothing more than labour-intensive and low-value-added assembling of radios, cassette recorders, and electronic watches.

The Chinese export strategy for the electronics and IT industry has basically followed that of the "four little dragons". Most of the producer enterprises are engaged in "original equipment manufacturing" (OEM) on behalf of global conglomerates. That is to say, the exported products are normally labelled with globally known brand names, rather than the producers' own trademarks. Unlike the "little dragons", however, China, with a virtually unlimited supply of the necessary labour, can always fall back on the vast hinterland to continue with labour-intensive manufacturing whenever the more advanced coastal areas are compelled by increased labour costs to promote capital-intensive technological upgrading. In other words, the "flying geese pattern" of regional specialization can take place within China itself, as has indeed been the case since the mid-1990s. As a result, one may expect that for many years to come, the country's electronics and IT exports will continue to be shared by both capital- and labour-intensive products.

Table 11.9 shows the export commodity composition of the Chinese electronics and IT industry by broad category. Several important points emerge:

First, by 2000, computers and peripheral equipment have already taken up the largest share, nearly one-third of China's total electronics and IT exports. The increases appear indeed to be quite consistent over the years since the early 1990s, when the comparable share amounted to only around 10%. While the exports tend to be dominated by hardware manufactures, especially minicomputers, they cover nevertheless a wide range of products, including cards, printers, display units, hard disk drives, floppy disk drives, computer cases, keyboards, floppy and hard disks.

Second, by contrast, the share of "consumer electronics", which include coloured TVs, hi-fi stereos, radios and cassette recorders, laser discs, video recorders and the like, has declined also quite consistently from a high of 47% in 1992 to around 20% in 2000. It is forecast to be reduced further in the years to come in favour of the share of computer and peripheral equipment.

Third, similar to the category of "computer and peripheral equipment", exports of "telecommunications equipment", which include notably, telephones, programme-controlled switchboards, mobile phones, optical fibres and optical cables, also increased quite drastically in the 1990s, to a high of 50% in 1998 as a share in total electronics and IT exports. However, the share tended to stabilize at just a little more than 10% by the early 2000s. It is forecast to increase in the next few years to only half the size of that of the "computer and peripheral equipment" category.

Last but not least of interest is the export share of the category "electronic components and apparatus", which includes, among other things, printed circuit boards, capacitors, transistor tubes, and most importantly, integrated circuits as well. Notice that by 2000, for the entire category taken as a whole, the share in total electronics and IT exports stood at around 30%, which is comparable to that of "computer and peripheral equipment". The accelerated increases in IC exports are especially noteworthy. It points to the fact that with increased technological upgrading, producer electronics are poised to assume a greater role in the country's electronics and IT exports. This is already clearly reflected in the shift, in relative terms, from "consumer electronics" as a category to "computer and peripheral equipment".

As a matter of fact, all major categories of electronics and IT exports have shown massive growth over the past fifteen years. Thus, as may be estimated from the data given in Table 11.9, the annual average rate of growth from 1991 to 2000 is 50% for "computers and peripheral equipment", 31% for "telecommunications equipment", 27% for "consumer electronics", and 39% for ICs (for 1996–2002). These figures all indicate phenomenal growth by any international standard.

More remarkable is the fact that accelerated expansion in production and exports has rapidly turned China into a net exporter for a wide range of electronics and IT products. As revealed in Table 11.10, the net export position is most pronounced with both coloured TV and telephone sets, but it is also clearly the case with facsimile equipment, minicomputers, display units, keyboards, printers, and others. However, the reverse is true with IC technology, for which the country is a very substantial net importer, and as it presently stands, there still is no sign for any reversal to take place in the foreseeable future. In other words, the country will likely have to rely on advanced Western countries for core technology to sustain its electronics and IT industry for many years to come.

Table 11.9 Export Composition of China's Electronics and IT Industry by Broad Product Category, 1991–2000 (realized) and 2001–2005 (forecast) (US$100 million and %)

	E/IT Exports total	Computer and peripheral equipment		Telecom products		Consumer electronics		Electronic apparatuses and components		Integrated circuits	
	value	value	%	value	%	value	%	value	%	value	%
1991	49	4.5	9.2	1.4	2.9	13.9	28.4	–	59.5	0.04	0.08
1992	61	10.7	17.5	6.7	11.0	28.7	47.4	–	24.1	0.00	0.00
1993	81	15.6	19.3	7.3	9.0	31.7	39.1	–	32.6	0.8	0.93
1994	124	28.0	22.6	14.6	11.8	51.2	41.3	–	24.3	1.6	1.29
1995	165	49.6	30.1	20.8	12.6	51.8	31.4	–	25.9	4.3	2.63
1996	215	64.7	30.1	89.4	41.6	44.8	20.8	–	7.5	12.6	5.86
1997	269	87.3	32.5	99.7	37.1	45.0	16.7	–	13.7	19.4	7.21
1998	258	68.9	26.7	130.2	50.5	38.7	15.0	–	7.8	12.0	4.65
1999	390	122.9	31.5	39.7	10.2	87.9	22.5	–	35.8	18.9	4.85
2000	552	175.3	31.8	68.5	12.4	120.9	21.9	170.4	28.7	19.7	4.36
2001	634	210.4	33.2	85.6	13.5	133.0	21.0	196.0	30.9	22.7	3.58
2002	730	252.4	34.6	107.0	14.7	146.3	20.1	225.4	30.9	26.1	3.58
2003	839	302.9	36.1	133.8	15.5	160.9	19.2	259.2	30.9	30.0	3.58
2004	965	363.5	37.7	167.2	17.3	177.0	18.3	298.0	30.9	34.5	3.58
2005	1,109.5	436.2	39.3	209.0	18.8	194.7	17.5	342.7	30.9	39.6	3.58

Sources: *CEITPERR* 2001.

Notice also from Table 11.10 that the strong export growth has persisted through the early 2000s for virtually all major electronics and IT products. Exports of "computer and peripheral equipment" taken as a category posted an annual average growth rate of 44% from 1996 to 2002, which is much higher than the 20% growth predicted in Table 11.9.[11] The same goes for coloured TVs, video cameras, carrier communications equipment and ICs; although for the relatively more mature products such as telephones, fax machines, cassette recorders, and perhaps speaker cabinets as well, the export growth tended to stabilize, to a greater or smaller degree, towards the later years (see Table 11.10).

Major export markets

For exports of the electronics and IT industry taken as a whole, the distribution among the major destinations are already highlighted under section C above. It is sufficient to refer to a couple of representative products to examine how they are tailored to the overseas markets. Several important points may be made from Table 11.11.

First, the US, European Union, Japan, and Hong Kong all remain, generally speaking, the largest markets for China's exports of electronics and IT commodities. However, the respective shares tend to vary from year to year, and indeed from product to product. Thus, the US share in China's exports of both coloured TV sets and mobile phones increased from 6% in 2001 to 26% in 2002 for the former, and from 12% to 31% for the latter. In absolute terms, the increases are by any measure also spectacular, by 528% (from some US$91 million in 2001 to US$569 million in 2002) for the former, and by 221% for the latter (from US$505 million to US$1,618 million). For exports to Japan, the share in coloured TV sets declined from 45% in 2001 to 30% in 2002; but the absolute amount still increased nevertheless, albeit slightly from US$650 million to US$654 million.

Second, in the case of the European Union, as represented by the five major countries—the United Kingdom, Germany, France, Italy, and the Netherlands (hereafter referred to as EU-5)—it is interesting to note that the share in China's electronics and IT exports varies very substantially from product to product, rather than from year to year for the same product. Thus, while for coloured TV sets the share stood at the negligible low of 1.8% in 2001 and 2.5% in 2002, it amounted to a high of 40% and 33% respectively for computer display

Table 11.10 Exports and Imports of Selected Electronics and IT Products, 1996–2002 (US$ million)

	1996	1997	1998	1999	2000	2001	2002	Annual Growth %
Computers								
Total X	369,632	536,371	706,797	792,195	1,099,475	1,309,625	2,013,483	43.54
M	96,520	113,452	181,010	325,333	451,644	498,150	673,328	38.23
X/M	3.83	4.73	3.91	2.44	2.43	2.63	2.99	
- Small PC								
X	–	–	–	12	266	184	736	–
M	6,697	3,268	4,609	11,869	19,334	24,238	23,747	23.48
X/M	–	–	–	0.001	0.001	0.008	0.031	
- Mini PC								
X	9,669	12,255	20,397	16,669	69,364	33,143	96,499	46.73
M	2,283	4,683	7,584	6,282	7,422	5,214	2,913	4.15
X/M	4.24	2.62	2.69	2.65	9.35	6.36	33.13	
- Display unit								
X	85,465	121,485	173,777	256,461	338,567	352,378	572,666	37.30
M	8,051	10,056	8,182	9,077	15,236	26,479	55,767	592.67
X/M	10.62	12.08	21.24	8.25	22.22	13.31	10.36	
- Printer								
X	65,355	80,930	97,839	108,982	160,032	212,163	260,701	25.93
M	3,377	7,504	23,262	43,027	59,081	65,280	74,627	67.52
X/M	19.35	10.78	4.21	2.53	2.71	3.25	3.49	
- Keyboard								
X	24,696	40,431	52,726	64,856	71,653	70,308	77,788	21.67
M	1,809	1,686	1,958	3,774	4,623	4,590	6,824	24.77
X/M	13.65	23.98	26.93	17.18	15.50	15.32	11.40	

Table 11.10 (to be continued)

Table 11.10 (continued)

	1996	1997	1998	1999	2000	2001	2002	Annual Growth %
- Diskette								
X	15,698	9,568	8,263	7,385	6,122	7,714	7,725	–11.15
M	2,650	2,263	7,968	9,908	3,625	4,959	22,638	42.98
X/M	5.92	4.23	1.03	0.75	1.69	1.56	0.34	
- Word processor								
X	10,390	3,965	4,055	4,343	2,369	1,368	1,252	–29.72
M	–	93	376	668	685	–	–	
X/M		42.65	10.78	6.50	3.46			
Household electronics								
- Colour TV								
X	62,206	50,554	52,590	63,782	111,848	143,350	220,608	23.49
M	277,207	17,016	13,040	14,266	5,919	3,386	3,515	–27.52
X/M	2.57	2.97	4.03	4.47	18.90	42.34	62.76	
- Tel sets								
X	86,470	94,796	130,412	152,201	169,283	140,968	140,457	8.42
M	1,563	2,337	1,659	4,168	1,550	2,042	1,964	3.88
X/M	55.32	40.56	78.61	36.52	109.22	69.03	71.52	
- Cassette recorder								
X	201,733	214,883	221,097	205,328	243,869	223,442	267,058	4.79
M	7,339	3,823	3,025	4,216	3,814	2,191	3,374	–12.15
X/M	27.49	56.21	73.09	48.70	63.94	101.98	79.15	
- Video camera								
X	3,207	5,633	9,856	14,305	35,420	54,803	98,552	76.98
M	838	1,685	1,626	4,854	7,261	8,575	11,363	54.42
X/M	3.83	3.34	6.06	2.95	4.88	6.39	8.67	

Table 11.10 (to be continued)

Table 11.10 (continued)

	1996	**1997**	**1998**	**1999**	**2000**	**2001**	**2002**	**Annual Growth %**
- Speak cabinet								
X	44,072	59,081	66,874	90,123	96,533	93,764	115,312	17.39
M	8,869	9,080	8,561	14,014	15,673	14,996	17,987	–12.51
X/M	4.97	6.51	7.81	6.43	6.16	6.25	6.41	
Others								
- ICs								
X	59,455	93,180	115,004	205,803	293,799	262,852	431,602	39.15
M	272,207	364,178	477,824	792,376	1,379,983	1,699,924	2,637,832	46.01
X/M	0.22	0.26	0.24	0.26	0.21	0.15	0.16	
- Carrier com. eq.								
X	1,121	1,125	5,451	11,628	30,867	50,969	86,402	106.29
M	19,086	10,671	66,280	87,183	172,108	282,737	148,650	40.79
X/M	0.059	0.105	0.082	0.133	0.179	0.180	0.581	
- Fax machine								
X	23,804	23,435	17,725	20,889	31,651	44,270	50,610	13.40
M	2,475	1,475	1,215	4,835	5,706	6,414	9,748	25.67
X/M	9.62	15.89	14.59	4.32	5.55	6.90	5.19	

Sources: *CFETYB*, various years.

units, or 24% and 21% for the broader category of "computers and components". The comparable EU-5 share for mobile phones was also quite substantial, at 22% in 2001 and 20% in 2002. Notice also that for the European Union as a whole, the share in China's mobile phones exports for 2001 amounted to 24% (i.e., only two percentage points higher than the 22% given for the EU-5). This seems to suggest that there still is considerable room for China to expand its exports to the other EU countries.

Third, even within the EU-5, the shares for most product categories tend to vary greatly between countries in a manner that is entirely disproportionate to the population and income size of the countries involved. For "computers and components", or the narrower category of "display units", the share of the Netherlands for 2001 stood respectively at 14% and 21%, and for 2002 at a comparable 12% and 18%. These are all much higher than the shares for the other major EU countries, which ranged from 0.7% to 4.6% for "computers and components", or 0.9% to 10% for the "display units" category. Does the Netherlands merely serve as an entrepôt for the other EU countries, or is it because the country is the home base of Philips, the global electronics giant? It would take further investigation to elucidate. In the same vein, Germany alone took up a hefty share of 17% in China's exports of mobile phones in both 2001 and 2002, while the other four EU countries' shares ranged from 0.02% to 1.75% for the two years. Is the Chinese "handi" (as the Germans refer to a mobile phone) of particular appeal to the Germans, or is it because Siemens is made in China on an OEM basis and shipped backed to Germany for sales? The same question may be raised with the disproportionately large share of Chinese electronics and IT exports to Finland, in relation to its gigantic neighbour, the Russian Federation (see Table 11.11). Is it because Finns are particularly fond of Nokia (their globally known national brand name), despite the fact that the mobile phone sets may all be made in China?

Fourth, Hong Kong tells a story similar to that of the EU-5, in that its share in China's electronics and IT exports also varies from product to product: an average of 21% for "computers and components", as against only 4.6% for "display units". Notice that for both the US and the Netherlands, the exact reverse is true, although the discrepancy may not appear to be as substantial. Likewise, Hong Kong's share in China's exports of mobile phones stood at 37% in 2001, or 25% in 2002, as against a negligible 4% for coloured TV sets.

Fifth, for the ASEAN-5 taken as a whole, the share in China's electronics and IT exports seems to be biased downwards, consistently across the different

Table 11.11 Share of Major Overseas Markets in China's Exports of Representative Electronics and IT Products, 2001–2002 (US$ million and %)

	Computers		Display units		Mobile phones		Coloured TV sets	
	2001	**2002**	**2001**	**2002**	**2001**	**2002**	**2001**	**2002**
World total	13,096	20,134	3,524	5,727	4,121	5,280	1,434	2,206
N. America								
- USA	26.66	28.04	28.39	36.76	12.25	30.65	6.32	25.79
- Canada	0.53	0.76	1.00	1.03	–	0.11	0.37	0.60
EU								
- UK	3.49	2.66	3.97	3.92	2.66	0.24	0.11	0.66
- Germany	4.50	4.61	10.46	8.67	16.86	6.90	1.09	1.02
- France	1.44	1.35	2.16	0.94	1.44	1.75	0.31	0.29
- Italy	0.66	0.74	1.61	1.58	0.07	0.02	0.14	0.24
- the Netherlands	14.22	11.71	21.38	17.83	0.80	1.23	0.13	0.31
- Belgium	0.84	0.57	0.96	0.78	–	–	0.27	0.30
- Finland	0.39	0.23	0.97	0.61	1.15	0.96	3.82	2.53
Russia	0.11	0.29	0.30	0.91	–	–	1.11	1.34
Japan	11.26	15.31	5.24	7.75	0.23	0.13	45.40	29.66
South Korea	2.47	1.38	2.72	1.41	7.28	5.94	0.64	0.36
Taiwan	1.77	2.85	1.11	1.98	0.01	0.06	0.45	0.72

Table 11.11 (to be continued)

Table 11.11 (continued)

	Computers		**Display units**		**Mobile phones**		**Coloured TV sets**	
	2001	**2002**	**2001**	**2002**	**2001**	**2002**	**2001**	**2002**
Hong Kong	20.62	20.40	4.61	4.60	37.41	24.82	5.06	3.43
ASEAN-5	4.01	3.43	3.15	2.63	11.60	7.39	10.12	7.32
- Indonesia	0.14	0.08	0.28	0.18	0.00	–	5.29	1.84
- Malaysia	0.44	0.72	0.35	0.42	7.26	1.85	0.53	1.31
- Thailand	0.31	0.26	0.52	0.41	1.55	2.73	0.42	0.47
- the Philippines	0.31	0.28	0.62	0.41	0.66	0.36	0.49	0.59
- Singapore	2.81	2.09	1.38	1.21	2.13	2.45	3.39	3.11
Australia	1.08	1.21	2.12	2.01	0.55	0.48	4.28	5.04
New Zealand	0.11	0.11	0.26	0.25	0.11	–	0.74	0.65
Others	5.82	4.30	9.6	6.27	7.54	9.30	19.71	19.76

Notes and sources: *CCSYB* (various years) for mobile phones, and *CFETYB* (various years) for computers (including peripheral equipment), display units (sum part of computers as above), and coloured TV sets.

products despite the entrepôt role played by Singapore (which takes up quite consistently a higher share for most of the product types). Perhaps the small shares for the ASEAN-5 combined conceal the fact that part of their imports from China are also channelled through Hong Kong, because such imports are, by international custom statistical practice, treated as exports from Hong Kong rather than China. However, the bulk of Hong Kong's re-exports of Chinese origin are normally destined to the US and Europe, rather than Japan and ASEAN countries. If this is the case, then here again, the share of the ASEAN-5 in China's electronics and IT exports seems to be disproportionately low, compared with that of Australia and New Zealand, in relation to the size of the countries.

Several points of interest or conclusions may be drawn from the above observations:

The first relates to the volatility of the shares for some major markets or block of countries in China's electronics and IT exports across the years, and the disproportionate discrepancy between the different sizes of importing economic entities and their shares in the different categories of products imported from China. The circumstances clearly suggest that there still exist substantial market potentials overseas that Chinese exporters may continue to exploit in the years to come.

The next point concerns the remarkably high share for Japan in China's exports of coloured TV sets (45% in 2001 and 30% in 2002). This truly flies in the face of the "kingdom of consumer electronics", which has for decades dominated the global supply of TV sets. The fact, however, is that not only all the familiar Japanese brand names sold in China today are all manufactured in the country, but those available in domestic Japanese markets are also increasingly imported from China as well. All the Japanese electronics giants have established their own manufacturing plants in China: Sony in Shanghai, Matsushita (National and Panasonic) in Jinan (Shandong Province), Toshiba in Dalian (Liaoning), Sharp in Nanjing (Jiangsu), Hitachi in Fuzhou (Fujian), and Sanyo in Shenzhen (Guangdong), alongside Korea's LG (Shenyang in Liaoning) and Samsung (Tianjin), and the Dutch-based conglomerate, Philips (Suzhou in Jiangsu). Obviously, the exceedingly high intake rates by the US of China's exports of mobile phones (31% in 2002), computer and components (28% in 2002), and display units (37% in 2002) may be similarly explained by Motorola's investment in Tianjin and by IBM and Compaq resorting to the

Dongguan municipality (the single largest computer manufacturing centre in China) as their global outsourcing base.

The third point is that while the US, European Union, and Japan are all being swiftly flooded with Chinese electronics and IT products, the day may not appear far away for a similar Chinese foray into neighbouring ASEAN countries as well.

A primary point of concern for the present study is how the emerging Chinese new industries may impinge upon the broader regional industrial setting in East Asia. For this purpose, we shall now look at how, in the first place, the massive Chinese electronics and IT export expansion into advanced Western countries—the United States in particular—may bear on rival exporting economies in the region.

Market shares and revealed comparative advantage in the US and Japan

Specifically, we estimate the revealed comparative advantage (RCA) index for China and the other major East Asian economies for their electronics and IT exports to the US (i.e., the single largest market for all), with a view to examining to what extent China may have eroded the export capability of its rivals over the past decade. Five major custom entities (viz., Japan, South Korea, Taiwan, Malaysia, and Singapore) are selected for comparative analysis with China. These are all important manufacturers-cum-exporters of electronics and IT commodities.

The RCA formula to be used for the estimation is familiar, as follows,

$$R_{ij}^{(k)} = \frac{X_i^k}{\sum_j Y_{ij}^k} \div \frac{\sum_i X_i^k}{\sum_i \sum_j Y_{ij}^k} = \frac{X_i^k}{\sum_i X_i^k} \div \frac{\sum_j Y_{ij}^k}{\sum_i \sum_j Y_{ij}^k}$$

Where *i* stands for the traded goods, *j* the exporting country, *k* the importing country (in this case the United States), X_i^k the sum total of *i* imported by *k* from the country under study, and Y_{ij}^k the sum total of *i* imported by *k* from *j*.

US Customs statistics, which apply the HS (Harmonized Commodity Description and Coding System) classification method, are used for the estimation. The following major electronics and IT commodities are included, representing different degrees of disaggregation:

HS code Commodity (short reference to be used hereinafter)

8471 computers & components, data processing machines, magnetic readers, etc. (computers and components)
8471–60010 display units, nesoi (display units)
8471–60020 display units, incorporating liquid crystal devices (LCD)
8471–603000 display units, not incorporating a cathode-ray-tube (CRT), having visual display diagonal not exceeding 30.5 cm (display units A)
8471–604580 display units, nesoi, not incorporating a CRT (display units B)
8471–606400 printers, nesoi, ink jet (printers)
8517 electric apparatuses for line telephones, etc.; parts (telephone sets)
8521 video apparatuses (video apparatuses)
8525 transmission apparatuses for radio-telephones, etc., TV cameras & recorders (TV cameras and recorders)
8528–1200 coloured TV sets with/without radios or players, recorders (coloured TV sets), and
8542 electronic integrated circuits and microassemblies, and parts (integrated circuits)

Before examining the estimated RCA indices, we should, however, look at the size contributions of the six East Asian economies to total imports of the US for all goods combined, as well as for the various major categories as classified above. In other words, we are looking at both the denominator and numerator for the RCA formula, in order to gauge the relative magnitude of the East Asian-6, taken both as a whole and separately, in the relevant US import measures. The figures in Table 11.12 provide some very important information.

First, the combined share of the East Asian-6 in total US imports amounted to a hefty 31% in 2004, although it has declined consistently from the high of 35% in 1995.

Table 11.12 Shares of China and Other East Asian Economies in Electronics and IT Imports by the United States, 1995–2004 (in %)

	All goods							8471						
Year	**C**	**J**	**K**	**T**	**M**	**S**	**Sum**	**C**	**J**	**K**	**T**	**M**	**S**	**Sum**
1995	6.13	16.62	3.25	3.9	2.35	2.5	34.75	3.67	29.43	4.23	10.25	7.04	23.82	78.44
1996	6.51	14.56	2.86	3.78	2.25	2.57	32.53	3.64	23.75	4.93	10.4	6.97	25.99	75.68
1997	7.19	13.95	2.66	3.75	2.07	2.31	31.93	4.59	22.79	4.93	11.42	7.07	21.97	72.77
1998	7.79	13.35	2.62	3.62	2.08	2.00	31.46	6.37	21.11	4.05	10.61	6.82	21.04	70.00
1999	7.98	12.82	3.05	3.43	2.09	1.77	31.14	9.33	19.23	7.50	10.20	7.51	16.96	70.73
2000	8.22	12.05	3.31	3.33	2.10	1.58	30.59	11.29	16.69	8.74	11.83	8.33	12.37	69.25
2001	8.96	11.08	2.93	2.93	1.96	1.31	29.17	12.53	12.44	6.62	12.08	10.14	11.94	65.75
2002	10.28	10.46	2.77	2.77	2.07	1.27	29.62	18.31	9.07	5.54	12.60	13.77	10.44	69.73
2003	12.10	9.37	2.51	2.51	2.02	1.20	29.71	29.36	6.54	4.12	8.85	14.96	9.52	73.35
2004	13.38	8.83	3.14	2.36	1.92	1.05	30.68	40.97	5.34	2.70	5.59	14.06	7.47	76.13

	8471–603000							8471–604580						
Year	**C**	**J**	**K**	**T**	**M**	**S**	**Sum**	**C**	**J**	**K**	**T**	**M**	**S**	**Sum**
1995	–	–	–	–	–	–	–	–	–	–	–	–	–	–
1996	0.02	82.95	2.20	5.79	1.50	0.29	92.75	0.11	74.65	6.88	6.96	0.04	0.01	88.65
1997	0.29	71.78	2.37	11.06	0.06	0.56	86.12	0.22	63.27	12.80	13.37	4.53	0.97	95.16
1998	0.76	77.38	0.87	6.84	0.02	0.28	86.15	0.14	77.53	8.14	8.91	0.06	0.15	94.93
1999	0.56	76.38	1.57	9.64	0.01	0.11	88.27	0.21	48.08	31.14	15.08	0.09	0.19	94.79
2000	1.00	75.93	0.69	11.52	0	0.14	89.28	3.57	28.15	39.86	25.03	2.02	0.07	98.70

Table 11.12 (to be continued)

Table 11.12 (continued)

	8471–603000							8471–604580						
Year	C	J	K	T	M	S	Sum	C	J	K	T	M	S	Sum
2001	4.31	57.98	6.58	18.16	0.20	0.54	87.77	8.63	18.47	31.05	26.04	3.71	0.01	87.91
2002	19.01	39.49	10.00	19.38	0.03	0.73	88.64	29.83	11.47	23.53	16.18	0.96	0.04	82.01
2003	46.52	22.24	5.77	14.97	0.12	0.71	90.33	49.21	5.02	13.42	10.95	2.07	0.04	80.71
2004	47.37	17.14	7.78	15.36	0.11	0.42	88.18	65.00	2.52	10.77	7.03	1.09	0.06	86.47

	8471–606400							8517						
Year	C	J	K	T	M	S	Sum	C	J	K	T	M	S	Sum
1995	–	–	–	–	–	–	–	9.35	26.80	1.77	4.09	7.56	2.88	52.45
1996	4.43	20.48	5.00	0	3.86	56.63	90.40	13.23	17.40	1.21	4.74	10.48	0.85	47.91
1997	9.97	14.93	4.74	0	0.60	61.76	92.00	13.86	15.69	1.00	5.00	7.67	0.38	43.60
1998	9.44	16.73	4.55	0	6.92	40.44	78.08	15.96	16.31	1.04	6.83	6.02	0.35	46.51
1999	12.46	8.58	1.75	0	20.68	20.26	63.73	14.46	16.33	0.67	4.47	4.89	1.19	42.01
2000	12.31	2.25	1.78	0.14	26.06	23.22	65.76	11.71	12.34	0.77	4.33	5.11	0.97	35.23
2001	19.39	1.88	3.78	0.08	24.06	23.13	72.32	16.85	11.23	0.87	5.88	6.14	0.73	41.70
2002	22.06	1.76	3.13	0	44.69	13.50	85.14	20.21	4.70	0.94	5.10	10.20	1.89	43.04
2003	21.95	0.19	0.02	0.02	55.73	10.08	87.99	21.14	4.31	1.12	3.78	16.51	0.11	46.97
2004	33.26	1.51	0.01	0.00	46.00	5.00	85.78	22.62	4.62	1.29	2.55	15.62	1.00	47.70

Table 11.12 (to be continued)

Table 11.12 (continued)

	8521							8525						
Year	C	J	K	T	M	S	Sum	C	J	K	T	M	S	Sum
1995	7.32	30.86	16.51	0.39	20.72	5.44	81.24	3.22	39.75	7.35	4.00	6.40	0.30	61.02
1996	8.60	31.57	9.54	0.46	21.64	4.70	76.51	4.35	41.83	4.66	6.25	2.57	0.52	60.18
1997	8.13	34.86	3.48	0.49	19.57	2.80	69.33	5.25	38.32	6.24	8.64	2.03	0.91	61.39
1998	11.50	38.79	5.40	0.26	16.84	0.56	73.35	4.71	35.79	9.36	8.23	2.00	0.70	60.79
1999	17.36	35.02	7.31	0.51	15.59	0.90	76.69	5.06	31.52	15.09	8.26	3.88	1.00	64.81
2000	27.44	24.48	10.12	0.57	16.26	0.93	79.80	5.74	24.19	16.00	6.04	6.31	0.75	59.03
2001	42.95	13.33	10.98	1.13	13.79	0.65	82.83	6.45	17.81	21.90	3.83	7.84	0.88	58.71
2002	53.84	8.88	11.62	0.61	6.80	0.93	82.68	12.73	19.31	21.25	2.66	6.45	0.56	62.96
2003	60.42	8.97	7.35	0.59	5.02	0.67	83.02	18.19	17.12	24.07	2.90	7.39	0.77	70.44
2004	63.03	7.71	6.59	1.04	4.01	0.49	82.87	25.92	14.09	27.23	2.65	5.91	1.68	77.48

	8528–1200							8542						
Year	C	J	K	T	M	S	Sum	C	J	K	T	M	S	Sum
1995	–	–	–	–	–	–	–	0.28	26.72	19.26	7.76	12.82	7.54	74.38
1996	0.72	2.95	0.55	0.09	12.46	0.18	16.95	0.42	22.85	18.27	8.14	13.66	8.50	71.84
1997	0.38	1.27	0.76	0.15	10.96	0.05	13.57	0.48	20.13	15.57	8.90	13.93	7.30	66.31
1998	0.42	0.69	1.01	0.11	8.34	0.02	10.59	1.07	16.28	17.34	9.50	12.42	6.69	63.30
1999	1.04	0.61	1.66	0.11	11.59	0.09	15.10	1.43	16.03	19.52	10.44	13.00	5.78	66.20
2000	1.69	0.86	1.27	0.26	11.81	0.06	15.95	1.15	15.78	17.99	11.40	12.84	7.68	66.84

Table 11.12 (to be continued)

Table 11.12 (continued)

	8528–1200							8542						
Year	**C**	**J**	**K**	**T**	**M**	**S**	**Sum**	**C**	**J**	**K**	**T**	**M**	**S**	**Sum**
2001	2.25	2.33	2.38	0.24	10.66	0.25	18.11	1.57	13.45	13.07	12.32	15.44	6.41	62.26
2002	7.70	4.79	2.73	0.47	13.78	0.04	29.51	1.98	9.50	14.98	12.80	16.65	5.35	61.26
2003	8.74	6.15	5.86	2.49	9.27	0.19	32.70	2.54	8.84	15.57	13.43	14.65	5.84	60.87
2004	8.36	5.51	6.02	5.21	5.24	0.11	30.45	4.03	9.58	17.00	15.56	13.63	6.26	66.06

Notes: C stands for China, J for Japan, K for South Korea, T for Taiwan, M for Malaysia, and S for Singapore.

Sources: *WTATLAS* 1993–2004 (Internet version accessed via Business Infocentre of HKTDC).

Second, except perhaps for HS 85281200 (coloured TV sets), the shares of the East Asian-6 in US imports of all the other eight major categories of electronics and IT products taken separately are all exceedingly high, compared to the "all goods" measure. That is to say, exports of the East Asian-6 to the US have been overwhelmingly dominated by electronics and IT goods over the years. Notice, however, that even for coloured TV sets, the share has continuously increased from 17% in 1996 to 30% in 2004, which is now above the average for all goods exported by the East Asian-6 to the US.

Third, virtually all display units (HS 8471–603000 and –604580 combined) and printers (HS 8471–606400) imported by the US are of East Asian origin. The same goes basically for video apparatuses (HS 8521), and to a lesser extent, TV cameras and recorders (HS 8525) as well. Over half of the ICs (HS 8542) imported by the US are also from the East Asian-6.

Viewed against this overall context of East Asian electronics exports to the US, it should be of great interest to see how as a result of the accelerated Chinese export expansion over the past decade, there might have come to a redistribution of the export shares among the East Asian-6 in the US market in favour of China. Several important points emerge from Table 10.12.

First, China's share in total US imports (all goods combined) has doubled from 6% in 1995 to 13% in 2004, while that of Japan has continuously been reduced from a high of 17% to 9% in the same period. The other East Asian-4 (South Korea, Taiwan, Malaysia, and Singapore) have indeed all seen their shares curtailed as well, to a greater or lesser degree.

Second, for the various categories of electronics and IT exports, the Chinese shares have increased even more substantially compared with the average for "all goods". The country has thus rapidly replaced Japan across the board to be the largest exporter to the United States. By 2004, 63% of the video apparatuses (HS 8521) imported by the US are of Chinese origin, up from merely 7% in 1995. For computer display units (HS 8471–60300 and –604580 combined), over half of US imports are now also from China, while just three or four years ago, the Chinese share was virtually zero. The same goes for printers (HS 8471–606400), telephone sets (HS 8517), and TV cameras and recorders (HS8525), for which China now makes up between 23% and 33% of total US imports, as against only 3% to 9% respectively in 1995 and 1996. With only one or two exceptions, the Chinese shares for all the last three types of exports to the US are also larger than that of the other East Asian economies.

Third, out of the nine major categories of exports under study, only in the case of coloured TV sets (HS 8528–1200) and integrated circuits (HS 8542) did China not command any particular competitive edge. Interestingly, despite accelerating its export drive in recent years, the country's share in US imports of coloured TV sets stands at a mere 8%. And for integrated circuits, the share (scarcely 4%) falls indeed well behind that of the East Asian-5, especially South Korea (17%), Taiwan (16%), and Malaysia (14%), as is also shown in Table 10.12.

Fourth, for US imports of printers, Malaysia commands an exceedingly large share of 56% in 2003, and 46% in 2004, compared to 22% (33%) and 10% (5%) respectively for China and Singapore. Likewise, South Korea's share in US imports of TV cameras and recorders in 2004 are also quite impressive, standing at 27%, as against 26% for China, or 14% for Japan. These discrepancies seem to suggest that despite increased overall Chinese dominance in East Asian exports to the US market, there may still be room for other exporting economies to carve out their own niche in the trade.

All said, the particular Chinese strengths in exports to the US or other major markets overseas should not be interpreted in oblivion of the important background that they are essentially built upon FDI and technology transfer from the US, Japan, Taiwan, and increasingly South Korea as well, with or without assuming the prevalent practice of OEM, ODM, or others. With this important qualification, we now look at the estimated RCA indices in order to gauge more precisely the comparative advantages of China in electronics and IT exports.

The standards for assessment adopted as an empirical rule are as follows: when the estimated RCA index is >2.5, the commodity concerned is considered to be highly competitive; 1.25–2.5, comparatively competitive; 0.8–1.25, of average competitiveness; and <0.8, comparatively less competitive.[12]

The estimated RCA indices are given in Table 11.13. The major findings may be summarized as follows:

First, out of the nine categories of electronics and IT exports to the US by 2004, China has five—namely, HS 8471 (computers and components) with breakdowns for -603000, -604580 (both display units), -606400 (printers), and HS 8521 (video apparatuses)—which are all ranked as "highly competitive" (RCA>2.5). Both Chinese computer display units (RCA around 4) and video apparatuses (RCA 5) appear to be particularly appealing to the US market. Two categories, HS 8517 (telephone sets) and HS 8525 (TV camera and recorders), fall within the range of "comparatively competitive" (RCA 1.25–2.50). The remaining two, HS 8528–1200 (coloured TV) and HS 8542 (integrated circuits) are ranked "comparatively less competitive" or not competitive at all, with their RCA indices being as low as 0.63 and 0.30 respectively. These figures all bear out the points made earlier about the net import-export balances for the various categories of electronics and IT commodities, as well as the discussion on the changing Chinese market shares in the US.

Second, the pace with which the various Chinese RCA values have been upgraded to "highly" or "comparatively" competitive over the past several years appears indeed most remarkable. This is clearly discernible in Table 11.13 and needs no further elaboration. The only notable exception concerns HS 8517 (telephone sets), for which the RCA index has more or less remained the same from 1995 to 2004, and is indeed consistently lower than that of Malaysia over the years.

Third, despite the accelerated Chinese foray into the US market, Malaysia and other East Asian economies have still been able to maintain or even improve their competitive edge for some categories of electronics and IT exports to the US in terms of the estimated RCA indices. This brings us to the question of how the emergence of China as an electronics and IT "giant" may bear on the East Asian production network for the industry. Before we turn to this broader regional issue, however, let us briefly look at the Chinese performance in the Japanese market.

As shown in Table 11.14, within nine years from 1995 to 2004, China's share in total Japanese imports (of all goods combined) has doubled from around 11% to 21%. Among the various categories of electronics and IT exports to Japan, China's share for "computers and components" (HS 8471) increased most substantially from hardly 3% in 1995 to 48% in 2004. By comparison, the increases in the country's share in US imports of the same commodity group, from 4% to 41% in the same period (see Table 11.12) appear to be somewhat more modest. The same goes for the Chinese exports of coloured TV sets (HS8528–1200) to Japan. The share in Japan's imports increased equally remarkably from hardly 10% in 1995 to 48% in 2003, although it then slowed down to 37% in 2004; whereas the comparable share in US imports rose by merely eight percentage points from 1% in 1995 to 9% in 2003, or 8% in 2004. As a result, the RCA indices for China in the related Japanese markets have all increased consistently and in fact most substantially, namely

Table 11.13 Estimated RCA Indices for China and Other East Asian Economies in Their Electronics and IT Exports to the United States, 1995–2003

	HS 8471						8471–603000					
Year	**C**	**J**	**K**	**T**	**M**	**S**	**C**	**J**	**K**	**T**	**M**	**S**
1995	0.60	1.77	1.30	2.63	3.00	9.53	–	–	–	–	–	–
1996	0.56	1.63	1.72	2.75	3.10	10.11	0.00	5.70	0.77	1.53	0.67	0.11
1997	0.64	1.63	1.85	3.05	3.42	9.51	0.04	5.15	0.89	2.95	0.03	0.24
1998	0.82	1.58	1.55	2.93	3.28	10.52	0.10	5.80	0.33	1.89	0.01	0.14
1999	1.17	1.51	2.46	2.93	3.59	9.58	0.07	5.96	0.51	2.81	0.00	0.06
2000	1.37	1.39	2.64	3.55	3.97	7.83	0.12	6.30	0.21	3.46	0.00	0.09
2001	1.40	1.12	2.26	4.12	5.17	9.11	0.48	5.23	2.25	6.20	0.10	0.41
2002	1.78	0.87	2.0	4.55	6.65	8.22	1.85	3.78	3.61	7.00	0.01	0.57
2003	2.43	0.70	1.64	3.55	7.41	7.93	3.85	2.37	2.30	5.96	0.06	0.59
2004	3.06	0.60	0.86	2.37	7.32	7.11	3.54	1.94	2.48	6.51	0.06	0.40

	8471–604580						8471–606400					
Year	**C**	**J**	**K**	**T**	**M**	**S**	**C**	**J**	**K**	**T**	**M**	**S**
1995	–	–	–	–	–	–	–	–	–	–	–	–
1996	0.02	5.13	2.41	1.84	0.02	0.00	0.68	1.41	1.75	0	1.72	22.04
1997	0.03	4.54	4.81	3.57	2.19	0.42	1.39	1.07	1.78	0	0.29	26.74

Table 11.13 (to be continued)

Table 11.13 (continued)

Year	8471–604580 C	J	K	T	M	S	8471–606400 C	J	K	T	M	S
1998	0.02	5.81	3.11	2.46	0.03	0.08	1.21	1.25	1.74	0	3.33	20.22
1999	0.03	3.75	10.21	4.40	0.04	0.11	1.56	0.67	0.57	0	9.89	11.45
2000	0.43	2.34	12.04	7.52	0.96	0.04	1.50	0.19	0.54	0.04	12.41	14.70
2001	0.96	1.67	10.60	8.89	1.89	0.01	2.16	0.17	1.29	0.03	12.28	17.66
2002	2.90	1.10	8.49	5.84	0.46	0.03	2.15	0.17	1.13	0	21.59	10.63
2003	4.07	0.54	5.35	4.36	1.02	0.03	1.81	0.02	0.01	0.01	27.59	8.40
2004	4.86	0.29	3.34	2.98	0.57	0.06	2.49	0.17	0.00	0.00	23.96	4.76

Year	8517 C	J	K	T	M	S	8521 C	J	K	T	M	S
1995	1.53	1.61	0.54	1.05	3.22	1.15	1.19	1.86	5.08	0.10	8.82	2.18
1996	2.03	1.20	0.42	1.25	4.66	0.33	1.32	2.17	3.34	0.12	9.62	1.83
1997	1.93	1.12	0.38	1.33	3.71	0.16	1.13	2.50	1.31	0.13	9.45	1.21
1998	2.05	1.22	0.40	1.89	2.89	0.18	1.48	2.91	2.02	0.07	8.10	0.28
1999	1.81	1.27	0.22	1.30	2.34	0.67	2.18	2.73	2.40	0.15	9.46	0.51
2000	1.42	1.02	0.23	1.30	2.43	0.61	3.34	2.03	3.06	0.17	7.74	0.59
2001	1.88	1.01	0.30	2.01	3.13	0.56	4.79	1.20	3.75	0.39	7.04	0.50
2002	1.97	1.45	0.34	1.84	4.93	1.48	5.24	0.85	4.19	0.22	3.29	0.73

Table 11.13 (to be continued)

Table 11.13 (continued)

	8517						8521					
Year	**C**	**J**	**K**	**T**	**M**	**S**	**C**	**J**	**K**	**T**	**M**	**S**
2003	1.75	1.46	0.45	1.5[illegible]	8.17	0.09	4.99	0.96	2.93	0.24	2.49	0.56
2004	1.69	0.52	0.41	1.08	8.14	0.95	4.71	0.87	2.10	0.44	2.09	0.47

	8525						8528–1200					
Year	**C**	**J**	**K**	**T**	**M**	**S**	**C**	**J**	**K**	**T**	**M**	**S**
1995	–	–	–	–	–	–	–	–	–	–	–	–
1996	0.67	2.87	1.63	1.65	1.14	0.20	0.11	0.20	0.19	0.02	5.54	0.07
1997	0.73	2.75	2.35	2.30	0.98	0.39	0.05	0.09	0.29	0.04	5.29	0.02
1998	0.60	2.68	3.57	2.27	0.96	0.35	0.05	0.05	0.39	0.03	4.01	0.01
1999	0.63	2.46	4.95	2.41	1.86	0.56	0.13	0.05	0.54	0.03	5.55	0.05
2000	0.70	2.01	4.83	1.81	3.00	0.47	0.21	0.07	0.38	0.08	5.62	0.04
2001	0.72	1.61	7.47	1.31	4.00	0.67	0.25	0.21	0.81	0.08	5.44	0.19
2002	1.24	1.85	7.67	0.96	3.12	0.44	0.75	0.46	0.99	0.17	6.66	0.03
2003	1.50	1.83	9.59	1.16	3.66	0.64	0.72	0.66	2.33	0.99	4.59	0.16
2004	1.94	1.60	8.67	1.12	3.08	1.60	0.63	0.62	1.92	2.21	2.73	0.10

Table 11.13 (to be continued)

Table 11.13 (continued)

			8542			
	C	**J**	**K**	**T**	**M**	**S**
1995	–	–	–	–	–	–
1996	0.06	1.57	6.39	2.15	6.07	3.31
1997	0.07	1.44	5.85	2.37	6.73	3.16
1998	0.14	1.22	6.62	2.62	5.97	3.35
1999	0.18	1.25	6.40	3.04	6.22	3.27
2000	0.14	1.31	5.44	3.42	6.11	4.86
2001	0.18	1.21	4.46	4.20	7.88	4.89
2002	0.19	0.91	5.41	4.62	8.04	4.21
2003	0.21	0.94	6.20	5.35	7.25	4.87
2004	0.30	1.08	5.41	6.59	7.10	5.96

Notes: C stands for China, J for Japan, K for Korea, T for Taiwan, M for Malaysia, and S for Singapore.

Sources: As Table 11.12.

Table 11.14 China's Market Share and RCA Indices in Japan's Imports—Total and by Major Electronics and IT Commodities, 1995–2004 (percent and ratio)

	All goods	HS 8471		8471–60010		8471–60020		HS 85281200	
		Share	**RCA**	**Share**	**RCA**	**Share**	**RCA**	**Share**	**RCA**
1995	10.72	2.52	0.24	–	–	–	–	–	–
1996	11.58	3.63	0.31	1.14	0.10	4.39	0.38	9.57	0.83
1997	12.36	4.12	0.33	0.03	0.00	22.26	1.80	13.84	1.12
1998	13.22	3.99	0.30	0.05	0.00	25.61	1.94	23.08	1.75
1999	13.82	4.25	0.31	0.56	0.04	30.25	2.19	24.15	1.75
2000	14.51	6.42	0.44	0.98	0.07	38.28	2.64	24.78	1.71
2001	16.57	12.49	0.75	5.93	0.36	47.96	2.89	34.47	2.08
2002	18.30	12.57	1.51	30.72	1.68	49.91	2.73	43.32	2.37
2003	19.70	41.61	2.11	42.75	2.17	56.55	2.87	48.08	2.44
2004	20.72	47.63	2.30	68.52	3.31	56.82	2.74	36.45	1.76

Notes: "All goods" refers to China's total exports to Japan as a share in Japan's total imports from the world.

Sources: As Table 11.12.

all from near-zero in 1995 to "highly competitive"(>2.5) or "comparatively competitive"(1.25–2.5) by 2003 or 2004 (see Table 11.14).

However, the accelerated increases in China's electronics and IT exports to Japan seem for the most part represented by exports manufactured in China by the various Japanese electronics giants located across the country, as alluded to earlier. The exceedingly large Chinese share (or "Japanese share-in-disguise") in Japan's total imports of coloured TV sets relative to that in the US import market (i.e., 36% versus 8% or 9%) may be explained by the fact that the Japanese market is simply more restrictive (by virtue of consumers preferring their own national brand names) than the vast multiracial US market, which allows for a greater degree of diversification of import sources.

Implications for the regional production network

Let us revert to the discussion about the changing RCA values among the East Asian-6. The figures given in Table 11.13 should be examined with care, in conjunction with Table 11.12.

First of all, let us look at the broad category of "computers and components" (HS 8471). Interestingly, in 1995–2004, the RCA index for Malaysia has consistently increased from 2.99 (already "highly competitive") further to the remarkable high of 7.32; whereas for China it has moved from 0.60 ("comparatively less competitive") to 3.06 ("comparatively competitive"). This has taken place against the backdrop of a drastic increase in the Chinese share in US imports of the same commodity group from 3.67% in 1995 to the startling high of 40.97% in 2004. By comparison, the Malaysian share has increased quite modestly, from only 7.04% to 14.06% in the same period (see Table 11.12).

A word or two should be said about the two seemingly conflicting quantitative trends between China and Malaysia: in light of the enormous Chinese foray into the US market for "computers and components" (HS 8471), Malaysia was being increasingly compelled to divert its effort to other types of exports either within or outside the same HS 8471 category. The statistics in both Tables 11.12 and 11.13 reveal indeed that Malaysia has moved out of both types of computer "display units" (HS 8471–60300 and –604580) to make room for China, in order to rigorously concentrate on the manufacturing of "printers" (HS 8471–606400) for export to the US market. The upshot for Malaysia to increasingly specialize on the export of "printers" (which constitute part of the broader "computers and components" (HS 8471) category is that Malaysia-made "printers" now, surprisingly, not only account for nearly half of total US imports (with a RCA index standing at as high as 23.96), but has also helped to raise the RCA for the "computers and components" (HS 8471) category taken as a whole to the high value of 7.32 as referred to above. By virtue of the RCA formula, given a more or less stable share of a country in total US imports (of all goods), an increased concentration on a particular group of commodity will understandably help to raise the share and hence the RCA index of that country in the relevant US imports.

Similar changes have taken place with the other East Asian economies. For example, Taiwan and South Korea have made relative shifts towards both types of "display units" (A and B), but not "printers". The real losers appear to be Singapore and Japan in particular. Singapore has seen its share in US imports of printers curtailed from a high of 57% in 1995 to a dwindling 5% in 2004 in favour of Malaysia, with its RCA index declining from 22.04 to 4.76 accordingly. Taking "computers and components" (HS 8471) as a whole, Singapore appears, nevertheless, to be quite resilient in the US market, being able to maintain a 7.47% share and a RCA index of 7.11 in 2004.

In the case of Japan, however, both its shares and RCA indices in the US market for "computers and components", including both types A and B display units and printers, have been drastically reduced across the board (see Tables 11.12 and 11.13). While in the mid- and late-1990s, Japan-made display units still absolutely dominated the US import market, it now appears that they would soon be all replaced by similar products from China. Here again, the same caveat as alluded to earlier must be given—that is, China-made display units sold in the US may essentially represent exports of "Japanese origin-in-disguise", or for that matter, exports that are similarly manufactured by Taiwanese and Korean firms that are based in mainland China.

Similar observations may be made relating to the sample subcategories of HS 85, which is broadly defined to include "electrical machinery and equipment and parts thereof; sound recorders and reproducers, TV image and sound recorders and reproducers; and parts and accessories of such articles". Thus, as is also revealed in Table 11.12, as a result of the massive increases of the Chinese share in US imports of HS 8521 (video apparatuses) from 7% in 1995 to 63% in 2004 (which cut deeply into the shares of all other East Asian exporters), Malaysia has strongly shifted its focus to the exports of HS 8517 (telephone sets), raising its share in US imports from 7% in 1995 to 16% in

2004. Malaysia has since the mid-1980s become the single largest country in Southeast Asia to host Japanese investment in the electronics industry. Most of the Sony telephone sets sold in the region or globally, for instance, are made in Malaysia. This probably explains why the country has been able to swiftly resort to its established competitive edge to expand exports of telephone sets to the United States.

Likewise, South Korea has been able to rapidly raise its share in US imports of HS 8525 (TV cameras and recorders) from 7% in 1995 to 27% in 2004, in order to compensate for its losses to China in exports of HS 8517 (telephone sets) to the United States. Taiwan has in turn managed to increase its share in US imports of HS 8542 (integrated circuits) from 6% to 7% respectively.

From Table 11.12, the increases in the respective shares for Malaysia (HS 8517), South Korea (HS 8525), and Taiwan (HS 8542) are also all wrought singularly at the expense of Japan, which has seen the relevant shares drastically curtailed across the board over the years under study.

Increased concentration by Malaysia, Taiwan, and South Korea on the respective HS 85 subcategories of exports has also greatly helped to raise their RCA indices, given that their overall shares in total US imports (of all goods) remained more or less the same for the period concerned. Thus, as shown in Table 11.13, the respective RCA indices for all three exporting economies have increased most substantially from 1995 to 2004: Malaysia's for HS 8517 (telephone sets) from 3.22 to 8.14, Korea's for HS 8525 (TV camera and recorders) from 1.63 to 8.67, and Taiwan's for HS 8542 (integrated circuits) from 2.15 to 6.59. These increases compare indeed very favourably with that of China, increasing respectively from 1.53 to 1.69, 0.67 to 1.94, and 0.06 to 0.30. If anything, these increases suggest that amidst overwhelming competition from China in the exports of HS 8521 (video apparatuses) to the United States, Malaysia, South Korea, and Taiwan have all been able to redivert their focus to alternative lines of exports for which they each command a particular competitive edge. We may call this as the "diversion effect" to refer to the gains obtained through increased intra-industrial specialization in exporting to third countries.

As a matter of fact, for both Korea and Taiwan, the absolute shares in US imports of HS 8525 and HS 8542, respectively, have remained consistently larger than that of China from 1995 through 2003. In other words, both South Korea and Taiwan remain absolutely more competitive than the Chinese mainland in this respect. As for Malaysia, the "diversion effect" has at least helped the country to maintain its absolute share in US imports of HS 8517, or prevent it from being further eroded.

Finally, let us look at the HS 8528–1200 (coloured TV sets) category. This seems to be the only category of East Asian exports to the US in which accelerated Chinese exports have not "crowded out" or substituted for the shares of the other East Asian exporters. That is to say, the "substitution effect", as observed in the other HS categories between China and its East Asian rival exporters did not take place. Rather, with the minor exception of Malaysia, all the others have seen their shares in US imports of this particular HS category (comprising coloured TV sets and other similar products) increasing in 1995–2004 alongside that of China (see Table 11.12). However, it is also very clear that the simultaneous increases are accounted for by an unusually heightened import demand by US consumers for coloured TV sets from the East Asian-6, at the expense of the rest of the world. The combined share of the East Asian-6 in US imports of HS 8528–1200 has doubled from 17% in 1996 to around 30% in 2004.

Even for Malaysia, after its share in US imports of HS 8528–1200 was reduced from 13% in 1995 to 9% in 2003 and 5% in 2004 (compared to 9% (or 8%) for China), its corresponding RCA index has nevertheless remained remarkably high at 4.59 in 2003, and 2.73 in 2004 (compared to the extremely low of 0.72 (0.73) for China).

The case of HS 8528–1200 stands therefore in sharp contrast to at least six of the other eight HS categories, for which the combined shares of the East Asian-6 have been consistently reduced, albeit marginally (see Table 11.12). This seems to imply that as it presently stands, and as long as US import demand is not unduly constrained for any reason, there may still be room for export expansion simultaneously by all East Asian-6.

The special case of HS 8528–1200 notwithstanding, our statistical analysis of the impact of China on the regional production networks for the electronics and IT industry from 1995 to 2004 may be summarized as follows:

First, the "substitution effect" by China has generally triggered a "diversion effect" on the part of the other affected East Asian economies—notably Malaysia, South Korea, and Taiwan. This has resulted in a higher degree of intra-industrial specialization in the region in exporting to the United States.

Second, despite overwhelming competition from China, virtually all the affected East Asian economies have gained from the "diversion effect" in absolute terms of the (percentage) shares in US imports of the particular lines of products on which they have increasingly focused their exports. As a matter of fact, the absolute size of the exports in which the respective economies specialize has also increased in response to heightened US import demand.

Third, relative to the overall share in total US imports of all goods, the gains from the "diversion effect" for the affected economies with respect to their special lines of exports are of course even more pronounced, hence resulting in a highly enhanced competitive edge, in terms of the estimated RCA indices in many cases.

Fourth, obviously as a result of the "substitution effect" by China, the overall shares in US imports of all goods of the other East Asian-5 have all declined. Nonetheless, except for Japan and Singapore, the absolute value of total exports by Malaysia, South Korea, and Taiwan to the United States have all recorded increases over the period under study.

Fifth, Japan and Singapore have turned out to be the biggest losers amidst the ongoing process of regional industrial realignment. Both countries have registered considerable losses in total exports of all goods to the United States, not only relative to increases in total US imports, but in terms of absolute volume as well. In the case of Japan, the losses were incurred across virtually all HS categories under study, and appeared indeed to be most substantial in both absolute and relative terms. For Singapore, the various HS shares have also either declined or remained stagnant.

Sixth, the consistent decline across the various HS shares for Japan (and for that matter, for Taiwan, South Korea, and Malaysia as well), should, however, be seen as a mirror image of the respective gains for China, noting that the Chinese electronics and IT industry has become very substantially dominated by FDI originating directly or redirected from these economies, and noting also that the exports from China are virtually all a matter of processing trade. The accelerated increases in the Chinese shares in Japan's imports of electronics and IT products may also be seen from the same perspective.

Seventh, China, nevertheless, still stands at the very end of the East Asian "flying geese formation", noting that (1) the country's share in US imports of integrated circuits (HS 8542), which is embedded with high technology, is still negligibly small at just 3% in 2004, compared to 6% for Singapore (the smallest share among the other East Asian exporting countries) in 2004; (2) the country actually depends greatly on outside supply of ICs to sustain and expand output of the electronics industry (to the extent of 80% of the domestic requirements); and especially (3) the bulk of ICs imported are not only from such advanced countries as Japan (24%) and the United States (9%), but also Taiwan (18%), Malaysia (10%), Korea (8%), and Singapore (4%) as well (all 2001 figures).

The question to be raised, finally, should be: what would the future hold for the Chinese electronics and IT industry within the broader East Asian production network? Or perhaps more specifically, in light of the enormous advances made by China in both output and exports of the industry in the recent past, would the other East Asian economies be eventually "crowded out" of the regional industrial scene?

The answer seems to be mixed. The accelerated Chinese foray into the US and global market for consumer electronics as taking place in the past two years captures essentially the initial big-push effect of the country's accession to WTO in 2001. The momentum is poised to continue unabated probably for some years. Moreover, China is also rapidly catching up with the neighbouring economies in developing or adopting new technology for IC manufacturing (see Box 1 for the interview with Dr Lee). Thus, the competition in exports against the other East Asian economies will likely further intensify in the years to come. However, this will inevitably lead to a higher degree of diversification and sophistication in the output structure of the industry. And there simply appears to be no reason why South Korea, Taiwan, Malaysia, or Singapore, let alone Japan will not be able to further engage in technological upgrading to enhance their competitive edge and carve out their own market niches for the industry, by emulating such tiny but highly successful countries as Finland (home of Nokia) and Sweden (Ericsson).

Furthermore, as it presently stands on the matter of semiconductor design (i.e., the very core technology of the industry), China still lags far behind Taiwan, not to mention Japan and the United States. As Dr Steven Lee sees it, the gap with Taiwan alone is still around eight years in this respect. Can the other East Asian neighbours not come in to join the technological race? Notice also that the entire Chinese electronics and IT industry, especially its export base, is by and large confined to two relatively small municipalities, Dongguan in Guangdong Province and Suzhou in Jiangsu.

The ascending automobile industry and potential regional impact

FDI and import substitution

In a way, the Chinese electronics and IT industry represents *faits accomplis*, which the automobile industry seems poised to emulate. But when will the latter be able to complete its highly import-substituting mission to turn around to be export-oriented as well? To answer the question, we have to first look at the role played by FDI in the Chinese automobile industry, noting that foreign investment is instrumental, as in the case of the electronics and IT and many other industrial branches in China, for promoting exports.

The figures in Table 11.15 show that the Chinese automobile industry is in fact also heavily dominated by FDI. Around a quarter of the GVIO (26%), total sales (26%), and fixed assets (23%) of the industry are all accountable by foreign investors in 2002, although the shares are still far less than that for the electronics and IT industry, respectively 54%, 52%, and 43% for 2001 (see Table 11.15). FDI's share in the automobile industry's total "export delivery" (at ex-factory prices), standing at 44% for 2002, also appears to be substantial, but it is again still far below that of 79% for the electronics and IT industry. In absolute terms, the discrepancy in "export delivery" by FDI between the two industries is indeed most substantial—14,849 million yuan for the automobile industry in 2001 (or 23,671 million yuan in 2002) versus 273,320 million yuan for the electronics and IT industry.

However, similar to the electronics and IT industry, foreign-invested manufacturing plants in the automobile industry also appear to be much larger in scale and hence more efficient. This is clearly reflected in their much larger shares in the industry's GVIO, total sales, and fixed assets, relative to the comparable shares in employment and the number of firms in the industry (Table 11.15). Their share in gross profits (50%) is also larger than that in total sales revenue and GVIO. This implies higher efficiency as well for FDI.

Notice nevertheless that the figures in Table 11.15 cover all types of motor vehicles (trucks, buses, and passenger cars) and motorcycles, as well as output of engine and vehicle parts and accessories. When the figures for sedan production are isolated, it is clear that the manufacturing and sales of passenger cars in China are virtually controlled by global conglomerates such as Volkswagen, Audi, General Motors, Renault, Ford, Honda, and now increasingly Toyota

Table 11.15 Share of FDI in China's Automobile Industry by Major Economic Indicators, 1992, 1995, 1999, 2000, and 2002 (million yuan and %)

	1992		1995		1999		2000		2002	
	value	%	value	%	value	%	value	%	value	%
No. of firms (unit)	2,555	1.7	2,479	6.8	2,362	11.4	2,326	11.5	2,436	14.7
Employees (100 persons)	18,095	2.5	19,525	6.6	18,068	9.8	17,813	9.7	15,705	12.2
- engineer technicians	–	–	1,660	9.0	1,606	10.8	1,643	10.4	1,680	12.6
GVIO	119,105	16.0	221,651	24.8	312,272	31.9	361,256	30.6	622,464	25.6
Investment completed	10,275	17.1	23,134	32.3	19,399	50.2	17,875	33.9	28,316	20.1
Fixed assets	16,033	21.3	115,002	15.1	222,361	25.1	254,576	23.9	364,233	23.4
Sales revenue	118,741	16.2	217,514	25.3	274,250	34.3	356,044	30.2	594,769	26.3
Exports	2,806	0.4	3,967	0.2	6,185	29.4	12,714	26.3	23,267	43.7
Gross profits	8,781	21.4	8,555	49.4	5,786	134.5	13,807	72.2	37,384	50.3
R&D outlay	699	0.8	–	–	3,818	54.7	6,774	36.3	8,619	19.2

Notes: The FDI shares cover both wholly-foreign-owned enterprises and Sino-foreign joint ventures, and include a relatively small proportion of investment from Hong Kong, Macao, and Taiwan combined. GVIO stands for gross value of industrial output at current prices. The value of fixed assets is based on original acquisition prices. The statistics cover all motor vehicles (including motorcycles) and output of engine and vehicle parts and accessories.

Sources: *CAIYB*, various years.

and Nissan as well, after the latter two Japanese automobile giants have synchronized with China's accession to WTO to make a most aggressive foray into the huge domestic car market.[13] All such other familiar brand names as Daimler-Chrysler, BMW, Volvo, Fiat, Mazda, and especially Hyundai, are now also represented in China.

As a matter of fact, all foreign carmakers in China operate as joint ventures with Chinese partners, and many have now increasingly come under the umbrella of the three largest Chinese automobile conglomerates—namely China First Auto Works (FAW) (based in Changchun, Jilin Province), Dongfeng Motors (Dongfeng) (based in Shiyan Municipality, Hubei), and Shanghai Automotive Industry Corporation (Shangqi) (based in Shanghai). As a result, the three Chinese automobile giants, FAW, Dongfeng, and Shangqi now increasingly function as holdings companies.

Shangqi (SQ) controls two major joint ventures, SQ-Volkswagen (VW) and SQ-General Motors (GM), but leaves both of them to operate as independent management entities. For VW, which was the first major global automobile giant to establish a joint venture in China as early as in 1985/1986, the "intrusion" of GM into its domain in the mid-1990s was of course an unwelcome event, as the author was told by Mr Wang Rongjun during a personal interview in Shanghai (op. cit.). Mr Wang saw it as an important factor why VW subsequently also wanted to team up with FAW. However, now that FAW's door is also open to other foreign carmakers as well, notably Nissan, VW has again found it profitable to "renew its interests in Shangqi". VW has indeed lately decided to extend its investment in Shanghai, by setting up its fourth manufacturing plant in the new Pudong district, where GM is also based.

The circumstances seem to suggest a two-pronged Chinese government policy on the automobile industry: one is to court as many global auto giants as possible to invest in China to enhance competition in the huge, newly born domestic market for passenger cars; the other is to push for further conglomeration and consolidation of the Chinese automobile industry by grouping the various joint ventures under the three state-run super conglomerates—FAW, Dongfeng, and Shangqi. Changchun, a well-established Chinese heavy industrial base in Northeast China, where the FAW is based, is now on the Chinese government's agenda to be promoted as the third largest vehicles manufacturing centre of the world (*TKP*, 12 March 2004; and *China Daily*, 8–9 May 2004).

Groups

Joint ventures/location	Share distribution	Main products
FAW (Changchun, Jilin)		
Volkswagen (Changchun)	VW40%	Audi(A6, A4), VW(Bora, Jetta, Golf)
FAW Xiali (Tianjin)	FAW 51%	Xiali, Xiali 2000, Echo, Vizi
Toyota (Tianjin)	FAW Xiali 50%	Toyota (Vios)
FAW Sedan (Changchun)	wholly-owned	Red Flag series, Mazda 6
FAW Hainan (Haikou)	wholly-owned	Mazda (Mazda 323, Primacy)
Dongfeng (DF) (Shiyan)		
Citroen (Wuhan)	PSA (France) 32%	Fukang, Citroën & Peugeot series
Fengshen (Guangzhou)	Yulong (Taiwan) 40%	Nissan Bluebird & Sunny
DF-Yueda-Kia (Yancheng)	Kia (Korea) 50%	Kia (Pride, Accent)
Dongfeng (Wuhan)	Nissan 50%	Nissan series
Shangqi (SQ) (Shanghai)		
SQ-VW (Shanghai)	SQ 25%, VW 50%	Passat, Santana, Polo, Golf
SQ-GM (Shanghai)	SQ 50%, GM 50%	Buick Sail
GM-Dongyue (Yantai)	GM(Shanghai) 50%, SQ 25%, GM 25%	Buick Sail (compact)
SQ-Qirui (Wuhu)	SQ 20%	Chery

Notes and sources: Huang Yonghe and Wu Songquan, "The automobile industry one year after China's accession to the WTO", in *CAIYB* 2003, p. 4; and *SCMP*, 19 May 2004, p. B1 for more details about Dongfeng's joint ventures with foreign partners.

Notice also that taken together, the three Chinese automobile groups presently already account for more than 50% of the country's total vehicle output and sales. If the other major five carmakers are included, including Honda in Guangzhou and Hyundai in Beijing, the share easily increases to around 80%.[14] As expected, with China now in WTO, the 100-odd small, unlikely

Chinese vehicle manufacturing plants are bound to be rendered out of business before too long.

As to when the tide may begin to turn to enable the country to target its vehicle output to the global market, obviously we have yet to first look at the relative degree of satiation of the Chinese domestic market and more importantly, the degree of technological sophistication attained in vehicle production, relative to the prevailing standards of overseas demand.

Scale of output and technological sophistication

We shall confine our consideration to the passenger car industry. Table 11.16 provides figures for China's output of vehicles, with particular reference to sedan production. While the production of goods trucks and buses to a lesser extent experienced a considerable setback in the mid-1990s (following massive economic retrenchment for curbing inflation),[15] sedan production continued to increase at high speed throughout most of the years since the early 1990s. The growth rate of sedan output averaged to a remarkable 26% per year from 1995 to 2003, compared to 7% for trucks and 14% for buses. As a result, the distribution ratio for trucks, buses, sedans narrowed in favour of sedan output from 63 : 25 : 11 in 1991 or 50 : 28 : 22 in 1995, to the equal distribution of 34: 33 : 34 in 2002, then swiftly to the "lopsided" development of 27 : 27 : 45 in 2003 (as may be calculated from the figures in Table 11.16).

Undoubtedly, joint ventures with foreign carmakers overwhelmingly dominate sedan production and sales in China, as shown in Table 11.17 below by the shares of the top ten manufacturers for 2003.

Except for Qirui (Chery) and Xiali which may be considered as homegrown models, the others produced and sold in China all carry familiar foreign brand names (see Table 11.17). Note also that Xiali is essentially based on imported technology as well.

Most importantly, by international standards, the scale of passenger cars or total vehicle output in China, taken either as a whole or separately by major producers, compares unfavourably with the other global automobile giants. Hyundai, which is Korea's top auto maker, controlling 42% of the country's auto market, for example, sold 1.899 million units of vehicles in 2003 and expects to increase its sales to 2.145 million in 2004 (including domestic sales of 639,000 units) (Reuters, 2 January 2004, via Google, accessed 31 January 2004). This represents nearly half of China's total vehicle output in

2003. Given that Hyundai's total output comprises essentially passenger cars, Hyundai should therefore compare favourably with any of the major carmakers in China, in terms of scale of output, as shown in the tabulation above.

However, the relatively small scale of production of carmakers in China does not necessarily imply that the car manufacturing technology will continue to drag behind that of its overseas counterparts. For one thing, most of the new technologies applied are already based on proven blueprints developed by relevant foreign carmakers. With enhanced protection of property rights under WTO, it seems that foreign partners may now feel more at ease to effect technology transfer to China. In fact, the author was told during an interview with Mr Wang Rongjun in Shanghai (op. cit.) that Chinese car manufacturers consider it as an "unexpected upshot" of the country's accession to WTO that all foreign carmakers investing in China have now become much more prepared to bring in new models and share their design and manufacturing technology, in light of the enhanced competition in the domestic market resulting from the increased influx of foreign carmakers in the past couple of years. Mr Wang also shared with the author the information that Shangqi's specialists have been invited by VW to their headquarters in Germany to engage in joint research and development for new VW models. This was all "inconceivable" prior to WTO accession, when foreign carmakers basically remained lethargic to the rigorous government promulgation to "open up the domestic market in exchange for technology" (a policy slogan personally coined in 1992 by the late Deng Xiaoping, China's paramount leader).

There are other important practical measures adopted by the Chinese government in compliance with WTO requirements that will encourage or even compel foreign carmakers investing in China to apply state-of-the-art technology used in their home countries.[16] These measures include: (1) the gradual reductions in import tariff (from 70–80% to 38–43% in 2003 and 25% by 2006) and the dismantling of import quotas (fully by 2005) for foreign cars, which will clearly help enhance competition in the domestic market; (2) elimination of the "local contents (localization rate)" requirements for foreign carmakers (effective 2002), which will facilitate global sourcing of parts and accessories of international quality standards; (3) lifting the restrictions on the class and model to be produced (in 2003), which will leave foreign carmakers free to make such decisions on a purely commercial basis and for the benefits of product diversification; (4) removing the limitation on Sino-foreign joint ventures for producing car engines and auto parts so as to allow for

Table 11.16 Growth of Vehicle Production in China, 1991–2003 (unit and %)

	Total	Chassis	Trucks		Buses		Sedans	
	(unit)	(unit)	(unit)	(%)	(unit)	(%)	(unit)	(%)
1991	708,820	122,873	45,203	–	175,742	–	81,055	–
1992	1,061,721	199,162	62,644	38.6	272,582	55.1	162,725	100.8
1993	1,296,778	171,769	77,488	23.8	292,213	7.2	229,697	41.2
1994	1,353,368	169,106	78,586	1.4	317,159	8.5	250,333	9.0
1995	1,452,737	162,713	72,182	–8.1	405,454	27.8	325,461	30.0
1996	1,474,905	167,651	68,864	–4.6	395,192	–2.5	391,099	20.2
1997	1,532,628	178,644	65,938	–4.3	439,615	10.2	487,695	24.7
1998	1,627,829	206,325	66,171	0.4	659,025	5.4	507,103	4.0
1999	1,831,596	229,113	75,632	14.3	509,179	10.9	566,105	11.6
2000	2,068,186	252,063	75,169	–0.7	709,042	39.3	607,455	7.3
2001	2,341,528	317,946	80,306	6.8	834,927	17.8	703,525	15.8
2002	3,253,655	425,601	109,256	36.1	1,068,347	28.0	1,092,762	55.3
2003	4,443,700	–	122,960	12.5	1,195,200	11.9	2,018,900	84.8
Annual Growth Rate 1995–2003	15.0			6.9		14.5		25.6

Sources: *CAIYB* 2003, p. 413 for 1991–2002, and www.xinhuanet.com, 20 January and 12 February 2004 for 2003.

Table 11.17 Market Shares of the Top Ten Car Manufacturers in China, 2003

Car manufacturers	Output		Sales	
	(unit)	share (%)	(unit)	share (%)
1. SQ-VW	405,252	20.00	396,023	20.00
2. FAW-VW	302,346	14.97	298,006	15.11
3. SQ-GM	168,991	8.37	201,282	10.21
4. FAW-Xiali	93,200	4.61	96,180	4.88
5. Guangzhou Honda	117,178	5.79	117,030	5.93 (5.8)
6. DF-Citroen	n.a.	n.a.	n.a.	(7.7)
7. Changan (Suzuki)	n.a.	n.a.	n.a.	(7.9)
8. SQ-Qirui	91,223	4.51	85,349	4.33
9. DF-Fengshen (Taiwan)	n.a.	n.a.	n.a	n.a.
10. Beijing Hyundai	55,113	2.72	52,128	2.64
Total	1,594,300	78.80	1,587,700	80.50

Notes and sources: Wu Peng, "Sedans production breaks record of two million units with reordering of the top ten (manufacturers) in China", in *Beijing Entertainment Times*, 3 February 2004, via www.xinhuanet.com, 20 January, and 3 and 10 February 2004. The figures for FAW-Xiali cover the most popular brand, Xiali, only. Figures for the other five or six different types of cars produced by the company, notably Xiali 2000, Echo and Vizi are not included, hence the total is smaller than that of Guangzhou Honda. Figures in parentheses are from HSBC—*CMR*, January 2004, p. 23, referring to 2002.

wholly-foreign-owned undertakings, which will further strengthen confidence in technology transfer to China; and perhaps most importantly, (5) the abolishment of the "foreign exchange balance requirement". As mentioned in the introduction to this study, this will greatly enable foreign carmakers to concentrate on manufacturing for the Chinese domestic market.

A word or two should be said about the last point made. For such global automobile giants as Toyota and Nissan, requiring them to export the cars manufactured in China (in order to be able to balance their own foreign exchange expenditure, as was the case in the pre-WTO accession era) would clearly be tantamount to creating a Frankenstein of Chinese competition that will undermine them in third-country markets. According to Mr Wang Rongjun (personal interview, op. cit.), this was the main factor that prevented the Japanese auto giants from investing in China in the past, although they were all highly interested in the huge China market. As for Volkswagen (VW), which started to gain a foothold in China as early as 1985, Mr Wang mentioned that the same "foreign exchange balance" rule applied as well, but VW was, nonetheless, willing and able to commit itself by manufacturing vehicle parts and accessories and car engines in China for export to Germany.

It seems that this German connection has now developed to be an important and integral part of the Chinese automobile industry and has indeed been rapidly maturing as a significant export undertaking, with total export value greatly surpassing that of finished vehicles in 2003, for example (*China Daily*, 8–9 May 2004; and *TKP*, 4 April 2004). As Mr Wang put it, it is also partly due to the increasing domestic availability of quality parts and accessories that the Japanese automobile conglomerates have become much more interested in China. Notice that the purchases of vehicle parts and accessories from Chinese domestic sources may not necessarily involve foreign exchange outlay, as foreign carmakers may pay with the Chinese currency (renminbi) that have been obtained from the sales of cars manufactured in China.

At any rate, China's accession to WTO has significantly altered the institutional parameters for foreign investment in the Chinese automobile industry, and has indeed resulted in the accelerated influx of foreign carmakers. This has lately prompted Standard and Poors to alert all involved to a potential overcapacity in the industry in the medium to long term.[17] In fact, since WTO accession, the industry has already seen price wars erupting repeatedly among the passenger cars manufacturers in China both large and small. Whatever the implications, this seems poised to eventually trigger a quality competition as well.

The Chinese government has also promulgated an array of technical measures since WTO accession to help bring the Chinese automobile industry in line with global standards. These include preferential treatment for carmakers which adopt environment-friendly exhaust fumes purifiers and catalysts, electronic fuel injection, anti-brake systems, airbags and so on, as well as the unified National Treatment standards of quality control for both imported and domestically manufactured vehicles (*CAIYB 2003*, p. 2).

Thus, as a Chinese commentator put it, "the new models produced in the past couple of years share one common characteristic: virtually all have reached the same advanced international standards for comparable classes [of passenger cars] produced elsewhere, yet their prices are by a clear margin lower than that of imported cars" (*CAIYB 2003*, p. 4). There seems to be some element of truth to the point made, judging at least by the fact that after WTO accession, the expected import influx of foreign-made passenger cars has been largely confined to high-class luxury saloons (*CAIYB 2003*, p. 227), while those produced in China are mostly small (compact and subcompact) and middle-size sedans (*CAIYB 2003*, p. 413), which for the reasons cited can well forestall competition from sedans of similar classes imported from abroad.

Thus, the days seem to have effectively gone, when the popular Santana model produced by Volkswagen in Shanghai could by no means be compared with its genuine German counterpart in terms of design sophistication and quality. In fact, before Buick manufactured by General Motors in Shanghai came into the scene, there were widespread complaints made in the country that the same Santana—the taxi image of China and Shanghai in particular—was reproduced over and over again, without a single trace of improvement since its inception in the late 1980s.

In the same vein, up to the eve of China's accession to WTO, the then highly publicized Buick New Century, also produced in Shanghai, and the new Honda VTI built in Guangzhou, as well as the Audi A6 of Changchun, all represented models that were more or less at the maturity stage of their life cycles in the West when they staged their debut in China.[18] But obviously this will no longer be the situation in the future.

The question is now, finally, whether the Chinese sedan industry is presently ripe for testing the Asia-Pacific waters, or even beyond.

Export potentials and implications for the region

Against the backdrop of the foregoing discussion, a number of points may be made about the export potentials of the Chinese automobile industry.

First, given the pace with which sedan production has been expanded in China in the recent past, and given as well, the accelerated adoption of advanced Western designs and manufacturing technology, the Chinese automobile industry seems poised to be fully integrated into the global network of production and marketing under the control of global automobile giants such as General Motors, Toyota, Nissan, and Volkswagen.

Second, on the eve of China's accession to WTO, it was still unknown whether the American approach to the China sedan market (i.e., exporting directly from home plants in order to take advantage of the reduced import tariff and import quota barriers) would eventually prevail.[19] But now the established EU approach as represented by Volkswagen of directly investing in China (import-substituting and tariff-jumping) has clearly gained the upper hand. Following WTO accession, the country has indeed seen most existing foreign carmakers expanding their scale of investment in China, and many newcomers, notably the Japanese auto giants, joining in the spree as well.[20] This will all greatly help raise the scale of output, which is bound to spill over to the export markets sooner or later, with or without the pressures of any excess production capacity.

Third, the belated initiatives taken by Toyota and Nissan towards China warrant some words. Various explanations were given as to why the two auto giants, among others, were not inclined to enter into any major deals with their Chinese counterparts until after the WTO accord was sealed in 2000. A frequently cited explanation was that the Japanese were particularly concerned about "forced technology transfer", or were wary of the inadequate Chinese record of property rights protection (were the Germans or Americans not concerned?). It is argued, however, that the Japanese conglomerates were actually already assured of sizeable market shares in China—in addition to the Chinese predilection for the relatively less expensive Japanese cars, most of the vehicles used by a great number of investors from Hong Kong and Taiwan were also made in Japan (and indeed shipped through Hong Kong to China), hence there appeared to be no urgency for the Japanese carmakers to invest in China.[21] Whatever the reasons, the fact is that Toyota and Nissan now simply cannot afford to ignore the enormous China automobile market, especially with the "foreign exchange balance" rule no longer in place. This also implies that such global auto conglomerates may eventually be prepared as well to risk creating a Frankenstein from China which will compromise their own overseas markets.

Fourth, the same WTO whirlwind has also vigorously sucked in FDI, increasingly from wholly-foreign-owned car manufacturers for production of car engines, parts and accessories. This has also triggered competitive efforts from domestic Chinese manufacturers to import advanced foreign technology to enhance output, in order to meet the increasingly sophisticated domestic demand. As a result, import demand for vehicle parts and components tended to decline, relative to the accelerated increases in exports in recent years (see Table 11.18). The upshot is that exports of parts and accessories have continued to exceed that of finished vehicles by an increasingly larger margin, accounting for two-thirds of total exports of all vehicle products combined in 2002. Many new products have indeed already become targets of global sourcing by international vehicle dealers.[22] This suggests that the Chinese sedan industry, which presently consists essentially of assembling plants, is now poised to become a vertically integrated industrial system. A recent report from the Chinese government reveals that the country has already formulated a grand plan for developing ten major regional bases for exports of vehicles and parts and accessories, targeting a combined export value of US$110 billion for year 2010 (*TKP*, 2004). This represents an annual growth rate of between 36% to 38% from the planned total export value of US$15 billion to US$20 billion for 2005.

Fifth, the present-day export capability of the Chinese automobile industry is by any measure miniscule. In 2002, the country exported only 28,645 vehicles (see Table 11.18). Of the total, trucks accounted for 37%; trailers and semi-trailers, 23%; and chassis, 20%. The number of sedans exported stood at a negligible low of 969 units (excluding 269 units of minibuses and 440 light SUVs).[23] Major export destinations were, in terms of value and in descending order: Hong Kong, Iraq, Liberia, Vietnam, the Sudan, and the Philippines.[24] These figures are self-explanatory when compared to those of Thailand, the largest auto manufacturer among ASEAN countries, concentrating especially on passenger cars. Thailand, where most of the global auto giants, such as GM, Toyota, Nissan, Ford, Honda, Mitsubishi, Mazda, BMW, and Renault have stakes of varying sizes, but which still cannot be ranked as a major global auto manufacturing base, exported a total of 173,382 cars out of the total number of 536,000 cars produced over the first nine months of 2003 (with the annual targets estimated by the Federation of Thai Industries to be 227,699 and 729,465 units respectively) (www.tradeportalofindia.com, 30 January 2004, accessed via www.google.com).

Sixth, there are, nonetheless, clear and early signs of an offensive taken by some major foreign carmakers in China to rigorously move into the global export markets. Honda tied up with Dongfeng Motors and the Guangzhou Automobile Group to secure a deal (in Beijing, July 2002) to establish an export base in Guangzhou's export processing zone for manufacturing compact Honda sedans exclusively for exporting, with an initial capacity of 50,000 units a year. More recently, Daimler-Chrysler "is seeking approval to set up a 250 million-euro joint venture with Dongnan (Fujian) Auto Industry to manufacture commercial vehicles for export to Southeast Asia, with an initial output of 20,000 units a year" (*HSBC–CMR*, January 2004, p. 22). In an

Table 11.18 China's Imports and Exports of Finished Vehicles and Vehicle Parts and Accessories, 1995–2002 (unit and US$100 thousand)

	Total finished vehicles (unit)		Trucks		Sedans		Parts/Accessories (US$ million)		Vehicle products total (US$ million)	
	M	X	M	X	M	X	M	X	M	X
1995	158,115	17,747	12,037	9,070	129,176	1,413	8,547	3,761	25,755	7,214
1996	75,863	15,112	6,256	6,256	57,942	635	10,776	3,821	25,002	8,165
1997	49,039	14,868	7,424	8,297	32,019	1,073	9,280	4,472	20,782	9,878
1998	40,216	13,627	4,373	6,306	18,016	653	8,049	4,896	20,579	8,834
1999	35,192	10,095	2,685	3,868	19,953	326	10,043	7,069	25,812	11,873
2000	42,703	27,136	3,085	7,093	21,620	523	21,128	11,254	40,475	24,785
2001	71,398	26,073	3,138	8,527	46,632	763	26,177	16,322	47,033	27,123
2002	128,195	28,645	6,692	10,520	70,329	969	29,587	22,101	65,999	33,589
2003				25,348		2,849				

Notes: The figures for trucks include chassis. Sedans do not include light SUVs and nine-seater (and smaller) buses. Import figures for parts and accessories do not include motorcycles and car engines. Export total of vehicle products cover car engines, as well as trailers and semi-trailers.

Sources: Wang Zude, "Imports and exports of our country's automobile industry in 2002: A general survey", in *CAIYB* 2003, p. 231 for 1995–2002, and www.xinhuanet.com, 23 January 2004 (accessed 25 January 2004) for 2003.

interview with the Chinese press, in June 2002, Mr Bernd Leissner, president of Volkswagen's Asia-Pacific Headquarters (which was then just moved to Beijing from Wolfsburg), was quoted as saying that Volkswagen "has vowed to export its made-in-China automobiles to eighty-four countries in the next three to five years (by slashing high costs)".[25] In fact, the first batch of VW's Passat was already shipped to Southeast Asia in May 2003 (www.xinhuanet.com, 20 May 2003, courtesy of Economic Reference Times, accessed 2 February 2004). This was followed by another shipment of 600 VW Polo to Australia late last year (information courtesy of Mr Wang Rongjun). Notice also that the total number of sedans exported by China increased from 969 units in 2002 to 2,849 units in 2003 (www.xinhuanet.com, 23 January 2004, accessed 25 January 2004).

Finally, the question is in what way may the Chinese advances bear on the East Asian production network of automobile manufacturing in the future. In a report published by the Japanese Research Institute in October 2001, which did not take into account in earnest the possible "China factor", the likely contour of the ASEAN automobile industry in the future was briefly highlighted on the premises that the ASEAN free trade area (AFTA) would soon become a reality.

First, Thailand, which is already home to by far the largest concentration of Japanese automobile and parts manufacturers in the ASEAN-4 (Thailand, Malaysia, Indonesia, and the Philippines), would become a base for exporting automobiles to the world. European (e.g., BMW) and American (specifically GM) automakers had also begun to see Thailand as a production and supply base for ASEAN and Asia.

Second, the regional production structure which is being reinforced by AFTA, would cause the Japanese firms, which have production bases in all of the ASEAN-4 countries, to "come up with a mutual complementary strategy that will allow them to utilize the particular characteristics of each base". Thus, the report saw a strong possibility that production of passenger cars would be concentrated in Thailand (e.g., by Toyota, Nissan, and Honda) while van-type commercial vehicles for developing nations as well as recreational vehicles would be centred in Indonesia (by Honda and Nissan).[26]

The same report refers to the "China factor" in passing, arguing that "if ASEAN's automobile industry is to maintain its presence in Asia, the realistic option would appear to be to increase the depth of the industry throughout the region, through complementary activities".[27]

Would some sort of a tacit agreement on regional specialization among the major Japanese carmakers really help, without factoring into the ASEAN context the rapidly emerging Chinese automobile industry? Nobody knows for sure at this stage. However, the single most important question that should be raised is whether the Frankenstein created in China by the Japanese or other global automobile giants would leave room for their own counterparts in ASEAN countries to manoeuver in the future. These are all realistic questions, especially when taking into consideration that the ASEAN 10+1 (China) FTA will soon become a reality. According to Mr Wang Rongjun, whom the author interviewed in Shanghai, the likely scenario initially would be that the various global giants would each come up with an arrangement for the different regional manufacturing plants to specialize in different classes and models of vehicles and different categories of auto parts and accessories: that is, to mutually engage in what the report of the Japan Research Institute suggests as "complementary activities". This would be similar to the emerging pattern of specialization between China and the other East Asian economies (as discussed in the previous section) with respect to their exports of electronics and IT products to the United States. However, given the enormous size of the China market, which seems capable of absorbing any classes and models of vehicles produced in the world in the long run, how long can the perceived regional specialization really sustain the continuous economic pressures for further regional conglomeration for the benefit of scale economies? We really do not know for sure. Perhaps this is too distant a question to warrant any further discussion.

Conclusion and implications for regional cooperation

The main points made in the chapter may be summarized as follows:

First, the electronics and IT industry represents the single largest branch of the new and high-technology industry in China. It is classified as a pillar industry, but is strongly dominated by foreign investment. The core technology is controlled essentially by foreign investors, notably from Japan, Taiwan, and the United States. The industry is highly export-oriented with exports essentially representing processing trade. In the past decade or so, and especially after China's accession to WTO, the volume of exports has increased drastically, threatening to cut deeply into the market shares of neighbouring East Asian economies such as South Korea, Taiwan, Malaysia, and Singapore, and most remarkably, even that of Japan as well. As a matter of survival, however, most of these affected exporting economies have managed to enhance their competitiveness by diverting resources to production and exports of particular lines of products for which they enjoy a competitive edge. As a result, the "China factor" tends to significantly help alter the shape of the East Asian production network for the electronics and IT industry, with the upshot of the structure of the industry becoming more and more diversified and competitive.

Second, the Chinese automobile industry, which is classified as a pillar industry as well, is likewise greatly endowed with foreign investment, and hence depends greatly on global automobile giants for the adoption of new core technology. Similar to the electronics and IT industry, the Chinese automobile industry is essentially made up of assembly plants, focusing on passenger cars in particular. It stands nonetheless in sharp contrast to the electronics and IT industry, in that foreign carmakers have hitherto been catering exclusively to the Chinese domestic market. The industry has therefore followed the Asian experience of hosting FDI for the purpose of "import substitution", whereas the electronics and IT represents a "leapfrog" from "import substitution" to "export orientation". However, there are now clear signs that the Chinese automobile industry is on the threshold of targeting the export market as well. Thus, given that most of the global auto giants investing in China also have similar and considerable stakes in ASEAN countries, the new reorientation towards the overseas market appears to be tantamount to creating a Frankenstein of Chinese competition to undermine their third-country markets. The existing regional network for automobile manufacturing seems therefore poised for a significant reshuffling as well. To ameliorate the situation, the various automobile giants will likely have to readjust their modus operandi, by assigning, for example, their manufacturing plants in different parts of the region to specialize in different models and classes of vehicles to be produced.

The ongoing or anticipated changes in the East Asian production network are bound to bear on the pattern of investment and trade flows in the region, given the enormous size of the "China factor" and its potential export capability. Put simply, the country's accession to WTO will likely continue for some years to serve as a great magnet for foreign investment in both the electronics and automobile industries. Japan, the United States, European Union, South Korea, and Taiwan as well, all seem poised to expand investment in China as a manufacturing base, either for exporting to third-country markets or for the purpose of avoiding high labour costs in meeting their own domestic demand.

The observed increases in electronics exports from China to Japan, the US, Germany and the Netherlands seem to represent exactly the latter type of trade flows. It remains of course a matter of conjecture as to whether the Chinese automobile industry will also be able to follow the same pattern of development in the future.

However, as a result of continuous income growth and increased purchasing power amidst the industrialization drive in China, one may expect the country to increasingly become a major export market for the other neighbouring developing East Asian economies as well, as it indeed already is for the US, Japan, and the European Union for high-technology products and advanced industrial consumer durables. If one considers, for example, that the entire Chinese computer export manufacturing industry is essentially confined to two relatively small municipalities (i.e., Dongguan and Suzhou), then there is obviously no reason why similar industrial slots cannot be developed in Southeast Asia. Malaysia is currently one of the few major exporters of integrated circuits to China. Whether in light of China's rapid advances with the same technology Malaysia will be able to hold on to that position is a question which should not detain us here. However, as industrialization advances in East Asia, the cross-Atlantic experience clearly suggests that there will be increased room for inter- and intra-industrial specialization and exchange between Northeast and Southeast Asia. It will of course all depend on the entrepreneurs and high-tech professionals to help carve out the market niche for the different countries involved. Under these circumstances, governments will certainly play the very important role of a facilitator. And the ASEAN 10+1 FTA agreement as hammered out in November 2002 has clearly helped to establish the necessary overall framework.

Acknowledgements

In preparing the manuscript, I have benefitted greatly from interviews granted separately by three key personalities and conducted in Shanghai as follows: i) Mr Wang Rongjun was managing director of Shanghai Volkswagen Automotive Company, Ltd. from the inception of this much celebrated Sino-German joint venture in 1985 or 1986 until his retirement a few years ago. He is now a member of the China National Automotive Industry Consultative Committee. ii) Dr Steven S. L. Lee, special assistant to CEO of the Taiwan-based VIA Technologies, Inc. VIA is one of the leading IC design houses in the world. The establishment features a total employment of more than 4,000 persons (80% are R&D experts and ICs designers) distributed among the Taiwan home base (2,500) and its branches in the United States (700–800) and in the Chinese mainland (in Shanghai, Beijing, Shenzhen, and Hangzhou, totaling about 1,000). Dr Lee, who holds two PhD degrees (in Engineering and Material Science) from the University of California at Los Angeles, was previously deputy executive managing director of US-based Lam Research, Inc., specializing in semiconductor manufacturing equipment (research and manufacturing as well). The firm is a major equipment supplier of the two largest electronic conglomerates in Taiwan, United Microelectronic, Inc. and World Semiconductor Manufacturing, Inc. iii) Mr Yenho Tree, managing director for Asia of US-based Centurion Wireless Technologies, Inc., based at Centurion Electronic (Shanghai) Ltd., with branches in Beijing (employment of 500 persons) and Penang (Malaysia) (about 1,000), in addition to Shanghai (400). Centurion specializes in R&D and manufacturing of mobile phones terminal antennae. It controls a global market share of 25–30%. Around 90% of its total global output is now manufactured in Shanghai, Beijing, and Malaysia.

I owe a great debt of gratitude to all three of them—Mr Wang, Dr Lee, and Mr Tree—for graciously sharing their great professional views and insights during the interviews. I am of course solely responsible for any errors and misinterpretations that I may have made in the manuscript.

My thanks also go to Mr Edward H. K. Leung, chief economist of the Hong Kong Trade Development Council for helpful guidance to research materials held by the HKTDC's Business Infocentre at the Hong Kong Exhibition and Convention Centre, and as well to Mr Benson Wong of the Infocentre for practical assistance in identifying and locating the useful materials.

12

China's WTO Accession, ASEAN 10+1, and ECFA

*"Open Regionalism" at Work**

A distinction may be made between the "full APEC" and "APEC Proper"; the latter should just cover member countries/regions of the Asia-Pacific rim, thus excluding the North and South American member countries. Within APEC proper, however, we may distinguish between North APEC and South APEC, using Hong Kong as the geographic dividing line.

Implications of WTO accession

The key question involved is, therefore, in what way China's entry into WTO in December 2001 may help to promote economic integration between China as a North APEC member and South APEC, ASEAN countries in particular. We will focus on trade and investment relations, in broad terms, in our discussion. Before we proceed, a few points should be made from the foregoing discussion[1] about the economic imperatives for China to yield to Western technological supremacy and the possible pattern of Western intrusion into the Chinese banking industry, following WTO accession.

---

* The first half of this chapter draws from the ending part of a broader monograph "China in the WTO and the prospects for regional economic integration—with special reference to the proposed ASEAN 10+1 FTA", which was presented to the Asian Development Research Forum (ADRF) Conference co-sponsored by the Thailand Research Fund and Canada's International Development Research Center (IDRC) and held in Bangkok, 2–3 December 2002. Consult ADRF Secretariat (http://www.adrf.org), *Asian Transition: Proceedings and Full Papers*, Bangkok, 2004 for details. An epilogue is added (in 2011) to extend the analysis to year 2010, i.e., the year of the formal launch of ASEAN 10+1 FTA. The last part of the chapter, newly written, discusses the region-wide implications of the signing of the Economic Cooperation Framework Agreement (ECFA) between the Chinese mainland and Taiwan on 29 June 2010.

First, in light of China's massive industrialization and modernization drive, it is clear that the country will continue to enhance technological supplies from such advanced countries as Japan, the United States and Western Europe—dubbed the Triad. At the same time, with China's own industrial system being increasingly maturing and diversified, we may also expect increasing intra-industrial trade between China and these major trading partners.

Second, WTO accession has already brought about clear signs of a drastic increase in China's FDI intake,[2] especially from major global conglomerates of Western origin, continuing the upsurge since 1992 when the Chinese strategy of "market-for-technology exchange" for courting foreign investment was promulgated. The Japanese car giants, Toyota and Nissan, hitherto wary of the Chinese investment environment for various reasons, are now all poised to rigorously move into the domestic market to compete with Volkswagen and General Motors.[3] Many similar foreign tariff-jumping import-substitution manufacturing investment initiatives are coming into the stream as well.

Third, enhanced trade and investment relations with the outside world also imply concomitant expansion in related foreign banking and financial activities in China. A good but nonetheless quite obscure case in point is that Hong Kong-based Japanese banking and financial institutions have helped to finance an overwhelming proportion of the SAR's FDI in China over the years, because the bulk of industrial materials, machine and equipment, as well as transport vehicles needed for their venture on the mainland are imported from Japan.[4] It is also for this reason that foreign-invested banks of Japanese and Hong Kong origin presently have the strongest presence in China, being responsible for import/export financing and foreign exchange clearing for their export manufacturing clientele in China.[5] Thus, with the accelerated FDI influx from Japan and the US following China's WTO entry, it can only be expected that financial flows between China and North APEC countries will take on greater momentum than with anywhere else.

To add on the weight of the strengthened economic integration between China and North APEC at large (the US included), there is of course the highly visible upsurge of Chinese exports since WTO accession. From January to September 2002, total Chinese exports have increased by nearly 20% year-on-year, and for October 2002 alone, the increase amounted to an even more spectacular 32%.[6] The exports are all predominantly destined for such high-income markets as Japan, the US, and the European Union.

Prospects for ASEAN 10+1

Viewed this way, what will the prospects hold for an ASEAN 10+1 (China) Free Trade Area (FTA), for which a framework agreement has been signed at the most recent ASEAN summit in Phnom Penh (4 November 2002), targeting its formal launch in year 2010? We should first take a closer look at the statistics on China's trade with ASEAN and other major trading blocs, in order to assess the potentials and relative economic significance of the ambitious ASEAN 10+ 1 FTA initiative. A number of points emerge from the figures in Table 12.1, in conjunction with Table 10.1 (in Chapter 10).

First, with a combined share of 43% in China's total external trade (imports plus exports) in 2000, North APEC proper taken as a whole (Hong Kong,

Table 12.1 Shares of ASEAN and Major Bloc of Countries in China's World Trade Total, 2000

	Exports		Imports		Exports + Imports	
	US$ m	%	US$ m	%	US$ m	%
World	249,195	100	225,175	100	474,310	100
AP proper	121,447	48.7	126,393	56.1	247,786	52.2
NA & EU	78,425	31.5	47,176	21.0	125,601	26.5
ROW	49,323	19.8	51,606	22.9	100,929	21.3
TRIAD	120,079	48.2	88,696	39.4	208,775	44.0
North APEC proper	102,507	41.1	99,656	44.3	202,163	42.6
(excl. Japan)	60,853	24.4	58,136	25.8	118,989	25.1
ASEAN-5	15,095	6.0	20,999	9.3	36,094	7.6
ASEAN-10	17,339	7.0	22,179	9.8	39,518	8.3
AUS & NZ	3,845	2.3	5,737	2.5	9,582	2.0

Notes: AP proper covers all Pacific-rim member countries only (including Australia and New Zealand, and Taiwan as well). NA & EU stands for North America (the USA and Canada) and European Union (as represented by France, Germany, Italy, and the United Kingdom only). ROW means the Rest of the World. TRIAD refers to NA & EU plus Japan. North APEC proper covers Japan, South Korea, Taiwan and Hong Kong. ASEAN-5 represents the five major founding member countries Indonesia, Malaysia, the Philippines, Singapore, and Thailand; while ASEAN-10 includes in addition the new member countries Brunei, Cambodia, Laos, Myanmar and Vietnam.

Sources: IMF—*DTSYB* 2006.

Taiwan, South Korea, and Japan, in particular) will clearly remain the single most important trading partner of China in the years to come.

Second, the Triad, which has already taken up a most significant proportion of China's total trade (ranging from a combined share of 36–52% over the past one-and-a-half decades, or 44% in 2000), will in all likelihood remain or become even more predominant as China's import suppliers as well as export markets, by virtue of the expected WTO effects as alluded to above.

Third, by contrast, ASEAN, as represented by the five major member countries (or the larger ASEAN-10), contributed a mere 7.6% (or 8.3%) to China's global trade in 2000, marginally up from 4.9% in 1980. If the most recent Chinese trade and investment statistics are of any indication of the long-term consequence of her entry into WTO, then it seems quite possible that ASEAN as a bloc may be further pushed to the peripheral of the Chinese trading system, similar to the continuous decline of the combined Australian and New Zealand share.

Can the new ASEAN 10+1 FTA initiative alter this long-term scenario in any significant way? I very much doubt so. That is of course not to say that amidst a relative decline in ASEAN's trade with China, there should be no room for an absolute growth in bilateral trade and investment relations. But where should then the sources of growth be within a FTA framework? The issues involved are certainly quite complex, deserving a fully-fledged paper for a more detailed analysis. Suffice it to highlight a few major points here.

It should, first of all, be noted that until the mid-1990s, total exports and imports of the ASEAN countries combined (excluding Singapore) were actually 25% and 45% larger than those of China. Apart from such primary commodities as timber, rubber, and palm oil, ASEAN exports had comprised increasingly light consumer manufactures destined to major Western markets, following the successful path of the "four little dragons". As for imports, they also relied essentially on Japan—the "engine of Asian growth"—for the supply of the necessary producer goods, as well as Japanese investment and technology for import-substitution manufacturing, such as electronics and car assembling. There are two important aspects to this familiar ASEAN industrializing experience that may bear on the potentials for further economic integration with China.

First is that the continuous ASEAN export drive is bound to be increasingly compromised by the rapid ascendancy of China in the global market, given that most of their manufacture exports are competitive, rather than complementary in the Western markets.[7] Second, and more importantly perhaps, is the evident implication that China—increasingly dubbed the "World Manufacturing Centre"—would potentially be able to produce whatever export manufactures ASEAN countries presently still command a comparative advantage on in third-country markets, given the enormous size and increased sophistication of China's industrial capabilities. This would of course limit ASEAN's access to the Chinese market in the future.

Take the electronics and information equipment industry for example. Just a decade ago, with the FDI blessing from the Japanese industrial giant, Sony Corporation, Malaysia had firmly established herself as the ASEAN base for the new industry, catering to both the domestic and overseas markets. But now Hong Kong, for example, is already being rapidly flooded with China-made telephone sets of various familiar brands, complete with all avant-garde functions. In the same vein, one may question whether sooner or later the Toyota plants in ASEAN would be made redundant as well, in favour of increased investment and manufacturing in China. In fact, Honda has just entered into a new joint venture agreement with the Chinese car giant, Dongfeng, and the Guangzhou Automobile Corporation, by securing an approval from the Chinese central government for a majority stake of over 50% (the first of its kind in China), in order to produce its popular sedan models (Accord and Odyssey) for the Asian and European markets.[8]

It therefore appears that ASEAN exports to China will continue to comprise essentially primary commodities for which the bloc truly enjoys absolute or clear cut comparative advantages, similar to the Australian exports of wool, beef, dairy products, and iron ore to North APEC countries. Such exports will surely increase with the growth of income and exports in China, but most typically have, nonetheless, relatively low price and income elasticities of demand.

Role of China

Let us turn to the other side of the story, i.e., ASEAN imports from China. Over the past two decades, ASEAN 5 have made up no more than 6% of Chinese total exports to the world, the bulk of which has clearly targeted consumers of Chinese origin in these countries. However, with China now emerging increasingly as an industrial giant—powerful but not necessarily a strong one—it should be expected that Chinese exports to ASEAN will gradually be dominated by industrial producer goods as well. Notice that ASEAN countries and South Korea presently take up a combined share of 90% in total Chinese steel exports, comprising essentially low- or lower-quality finished steel products. Meanwhile, China herself has to continuously rely on Japan and other advanced countries for the supply of various types of high-quality and high value-added steel products, which amounted, in recent years, in value terms, to around one-third of the country's total steel output. This "flying geese" pattern of international/regional trading in steel products will likely be substantially enhanced, with China now being a member of WTO and import tariff and other trade barriers reduced/abolished among the countries concerned in the years to come. Obviously, any further measures of trade liberalization to be adopted towards the creation of the ASEAN 10+1 FTA will only help to further promote Chinese exports of industrial producer goods and "appropriate technology" to ASEAN countries.

At a press conference held in conjunction with the 16th National Party Congress in Beijing (13 November 2002), the Chinese minister of Foreign Trade and Economic Cooperation (MOFTEC), Mr Shi Guangsheng, also expected that under China's "going out" strategy, an increased number of Chinese multinational corporations will also strengthen their overseas investment, especially in the neighbouring, viz. ASEAN countries. This should probably not be taken to imply merely following the Chinese experience of investing in, say, Australia's aluminium-smelting plant or iron ore development projects.

Rather, as I put it in a concluding statement of a paper presented at an international conference held at the University of Queensland in Brisbane in 1996 (reprinted as Chapter 11 of this volume), "a more likely scenario is that as China gradually becomes an industrial powerhouse of Asia, it will fuel growth and industrialization within APEC proper, joining Japan to become a crucial source of supplying the bulk of industrial producer goods to her Asian neighbours". And although "China currently represents the very tail of the 'flying geese' formation by reason of its comparative advantage in labour-intensive manufactures exports…, the Asia-Pacific region must anticipate the time when the emerging industrial giant will join Japan as the dragon head of economic growth in the region". Nonetheless, I also said that "the huge and highly diversified Chinese economy will one way or the other promise to provide sufficient market niches for the highly export-oriented ASEAN countries to diversify their overseas markets", although it remains yet to be identified where exactly those niches might be.

Moreover, there should also be room for regional economic cooperation on selective geographic spots. The Joint Mekong Basin Development project is a good case in point. China has indeed also decided to fully revamp and upgrade the Chinese section of the Kunming-Hanoi railway as part of the proposed Pan-Asia rail link. However, these all appear to be relatively small undertakings, viewed from the broader context of the North-South APEC dichotomy.

Forecast to 2010

According to Chinese estimates, upon the establishment of the ASEAN 10+1 FTA in 2010, Chinese exports to ASEAN will increase by 55% or a total of US$10.6 billion. The country's imports from ASEAN will in turn increase by 48% or a total of US$13 billion.[9] Three important points may be made from these figures to conclude our discussion.

First, there is a clear element of truth in the quoted Chinese prediction for a faster growth in Chinese exports (55%) to ASEAN than imports (48%) from ASEAN. And if China is to truly emerge as an "engine of Asian growth" alongside Japan, her exports to ASEAN in the years to come will probably increase by a much greater measure than the one suggested.

Second, the same Chinese forecast clearly suggests that the bilateral trade balance will basically remain to be in ASEAN's favour, continuing the trend since the mid-1990s (see Table 12.1 and Table 10.1). I would rather argue, however, that the meagre trade surplus presently earned by ASEAN will likely quickly turn into a trade deficit well before the formal launch of the ASEAN 10+1 FTA in 2010, given the anticipated momentum of Chinese export growth.

Third, and perhaps more importantly, the Chinese forecast clearly implies an annual average growth rate of trade volume between China and ASEAN that is considerably lower than MOFTEC's own estimates of 7.2% for China's overall global trade in 2010 (amounting to a doubling) and 2020 (quadrupling).[10] That is to say, ASEAN's share in China's total global trade will continue to decline in favour of that of the Triad, for example.

Epilogue: Forecast realized and implications

From the vantage point of 2011, the China-ASEAN trade statistics for 2002 to 2009, as shown in Table 12.2, basically bear out the forecasts and conclusions made in the foregoing sections. Several points may be made.

Table 12.2 Share of ASEAN in China's Total Exports and Imports, and Rate of Growth in Comparison with China's World Trade Total, 2002–2009 (US$ million and %)

	2002			**2009**		
	Exports	**Imports**	**X + M**	**Exports**	**Imports**	**X + M**
China's world	325,711	295,440	621,151	1,203,420	1,003,910	2,207,330
total (%)	(100)	(100)	(100)	(100)	(100)	(100)
ASEAN 5						
Major	20,372	29,666	50,038	86,386	100,279	186,665
	(6.3)	(10.0)	(8.1)	(7.2)	(10.0)	(8.5)
Minor	3,202	1,529	4,731	20,004	6,042	26,045
	(1.0)	(0.5)	(0.8)	(1.7)	(0.6)	(1.2)
ASEAN 10	23,574	31,195	54,769	106,389	106,321	212,710
	(7.2)	(10.6)	(8.8)	(8.8)	(10.6)	(9.6)
2002–2009	**Average annual growth rate (%)**					
	Exports	**Imports**	**X + M**			
China's world	20.5	19.1	19.9			
total						
ASEAN 5						
Major	22.9	19.0	20.7			
Minor	29.9	21.7	27.6			
ASEAN 10	24.0	19.2	21.4			

Notes: See notes to Table 12.1 for definition of ASEAN-5 (major and minor); ASEAN-10 covers both categories.

Sources: IMF—*DTSYB*, various issues.

First, China's exports to ASEAN 10 has indeed increased—as I predicted in 2002—at a much faster rate of 24% annually, than imports from ASEAN 10, which recorded an annual increase of 19%. This is especially marked with respect to the new member countries (defined as ASEAN 5 minor), which recorded increases of 30% and 22% respectively. Being the largest and most significant new member country, Vietnam played a most crucial role in this regard, with average annual rates of increase of 34% and 23% respectively.

Second, again, contrary to the Chinese forecast made in November 2002, as I then predicted, the bilateral trade balance in favour of ASEAN 10 has indeed turned from a surplus of US$7,621 million (or 14% of exports and imports combined) to a deficit of US$68 million (or minus 0.03% of exports and imports combined) against the entire Southeast Asian trading bloc. Note that for ASEAN 5 major alone, the bilateral trade balance did indeed remain in its favour; but in relation to total bilateral trade (exports plus imports), it has declined from the high of 19% to a meagre 7% (as estimated from the figures in Table 12.2). The trends will likely persist through the years to come, save that for geopolitical considerations, for example, China might find it in her interest to greatly boost imports from ASEAN viewed as a political grouping.

Third, for sheer economic factors within the global context as elaborated, however, it is difficult for ASEAN as a trading bloc to encroach, to any substantial extent, the shares of North APEC proper or the Triad in China's exports and/or imports in the foreseeable future. As reflected by the statistics in Table 12.2, the growth rates of ASEAN's exports to and imports from China in 2002–2009, though appearing to be much higher than the ones predicted when the ASEAN 10+1 agreement was signed in November 2002, can barely keep pace with China's total trade growth. In fact, the statistics in Table 12.2 reveal that the shares of the major ASEAN 5 in China's total trade in 2002 (8.1%) and 2009 (8.5%) represent hardly any marked improvement over the figures from the past two decades—6.0% in 1990, 6.6% in 1995, and 7.6% in 2000—as may be inferred from the same IMF statistics (see also Table 12.1 and Table 10.2).

If the trade statistics of the minor ASEAN 5 are included, the scenario is in fact not altered to any significant extent (as is also shown in Table 12.2) to the detriment of North APEC proper countries/regions, or for that matter, the Triad, for which the combined trade shares in China's global trade total are namely 47.4% (in 2002) and 34.8% (2009), compared with 36% (1990), 46.4% (1995), and 44.0% (2000).[11] If anything, the recent signing (in June 2010) of ECFA (Economic Cooperation Framework Agreement) across the Taiwan Strait will only help to further strongly promote economic integration within North APEC proper, and dilute (or even preempt) the potential positive effects of the much celebrated ASEAN 10+1 FTA.

ECFA and "open regionalism"

ECFA represents clearly a desperate attempt on the part of Taiwan to board the ASEAN 10+1 bandwagon, for fear of being "marginalized". The breakaway

Chinese province, adamant for years that it should remain both politically and economically independent from the motherland, finally could not help but yield to the enticing economic imperatives to cash in the huge trade and investment potentials offered across the Taiwan Strait. Briefly, ECFA is very much a lopsided agreement in favour of the island province, as shown in Table 12.3.

Notice that first of all, under the Early Harvest Programme of the trade pact, tariff concessions made by the Chinese mainland to Taiwan were by far much more extensive, covering 539 Taiwanese export commodities worth US$13.84 billion, than the reciprocal offers by Taiwan for 267 mainland export items, valued at only US$2.86 billion. The tariffs for all these exports, which make up, in value terms, 16.1% and 10.5% respectively of Taiwan's and mainland China's total exports to the other party, will all be phased out to zero in three stages within two years.

Secondly, as is also shown is Table 12.3, the tariff concession made by mainland China for the agricultural sector is unilateral, i.e., not at all reciprocated by Taiwan.[12] Moreover, the tariff reductions given by both sides cut across a wide range of industrial products for which the import tariffs were, on average, much higher in the mainland than in Taiwan, except for transport equipment. This can also be seen simply by comparing the ratio DV/NB for

Table 12.3 ECFA's Early Harvest Programme: Number (NB) of Broad Commodity Categories Involved and Dollar Value (DV) of Tariff Concessions made by Mainland China (MC) and Taiwan (TW) to Each Other Effective January 2011 (value in US$ 100 million)

Major industries	**Petro-chemical**	**Textiles**	**Machinery**	**Transport equipment**	**Agriculture**	**Others**	**Total**
MC to TW							
(1) NB	88	136	107	50	18	140	539
(2) DV	59.44	15.88	11.43	1.48	0.16	49.97	138.36
TW to MC							
(3) NB	42	22	69	17	0	117	267
(4) DV	3.29	1.16	4.74	4.09	0	15.3	28.58
(5) = (3)/(1)	0.48	0.16	0.64	0.34	0	0.83	0.50
(6) = (4)/(2)	0.06	0.07	0.41	2.76	0	0.31	0.21

Sources: *Xinbao*, 19 August 2010.

the mainland against Taiwan. That is to say, the tariff concessions made by mainland China are much more substantial in both absolute value and relative to the number of commodities included in the "early harvests" list (compare rows 4 and 5 in Table 12.3).

Third, in assessing the potential impact of ECFA on North APEC proper economic integration, it should, however, be noted that the "early harvests" list involves in fact only a relatively small proportion of Taiwan's exports to and imports from the Chinese mainland. In other words, the full weight of the FTA (Free Trade Agreement) is yet to be unfolded. Moreover, trade and investment flows, as well as services exports and imports involving the banking and financial sectors in particular, are all fellow travellers. While over the past two decades, Taiwan's growing FDI in the Chinese mainland, especially in electronics/computer industries, has generated enormous exports from the island of relevant components/parts and accessories to the mainland for export processing, complementary banking and financial services from Taiwan are considered seriously lacking. On this account, ECFA consistently grants Taiwanese banking, insurance and financial companies access to the mainland market, and as well allows the profitable banks to conduct renminbi business with Taiwanese-invested firms. These and the other provisions for Taiwan to expand its services industries (including medical and health services) into the mainland markets are indeed widely considered in Taiwan as much more substantial than the trade pact itself. In return, however, the mainland's financial counterparts are generally not reciprocated with similar benefits, although the major state-owned banks are now all poised to invest in participatory shares in Taiwanese financial institutions, hopeful of an early lifting of the highly restrictive regulations in this respect.

And fourth, ECFA has also come at a time when Taiwan is still very much in need of boosting her exports to compensate for reduced demand from Western markets in the aftermath of the global financial crisis. And this has indeed coincided with Beijing's attempt to promote domestic investment expenditure and especially domestic consumption to compensate for similar export shortfall, in order to sustain the desired GDP growth. As a matter of fact, Beijing is also increasingly wary of excessive reliance on the US market and American trade protectionism, in addition to the predicament faced of the faltering value of US treasury bills which the country has unceasingly accumulated over the years with the trade surplus generated. In short, ECFA, coupled with Beijing's remarkable policy reorientation towards the domestic sectors, will undoubtedly strongly render the two Chinese economies to be closely knitted together in the years to come.

Not only will there come to a significant reorientation on the part of Taiwanese exporters towards the mainland's domestic market, but mainland-based OEM (original equipment manufacturing) enterprises of Taiwanese origin are also expected to increasingly retarget the local markets as well, especially in light of continuous appreciation of renminbi against the US dollar that curtails export earnings but prompts wage-costs increases in the mainland. A good case in point is the consumer electronics OEM giant, Foxconn, of Taiwan origin, which was forced to substantially raise wages in 2010 due to increased labour unrest. The company announced earlier in 2010 its launch of a bold initiative, dubbed the "Galloping Horses" (萬馬奔騰) programme, for expanding its retailer network in mainland China.[13] Note that following China's accession to WTO, the mandatory requirement for export-oriented foreign investors to export at least 30% of their output overseas for earning sufficient foreign exchange to "balance [their own] foreign exchange expenditure incurred in investing in China" was already lifted, but until lately, however, "retargeting the domestic market" among foreign investors (labour-intensive manufacturers from Taiwan and Hong Kong included) seems not to have really gained in momentum.

In a way, ECFA is a duplicate of the CEPA (Closer Economic Partnership Arrangement) agreement signed between Hong Kong and mainland China on 29 June 2003, i.e., seven years earlier exactly to the date. After seven consecutive sets of supplementary agreements signed since then, the largely services-based HKSAR economy is virtually fully integrated with the motherland's these days. Interestingly, while CEPA was meant to be a rescue for Hong Kong under the enormous adverse impact of the Asian financial crisis, ECFA is similarly poised to redress the havoc wrought on Taiwan by the 2008/2009 global financial tsunami. Falling back on the Hong Kong experience, ECFA will probably be completed and enforced at a much quicker pace with supplementary agreements, barring any political interference on the part of Taiwan. Thus, the scenario seems to be already rapidly arising from the horizon for the Greater China triangle to be fully integrated as a quasi-single economic entity. And if ECFA is deemed as being prompted by ASEAN 10+1, or by CEPA as well, then the path has clearly already been set for "open regionalism" to work towards the envisioned APEC-wide FTAAP, i.e., to "link the emerging Asia-Pacific FTAs in one large FTA, the Free Trade Agreement of the Asia Pacific".[14]

Indeed, both South Korea and Japan are long poised to help expand the FTA between China and ASEAN into an ASEAN 10+3. And especially following ECFA, these two North APEC countries neighbouring Taiwan are keen to strike a similar deal with China to withstand potential export competition from the island. As an estimate puts it, the "early harvests" provisions of ECFA alone should already help to curtail competitive electronics exports from South Korea and Japan to mainland China to a combined total of some US$2,300 million.[15] Moreover, after ECFA, Taiwan "as a WTO member could pursue (similar trade) pacts with other member economies, sidestepping sensitive issues of sovereignty".[16] Pending the emergence of FTAAP, however, we should from a broad regional perspective briefly say something about how ECFA may bear on Taiwan's ASEAN counterparts in the long run.

ECFA and ASEAN 10+1 at loggerheads

Let it be noted first of all, that Taiwan, tiny as it may appear to be with a population of some 23 millions population, compared with 600 million for ASEAN 10 taken as a whole, produced a GDP of US$738.8 billion in 2010, which is equal to 41% of the combined total of US$1,800.3 billion for ASEAN 10. In per capita terms, the island's GDP amounted to US$17,660 in 2010, compared to a meagre average of US$3,246 for ASEAN 10.[17] Viewed against this backdrop, Taiwan's share of 4.8% in China's total external trade (exports and imports combined) in 2010, should be considered as basically commensurate with ASEAN 10's share of 9.6% (see Table 12.2). Should the 4.8% share be deemed as more than proportionate to the difference in absolute GDP size, however, it may rightly be accounted for by the discrepancy in per capita GDP in favour of Taiwan.

Nonetheless, the important point to be made here is that Taiwan's comparatively higher trade share in mainland China's total is overwhelming dominated by imports from Taiwan (a share of 8.5% in 2009) rather than exports to the island (only 1.7%). This clearly reflects the hitherto highly lopsided trade relationship across the Taiwan Strait. And it remains to be seen, how and to what extent ECFA may further help to redress the imbalance.

More importantly, the high share of Taiwan in China's imports is in turn exceedingly weighted by exports from the island of semi-manufactures (as alluded to in the previous section) for export processing rather than final goods for domestic consumption in the mainland. In other words, with ECFA, bilateral trade proper across the Taiwan Strait is now bound to be expanded much more rigorously than between ASEAN 10 and China in the years to come. And the potentials appear indeed to be most forceful, especially in view of the much more industrialized economic structure of Taiwan, as compared to ASEAN countries, or with reference to the transatlantic (viz. Europe and North America) trading experience.

Specifically, by sectoral origin, Taiwan's GDP is now composed of a contribution by industry of 23.1%, the services branch of 75.2%, and the agricultural sector of a dwindling 1.7% (2010 figures). This structure resembles more or less that of an advanced Western economy, and is indeed being increasingly approximated by the major industrialized cosmopolitan centres along the Chinese coastal belt, but not quite so by the largely less sophisticated ASEAN bloc. Thus, broadly speaking, intra-industrial trading exchanges between the Chinese mainland and Taiwan following ECFA may rapidly turn out to be much more substantial than that of the North-South type exchanges of manufactures for resource-based primary commodities between the Chinese mainland and ASEAN within the 10+1 FTA framework.

Equally important is that, similar to the expected impact on South Korea and Japan as mentioned, ECFA will likely help to enhance Taiwan's competitiveness to "crowd out" the electronics exports of ASEAN countries in the Chinese market. Note that the trading bloc, representing the very tail of the Asian "flying geese line-up", has nevertheless actually been quite successful with its electronics/computer industries in entering and penetrating the China market throughout the 1990s. As a senior officer from ASEAN's secretariat put it, as a share of ASEAN's total exports to China, manufacture goods—especially electrical machinery and computer equipment—went up from 12% in the early 1990s to 38% in 1999.[18] However, after China's entry into WTO in December 2001, even Malaysia and Singapore—both being the very hub of ASEAN's electronics industries—could not withstand the massive Chinese competition in the imports market of the US, as verified and shown in great detail in chapter 11 of this volume. How could then ASEAN taken as a whole possibly ward off Taiwan's pre-emptive superiority in the China market in this respect, now that ECFA is effectively sealed?

On the eve of China's WTO accession, the same senior officer from ASEAN's secretariat as cited, was then quite thrilled with the "retrospect" that "resource-based commodities—especially hydrocarbon, wood, and fat and oil products—accounted for two-thirds of the total export value of ASEAN to China in the early 1990s, but only 22% in 1999".[19] But now with ECFA across the Taiwan Strait in place, one wonders really whether the trend would be rapidly reversed, barring any powerful geopolitical consideration, say, on the part of China, to help forestall the inevitable for Greater China, or for North APEC proper taken as a whole, to reassume a largely North-South type economic and trade relationship with ASEAN, and as well with the remote Anzac clique, which are fortunately richly endowed with wheat, cattle, sheep, aluminium, iron ore, and not least, crocodile and snake of a wide variety as well.

Concluding remarks on long-term prospects

The wide-ranging regional realignment of economic forces in the Asia Pacific as highlighted surely does not necessarily spell doomsday for ASEAN. There are market niches remaining to be carved by the disadvantaged. A good case in point is that amidst enormous competitive pressures from China in the US market for electronics and IT products following China's WTO accession, Malaysia was able to swiftly divert resources and technological capability to concentrate on printer production, and thus successfully maintained her market shares for the broad category of computers and components in the early 2000s (see Chapter 11).

More importantly, with "open regionalism" now being forcefully at work, ASEAN 10+3 is poised, *fait accompli*, to help Japan and South Korea, in addition to China and Greater China, to greatly generate investment and trade flows with ASEAN countries. The Southeast Asian economic-cum-political grouping may presently appear to be a "backyard", but with a combined population of some 600 million and the blessing of the North APEC growth engine, the prospect seems not at all remote for it to emerge as another "golden brick" to be the next BRICS member, following the unlikely candidate of South Africa.

13
Conclusion
Pax Sinica Looming on the Asia-Pacific Horizon

Looking back, the far-flung regional realignment of the production network and the ensuing forceful trends of economic integration within APEC—whether APEC proper or encompassing the American-Pacific member states across the Pacific—have obviously all been triggered by China's economic reform and opening up to the West over the past three decades. Specifically, the gradual and successful conversion of China's centrally planned and controlled system into a decentralized market-oriented and open economy as it is today has allowed the Ricardian "principle of comparative advantage" and the Heckscher-Ohlin theorem, or the so-called "Leontief paradox", to unfold powerfully, though in practicum in gradual steps over the years. As a result, the Chinese economy is nowadays inextricably linked up with other APEC economies, large or small, to various extents.

In addition to WTO serving as a common foundation for enhancing trade and investment flows between China and the member economies, CEPA, ASEAN 10+1 FTA, ECFA, and the China-New Zealand FTA have all helped to intensify economic cooperation and integration. It seems likely that South Korea, and notably Japan, will sooner or later also be brought into the nexus as well. And with "open regionalism" prevailing, ASEAN 10+3 may be just a stone's throw away. Should all these network FTA cornerstones consolidate into the envisaged APEC-wide FTAAP, i.e., the "Free Trade Agreement of the Asia Pacific", then by virtue of her economic size, China—surpassing Japan since 2010 as the second largest economy in term of GDP, next only to the United States—would clearly become the gravity of the "geoeconomic" power in the region. This will be achieved with strong underpinning from Japan and the US—both being pivotal partner cornerstones of China within APEC. And if the pace and pattern of developments as highlighted in the foregoing chapters are of any indication, the continuous regional economic agglomeration towards and around the Chinese system will likely remain as coherent and powerful to defy any possible geopolitical interference.

Cases of geopolitical clashes indeed abound, but all were eventually overridden by imperatives for regional economic synergy. Such clashes include, among others: the Diaoyutai (Senkaku islands in Japanese terms) incident on 7 September 2010, which set off the most serious China-Japan conflict in decades; earlier on, the "mid-air collision" on 1 April 2001 near Hainan Island between the US and China, which threatened to derail the hard-won improvements in diplomatic and political relations; the large-scale "missile test" by China off the Taiwan coasts in March 1996, which prompted the US to send two aircraft carriers to the vicinity; and the conflicting territorial claims between ASEAN countries, notably that of Vietnam and the Philippines against China over the Paracel and Spratly Islands in South China Sea, which have resurfaced time and again, and latterly in July 2011, arousing global concern. It seems unlikely, if at all, that such and other similar geopolitical hiccups—serious as they may at times appear to be—would erupt into large-scale political confrontation or even warfare to entirely forestall the compelling forces for regional economic integration.

Viewed this way, the highly provocative tirade by Secretary Hillary Clinton, delivered consecutively on her Asian tours from Honolulu to Canberra and then Hanoi in 2010 to resurrect US interest in Southeast Asia is indeed tantamount to *wudifangshi* (shooting aimlessly) in Chinese parlance—nothing short of an anti-China rallying.[1] For one thing, being oblivious of the built-in regional dynamism for economic convergence, Clinton seemed little aware of just how the four little dragons, once serving as the frontier of the American-led "free world" against communism, have been drawn into the Chinese economic axis over the past two decades; and how even within Japan, the US's most trusted ally, political factions have already been wrangling to reconcile the country's enhanced stakes in the emerging economic giant across the Yellow Sea with the protective American umbrella.[2]

It would be misguided for Secretary Clinton to mistake the oriental courtesy of a couple of ASEAN leaders as political ambivalence to be exploited. This is especially so in view of the remarkable rapprochement and accelerated pace of economic cooperation between the two former rival communist giants, USSR and China, over the past two decades, which may possibly help to redress the gross deficiency arising from the unipolar dominance by the US. Indeed, as a high-ranking official in an ASEAN country is quoted by a

Stanford University academic as saying, "for us in Asia, the US is geopolitical, but China is geographical". "In other words", as the author further interprets, "faraway friends are welcome and helpful, but the local landscape is a permanent fact. One has to adapt to it—and to the seascape—to survive".[3] And here, "to survive" clearly means to yield to the economic imperatives for regional economic cooperation for mutually sustainable growth, while avoiding the risk of negative-sum military confrontations or clashes.

American politics seems also to be "haunted" increasingly by such strikingly new concepts as "G2" (the USA and China) and "Pax Sinica in the offing" in world politics, in the aftermath of the 2008/2009 global financial crisis, from which China has emerged largely unscathed while the US hegemony appears to be in tatters. Perhaps Clinton's tirade on her Asian tour should rather be regarded as a rallying cry to her fellow countrymen to reassert American confidence, or as a Freudian slip of a lack of confidence. Whatever the case, it is by any standard wildly premature to talk of a "Pax Sinica" arising to overshadow, let alone replace, Pax Americana. At best, one might speak of a Pax Sinica looming on the Asia-Pacific horizon by referring to some newly emerging "China factors" from the global crisis.

First of all, we should look at what constitutes Pax Americana as a baseline for gauging "Pax Sinica" as a rising potential. According to the influential global economist, Professor Nouriel Roubini, under its military and political clout, Pax Americana not only provided "security to most of Western Europe, Asia, the Middle East, and Latin America . . ., [but] also dominated the Bretton Woods institutions—the IMF and the World Bank, and, later, WTO—to determine the global and trade and financial rules, with the dollar as the main reserve currency". However, following the global financial crisis, "the US 'empire' is in relative decline and fiscally over-stretched", and the expansion of G7 into a broader, less coherent G20 has virtually left behind a "power vacuum" (hence the buzzword G0, or G-Zero). This referred to the absence of a global leadership to tackle international current-account imbalances, currency and trade wars, trade and financial protectionism; and to regulate and supervise financial institutions, let alone "reform an international monetary system based on flexible exchange rates and the dollar's central role as the leading reserve currency".[4]

Viewed this way, how could in the first place, say, the few Chinese naval warships patrolling off Somali waters possibly wrangle with the mighty aircraft carriers of the US 5th Fleet in the Arabia Gulf and Indian Ocean? Or, for that matter, that of the 7th Fleet off the East China coast, the 6th Fleet in the Mediterranean, or the 2nd Fleet in the Atlantic? We note, incidentally, that China's first ever aircraft carrier, which made her debut on 27 July 2011, represented nothing more than a defunct Varyag model bought from Ukraine in 1998 to be fitted for purposes of training and scientific research, as against the original objective of the firsthand buyer (a Hong Kong businessman) of having it converted into a floating casino in Macau.

Setting aside America's global and overwhelming military clout, it remains hard to envisage how China could any sooner overrule America to be a leader in the world economic arena. In this regard, a flexible exchange rate regime may not necessarily be a prerequisite, given that prior to its collapse in the early 1970s, the original Britton Woods agreement was actually built upon a fixed rate system. The greater question is how the renminbi could possibly challenge the greenback as the "leading reserve currency" or the "global medium of exchange"—certainly not courtesy of a few currency swap agreements signed amidst the global financial crisis between China and a couple of relatively minor trading partners to allow the parties concerned to bypass the vulnerable US dollar as a medium of exchange.[5]

Similarly, in calling for IMF's Special Drawing Rights to replace the US dollar as the world's de facto reserve currency, Zhou Xiaochuan (China's central bank governor) was clearly helplessly wary of the US government's resorting anew to note-printing to make ends meet, as the ensuing inflation would grossly curtail the value of China's enormous holdings of US treasury bills.[6] Indeed, what stands behind China's colossal foreign exchange reserves (amounting to US$2.850 trillion in the last quarter of 2010 and rapidly growing to a startling total of US$3.197 trillion by the end of June 2011, of which more than one-third, or US$1.1655 trillion, are held in US treasury bills)[7] is clearly, à la Professor Paul Krugman—Nobel Laureate in Economics—the "perspiration" of hundreds of millions of Chinese factory workers who deserve to be respected and honoured for what they have created with blood, sweat, and tears.[8]

Moreover, China's growing visibility in space technology and intercontinental ballistic missiles have very often conjured up a rising Pax Sinica to overshadow the globe. However, the country's number of nuclear warheads in stock or production potentials, or delivery capacity taken together, is likely still a far cry from the US and the Russian Federation, as is also widely known. Rather, one might hope that its relatively modest capability may hold the regional and global powers in balance to prevent any negative-sum military confrontation from taking place in the Asia Pacific.

To conclude, an attempt should be made to gauge how the interplay of geopolitics and geoeconomics within the broader global and regional context may help to shape the possible parameters for the scenario of a rising Pax Sinica. Several points emerge.

First, it seems simply surreal, in the first place, to envisage a China superpower emerging in the foreseeable future to replace Pax Americana in its totality—encompassing military, political, economic, and even cultural and moral clout; or even in the narrower sense, as Professor Roubini has delineated with reference to the US military might and economic power.

Second, a Pax Sinica may at best emerge in the Asia-Pacific context, but essentially as an economic phenomenon—meaning, the rise of China as an economic giant with far-reaching forward and backward industrial linkages to other APEC economies. Such a China-based APEC proper economic agglomeration will, as it expands over time, likely spill over to Russia, and the South Asia subcontinent as well.

Third, Pax Sinica, or rather, Pax Pacifica—or perhaps more aptly, the Pacific century (as the term was coined in the late 1980s and early 1990s)—will inevitably continue to interface with a moderated Pax Americana and its European allies. But this will in future take place on the basis of more equitable global economic and financial rules, as may be fixed for the IMF and the World Bank within, e.g., the G20 framework. Currently, the few agreements signed by China for "currency swap" represent really nothing more than a passive hedge against the US dollar dominance.

Fourth, within Pax Sinica itself, China's economic-industrial structure is poised to be consistently upgraded with progress in science and technology, behind the façade of the "world factory" (as China is often so dubbed). And apart from civilian industries, aerospace technology and military capability seem to have already entered a self-augmenting stage to emulate and eventually help counter US advances.[9]

Fifth, and a most poignant point, as a Taiwan-based press commentary put it, "If this (China at the head of Pax Sinica) materializes, China will be the only global power in history to have become a veritable superpower by relying on its own vast territory, huge manpower, science and technology and market system, without having to overstretch itself by maintaining military bases overseas. This will also be unprecedented in the history of mankind."[10]

The perception clearly stands in sharp contrast to the Greater East Asia Co-Prosperity Sphere envisaged by prewar Japan to be imposed upon China and other Pacific-rim countries with blood and iron.

Finally, given the resurrection of Confucianism in China over the past two decades or so, one may also anticipate a Pax Sinica to emerge with cultural and moral clout to help sustain peace and prosperity in the Asia Pacific. Japan, Korea, Vietnam, and to a certain extent Thailand, Malaysia, Singapore, and Indonesia—i.e., the majority of ASEAN member countries—all used to be under the influence of "Confucianism-cum-Buddhism" historically. The ethical and philosophical system is itself an incarnation of "soft power" (not necessarily entirely in accord with the definition of Joseph Nye Jr., who invented the term), as opposed to an exercise of "hard power" (i.e., by military, economic or financial coercion on the contemporary global political stage).[11]

Postscript on US TPP initiatives[12]

While the highly provocative tirade launched into by Secretary Hillary Clinton in 2010 for the US to "return to and stay back in Asia" appeared to have essentially translated into her government's pushing for the South China Sea disputes to be subjected to multilateral negotiations involving the US as a stakeholder,[13] the rigorous initiative taken by current US President Barack Obama to promote the Trans-Pacific Partnership (TPP) at the 2011 APEC summit seems indeed to represent quite a tactical approach to counterweigh China's rise within the Asia Pacific as a global power. It has, without doubt, helped to refresh and reinforce the emerging global image of a G2 scenario, but probably more in the sense of a bipolar rivalry rather than a possible strategic partnership in reigning in the tumultuous global affairs.

Briefly recast, TPP, which initially embraced only a very few minor South Pacific countries (specifically Singapore, New Zealand, Chile, and latterly Brunei as well) was hardly visible prior to late 2009. Around that time, it started to attract US interest, which prompted in turn Australia, Peru, Vietnam, and Malaysia to be included in a formal nine-party negotiation in 2010. On the eve of the 2011 APEC summit in Honolulu, Obama had rushed to conclude long-expected FTA agreements with South Korea, Panama, and Colombia. He also announced with high-flown rhetoric at the margins of the summit to have already hammered out an overarching TPP framework agreement with the other eight interested APEC members referred to above. Both Japan and

South Korea were reported to be interested as well. But China was not invited, presumably because the country's tariff and non-tariff barriers still remained relatively high, while TPP required tariff reduction to zero or near-zero, in addition to enhanced intellectual property rights protection, high-standard access to goods and services markets, as well as increased liberalization of the financial sectors.[14]

The selective exclusion of China inevitably conveys the impression that the US's TPP approach assumes strong geopolitical overtones, rather than a mere orientation towards a fully-fledged trade and investment liberalization across the Pacific. In fact, as Secretary Clinton put it, shortly ahead of Obama's announcement at the APEC summit, the US and its European allies had successfully established the postwar transatlantic system, and now a trans-Pacific system is needed.[15] Clearly, from the US perspective, the TPP initiative should play an embryo to NATO in Asia—and China, with or without the Shanghai Five,[16] the Warsaw Pact to NATO.

Whether the analogy holds should not detain us. But briefly, any affirmative academic comments made in this respect would do injustice to the post-Mao history of a China being steadily integrated with the outside world over the past three decades, and now, as it stands, being fully knitted into the global economic fabric. This is all the more remarkable considering that the former Soviet Union and its allies were then all virtually fully insulated from the West, and absolutely so in economic terms, for more than four decades from the mid-1940s through to the early 1990s.[17]

This seems to suggest that geopolitics prevails, irrespective of any fundamental differentiation in economic regimes, or in other non-economic values among nations. And the visit by Secretary Clinton to Myanmar in early December 2011, the first ever since that of her early predecessor, Secretary of State John Foster Dulles in 1955, seems to unequivocally endorse this point, especially given that by any human right standards, Myanmar under the prolonged military dictatorship should certainly be much less conducive than China to a genuine rapprochement with the United States.

Admittedly, Clinton's visit was prompted by the encouraging signs from the new Myanmar leadership of an increased relaxation in domestic control, given the sanguine US aspirations for spreading the values of liberty, democracy, and human rights across the globe. One can only hope that the offer she rushed to make for Myanmar—the Upper-Mekong country bordering China—to be incorporated into her celebrated Lower-Mekong Initiative[18] would not be a finishing ply to extending the Truman/Dulles containment of China from along the East China coastal belt to the Southwest land mass of the country.[19]

Now let me revert to the US TPP initiative, as it may bear on the APEC vision in relation to the geopolitical dynamics in the region. Our comments can only be made with relative brevity, given that the TPP framework agreement is yet to take effect from 2012, and pending supplementary proclamations on the details of implementation.

First of all, the US-led TPP initiative purports to pre-empt the given APEC agenda in favour of a "leapfrog" to the long-term vision of a FTAAP. The question is of course whether it would really help towards achieving the goal, geopolitical implications aside. Compared against the 1994 Bogor agenda of APEC, which prescribed for the removable of tariff and non-tariff barriers to the free flow of goods, services and capital among APEC economies by 2010 for industrialized economies and 2020 for developing economies, TPP would commit the less-advanced APEC economies to a full liberalization of trade and investment flows well ahead of the Bogor schedule. This should not pose too much of a problem for such minor APEC economies as Singapore, Brunei and New Zealand which are tightly tied in with the US economy. But for the other major APEC members—Malaysia, Vietnam, and especially Indonesia (the latter as yet not included in the TPP initiative)—which all exhibit a much more complex economic structure characteristic of an industry-agriculture dichotomy, accelerated liberalization may indeed run the risk of comprising their independent industrialization pursuit. Nor is it a straightforward issue for the much more industrialized South Korea and Japan (both of which have expressed an interest in TPP), especially with regard to the nations' highly disadvantaged agricultural sectors.[20]

Secondly, it is obvious that for Vietnam and the Philippines, TPP is bound up with an added security umbrella in light of the South China Sea disputes. The agreement may help to enhance the position of the US as a stakeholder in the region, and thus offer the necessary pretext for involvement in regional affairs. Besides, for the Philippines, the possible opportunity costs associated with the anticipated TPP bonanza should be minimal, if any at all. The country seems prepared to take advantage of enhanced access to the US market, and to be fully exposed to the influx of any amount and type of goods and capital from the US as in its colonial past, as this would clearly help to boost economic development and much needed employment opportunities.

Thirdly, from the US perspective, geopolitics apart, TPP as construed should clearly bring considerable trade and investment benefits, and thus much needed domestic employment gains. Perhaps it is not mere coincidence that the new initiative was launched exactly at a time when the US economy was and still is bearing the brunt of the 2008/2009 global financial tsunami.[21]

Fourthly, this is obviously not the place for making any simulative assessment about the potential total gains for the TPP initiative, in terms of extra volume of trade and investment flows generated within the TPP bloc. However, the more crucial question to be asked is whether TPP without China would help to expedite the Bogor agenda, and with that, progress towards FTAAP. The agreement would seem to be shirking its purported goals should the second largest economic entity of the world not be embraced into this new economic architecture. And an even more crucial question is whether TPP would lead to China-bound trade and investment flows being diverted to the US or elsewhere. This would certainly help to allay the apprehension felt by many for the rise of China to be a regional or global power.

This last hypothetical question is worth pondering, even if just briefly, for the conclusion of our discussion. But this should be preceded by a few words about the geopolitical undertones prevailing in Japan, bearing in mind that alongside China, Japan represents the single most important linchpin of APEC proper. As widespread press comments put it, Mr Yoshihiko Noda, the new Premier (the sixth in five years, mirroring frequent cabinet reshuffles amidst highly diverse and conflicting political-factional interests), is indeed facing insurmountable dilemma associated with Obama's TPP initiative.

For one thing, "popular fear of the rise of China" has tended to coerce the political leadership into a new military alliance with the United States via the TPP initiative, and therewith also gaining support from most of ASEAN's member countries. Political realists also abound, however, who, being wary of the track record of American political ambiguities (e.g., the "unexpected" normalization of Sino-American relations which had then caught Japan in great surprise), strongly caution against the possibility of a "TPP trap"—should the US come to an about-face to involve China in the new initiative, Japan would be sidelined as number three. The scepticism has prompted a number of scholars, though in the minority, to advocate for adherence to the conventional trading regime in the new era, by promoting closer trade and economic relations with China, rather than "trimming one's head to fit into the grotesque TPP structure". [22]

The point made by these scholars and political realists clearly brings home once again the notion enunciated earlier that the Japanese economy is these days inextricably linked up with the Chinese economy. The same goes for South APEC proper, Vietnam and the Philippines included, for similar reasons of geoeconomic factors. And the manifest economic nexus will likely continue to defy geopolitical manipulations in the years to come. As the Stanford University scholar puts it, China to ASEAN economies must be dealt with as a permanent geographical verity, while the United States remains largely geopolitical.[23]

Notes

Chapter 1 Introduction

1. See Christopher B. Howe, Y. Y. Kueh, and Robert Ash, *China's Economic Reform: A Study with Documents,* London and New York: RoutledgeCurzon Press, 2003, especially my own contributions (Chapters 3, 4, and 7) therein about "Creating a market-oriented industrial and economic system" and the chronology (Chapter 3), "Industrial change and technological upgrading" (Chapter 4), and "China's foreign economic relations" (Chapter 7) for a concise interpretative study of China's economic reforms and opening up.
2. For a Chinese interpretation of *taoguang yanghui* see Xiong Guangkai (former Deputy Chief of Staff of the Chinese People's Liberation Army), "China's diplomatic strategy: Implication and translation of *Tao Guang Yang Hui*", in *Foreign Affairs Journal* (published quarterly by The Chinese People's Institute of Foreign Affairs), No. 98 (Winter 2010).
3. Vis-à-vis the state-owned Soviet export monopolies, Chinese import buyers are clearly the weaker trading partners, despite their acting more or less as monopsonists. Cf. for example, John F. Nash, Jr., "The bargaining problem", *Econometrica*, Vol. 18, No. 2. (April 1950), pp. 155–62 for a theoretical exposition of the market form of "monopoly versus monopsony".
4. See Guo Yi Yao (Y. Y. Kueh), "Political and economic trends on the Chinese mainland and the prospects for (political) reunification across the Taiwan Straits", in *TKP*, 1–4 February 2000. I then also explicitly noted that the "equalizing" trends were already highly visible especially with respect to such major metropolitans on the mainland as Beijing, Tianjin, Shanghai and Guangzhou, in relation to Taipei; and one need not indeed expect a full equalization for the purpose of reunification in terms of average nominal GDP per capita, given that the combined absolute number of, say, the "middle class" in the mainland cities should be largely comparable, if not more than its counterpart on the island.
5. These are all official statistics from Japan given in http://www.stat.go.jp/english/data/handbook/c11cont.htm for 2009.
6. Staffan Burenstam Linder, *The Pacific Century Economic and Political Consequences of Asia-Pacific Dynamism*, Stanford: Stanford University Press, 1986, p. 116.
7. This happened in fact already nearly a decade ago; see United States General Accounting Office, *Rapid Advances in China's Semiconductor Industry*

Underscore Need for Fundamental US Policy Review, Washington DC, April 2002. The US report, defining the technological gap in terms of "feature size" (measured in microns) argues that "since 1986, China's efforts to improve its semiconductor manufacturing capability have narrowed the gap between US and Chinese semiconductor manufacturing technology from between seven to ten years to two years or less".

8. And also clearly alluded to in my paper presented at the Asian Development Research Forum (ADRF) conference held in Bangkok, 2–3 December 2002, shortly after the official signing of the ASEAN 10+1 FTA agreement (see asterisk note in Chapter 12 for details).
9. Immediately following my oral presentation at the ADRF conference (*ibid.*), I was rigorously challenged by a senior ASEAN official by the question, "Why then ASEAN 10+1 after all?" The question was obviously directed against the somewhat "unpleasant" point I had made that ASEAN 10+1 FTA would not help to substantially alter the long-term scenario of ASEAN as a trading bloc remaining "peripheral to the Chinese trading system" (see Chapter 12). My immediate response was: "Without ASEAN 10+1 FTA, you would be even worse off!"

Chapter 2 The Emergence of the Greater China Economic Circle

1. For most purposes of this article, we define "Greater China" in terms of the two southern provinces of Guangdong and Fujian, Hong Kong and Taiwan. Occasionally, however, our analysis extends to mainland China as a whole.
2. Global trade grew by 7.93% per annum, Taiwan's by 13.61%, Hong Kong's by 16.00%. See IMF—*IFSYB 1992*, pp. 108–15. Note that in 1992, China's merchandise trade expanded by a further 22% (*ZGTJZY 1993*, p. 101).
3. IMF data for China reveal a reversal of the pattern of trade expansion in the first and second halves of the 1980s. In the earlier period, import growth sharply exceeded that of exports; latterly, the opposite was the case. In Hong Kong and Taiwan, the second half of the decade witnessed an acceleration of growth of both exports and imports.
4. See, for example, Yun-wing Sung, *The China-Hong Kong Connection: The Key to China's Open Door Policy*, Cambridge: Cambridge University Press, 1991.
5. This role is a major complicating factor in compiling and interpreting trade statistics between China and the region. Goods flowing from (to) Hong Kong to (from) China comprise some which are part of a purely bilateral trade flow and others which have their origin or destination in a third country. It is important to distinguish between the two categories and to allow for a "re-export margin" added to goods which have passed through Hong Kong. In this article, re-exported Chinese imports into Hong Kong are discounted on the basis of an assumed re-export margin of 25%; for commodities coming from other countries, a rate of 14% is thought more appropriate.

6. These estimates are derived from data in the 1930s, cited in Yun-wing Sung, *The China-Hong Kong Connection*, p. 19.
7. Including re-exports.
8. Calculations suggest that it would have declined by about three percentage points.
9. HKGCSD—*HKMDS*, January 1981, pp. 19–21, January 1987, pp. 19–22, and December 1991, pp. 19–22. By the beginning of 1993, re-exports accounted for 78% of Hong Kong's total exports as reported in *SCMP*, 14 May 1993, which also noted that " . . . the market in China for goods re-exported through Hong Kong is now almost double the size of the United States market . . .".
10. China's share of Hong Kong imports rose in every single year between 1978 and 1991, from 19% to 38%. HKGCSD—*HKMDS*, January 1981, pp. 19–21, January 1987, pp. 19–22, and December 1991, pp. 19–22.
11. Re-exported imports to countries other than China showed a similar surge during the first half of the decade, but thereafter stabilized. *Ibid*.
12. To state it differently, in 1980, re-exports of Chinese imports accounted for 26% of all Hong Kong's re-exports; by 1990, the figure had risen to 56%.
13. The extent of the decline depends critically on assumptions made about the value of the re-export margin.
14. The very fact of such integration does, however, make interpretation of re-export data hazardous. Conventional practice regards any movement of goods across a border as trade. But cross-border shipments for processing purposes will lend an inflationary bias to measures of the volume of trade. Take the case of imported components from Taiwan, re-exported from Hong Kong to Guangdong, and subsequently shipped back in processed form (as Chinese exports) for re-export elsewhere (perhaps even to China itself!). Such a process will earn several separate entries in customs statistics, threatening to disguise the true value-added element embodied in each stage. The extent of the underlying interpretative problem is suggested by the finding that by 1991, the share of outward processing trade in Hong Kong's gross imports from China had reached 67.6%.
15. These and other estimates cited in this paragraph are derived from statistics in HKGCSD—*HKMDS*.
16. It increased from US$1.11 million to US$72.54 million between 1978 and 1991.
17. In the early eighteenth century, some 3,000 small-scale boats plied across the Taiwan Straits, carrying large quantities of sugar and rice to the mainland in exchange for cotton cloth, silk, paper and timber. See Zhou Shulian et al. (eds.), *Haixia Liangan ji Xianggang Jingji Hezuo Qianjing* (Prospects for Economic Co-operation across the Taiwan Straits and with Hong Kong), Beijing: Economic Management Publishing House, 1991, p. 156.
18. *Ibid*., pp. 156–7.

19. The estimates are "suggestive" in the sense that they are derived from data which only show *indirect* trade between Taiwan and the Chinese mainland, conducted through Hong Kong. Such trade dominates transactions across the Taiwan Straits, but also underestimates their true extent by excluding indirect trade through other countries (for example, Japan and Singapore), as well as genuinely direct—but minor—trade with coastal mainland ports. See Kao Charng, Yen Chong-ta et al. (eds.), *Liangan Jingji Jiaoliu Xiankuang ji Fazhan Qushi Yanjiu* (A Study of Economic Exchanges across the Taiwan Straits: The Current Situation and Trends of Development), Taipei: Zhonghua Institute for Economic Research, 1992, pp. 14–6.
20. Notice that in 1991 alone, the PRC's share of all Taiwan's exports rose from 4.89% to 6.13%.
21. *TKP*, 30 December 1992.
22. Sources as in Table 2.4.
23. Since the late 1980s, Taiwan's trade balance has also improved with ASEAN countries, but deteriorated against the United States. The changing pattern is not coincidental. On the one hand, growing American protectionism has forced Taiwan to diversify its export markets; on the other, increased FDI by Taiwanese entrepreneurs in both the Chinese mainland and ASEAN countries has given added impetus to trade expansion with these countries.
24. TIR is given by the following formula:
TIR = $(X_{ij} / X_i) \div (M_j / M_w)$ where X_{ij} are the exports of country i to country j; X_i are the total exports of country i; M_j are the total imports of country j; and M_w are global imports.
25. That is, TIR $\geq$ 1. See above.
26. From 18.9 (1980) to 8.52 (1989).
27. By the end of the 1980s, such shipments included a large proportion of goods destined for outward processing.
28. Also relevant are data cited in *TKP*, 31 May 1993.
29. Between 1980 and 1991, the share of primary products in China's total exports fell from 50.2% to 22.5%, whilst that of manufactured goods (mainly produced by labour-intensive methods) rose from 49.8% to 77.5% (*ZGSYWJTJZL* 1952–1988, p. 430) and *ZGTJNJ* 1992, p. 630). Since 1970, the share of labour-intensive manufactures in Hong Kong's exports has fallen steadily (e.g. from 75% to 55% during 1970–87) in favour of an expansion of capital-intensive goods (up from 21% to 41%) (data cited in Ross Garnaut, *Australia and the Northeast Asian Ascendancy*, Canberra: Australian Government Publishing Service, 1989, p. 54). The same period saw the simultaneous expansion of the export shares of labour and capital-intensive products in Taiwan, although it is only in recent years that the latter category has come to predominate (*ibid.*).
30. During the 1980s, the proportion of total Chinese food exports retained in Hong Kong fell by more than half.
31. Ironically, more and more goods labelled "Made in China" have in fact been produced by subsidiaries of Hong Kong parent companies, sited in Guangdong.

32. Yun-wing Sung, *The China-Hong Kong Connection*, Chapter 7.
33. A kind of technological complementarity is also evident. That Hong Kong's textile machinery does not embody the most up-to-date technology makes it appropriate for use in labour-intensive operations, such as China's resource-endowment favours.
34. Although their relative importance did decline, in 1990 such products still accounted for 76.69% of Taiwan's exports to China.
35. The share of chemicals and related exports rose from 2.24% to 12.65% between 1985 and 1990.
36. See Maruyama Nobuo (ed.), *Kanan keizaiken: Hirakareta Chiiki Shugi* (The South China Economic Region), Tokyo: Institute of Developing Economies, 1992, pp. 299–302 for a useful summary of cross-Straits trade policies emerging from Beijing and Taipei between 1977 and 1991.
37. As a proportion of total PRC exports to Taiwan, goods under SITC 0 and 2 fell from 74.93% to 31.85% (1985–90), whilst those under SITC 6, 7 and 8 increased from 13.39% to 54.26%.
38. Notice too that as Taiwan has become increasingly involved in southern China, its investment in Hong Kong has risen dramatically (in 1991, Hong Kong was the destination of 43% of all Taiwanese FDI in Asia). This sharp rise no doubt reflects the need to make appropriate servicing arrangements in Hong Kong for the operations of subsidiary companies in China.
39. See, for example, Alan J. Day (ed.), *The Annual Register*, 1992, Harlow, Essex: Longman Group, 1991, p. 360; and British Broadcasting Corporation, Summary of World Broadcasts, *Part 3: The Far East (Weekly Economic Report)*, FE/W0244, 19 August 1992, p. A/I.
40. *QGGSZZLSTJZLHB 1948–1989*, pp. 434 and 618. These figures imply an average addition of some 400,000 (Fujian) and 800,000 (Guangdong) labour recruits each year. Notice too that secondary-and tertiary sector employment growth in both provinces has easily outstripped that of the primary sector (*ibid.*).
41. Guangdong recorded an average annual rate of growth of 20.27% during 1978–1991 (*GDTJNJ 1992*, p. 342); the corresponding figure for Fujian was even higher (*FITJNJ 1992*). Fujian's faster trade growth needs to be set against a much smaller base level than in Guangdong. Compare these figures with the estimates for Hong Kong and Taiwan presented earlier (see supra note 2).
42. In 1970, Guangdong accounted for 19.2% of all China's exports; in 1991, the corresponding figure was 19.0% (*GDTJNJ 1992*, p. 342 and *ZGSYWJTJZL*, p. 502). Note that preliminary estimates indicate that Guangdong exports grew by a further 32% in 1992 (*TKP*, 1 January 1993).
43. To cite just one example: available evidence suggests that without Guangdong and Fujian, China's trade surplus in 1990 would have been reduced by 70%!
44. During the same period, Shanghai's share of imports rose from 1.2% to 3.6%. By way of comparison, Guangdong's share of China's trade increased from

1.78% to 13.34% (imports), and from 12.11% to 19.03% (exports). The corresponding increases in Fujian were from 0.71% to 2.21% (imports), and from 2.01% to 4.07% (exports). National data from *ZGSYWJTJZL*, pp. 432–3 and 438–9; Shanghai data from *SHTJNJ* 1992, pp. 349 and 352. The sources for Guangdong and Fujian estimates are shown in Table 2.4. However, these figures conceal the fact that the shares of both Guangdong and Fujian in total exports declined between 1980 and 1985, thereafter rising in a spectacular fashion. Given the more consistent downward trend in Shanghai, it is clear that during the early 1980s, the export performance of other parts of China outstripped that of all three regions. In this respect, it is noteworthy that in 1985 Liaoning's export share was the highest in the country (19.34%), even though just three years later its contribution had almost halved. Shandong was another province which experienced a significant relative decline (*ZGSYWJTJZL*, p. 510).

45. The average growth rate during 1985–91 was 27.94% per annum. The estimates show imports to have grown by 17.44% per annum during 1985–91.
46. Guangdong's export surplus vis-à-vis Hong Kong almost doubled in two years, rising from US$2,960 million to US$5,290 million between 1989 and 1991.
47. For 1985–90, the corresponding figure is over 33% per annum.
48. Average annual growth of imports from Hong Kong was only 14.23% during 1985–91, compared with 42.90% during 1980–85.
49. This phrase (literally, "three foreign-funded") refers to the activities of equity and contractual joint ventures and firms wholly under foreign ownership.
50. That is, processing operations based on the provision of raw materials, assembly operations based on the supply of components, manufacturing based on supplied designs (*sanlai*), and exchange through the practice of compensation trade (*yibu*).
51. The difference between total exports and those associated with commissioned processing, compensation trade and FDI ventures provides a measure of merchandise exports.
52. No doubt the figure would be even higher if provincial exports to Hong Kong alone were considered.
53. The available evidence also suggests that Taiwan's relationship with southern China has mirrored that of Hong Kong. Since shipments between Guangdong, Fujian and Taiwan must formally pass through Hong Kong, the extent of Taiwan's linkages with the two Chinese provinces is partly concealed within the British colony's own statistical records.
54. *TKP*, 1 January 1993, stated that China's trade balance with the USA had declined by 5% in 1992. However, another Hong Kong source subsequently revealed that the American deficit had further widened during the early months of 1993 (*SCMP*, 20 May 1993).
55. In the context of the accelerated relocation of manufacturing activity on the Chinese mainland, specific mention should be made of the Plaza Accord (1985), which forced Japan and Asian NIEs (newly industrializing economies) to

appreciate their currencies against the US dollar and thereby encouraged large-scale transfers of manufacturing operations within the Asia-Pacific region.

56. For a detailed analysis of quantitative trends in foreign investment and its distribution amongst "economically opened coastal areas" in China, as well as consideration of its impact on output and income growth, see Y. Y. Kueh, "Foreign investment and economic change in China", *The China Quarterly* (*CQ*), No. 131 (September 1992).
57. But in terms of AFI stock growth, Fujian and Shenzhen are almost identical.
58. The figures for investment in all China are 53.2% per annum (FDI stock) and 55.2% per annum (AFI stock).
59. For an elaboration of this point, see Kueh, "Foreign investment and economic change in China", pp. 652–5. See also *TKP*, 10 February 1993, which argues that although the Pearl River Delta remains the principal destination of Hong Kong investment, signs of a northward extension of capital flows (to Shanghai, Jiangsu, Zhejiang, etc.) are also in evidence.
60. The momentum of Taiwanese investment in mainland China accelerated after an official government declaration (Taipei, November 1987) that Chinese from Taiwan would be allowed to visit relatives across the Taiwan Straits. The continued and active interest shown by Taiwanese entrepreneurs in seeking investment opportunities in the PRC eventually brought official approval (in 1991) of investment conducted "through a third country". For further details, see Tzong-biao Lin, "Economic nexus between the two sides of the Taiwan Straits", paper presented at Conference on the Economic Development of ROC and the Pacific Rim in the 1990s and Beyond: Taipei, 25–29 May 1992; and Charng Kao, "Economic interaction between the two sides of the Taiwan Straits", paper presented at Conference on the Evolution of Taiwan within a New World Economic Order: Taipei, May 1993.
61. *TKP*, 2 June 1993.
62. See Charles H. C. Kao, Joseph S. Lee and Chu-chia Steve Lin, *Taiwan Tupuo: Liangan Jingmao Zhuizhong* (An Empirical Study of Taiwanese Investment in Mainland China; hereafter, *Taiwan Tupuo*), Taipei: Taipei Commonwealth Publishing Company Ltd., p. 12. The actual number of Taiwanese firms then operating in mainland China was thought to be between 3,000 and 3,500. Different estimates again are available in other Taiwanese sources. For example, the prestigious Chung-Hua Institution for Economic Research suggested that as of April 1983, some 2,700 Taiwanese firms were operating on the mainland with a total investment of US$3.7 billion (see King Pei and Hsu Chia-xian, "Trends and prospects of economic interaction between the two sides of the Taiwan Straits", paper presented at a Symposium on the Current State of Economic Management in the Mainland, Taiwan and Hong Kong: Hong Kong, December 1991). King and Hsu also gave a cumulative total of US$100 million in Taiwanese investment in mainland China for 1979–87. This figure increased by US$300 million (1988) and 600 million (1989) (see

Lin, "Economic nexus between the two sides of the Taiwan Straits") to raise the cumulative total to US$l billion. None of these figures is compatible with the official PRC statistics. The discrepancy is likely to reflect differences in the definition of FDI of Taiwanese origin (which may or may not include investment originating in Taiwanese firms based outside Taiwan, e.g., in Hong Kong or Southeast Asia, and which have become detached from their parent companies). The cumulative total given in the Ministry of Economic Affairs 1991 survey (US$750 million) seems most reconcilable with the incomplete official PRC estimates shown in Table 2.7.

63. For example, any attempt to estimate FDI's contribution to China's domestic capital formation and GNP growth should take account of possible distortions arising out of erratic exchange rate adjustments in converting foreign capital into *renminbi* (RMB) equivalent. See Kueh, "Foreign investment and economic change", p. 657.
64. These estimates were obtained by applying Hong Kong's shares (HKS) in the total intake of foreign investment of all kinds (FDI and capital borrowing) received by Guangdong, Shenzhen and Fujian to the respective percentage contributions of *all* foreign investments to total investment in fixed assets (CFA) in the corresponding areas. HKS are calculated from the absolute dollar figures shown in Table 2.7 and in Kueh, "Foreign investment and economic change in China", Appendix A, p. 683. CFA are given in *ibid*., p. 656.
65. For an elaboration of this point, see Kueh, "Foreign investment and economic change", p. 658.
66. Kwong-yiu Tang, "Outward processing in China and its implications for the Hong Kong economy", paper presented at Symposium on Asian Newly-Industrializing Economies: Past Success and Future Challenge: Hong Kong, May 1991.
67. Kao, Lee and Lin, *Taiwan Tupuo*, pp. 90–1.
68. See Y. Y. Kueh, "The Maoist legacy and China's new industrialization strategy", *CQ*, No. 119 (September 1989), pp. 422–4.
69. Shenzhen seems to be the only exception, its tertiary share in GDP having fallen from 45% (1980 and 1985) to 35% (1991). This decline was offset by a rapid increase in industry's GDP share (from 26% to 60%, 1980–91).
70. We are grateful to Joseph C. H. Chai for raising the points outlined in this paragraph.
71. These are the Hong Kong government's own estimates, made in March 1992 in the wake of the annual US review. The same report predicted that China's loss of MFN status would reduce Hong Kong's GDP growth in 1992 (forecast at 5%) by half. See *SCMP*, 14 March 1992; also *The China Business Review*, May–June 1992, p. 14. For consideration of the impact on the US of the decision to revoke China's MFN status, see *SCMP*, 23 May 1993.
72. But see also below.
73. The capital/labour ratio provides one measure of the extent of industrialization.

74. See Y.P. Ho, *Trade, Industrial Restructuring and Development in Hong Kong*, London/Honolulu: Macmillan Press/University of Hawaii Press, 1992, Ch. 10.
75. Yuh-jiun Lin and Chin-shu Huang, "Development of trade and investment between the two sides of the Taiwan Straits", paper presented at Conference on Global Interdependence and Asia-Pacific Cooperation, Hong Kong, 8–10 June 1992, pp. 8 and 10.
76. See Kao, Lee and Lin, *Taiwan Tupuo*, p. 42.
77. *Ibid.*, p. 65.

Chapter 3 Hong Kong Surviving the Open-Door, Reforming Chinese Economy

1. The movement of capital in and out of Hong Kong is unrestricted, and it can take place at any time by simply keying in the figures on a computer for outward remittance via fax machine. Import levies are virtually non-existent, except for the "domestic consumption taxes", referred to as "duties" in Hong Kong, which are currently imposed on three groups of commodities—tobacco, alcohol and fuel—irrespective of whether they are imported or manufactured locally.
2. As an island economy, Hong Kong's terrain is rocky and hilly. Of this tiny land area, however, only rather more than 14% is built up and less than 9% is suitable for crop and fish farming.
3. See Robert Ash and Y. Y. Kueh, "Economic integration within Greater China", *The China Quarterly* (*CQ*), No. 136 (December 1993) for the comparative Chinese GNP figures (the article is reprinted as Chapter 2 in this volume).
4. For a comprehensive review of the economic situation in China following the introduction of its market-oriented economic reforms in late 1978, see World Bank, Country Operations Division, China and Mongolia Department, and East Asia Pacific Region, *China: Country Economic Memorandum—Reform and the Role of the Plan in the 1990s*, Report No. 10199-CHA (19 July 1992).
5. The "gradualism" and the "big bang" models have now been almost unanimously identified as the two main models of transition from a Soviet-type *dirigisme* to a market-oriented system. Roughly speaking, China has taken gradualism, while all the East European countries and the former Soviet Union have followed the big bang. Such a dichotomy is, of course, not quite correct. Hungary and Poland had practised gradualism before the big bang. Even the former Soviet Union had engaged in gradualism before the collapse of its communist regime.
6. In terms of land surface area, China's is the world's third largest country encompassing an area of about 9.6 million square kilometres. Its 1.18 billion population represents some 22% of the world's population.
7. Lawrence H. Summers, "The Rise of China", *International Economic Insights* (May–June 1992). The departure growth rates for Summers' extrapolation are: during the 1980s, China's annual GDP growth averaged about 8.7%, while the United States equivalent was 2.3%. By Summers' reckoning, even if that growth differential were cut in half, China's total GDP would surpass that of the United States by 2014.

8. See Gao Shangquan (former vice minister of China's State Commission for Restructuring the Economy), "Taking a market-oriented direction and pushing forward in a gradual way—a basic experience of China's economic reform", paper delivered at the International Symposium on the Theoretical and Practical Issues of the Transition Towards the Market Economy in China organized by China (Hainan) Institute for Reform and Development, held in Haikou, Hainan, 1–3 July 1993, p. 3.
9. For a fuller discussion concerning the role of foreign investment and trade in China's economy, see, for example, Y. Y. Kueh, "Foreign Investment and economic change in China", *CQ*, No. 131 (September 1992), pp. 637–90; Nicholas R. Lardy, *Foreign Trade and Economic Reform in China, 1978–1990*, Cambridge: Cambridge University Press, 1992; and Yin-Ping Ho, "China's foreign trade and the reform of the foreign trade system", in Joseph Cheng Yu-shek and Maurice Brosseau (eds.), *China Review 1993*, Hong Kong: Chinese University Press, 1993, chapter 17.
10. See Zhou Zhenxing (senior deputy general manager of Bank of China's Hong Kong Branch), "Hong Kong the hub of massive growth", *SCMP*, 4 May 1992.
11. HKTDC—*SHKDERXTT* (November 1991).
12. A succinct account of these four pivotal roles of Hong Kong can be found in Yun-Wing Sung, *The China-Hong Kong Connection: The Key to China's Open-Door Policy*, Cambridge: Cambridge University Press, 1991.
13. HKGSESB, *1992 Economic Background*, p. 21.
14. For details see HKTDC Research Staff, "Cross-Straits trade boom", *International Market News* (July–August 1992).
15. See Masahiro Hirano, "Recent trends in investment and operations of foreign affiliates", *JETRO China Newsletter*, No. 104 (May–June 1993).
16. A lucid analysis pertaining to this important facet of the Sino-Hong Kong connection is given in K. Y. Tang, "Outward processing in China and Its implications for the Hong Kong economy", paper presented at the Symposium on Asian NIEs: Past Success and Future Challenge organized by Lo Fung Learned Society, held in Hong Kong, 30–31 May 1991.
17. Burton Levin, "The Hong Kong-China phenomenon", in Hong Kong Government Information Services, *Hong Kong 1993*, Hong Kong: Government Printer, 1993, Chapter 1; cf. also HKTDC Research Staff, "Hong Kong's role in China's economic reforms", *International Market News* (October–November 1992).
18. Hong Kong Bank, "Monetary integration between Hong Kong and China", *Economic Report* (February 1993); see also, "HK$ currency in southern China—an updated estimate", *Asian Monetary Monitor*, Vol. 16, No. 6 (November–December 1992), pp. 34 et seq.
19. Originally, the Jackson-Vanik Amendment was enacted in 1974 to address concerns about the Soviet Union's restrictions on emigration by its Jewish citizens.

20. HKTDC—*SHKDERXTT* (November 1991), supra. In his "Non-institutional economic integration via cultural affinity: The case of mainland China, Taiwan and Hong Kong", Hong Kong Institute of Asia-Pacific Studies, Occasional Paper No. 13 (July 1992), pp. 10 *et seq*., Yun-Wing Sung argues that re-export markups are, in fact, higher for trade flows with China, with 25% being a more realistic estimate for such margins, otherwise Hong Kong official trade statistics would imply that retained imports, when conventionally defined as imports net of re-exports, from China were actually negative in both 1990 and 1991.
21. See Hamish Macleod, *Building on Success: The 1993–94 Budge*t (Speech by the Financial Secretary, moving the Second Reading of the Appropriation Bill, 1993), Hong Kong: Government Printer, 3 March 1993, p. 12.
22. *Ibid*.; see also Barber B. Conable Jr. and John C. Whitehead (co-chairs), and David M. Lampton and Alfred D. Wilhelm Jr. (co-rapporteurs), *United States and China Relations at a Crossroad*, Policy Paper, Washington DC and New York: The Atlantic Council of the United States and National Committee on United States-China Relations, February 1993, p. 15.
23. See USIS, "Greater China trade with the United States, 1987–92: The trend", *Economic Policy Backgrounder* (23 March 1993).
24. See Douglas Hurd (Secretary of State for Foreign and Commonwealth Affairs), *White Paper on the Annual Report on Hong Kong 1992 to Parliament*, Hong Kong: Government Printer, March 1993, p. 4; see also Levin, "The Hong Kong-China phenomenon", supra 17.
25. Hang Seng Bank, "The current state of the Chinese economy and its impact on Hong Kong", HSB– *HSEM*, July 1993.
26. For a further discussion, see Y. Y. Kueh, "Industrial deregulation and economic restructuring in China: A GATT perspective" (paper presented at the 34th International Congress on Asian and North African Studies, held in Hong Kong, 22–28 August 1993); a revised version is available in Dieter Cassel and Carsten Hermann-Pillath (eds.), *The East, the West, and China's Growth: Challenge and Response*, Baden-Baden: Nomos Verlagsgesellschaft, 1995, pp. 309–34.

Chapter 4 Guangdong Province Ascending as the "Fifth Dragon"

1. During his tour of southern China *[nanxun]* between January and February 1992, Deng Xiaoping described Guangdong as the "leading force for economic development" and explicitly urged the region to catch up with the "four little dragons" during the next twenty years. The four dragons are South Korea, Taiwan, Hong Kong, and Singapore.
2. Lardy points out that by the mid-1980s, Guangdong "was able to spend most of its fiscal revenues", its quota for tax remission to the centre having been reduced from US$1.0 billion to US$0.772 billion between 1980–82 and 1986–90. See Nicholas R. Lardy, *Foreign Trade and Economic Reform in China, 1978–1990*, Cambridge: Cambridge University Press, 1992, pp. 55 and 135.

3. Shenzhen, Zhuhai, and Shantou SEZs were set up in Guangdong in 1980. The fourth SEZ was Xiamen in Fujian Province.
4. Only South Korea, with a population of 43 million and a land mass of 0.099 million square kilometres, approaches it. Taiwan falls far behind, with a population one-third, and a surface area one-fifth of that of Guangdong. The city-states of Hong Kong and Singapore are of course minuscule by comparison.
5. See also Robert F. Ash and Y. Y. Kueh, "Economic integration within Greater China: Trade and investment flows between China, Hong Kong and Taiwan", *The China Quarterly* (*CQ*), No. 136 (December 1993), Table 11 and p. 743 (the article is reprinted as Chapter 2 in this volume).
6. GDP growth averaged 9.0% and 13.3% per annum in China and Guangdong, respectively, between 1979 and 1992.
7. The figures are derived from the estimates of absolute GDP in Table 4.2 and of sectoral contributions to GDP in Table 4.5. They are consistent with Guangdong's shares in national GVIO and GVAO, shown in Table 4.2.
8. The disappointing performance of the grain sector in southern China (of which Guangdong is a part) is touched on in Robert F. Ash, "The agricultural sector in China: Performance and policy dilemmas during the 1990s", *CQ*, No. 131 (September 1992). By 1993–94, the urgency of the situation, associated in particular with a sharp decline in the grain sown area, was reflected in calls of the provincial government to prevent further loss of land and to increase investment in order to restore levels of grain production.
9. GVAO embraces not only crop farming, but also fishing, animal husbandry, forestry, and subsidiaries. RSVO (rural social value output) extends the coverage by including the value of production of rural industries.
10. In fairness, it should be said that with the exception of South Korea between 1986 and 1992, China also achieved faster growth than the four dragons during 1979 and 1992, and 1986 and 1992. But in the case of Guangdong, the gap was much narrower and the growth record of all five regions was in fact quite similar.
11. From 12% to 15% in aggregate terms; and from 10% to 12% in per capita terms.
12. In 1994 foreign capital still accounted for a significant proportion of total fixed capital formation in Guangdong.
13. Notice, however, that the process has been more pronounced in Guangdong than in the rest of the country—this, in turn, reflecting improved capital productivity rather than the use of more physical capital..
14. Guangdong's per capita growth performance also easily outpaced that of every one of the four dragons. See Table 4.3.
15. Between 1980 and 1992, the share of agriculture in total employment fell from 71% to 47% in Guangdong, and from 69% to 59% in China. During the same period, the employment share of industry increased from 17% to 30%

(Guangdong), but from 18% to 22% (China); and in services from 12% to 22% (Guangdong), but from 13% to 20% (China).

16. Relevant data are available in Anis Chowdhury and Iyanatul Islam, *The Newly Industrialising Economies of East Asia*, London: Routledge, 1993, Tables 1.5 and 1.7.
17. A major part of the background to Guangdong's recent economic expansion has undoubtedly been increased inter-regional mobility within the province, as well as large-scale migration from outside in order to take advantage of employment opportunities. The associated pressures have contributed to the breakdown of administrative barriers (notably, the "household registration" [*hukou*] system), which since the early 1950s had prevented large-scale rural-urban movements of population. They have also given rise to an enormous "floating population" and many millions of "illegal" or "temporary" residents in major cities. To what extent these urban dwellers should be accorded proper urban entitlements and benefits is a major problem now facing the government. See *TKP*, 16 January 1994, p. 2.
18. In numerical terms, the sources of improvements in productivity are a residual, left over after the relative contributions of physical increases in labour and capital to income growth have been isolated. Their verification at an aggregate level is not readily susceptible to econometric testing (especially if reference is made to X-efficiency considerations).
19. Foreign domestic investment (FDI) into Guangdong rose by 95% in 1992 (but by 152% in China); the corresponding figures for all foreign capital were 88% and 66% (see Table 4.9). In 1993, Guangdong's realized FDI and total foreign capital inflows increased, respectively, by a further 113% and 75%, to reach US$6.2 billion and US$8.5 billion. See *TKP*, 3 January 1994 and Table 4.9.
20. The prediction was made in Y. Y. Kueh, "Foreign investment and economic change in China", *CQ*, No. 131 (September 1992). By 1994, Guangdong's share of national FDI had fallen further to under 28% (*ZGTJNJ 1995*, p. 557).
21. On the basis of inflows of all foreign capital, the figure is significantly higher—around 30% during 1991 and 1992.
22. Kueh, "Foreign investment and economic change in China", p. 658. The combination of a stable US dollar and accelerated price inflation in China in recent years suggests that the 3:1 ratio needs to be revised upwards.
23. A detailed analysis of Guangdong's foreign trade reforms and their impact is given by John Kamm, "Reforming foreign trade", in Ezra F. Vogel, *One Step Ahead in China: Guangdong under Reform*, Cambridge, Mass.: Harvard University Press, 1989.
24. For detailed consideration of Guangdong's foreign trade since 1978, see Ash and Kueh, "Economic integration within Greater China".
25. *TKP*, 3 January 1994.
26. The conversion of US dollar-into renminbi-based trade figures in order to facilitate comparison with yuan-based GDP estimates is likely to exaggerate

imports and exports under the impact of erratic yuan depreciations during the second half of the 1980s.

27. That is, both Guangdong and China experienced a relative rise in the contribution of export demand, but a relative decline in that of domestic demand.
28. For more detailed consideration of this aspect, see Ash and Kueh, "Economic integration within Greater China".
29. A useful account of Guangdong's SEZs and their early experience is given in "Special Economic Zones: Experiment in new systems", in Vogel, *One Step Ahead in China*, op. cit.
30. The three SEZs (Shenzhen, Zhuhai, and Shantou) were set up in 1980. In 1984, Guangzhou (the provincial capital) was included amongst the 14 coastal cities designated by the central government to be opened to foreign investment. In 1988, several other major provincial municipalities were added to the list.
31. Kueh, "Foreign investment and economic change in China"; and Ash and Kueh, "Economic integration within Greater China".
32. Prior to 1985, the corresponding figure was even higher—a reflection of the even greater importance of Guangdong as a recipient of foreign capital.
33. Exorbitant increases in land rents and persistent labour shortages have prompted this transfer of manufacturing activity. In so doing, they have contributed to a complex process of de-industrialization, which has fundamentally changed the economic structure of Hong Kong. See Ash and Kueh, "Economic integration within Greater China", and Y. P. Ho and Y. Y. Kueh, "Whither Hong Kong in an open-door, reforming Chinese economy?" *The Pacific Review* (London), Vol. 6, No. 4 (December 1993). The latter article is reprinted as Chapter 3 in this volume.
34. *Ibid.*, p. 339.
35. This is demonstrated by estimates of the relationship between the ratio of total state budget (revenue and expenditure) to GNP in 1992 and 1978. The calculated figures are 0.54 for Guangdong and 0.55 for China.
36. In 1978, Guangdong's ratio of revenue (expenditure) to GNP was 21% (15%). The corresponding figures for China were 34% (31%).
37. In general, both the revenue/GNP and expenditure/GNP ratios for Guangdong were between 50% and 60% of the national figures after 1980.
38. Perhaps this also explains some of the less positive factors associated with recent reforms, such as severe urban traffic congestion, environmental pollution, and deteriorating medical services and health care.
39. Compare Table 4.3 and Kihwan Kim and Kwang Choi, "Strategies for structural adjustment and rapid development in Korea", paper presented at the Western Economic Association International Pacific Rim Conference, 8–13 January 1994, Hong Kong.
40. These figures are taken from *Draft Programme for Economic and Social Development in Guangdong* (1990–2010), as cited in *TKP*, 22 February 1994.
41. Compare the following provincial annual growth rates: 1991, 14.3%; 1992, 19.9%; and 1993, 21% (Table 5.3 and *TKP*, 22 February 1994).

42. Zhu Senlin himself has referred to internal irrationalities within Guangdong's agricultural and manufacturing sectors, as well as to the lagging performance of the tertiary sector. By 2010, the ratio of value-output of primary to secondary to tertiary sectors is planned to change from 26:40:34 (1990) to 5:31:64 (*TKP*, 22 February 1994).
43. The benefits of rapid provincial growth have accrued disproportionately to the three SEZs and the Pearl River Delta region.
44. This point was developed by Simon Kuznets in his assessment of Taiwan's modern economic transformation. See his "Economic growth and structural change" in W. Galenson (ed.), *Economic Development and Structural Change in Taiwan: The Postwar Experience of the Republic of China*, Ithaca: Cornell University Press, 1979.

Chapter 5 The US Connection of Hong Kong in China's "One Country, Two Economies" System

1. The Chinese acronym *sanlai yibu* refers literally to the "three (*san*) comings (*lai*)" (or supplies from outside), plus "one (*yi*) compensation (*yibu*)"; see notes to Table 2.5 (in Chapter 2) for details of definition. Hereafter we will use the term "outward processing" and *sanlai yibu* interchangeably depending on whether it is looked at from the mainland Chinese or Hong Kong perspective. In short, in outward processing, all or part of the raw materials or semi-manufactures are exported from or through Hong Kong to China for processing/reprocessing with a contractual arrangement for subsequent re-importation of the processed goods into Hong Kong. Export proper is common to the world's export trade, but *sanlai yibu* is particular to the China-Hong Kong common production region.
2. USIS—Hong Kong, *Economic Backgrounder* (11 April 1994), p. 2. This appears to be a grossly inaccurate generalization. Apart perhaps from the *sanlai yibu* type of exports, in the early 1980s, regular Chinese exports are normally priced with gross output value rather than value-added. And from 1985, *sanlai yibu* exports have been assumed into official Chinese customs statistics at full value, instead of just the "processing" fee (*gongjiao fei*).
3. Since *sanlai yibu* involves essentially small-scale, labour-intensive manufacturing activities and their outputs are virtually all destined for export, the phenomenon stands in sharp contrast to investments by multinational corporations (MNCs) in third countries that are primarily for import substitution and deal with large-scale, capital-intensive technology. Another difference is that, where possible, MNCs normally make use of locally available materials rather than semi-manufactured products brought in from home countries, and where their outputs are destined for third countries, they are often exported directly from the countries in which funds were invested rather than being shipped back to home countries for re-export, as is the case with *sanlai yibu* within the Hong Kong-Guangdong context.

4. Hong Kong generally accounted for 50–70% of China's realized foreign direct investment (FDI) intake since 1984; see Y. Y. Kueh, "Foreign investment and economic change in China", *The China Quarterly* (*CQ*), No. 131 (September 1992), p. 674. The latest available figure for 1995 is given as 61% by a senior Chinese official from the Ministry of Foreign Trade and Economic Cooperation (see *TKP*, May 1995). For Guangdong Province alone, Hong Kong's FDI share ranges generally from 70–90%; see Y. Y. Kueh and Robert Ash, "The fifth dragon: Economic development", in Brian Hook (ed.), *Guangdong: China's Promised Land*, Hong Kong: Oxford University Press, 1996 (reprinted as Chapter 3 in this volume).
5. A good example is curtain supplies in Hong Kong. In the past, tens of thousands of small curtain shops normally did their own cutting and sewing at the back of the shops. But these days, the processing is all done on specifications across the border in Shenzhen by regular weekly or daily consignments on behalf of Hong Kong clients, rather than overseas customers.
6. The Hong Kong Census and Statistics Department only began to compile statistics on domestic exports and re-exports to China for outward processing purposes in the third quarter of 1988, and the statistics on imports from China related to outward processing in the first quarter of 1989.
7. Y. P. Ho and Y. Y. Kueh, "Whither Hong Kong in an open-door, reforming Chinese Economy", *The Pacific Review*, Vol. 6, No. 4 (December 1993), p. 340 for 1980, 1985, 1990, and same sources as given therein for 1993 (the article is reprinted as Chapter 4 in this volume).
8. *Ibid.*, p. 341, the spectacular increase in 1985 to 43% of China's share in Hong Kong's total re-exports was probably caused by two factors. The first is the so-called Hainan "car scandal" when the island's government made use of its special privileges in foreign trade autonomy to import, "illicitly" through Hong Kong, a large consignment of Japanese cars (with foreign currencies obtained from the black market in exchange for a special renminbi development grant from the central government) for resale in the inland market for profiteering. The second factor is that the central government had to spend a large amount of its precious foreign exchange reserves (totalling some US$2 million) to import relatively luxurious commodities in order to soak up excessive renminbi supply which was brought about in late 1984 as a result of misconceived wage and banking policies. A large proportion of the imports were probably hastily channelled through Hong Kong as an efficient trade mediator. See Y. Y. Kueh, "Economic reforms in China: Approach, vision, and constraints", in Dieter Cassel (ed.), *Wirtschaftssysteme im Umbruch: Sowjetunion, China und industrialisierte Marktwirtschaften zwischen internationalen Anpassungszwang und nationalen Reformbedarf*, Munich: Franz Vahlen Press, 1990.
9. See Table 5.1 (panel C) and Y. P. Ho and Y. Y. Kueh, "Wither Hong Kong in an open-door, reforming Chinese economy", p. 342.
10. See Yun-wing Sung, "Foreign trade and investment", *China Review*, Hong Kong: The Chinese University Press, 1991, pp. 15.1–21.

11. See *TKP*, 5 April 1995. However, the implied national total of US$18.2 billion (= US$15.1 billion/0.83) for *sanlai yibu* exports in 1994 is substantially lower than the Hong Kong dollar equivalent of US$46 billion (= HK$355 billion) given by the Hong Kong Government Census and Statistics Department (HKGCSD), as cited in Table 4.1, panel A, column (2). Comparable statistics for 1992 also reveal a similar discrepancy, with a HKGCSD survey showing that Guangdong Province alone accounted for 93% of total Chinese *sanlai yibu* exports to Hong Kong in 1992. It is difficult to reconcile the discrepancy. One possible explanation is that the HKGCSD figure (US$46 billion), which is 60% higher than the Chinese one (US$18.2 billion), may, FOB/CIF gap apart, represent exactly the margin earned by Hong Kong manufacturers. If correct, then the margin may indeed loom larger, to the extent that the Chinese figure refers to their *sanlai yibu* exports at large, including those exported directly from China. Another possible explanation for the discrepancy is that the lower Chinese figure represents some kind of estimate made by the Chinese authorities of their own share in total *sanlai yibu* exports, in a way perhaps similar to the attempt to be made in the following section of this chapter. We are unable to determine for sure how the Chinese figure is calculated.
12. A fraction of *sanlai yibu* exports by Hong Kong- and Taiwan-based investors in provinces other than Guangdong is directly exported to the United States; see Q. Luo and C. Howe, "Direct investment and economic integration in the Asia Pacific: The case of Taiwanese investment in Xiamen", *CQ*, No. 137 (December 1993), p. 746. However, detailed statistics are not available. We therefore will only estimate the re-export margin earned by Hong Kong.
13. If capital is borrowed, we estimate the capital cost in terms of interest repayment plus the costs of maintaining and replacing buildings, machinery and fixtures.
14. The average profit margin for the five surveyed companies is 10% (see the Appendix to this chapter), which is lower than that (15%) estimated by HKTDC in 1991, indicating that profit could have fallen in recent years. We attribute the 10% profit margin to the Hong Kong share to make it a total of 71.5% as a basis for apportioning the total *sanlai yibu* exports to the total China versus Hong Kong shares (for explanation, see the Appendix to this chapter). Note, however, that the validity of our surveyed results may be weakened by the small sample size used and by the limited range of company types chosen, which could, collectively, give rise to the limiting nature of our estimates. Nevertheless, pending a more comprehensive and rigorous survey, we propose to estimate the OP-related export margin earned by Hong Kong for both the direct and indirect export enterprises using the preliminary survey results.
15. In the case of US exports to China, we do not net out the re-export margin for two main reasons. Firstly, little production in the United States has an outward processing origin. Secondly, the redistribution margin earned by Hong Kong in the case of US indirect exports to China via Hong Kong has been netted out since US FOB prices were used in compiling the US statistics.

16. Nicholas R. Lardy, *Re-defining US-China Economic Relations*, Analysis Monograph Series, No. 5, Seattle, Washington: National Bureau of Asian and Soviet Research, June 1993.
17. Joseph C. H. Chai, "US-China trade conflict and its implication for Australia's agricultural trade", in Y. Y. Kueh (ed.), *The Political Economy of Sino-American Relations—A Greater China Perspective*, Hong Kong: Hong Kong University Press, 1997, pp. 223–42.
18. *Financial Times* (London), 22 May 1993 (Interview with Y.Y. Kueh); see also Robert Ash and Y. Y. Kueh, "Economic integration with greater China: Trade and investment flows between China, Hong Kong and Taiwan", *CQ*, No. 136 (December 1993), p. 727 (the article is reprinted as Chapter 2 in this volume).
19. Note that in our estimates, we have also ignored the parallel curtailment in the Chinese share of OP-type exports through Hong Kong, and the possible impact of a Chinese retaliation on US re-exports via Hong Kong to China.
20. For an excellent, full-scale study of industrial changes in Hong Kong, see Y. P. Ho, *Trade, Industrial Restructuring and Development in Hong Kong*, London/Honolulu: Macmillan Press/University of Hawaii Press, 1992.

Chapter 6 Hong Kong Weathering the Asian Financial Storm

1. See appendix to this chapter for a chronological illustration of the development of the Asian financial crisis, as it bears on Hong Kong.
2. Following relocation of tens of thousands of manufacturing plants from Hong Kong to the Chinese hinterland, starting especially from the mid-1980s, Hong Kong's gross domestic product had continued to grow at the rate of 5–6% per year through the advent of the Asian crisis. Domestic labour supply could increase, however, by only around 1% per year during the same period. These occurred, most remarkably, against the background of a declining workforce in the manufacturing sector from some 930,000 in 1986 to not more than 250,000 by 1997, as a result of the accelerated exodus of Hong Kong manufacturers. By 1998, the manufacturing sector's contribution to GDP had fallen to a mere 8% from 29.6% in 1985 and 24.9% in 1991, while the share of the services sector meanwhile rapidly expanded to over 90% from 69.7% and 74.8%, respectively. The entire Hong Kong economy has, therefore, been radically transformed into a Manhattan-type services industry. This is, by any historical measure, a massive and radical transformation.
3. In the first of its annual reports on Hong Kong released in January 1999, the European Commission also found "basic rights, freedoms and autonomy have been broadly upheld" (*SCMP*, 10 January 1999).
4. For a detailed analysis of the relative contributions of Hong Kong to China's total foreign exchange earnings and the role the SAR plays in the broader context of facilitating China's trade with the United States and the outside world in general, see Y. Y. Kueh and Thomas Voon, "The role of Hong Kong in Sino-American economic relations", in Y. Y. Kueh (ed.), *The Political Economy of*

Sino-American Relations: A Greater China Perspective, Hong Kong: Hong Kong University Press, 1997, especially pp. 61–83 (the article is reprinted as Chapter 5 in this volume).

5. See attached chronology for this and subsequent reassurances given by Chinese leaders that China would uphold the value of the renminbi in support of the Hong Kong government's defence of the US dollar peg.
6. For an excellent full-fledged study of the Currency Board as it is adopted in Hong Kong, see Y. C. Jao, "The working of the Currency Board: The experience of Hong Kong 1935–1997", *Pacific Economic Review*, No. 3 (October 1998), especially pp. 224–39.
7. This and the following one or two paragraphs, as well as Figure 6.1, derive from *HSEM*, September/October 1998, p. 3.
8. In a recent personal communication (March 1999), a major Hong Kong investor was resolute that he would only invest more in the mainland, if the renminbi were to depreciate in the present context.
9. For a detailed study in this respect, see Y. Y. Kueh, "The Greater China growth triangle in the Asian financial crisis", in Shahid Jusuf, Simon Evenett, and Weiping Wu (eds.), *Facets of Globalization: International and Local Dimensions of Development*, Washington DC: The World Bank, 2001, pp. 57–77 (reprinted as Chapter 7 in this volume).
10. These are all official statistics released at the 9th National People's Congress held in early March 1999; see *TKP*, 7 and 12 March 1999.
11. The realized GDP growth rate for 1998 was confirmed, in March 1999, to be 7.8%.
12. The reasons for this are familiar: Chinese domestic prices are normally not comparable to the free market prices in Hong Kong or elsewhere in the world. A straightforward conversion from renminbi prices for the export goods concerned on the basis of the given exchange rate, may not therefore yield an export quotation that is comparable to those offered for similar products from other sources in the Hong Kong market. Moreover, the officially fixed exchange rates used for the conversion are normally not in accord with the purchasing power parity to complicate the matter. Hence, China, as well as all other former Soviet-type economies, being deprived of reliable scarcity price signals (due to distortions in official price setting) are said to have been "trading in the dark", by relying on the changing world market prices.
13. This point is also strongly shared by Jeffrey Sachs, the Harvard economist, at the Asian Investment Conference sponsored by Credit Suisse First Boston in Hong Kong (*SCMP*, 25 March 1999).
14. This is the familiar acronym for various incarnations of what is known as "international trust and investment corporation". The most well-known ones include CITIC (China International Trust and Investment Corporation), a national-level agency based in Beijing, and the notorious GITIC—a Guangdong provincial agency that collapsed in late 1998 prompting several major

banks in Hong Kong to provide, for the first time, under such circumstances, full debt provisions in the balance statements.

15. Personal communication from a major Taiwan investor in the food processing industry.
16. Readers interested in the process should consult the chronology given in the appendix.
17. See HKMA, *Strengthening of Currency Board Arrangements in Hong Kong*, http://www.info.gov.hklhkmalnew/press/others/980905e.htm (September 1998) for details, and *HSEM* (October 1998) for a brief interpretative study.
18. Hong Kong Government Financial Secretary, *The 1999/2000 Budget*, 3 March 1999.

Chapter 7 The Greater China Growth Triangle in the Asian Financial Crisis

1. Viewed this way, FDI flowing from Hong Kong (and Taiwan) into mainland China represents a complete migration of manufacturing plants.
2. Because the complete transfer of manufacturing operations from Hong Kong to mainland China is generally to take advantage of abundant cheap labour across the border, it is normally not associated with investment in new technology. That is not to say, however, that FDI's impact on Chinese economic growth is minimal. The fact is that, in addition to employment and income creation in China, the highly export-oriented FDI from Hong Kong and Taiwan also helps to ease China's foreign exchange constraints, enabling the country to import more advanced technology from the West, as embodied in new machines and equipment, for accelerating industrial modernization. Note that more than 40% of China's total exports for 1997 were exports from various types of foreign-invested enterprises (*ZGTJNJ 1999*, pp. 592–3).
3. These used to be the single most important source of China's foreign exchange earnings in the past, accounting for one-quarter to one-third of the country's total. From the Hong Kong perspective, the imports were inputs needed for its own export manufacturing. With the relocation of Hong Kong factories to the hinterland, however, Chinese exports previously retained in Hong Kong for local consumption have now become China's liability in exchange for its claims on part of Hong Kong's foreign earnings in the form of what is commonly referred to by the Chinese as *gongjiaofei* (processing fees). For an elaboration and interpretation of this changing regional context of specialization within Greater China; see Kueh and Voon, "The role of Hong Kong in Sino-American economic relations", in Y. Y. Kueh (ed.), *The Political Economy of Sino-American Relations: A Greater China Perspective*. Hong Kong, China: Hong Kong University Press, 1997, pp. 61–3 (reprinted as Chapter 5 in this volume).
4. See Y. C. Jao, "Hong Kong as a financial center for Greater China", in Joseph C. H. Chai, Y. Y. Kueh, and Clement Tisdell, (eds.), *China and the Asia Pacific Economy*, New York: Nova Science Publishers, 1997, for an excellent discussion of the various aspects of Hong Kong as an international financial centre.

5. According to the head of the Industry Bureau in Taipei, the large-scale transfer of sunset industries to mainland China has more than anything else accounted for the rapid increase of heavy industry's share in total manufacturing output in recent years from 47% in 1986 to 56% in 1991; see Charles H. C. Kao, Joseph S. Lee, and Chu-Chia Steve Lin, *Taiwan tupuo: liangan jingmao zhuizhong* (An Empirical Study of Taiwanese Investment in Mainland China; hereafter, *Taiwan Tupuo*), Taipei: Taipei Commonwealth Publishing Company Ltd., 1992, pp. 90–1.
6. HKTDC, *Topical Paper: Economic Relations between Hong Kong and the Chinese Mainland,* 1998; and *Market Profile: Chinese Mainland,* 1998.
7. HKTDC, *Hong Kong Economy Profile, 1998.*
8. See Table 5.1. Nonetheless, the decline has proved to be short-lived. Latest official statistics show that for the first three quarters of 2000, FDI approval already amounted to US$378.58 million, a hefty increase of 27.86% over the comparable 1998 period. Actual FDI intake did decline by 8.7% in the same period in 2000, due to the reduction in 1999 of FDI approval (*TKP*, 15 October 2000), but given the remarkable rebound just cited, it is almost certain that 2001 will see a strong recovery of actual FDI intake in China.
9. FDI in infrastructure (and in services) is still quite limited in China. For example, FDI pledged in electric power plant and gas and water supply declined from US$5.2 billion in 1996 to US$3.7 billion in 1997, while FDI approved for the combined category of transportation, storage, and postal and telecommunications services increased from US$1.2 billion in 1996 to only US$2.6 billion in 1997. Taken together, FDI in infrastructure and services amounted to only 12% of total FDI approval in 1997, compared with 53% for manufacturing (*ZGTJNJ 1998,* p. 645). Similarly, while an increased number of foreign firms have been able to gain a foothold in China's wholesale and retail trade and catering services in recent years (e.g., McDonalds, KFC, and notably the well-known garment brand, Goldlion, from Hong Kong), foreign capital registered by the end of 1997 for this sector was no more than 4% of the total, compared with 58% for manufacturing (*ibid.*, p. 643).
10. As a rough estimate, the export markup rate is simply taken as the percentage difference between the value of columns (9) and (7) in Table 7.2. To the extent that part of the imports of outward processing goods from China may be retained in Hong Kong for local consumption, the estimated markup rate is clearly biased on the low side.
11. See Kueh and Voon, "The role of Hong Kong in Sino-American economic relations", p. 66.
12. Y. Y. Kueh, "Foreign investment and economic change in China", *The China Quarterly* (*CQ*), No. 131 (September 1992), pp. 637–90.
13. UNCTAD—*WIR 1998,* p. 203.
14. Y. Y. Kueh, "Financial restructuring for economic recovery in China and Hong Kong", paper presented at the international symposium, Financial Restructuring

and Economic Perspective in East Asia, sponsored jointly by The United Nations University Institute of Advanced Studies and Asian Development Bank Institute, Tokyo, 12 May 1999 (published by UNUIAS, 2000, and reprinted as Chapter 8 in this volume).

15. Y. Y. Kueh, "Weathering the Asian financial storm in Hong Kong", in James C. Hsiung (ed.), *Hong Kong the Super Paradox: Life After Return to China*, New York: St. Martin's Press, 2000, pp. 235–64 (reprinted as Chapter 6 in this volume).
16. For the first eight months of 1998, China's trade surplus and net FDI inflows amounted to US$58.7 billion, but total foreign exchange reserves increased by only US$1.2 billion (*TKP*, 28 November 1998). The leakage is attributed to defaults in bank clearing of foreign exchange earnings, illicit remittances overseas by way of fake import documentation, and other illegal practices.
17. *JJXXXB*, 1 May 1998.
18. Beijing University, Macroeconomic Group of China Economic Research Center, "Monetary policy or fiscal policy?" in *Jingji Yanjiu,* No. 10 (October 1998), pp. 11–9.
19. Since 1995, the US-based Heritage Foundation and the *Wall Street Journal* have compiled the Index of Economic Freedom for comparing more than 160 economies. Hong Kong was rated first for the first five consecutive years.
20. See HKMA, *Strengthening of Currency Board Arrangements in Hong Kong*. Hong Kong, China, 1998 (available on http://www.info.gov.hk/hkma/new/press/others/980905e.htm) for details; and *HSEM*, September/October 1998 for an interpretative study.
21. Yi-Chi Chen, "Country report on Taiwan", in Kar-Yiu Wong, (ed.), *The Asian Crisis: What Has Happened and Why.* Seattle, Washington: University of Washington, 1998, p. 5.
22. George Soros, *The Crisis of Global Capitalism: Open Society Endangered,* New York: Perseus Book, 1998.
23. Hong Kong Government Financial Secretary, *The 1999–2000 Budget,* p. 3.
24. This was also later confirmed by the financial secretary when he explained that "our exports to the United States and Europe grew, but this growth was unable to compensate for the marked shrinkage in our exports to East Asia. The growing volume of mainland products being shipped out directly from mainland ports instead of through Hong Kong also trimmed our export performance", *ibid*.
25. This view is strongly shared by Harvard economist Jeffrey Sachs. For a rigorous analysis of his views of the nature of contagion in the East Asian crisis, see Steven Radelet and Jeffrey Sachs, *The Onset of the East Asian Financial Crisis*, unpublished manuscript, as cited in Sweta C. Saxena, "Country report on Indonesia", in Kar-yiu Wong, *The Asian Crisis: What Has Happened and Why.*
26. Y. Y. Kueh, "Growth imperatives, economic recentralization, and China's 0pen-door Policy", *Australian Journal of Chinese Affairs* (renamed *The China*

Journal in 1995), No. 24 (July 1990), pp. 93–119; and Y. Y. Kueh, "China and the prospects for economic integration within APEC", in Chai, Kueh, and Tisdell, (eds.), *China and the Asia Pacific Economy,* pp. 29–47 (the latter article is reprinted as Chapter 10 in this volume).

27. A high-powered Commission on Innovation and Technology was established under the chief executive's office in late 1997. Headed by the prominent Chinese-American scholar Tien Chang-Lin, former president of the University of California at Berkeley, the commission's objective is to draw up a blueprint for long-term technological development in Hong Kong. A special mandate is to explore feasible ways to capitalize on the mainland's expertise in high technology and basic research for commercial applications and international marketing.

Chapter 8 Financial Restructuring for Economic Recovery in China and the Hong Kong SAR

1. The "complete migration" as referred to also raises the question as to whether investment made by Hong Kong manufacturers in mainland China should be regarded as FDI in the usual sense, quite apart from the implications of political reunification of Hong Kong with China in 1997.
2. As a matter of fact, a renminbi devaluation would appear only to help reduce Hong Kong manufacturers' investment costs in the mainland. Neither does there seem to be a reason to suggest that the non-devaluation, or rather, the de facto appreciation of the Chinese renminbi relative to the devalued Southeast Asian currencies, would fundamentally break the established "flying geese pattern" of regional industrial specialization at the expense of the labour-intensive Hong Kong/China joint venture exports from the mainland. This is of course not to say that Chinese exports to third-country markets are absolutely unaffected by the currency devaluations in Southeast Asia, bearing in mind that Chinese exports to the US overlap to a certain extent with those from Southeast Asia (by around 15% as estimated by Dai Xianglong, Governor of the People's Bank of China; or by between 20% and 30% according to the estimates of the director of the Institute of Finance and Trade in the Chinese Academy of Social Science). For an elaboration of the possible implications of a devaluation or non-devaluation of the renminbi and the Hong Kong dollar for both Hong Kong and China in the broader context of the economic synergy between the Chinese duo as illustrated above, see Chapters 6 and 7.
3. These are all year-end 1997 figures. Note that the SAR's foreign reserves stood by only 33% behind that of mainland China; and surprisingly, dollar by dollar (i.e., without adjusting for the purchasing power parities between the Hong Kong dollar and the renminbi), its GDP and total budget expenditure were, also in 1997, already separately equal to a most impressive 20% of mainland China's (cf. Chapter 7). This underscores the economic significance of Hong Kong to the mainland as a source of FDI intake and exports.

4. These measures are all given in the government's "five-point" and "seven-point" policy packages for rescuing the economy, released respectively on 29 May and 22 June 1998. Especially noteworthy is the ambitious housing strategy of building 85,000 units per year to mitigate the enormous housing pressures and increase home ownership to 70% in Hong Kong. The plan was initially given in the policy address by the chief executive of the HKSAR government in October 1997. It is seen by a Hong Kong-based academic as having essentially contributed to the drastic downturn of the property market, quite independent of the impact of the Asian crisis; see Lok-Sang Ho, "Hong Kong in the midst of a currency crisis", in James C. Hsiung (ed.), *Hong Kong the Super Paradox: Life After Return to China*, New York: St. Martin Press, 1999.
5. Cf. Edward K. Y. Chen and Raymond Ng, "Regaining international competitiveness: Hong Kong after the Asian financial crisis", paper presented at the AT10 Researchers' Meeting on Restoring East Asia Dynamism, The Tokyo Club Foundation on Global Studies, Nomura Research Institute, Tokyo, 28–29 January 1999.
6. See HKMA, *Strengthening of Currency Board Arrangements in Hong Kong*, September 1998.
7. This is part of a spectacular region-wide rally which lifted both the Bangkok SET and the Jakarta Composite Index to a thirteen-month high, and both the Singapore Straits Times Index and Manila Composite Index to a twenty-month high; see *SCMP*, 5 May 1999.
8. Interview on local TV, 4 May 1999.
9. According to the World Bank, by 1995 FDI inflows accounted for 25% of domestic investment, 13% of industrial output, 11% of tax revenues, 31% of total exports, and 16 million jobs. The export share was increased to nearly 50% in 1998. Since FDI from Hong Kong contributed around 50% of China's total FDI intake in 1998, or two-third of total cumulative FDI stock since 1979, the SAR's share in domestic capital formation may be roughly estimated to be 12.5% in 1998 and much more for the 1979–98 average. Exports by foreign-funded enterprises are of course almost all dominated by Hong Kong (and Taiwan) investors, and they all represent labour-intensive manufacturing. See World Bank, *China 2020: Integration with the Global Economy*, Washington, DC, 1997, p. 21 for details.
10. The author was told by a former Japanese consul general based in Hong Kong in 1995 that over half of Hong Kong's FDI in China was so financed.
11. This view was strongly promulgated by the Harvard economist, Jeffrey Sachs, in a public lecture entitled "The East Asian financial crisis: The way forward", delivered on 10 November 1998 immediately following the conferment of a Ph.D. degree honoris causa by Lingnan University, in Hong Kong.
12. According to a State Council analyst, the effect of a 1% increase in rebate of the VAT (set at 17%) is comparable to a 1% reduction in the export costs for general merchandise (*TKP*, 24 June 1998).

13. See *JJXXXB*, 1 May 1998. Another similar estimate puts the contribution of net exports at an average of 25% between 1994 and 1997 (*TKP*, 27 August 1998).
14. Beijing University, Macroeconomic Group of China Economic Research Centre, CERC "Monetary policy or fiscal policy?" in *Jingji Yanjiu* (*Monthly*), No. 10 (October 1998), pp. 11–9.
15. The "write-off" funds are generally tied in with enterprise restructuring, in the form of a merger of two or more state-owned firms. The allocation began in 1996 with RMB20 billion. It was increased to RMB30 billion in 1997, and RMB40 billion in 1998, with further increases to follow in 1999 and 2000; see Nicholas R. Lardy, *China's Unfinished Economic Revolution*, Washington, D.C.: Brookings Institution Press, 1998, p. 207.
16. Zhao Haoshen, "China's policy towards the Asian financial crisis" (interview with Dai Xianglong, Governor of the People's Bank of China), in *TKP*, 4 November 1998, p. 8.
17. See Fang Hangting, "Storm in the Chinese reforms of the financial system", in *TKP*, 21 March 1999, p. c7; note that the figure is even larger than China's total exports of US$183.76 billion in 1998. The disasters have presumably been brought about by massive losses from property and stock markets speculation in Hong Kong and elsewhere amidst the Asian crisis.
18. See Lardy, *China's Unfinished Economic Revolution*, p. 203.
19. See Fang, "Storm in the Chinese reforms of the financial system".
20. For an interesting discussion on this point, see Lardy, *China's Unfinished Economic Revolution*, pp. 161–5.
21. The "J-curve" suggests that at the initial stage of a currency devaluation, exports of the country concerned lag behind increases in imports, but the simulative effect of the devaluation will, after a certain time lag, help to accelerate the increases in exports. This is also revealed by the recent experience of most Southeast Asian countries in conjunction with the Asian financial crisis; see Peng Weihong, "The J-curve in the Asian currency devaluations amidst the financial crisis", *in TKP*, 29 March 1999, for a more detailed discussion.
22. Year-on-year, Chinese exports for the period January to May 1999 recorded a negative growth of 5.3%. Following consecutive monthly decline for the first four months, total exports for May 1999 reversed to a positive gain of 4.2%; but it is not at all certain whether the reversal will be sustainable (*TKP*, 15 June 1999).
23. Professor Lawrence Klein made the points in response to queries I raised during the discussion session at the international forum sponsored by United Nations University Institute of Advanced Studies (UNUIIAS), in collaboration with the Asian Development Bank Institute, and held in Tokyo, 12 May 1999 (the forum gave rise to the volume *Financial Restructuring and Economic Perspectives in East Asia* edited by Fu-chen Lo and T. Palanival and published by UNUIAS in 2000, which includes the present chapter). Shortly after the Tokyo forum, Professor Liu Wei, vice president of the School of Economic

Management at Beijing University, told me at a seminar in Hong Kong that according to a similar Chinese estimate made by the State Statistical Bureau, the total export losses incurred with ASEAN countries in the wake of the 1994 RMB devaluation should amount to only 7%, compared with the 20% estimate made by Professor Klein.

24. See USTRO, *Market Access Commitments of the Government of China on Goods, Services and Agriculture*, Washington DC, 8 April 1999, pp. 11–2.

Chapter 9 The "China Factor" vs. the "US Dollar Peg" in the Success Story of Hong Kong

1. The move was preceded by the establishment in 1979/1980 of the four Special Economic Zones (SEZs) in Guangdong and Fujian provinces. However, while SEZs were little different from the small export processing zones established in many other countries, the April 1984 opening of fourteen major coastal cities represented the most significant initial step in the opening of the entire country for foreign investment and trade. It was followed, only four years later in early 1988, by the even more spectacular opening of eleven coastal provinces, comprising a total of 288 "opened" municipalities and counties (*xian*); and subsequently by the even more strategic decision, made by Deng Xiaoping himself after his celebrated "South China tour" in early 1992, to open up China further not only in geographic terms but institutionally as well. For a detailed study of this opening process, see Y. Y. Kueh, "Foreign investment and economic change in China", in *The China Quarterly* (*CQ*), No. 131 (September 1992), pp. 637–90.
2. On 23 and 24 September 1983, the value of the Hong Kong dollar plummeted by some 15% to as low as HK$9.5 per US dollar amidst massive selling. It had been around HK$5.6 to the US dollar.
3. "Cash arbitrage" occurs when a financial institution takes advantage of the widening differential between the free market exchange rate and the official parity. For example, when the market rate against the US dollar is under devaluation pressure, commercial banks will obtain US dollars from the Hong Kong Monetary Authority (through the note-issuing banks) and sell them on the foreign exchange market. This process will continue until the differential narrows to cover the cost of arbitrage only. It helps to contain the market exchange rate within a narrow range around the linked level. "Interest rate arbitrage" takes place when interest rate differentials cause capital to move to a country where there is a higher interest rate. If Hong Kong dollars come under devaluation pressure caused, for example, by capital outflows or a current account deficit, the interbank market strains and interest rates rise relative to the US dollar interest rate. This will in turn attract capital inflows, and offset the initial devaluation pressure.
4. A decree made by the Hong Kong Monetary Authority specified that all mortgage loans were to be capped at 70% of the assessed value of the property.

Other measures adopted by the government to cool down the market included increasing the supply of land and housing, tightening the control over the resale of uncompleted flats, and prohibiting the resale of uncompleted flats before assignment.

5. See Y. Y. Kueh and Robert Ash, "The fifth dragon: Economic development", in Brian Hook (ed.), *Guangdong: China's Promised Land*, Hong Kong: Oxford University Press, 1996, pp. 149–92 (reprinted as Chapter 4 in this volume).
6. This figure was frequently quoted in the Hong Kong press. By 1995, total employment by foreign-invested enterprises (FIEs) in China was reported by the World Bank to be around 16 million; see World Bank, *China 2020: Integration with the World Economy* (Washington DC, 1997), p. 21. As Hong Kong investors account for about two-thirds of the cumulative FDI stock in China, and the overwhelming proportion (roughly 80%) of this is based in Guangdong (see Kueh and Ash, "The fifth dragon", p. 178), the figure of five million seems actually to have grossly understated the SAR's contribution to employment in the province. Moreover, most FIEs of Hong Kong origin are generally more labour-intensive than those from elsewhere.
7. HKSGCSD—*HKADS, 1987* and *1999*.
8. See Hiroyuki Imai, "Structural transformation and economic growth in Hong Kong: another look at Young's Hong Kong thesis", *Journal of Comparative Economics*, Vol. 29, No. 2 (June 2001), pp. 366–82, for the figures and for a discussion of the productivity implications arising from the structural changes in Hong Kong since the early 1980s.
9. HKGCSD—*HKADS, 1985*; and —*HKMDS*, March 2000.
10. A first attempt in this direction was made in Y. Y. Kueh and Thomas J. Voon, "The role of Hong Kong in Sino-American economic relations", in Y. Y. Kueh (ed.), *The Political Economy of Sino-American Relations: A Greater China Perspective*, Hong Kong: University of Hong Kong Press, 1997, pp. 61–92 (reprinted as Chapter 5 in this volume). Based on a small sample of joint ventures in Guangdong Province, the export share between the Hong Kong and Chinese partners was estimated to be 71.8% to 27.2% relative to their input contributions (comprising capital, rent, labour, raw materials, fuel charges and distribution costs); pp. 82 and 91. For an update, see Thomas Voon and Y. Y. Kueh, "Country of origin, China's value-added exports and Sino-US trade balance reconciliation", *Journal of World Trade* (Geneva), Vol. 34, No. 5 (October 2000), pp. 123–36.
11. The major branches included in the OP import and export statistics are: textile material, yarn, fabrics and articles other than textile garments; articles of apparel and clothing accessories (textile garments); plastics and articles; machinery and mechanical appliances; electrical equipment; sound recorders and reproducers, television image; clocks and watches; toys, games and sports requisites, and parts and accessories; base metals and metal products; and other (excluding commodities and transactions not classified according to kind).

Taken together, the processing margin as defined falls within the range of 50–60% in recent years. The OP re-export margin ranges in turn between 18% and 24%. If anything, these figures probably all underestimate the true margin of value added. For a discussion on this point, see Y. Y. Kueh, "The Greater China growth triangle in the Asian financial crisis", in Shahid Jusuf, Simon Evenett and Weiping Wu (eds.), *Facets of Globalization: International and Local Dimensions of Development*, Washington DC: The World Bank, 2001, pp. 57–77 (reprinted as Chapter 7 in this volume).

12. If anything, the estimated expansion in export capacity should err on the low side, simply because due to physical constraints in Hong Kong (land scarcity, in particular), domestic exports should not be able to grow as fast as the trend line in Figure 9.4 projects.
13. For a more detailed study, see Y. Y. Kueh, "Weathering the Asian financial storm in Hong Kong", in James C. Hsiung (ed.), *Hong Kong the Super Paradox: Life After Return to China*, New York: St. Martin Press, 2000, pp. 235–64 (reprinted as Chapter 6 in this volume).
14. By year-end 1997, the reserves stood at US$92.8 billion, equal to two-thirds of China's US$139.9 billion and 40% of Japan's US$220.8 billion. Note that until then, Hong Kong had neither a budget deficit nor any significant amount of external debt.
15. The case of Taiwan may not be exactly comparable. The island lags far behind Hong Kong in financial liberalization, although it is not as restrictive as the Chinese mainland in terms of capital account control. This made it less vulnerable to speculative currency attacks by international hedge funds. Nevertheless, after an abortive defence in late 1997, the NT dollar was floated and eventually settled at NT$34.5 to the US dollar in January 1988, down by only 19%, compared with the precipitous fall of the Thai baht by 55%, the Indonesian rupiah by 70%, the Malaysian ringgit by 42% and the South Korean won by 50%. For elaboration on this point, see Kueh, "The Greater China growth triangle". In the more comparable case of Singapore which has a currency board system similar to that in Hong Kong, the Singapore dollar was devalued by only around 17% at the peak of the speculative assaults in January 1998.
16. See Y. Y. Kueh, "Financial restructuring for economic recovery in China and Hong Kong", in Fu-chen Lo and T. Palanivel (eds.), *Financial Restructuring and Economic Perspective in East Asia*, Tokyo: United Nations University Institute of Advanced Studies, 2000, pp. 127–44 (reprinted as Chapter 8 in this volume).
17. As Joseph Yam, the chief executive of the Hong Kong Monetary Authority put it at a meeting of the Manila Framework Group of APEC held in Hong Kong on 20 March 2000, in the wake of a "renewed flood of capital into Asia's economies there was a danger the pain of the crisis that began in mid-1997 had been forgotten". According to Yam, net private capital flow into Asia's

emerging markets increased nearly six-fold from 1998 to US$39 billion in 1999, and the inflow was forecast to increase by more than 50% to US$59 billion in 2000. He called for "more progress to be made in coping with the potentially destabilizing impact on markets of what were formerly known as hedge funds"; see *SCMP* (Business Post Section), 21 March 2000, p. 1.

18. See Chi-hung Kwan, "Sayonaro dollar peg: Asia in search of a new exchange rate regime", Nomura Research Institute, Tokyo, December 1999 (mimeo).
19. The reduced FDI flow to China was partly a matter of increased removal by Hong Kong investors, and Taiwanese as well, of their registered company sites to the British Virgin Islands in the Caribbean Sea and Samoa in the remote South Pacific. The "re-registering" accelerated in the wake of Hong Kong's reversion to Chinese sovereignty in 1997. For more details see Kueh, "The Greater China growth triangle in the Asian financial crisis".
20. This is not unrelated to the peculiar circumstances prevalent in China since 1996 of declining interest rates, negative deflation, and inadequate consumption and investment expenditure. Note especially that the Chinese government already had to resort to prime-jumping deficit spending to prop up aggregate demand before the impact of the Asian financial crisis (by way of reduced export demand) was felt. See *ibid.*
21. See *TKP*, 24 June 1998. The estimate refers primarily to general merchandise trade.
22. See The Financial Secretary of Hong Kong Government, *The 1999–2000 Budget*, 3 March 1999, p. 3.
23. This is a very general statement. In fact, the two categories of exports involve different product ranges, different market destinations and different end-users.
24. These figures cover only the first ten months of 1998 (see *TKP*, 6 December 1998). The 47% share includes, of course, exports to Hong Kong as well. The same source also quotes the president of the Hong Kong Exporters Association as saying that at least for Hong Kong toys manufacturers based in the mainland who export directly through the Chinese ports (rather than Hong Kong), total exports for the first three quarters of 1998 recorded a 6% growth. Direct export to a third country implies less employment and income generation in Hong Kong, though the losses may nevertheless also be compensated for by increased factor income through profit repatriation to Hong Kong.
25. The "flying geese model", as coined by the Japanese economist, Kaname Akamatsu in the 1930s, refers to the continuous process of transferring relatively developed and internationally competitive manufacturing industries from industrialized countries (such as Japan) to the newly industrializing economies (such as Hong Kong, Singapore, Taiwan and South Korea), which will in turn delegate theirs to the less developed countries (China, Indonesia, etc.), as each economic entity is attempting to scale the ladder of industrialization in an ascending order similar to the flying geese line-up. The process is largely driven by the attempt to improve competitive edge, and to offset currency appreciation, labour shortages and rising wage costs.

26. The single most important source of the remarkable decline in Hong Kong's exports in 1998 was when Japan, South Korea and Southeast Asian countries all saw their import capabilities seriously curtailed as a result of massive currency devaluations in 1997/1998. By contrast, Hong Kong's most significant export markets, the US and Western Europe, were only marginally affected, perhaps as a result of enhanced export competitiveness from the devalued Southeast Asian economies. For a more detailed study on this, see Kueh, "Weathering the Asian financial storm in Hong Kong".
27. Cf. Kueh and Voon, "The role of Hong Kong in Sino-American economic relations", p. 81.
28. See note 12 of Chapter 6 for a detailed explanation.
29. According to the World Bank, by 1995, FDI inflows accounted for 25% of domestic investment, 13% of industrial output, 11% of tax revenues, 31% of total exports and 16 million jobs (n. 6). The export share was increased to nearly 50% in 1998. Since FDI from Hong Kong contributed around 50% of China's total FDI intake in 1998, the SAR's share in domestic capital formation may be roughly estimated to be 12.5% in 1998. Exports by foreign-funded enterprises are of course almost all dominated by Hong Kong and Taiwanese investors, and they all represent labour-intensive manufacturing.
30. Personal communication from a major Taiwanese investor in the food processing industry on the mainland.
31. This was aired by Liberal Party Chairman and Legislator James Tien Pei-chun. He insisted that "the policy adopted in 1983 was the major obstacle to economic recovery" and said "the Hong Kong dollar would depreciate by no more than 20% if the peg was scrapped"; see *SCMP*, 5 September 2001.
32. See Joseph Yam, "Building stability in unstable times" (talk given at the Hong Kong Institute of Bankers), 24 October 2001 (http://www.info.gov.hk/hkma/eng/speeches/speechs/ josephl20011024e_index.htm). Defending the peg, Yam also argues that "Hong Kong's currency was delivering competitive gains, . . . [in that] the REER [real effective exchange rate] for the Hong Kong dollar has depreciated by around 13% since the crisis period in 1998, . . . while the Reers for Asian currencies have appreciated by various degrees" (*ibid.*). This is of course a matter of judgment as to what extent the competitive gap between the currencies of Hong Kong and other Asian countries has narrowed, given that at the peak of the Asian crisis, most Southeast Asian currencies depreciated by 40–60%.

Chapter 10 China and the Prospects for Economic Integration within APEC

1. As reported in *ZGTJNJ 1995*, p. 21, China's GNP/GDP grew at an annual average rate of 9.8% and population 1.4% from 1980 to 1994.
2. The figure is obtained by applying the GDP growth rates of the province for 1992–1994 (*ZGTJNJ 1995*, p. 33) to the estimated 1992 GDP of US$2,806 as given in Y. Y. Kueh and Robert Ash, "The fifth dragon: Economic development",

in Brian Hook (ed.), *Guangdong: China's Promised Land*, Hong Kong: Oxford University Press, 1996, p. 151 (reprinted as Chapter 4 in this volume).
3. Cf. Kueh and Ash, "The fifth dragon: Economic development".
4. An alternative estimate was made by Nicholas Lardy, *Foreign Trade and Economic Reform in China, 1978–1990*, Cambridge: Cambridge University Press, 1992, pp. 150–5, for the trade ratio for 1988. Lardy made use of the comparative indices of growth of GNP and trade (in real terms) for 1978 to 1988 (which are made available in official sources), and related the growing discrepancy to two different Western PPP-based estimates of China's GNP for 1980, respectively by Herbert Block, and Robert Summers and Alan Heston. The first estimate gives a trade/GNP ratio of 5.8% (in 1978) and 9.4% by (1988), while the second generated corresponding figures of 2.1% (1978) and 3.4% (1988). Lardy regards the higher estimate as more acceptable. However, it seems quite curious, in our view, that China's trade ratio could already stand at as high as 5.4% in 1978, after decades of self-imposed trade autarky.
5. China and Indonesia re-established normal diplomatic relations in 1990 after a long break and the normalization was then expected to give a great boost to bilateral trade.
6. See Y. Y. Kueh and Thomas Voon, "The role of Hong Kong in Sino-American economic relations", in Y. Y. Kueh (ed.), *The Political Economy of Sino-American Relations: A Greater China Perspective*, Hong Kong: Hong Kong University Press, 1997 for more details in this respect (the article is reprinted as Chapter 5 in this volume).
7. As shown in Table 10.2, IMF statistics give a separate entry for Taiwan's trade with mainland China, as part of the catch-all category of "Asia not specified" in the original IMF compilation. It is not known, however, how the statistics are exactly obtained. Perhaps they are derived from the given statistics on Taiwan's trade with Hong Kong as shown in Figure 10.1. This would imply the possibility of double counting in Table 10.2. However, it seems nonetheless inappropriate to assume that IMF should engage in such double counting.
8. For a detailed study and interpretation of the significance of the role played by Hong Kong in Sino-American economic relations, see Kueh and Voon, "The role of Hong Kong in Sino-American economic relations". Consult also Y. P. Ho and Y. Y. Kueh, "Whither Hong Kong in an open-door, reforming Chinese economy", in *The Pacific Review*, Vol. 6, No. 4 (December 1993) for the increasing magnitude of Hong Kong's re-export business in general (the article is reprinted as Chapter 3 in this volume).
9. For a more comprehensive study of FDI in China and the importance of Hong Kong and Taiwan as FDI supplier in Guangdong Province and in China as a whole, see Y. Y. Kueh, "Foreign investment and economic change in China", in *The China Quarterly* (*CQ*), No. 131 (September 1992), pp. 637–90; and Kueh and Ash, "The fifth dragon: Economic development".

10. See Ash and Kueh, "Economic integration within Greater China: Trade and investment flows between Hong Kong, Mainland China and Taiwan", in *CQ*, No. 136 (December 1993) (reprinted as Chapter 2 in this volume); and especially K. C. Lei, "China-Taiwan trade and investment relations and their impact on Taiwan's income distribution", in Kueh, *The Political Economy of Sino-American Relations: A Greater China Perspective*, for a more systematic input-output analysis of the impact on the Taiwanese economy of increased FDI outflows to the Chinese mainland.
11. For an elaboration on this point, see Y. Y. Kueh "Growth imperatives, economic recentralization, and China's open-door policy", in *Australian Journal of Chinese Affairs* (renamed *China Journal*), No. 24 (July 1990), pp. 93–119.
12. See Kueh and Voon, "The role of Hong Kong in Sino-American economic relations" for details.
13. Thomas J. Voon and Xiangdong Wei, "Export competition among China and ASEAN in the US market: Application of market share model", in Joseph C. H. Chai, Y. Y. Kueh, and Clement Tisdell (eds.), *China and the Asia Pacific Economy*, pp. 198–206, gives a detailed analysis in this respect.
14. Elspeth Thomson, "Japanese FDI, exports and technology transfer to China", in Chai, Kueh and Tisdell, *China and the Asia Pacific Economy*, reveals that Japanese exports to China are barely related to their FDI in China.
15. For an illustration of the comparative tariff and non-tariff trade barriers existing among APEC countries, see the recent comprehensive survey made by Pacific Economic Cooperation Council (PECC), *Milestones in APEC Liberalization: A Map of Market Opening Measures by APEC Economies* (a report by PECC and APEC), Singapore, 1995.
16. Y. Y. Kueh, "Industrial Deregulation and Economic Consequences for China: A GATT Perspective", in Dieter Cassel and Carsten Hermann-Pillath (eds.), *The East, the West, and China's Growth: Challenge and Response*, Baden-Baden: Nomos Verlagsgesellschaft, 1995, pp. 309–34.

Chapter 11 China's New Industries and Regional Economic Realignment in the Asia Pacific

1. See Y. Y. Kueh, "Coping with globalization in China: Strategic implications of WTO accession", in *Journal of World Investment* (Geneva), Vol. 3, No. 1 (February 2002), pp. 37–63.
2. A reclassification of the enterprises seems to have taken place in 1998, with a great number of enterprises being excluded from the new definition for some reason. However, as the reclassification applies to both high-tech and non-high-tech enterprises, albeit perhaps somewhat differently, this should not affect our comparative analysis to any great extent.
3. Kueh, "Coping with globalization in China".
4. By 2002, every urban household in China had 1.26 coloured TV on average. In the rural areas, the rate was 60.45 per 100 households; see *CSYB 2003*, p. 342.

5. *CST* via www.xinhuanet.com, 26 November 2003. The sanction was formally endorsed by the US Department of Commerce on 14 May 2004; see *TKP*, 15 May 2004.
6. Alpha Research Co. Limited, *Thailand in Figures 2002/2003*, Bangkok, January 2003, p. 439.
7. Christopher Howe, Y. Y. Kueh and Robert Ash, *China's Economic Reform: A Study with Documents*, London and New York: RoutledgeCurzon Press, 2003, p. 152.
8. Mr Tree also informed the author that Bird (or *Bodao* in Chinese, which is tied up with Siemens of Germany and Seagam of France), TCL, and Amoi taken together, now account for about 50% of total sales of mobile phones in China. According to *Shanghai Daily*, 8–9, and 10 May 2004, Bird clamshell phones are well received in both Europe and the United States. The Ningbo-based Bird Mobile Communications Co. Ltd. has lately signed a cooperation agreement with AT&T, the largest telecom operator in the US. In 2004, Bird Mobile expects to export two million mobile phones, over four times more than the previous year, and most will be clamshell.
9. Huang Fanzhang. "The new era of Shenzhen: New opportunities, new positioning, and new development" in *TQJJ*, No. 180 (January 2004), p. 7.
10. This is a joint venture with the globally known Taiwan-based Worldwide Semiconductor Manufacturing Corporation (WSMC). SMIC, now the largest semiconductor manufacturer in China was floated in both the Hong Kong Stock Exchange and New York Stock Exchange in March 2004. It is billed as China's answer to Taiwan's WSMC and United Microelectronics Corporation.
11. The coverage of the two statistical series in Tables 11.9 and 11.10 differs to a certain extent. The two series are therefore not exactly comparable.
12. Jin Pei, *The International Competitiveness of the Chinese Industries: Theory, Methodology, and Empirical Research*, Beijing: Jingji Guanli Chubanshe, 1997, p. 147.
13. Y. Y. Kueh, "Sino-Japanese economic relations and the prospects of trade liberalization in East Asia", in Lim Hua-sing and Nyaw Mee-kau (eds.), *ASEAN and Japan in Economic Cooperation within the Chinese Economic Areas* (in Chinese), Singapore: World Scientific Publishing Co., December 2003, p. 522.
14. Huang Yonghe and Wu Songquan. "The automobile industry one year after China's accession to the WTO", in *CAIYB 2003*, p. 4.
15. Y. Y. Kueh, Joseph C. H. Chai, and Gang Fan. *Industrial Reform and Macroeconomic Instability in China*, Oxford: Oxford University (Clarendon) Press, 1999, pp. 270–3.
16. Huang and Wu, "The automobile industry one year after China's accession to the WTO", p. 2.
17. For an earlier estimation of the possible size of overcapacity in the Chinese automobile industry, in relation to estimated income and purchasing power in China, see P. Ryan, "China car market goes into overdrive: Over-capacity

scenario in the midterm", *ERMRI*, October 2002 (available at www.marubeni.co.jp/research/eindex/0210/body.html via www.google.com, accessed 31 January 2004).
18. Kueh, "Coping with globalization in China", p. 51.
19. Kueh, "Coping with globalization in China", pp. 50–1.
20. For a more detailed listing of the automobile joint ventures in China, see *HSBC–CMR*, January 2004, pp. 21–2 and 26–7.
21. Y. Y. Kueh, "China and the prospects for economic integration within APEC", in Joseph C. H. Chai, Y. Y. Kueh and Clement A. Tisdell (eds.), *China and the Asia Pacific Economy*, New York: Nova Science Publishers, Inc., 1997, pp. 44–5.
22. Wang Zude, "Imports and exports of our country's automobile industry in 2002: A general survey", in *CAIYB 2003*, p. 227.
23. *Ibid.*, p. 229.
24. *Ibid.*, p. 228.
25. Bernd Leissner, "Volkswagen to power China's auto exports", (interview in *People's Daily*, 5 June 2002; see www.china.org.cn via www.google.com, accessed 31 January 2004).
26. Minako Mori, "Automobile manufacturers unveil new ASEAN strategies", in *AMJRI*, October 2001, p. 2.
27. *Ibid.*, p.3.

Chapter 12 China's WTO Accession, ASEAN 10+1, and ECFA

1. This refers to the earlier parts of the ADRF monograph cited above.
2. CCTV-4 reported on 12 November 2002 that for the first three quarters of 2002, FDI pledged in China amounted to US$68.38 billion, up by 34% year-on-year, and FDI realized surpassed the benchmark of US$50 billion for the first time.
3. In 1999, Toyota signed an agreement with the Tianjin Automotive Industry Group to produce 100 to 150 thousand small sedans annually, starting in 2001 (see *CAIYB 2000*, p. 176). On 29 August 2002, Toyota further agreed with the top Chinese car manufacturer, First Automotive Work (FAW), to build 300,000 to 400,000 cars by 2010 (*SCMP*, 30 August 2002). Prior to this, Toyota's involvement in China was just to provide licence to Tianjin Automotive Corporation for producing the Daihatsu-designed Charade, a compact car marketed in China under the name Xiali, which has become the most popular model next to Volkswagen's Santana. The Toyota-FAW move was immediately followed, on 19 September 2002, by Nissan's agreement with Dongfeng, the second largest carmaker in China to invest US$1.28 billion to produce 900,000 vehicles within ten years (*SCMP*, 20 September 2002).
4. See, Y. Y. Kueh, "Coping with globalization in China: Strategic implications of WTO accession", *Journal of World Investment* (Geneva), Vol. 3, No. 1 (2002), pp. 37–64.

5. Hiu-Kwong Leung, *Zhongguo Yinhang Zai Zhongguo Jingjiji Jinrong Gaige Xia de Fazhan* (The Bank of China in China's Economic and Financial Reforms), MPhil thesis, Lingnan University, Hong Kong, 2001.
6. China Central Television Channel 4 (CCTV-4), 12 November 2002.
7. Thomas Voon and Xiangdong Wei, "Export competition among China and ASEAN in the US market: Application of market share models", in Joseph C. H. Chai, Y. Y. Kueh and Clement A. Tisdell, *China and Asia Pacific Economy*, Commack, New York: Nova Science Publishers, Inc., 1997. Epilogue: as a more recent report "China links up with ASEAN to boost trade" published in the *Bangkok Post–Business* (8 March 2010) put it, electrical machinery represents the top export product category (comprising nuclear reactors, boilers, machinery and mechanical appliances) for both ASEAN and China, making up respectively 23.4% and 23.9% (in 2008) of their total exports. "Therefore, the trade relationship between China and ASEAN is mostly competitive, not complementary." And in fact, "one month before the launching of CAFTA (ASEAN 10+1), Indonesia's fourteen industrial associations expressed concern over the zero tariff, which may damage Indonesia's own industries, in the hopes of delaying the agreement" (*ibid.*).
8. *TKP*, 16 November 2002.
9. *TKP*, 5 November 2002.
10. *TKP*, 14 November 2002.
11. The drastic decline in the Triad's share in 2009 in China's global trade total reflects clearly the impact of the 2008/2009 global financial crisis originating from the United States and affecting much more strongly its advanced Western counterparts rather than Asian countries, ASEAN included. Both China's exports to and imports from the Triad were markedly curtailed: exports were curtailed due to drastically reduced import demand from the Triad, and imports also, in favour of the Chinese government's massive "pump-priming" for forestalling accelerating unemployment resulting from reduced exports. Of course, the decline in the Triad's share in 2009 may also be a matter of long-term market diversification of Chinese exports and imports away from the Triad since WTO accession. The diversification seems indeed to have spread across the continents, hence the very marginal increases in ASEAN's share as shown in Table 12.2 and explained in the text.
12. This is obviously an attempt to woo the mainly agriculture-based Southern Taiwanese who traditionally advocate strongly for "political independence" of the island from the Beijing authority.
13. See *Xinbao*, 3 July 2010.
14. Ross Garnaut, "A new open regionalism in the Asia Pacific", paper presented at the International Conference on World Economy, Colima, Mexico, 25 November, 2004. See also C. Fred Bergsten, *Open Regionalism*, Working Paper 97–3, Washington DC: Peterson Institute for International Economics, 1997, for comparative definitions of "open regionalism".

15. This is an estimate verbally given by Professor Lin Chien-fu of National Taiwan University at a public conference held at the Hong Kong Convention and Exhibition Centre, 1 September 2010. The figure is from the notes I took, subject to further verification.
16. *SCMP*, 7 July 2010.
17. In terms of PPP (purchasing power parity) estimates, respectively US$34,743 and US$5,401 (IMF figures), the gap is even wider—Taiwan by a multiple of 6.43 higher compared with 5.44 for the nominal difference. Singapore is the only ASEAN country which has a per capita GDP higher than Taiwan, but it has a small population of 4.6 million only.
18. See Thitapha Wattanapruttipaisan (senior officer of industrial co-operation, ASEAN secretariat), "ASEAN-China economic relationships and cooperation in trade and investment: Patterns and potential", paper presented at the Symposium on China-ASEAN Entrepreneur Exchanges, China National Committee for Pacific Economic Co-operation, Chengdu, China, 22–23 October 2001.
19. *Ibid*.

Chapter 13 Conclusion

1. As Secretary Hillary Clinton put it categorically, on 13 January 2010, on the eve of her trip to Australia, "I don't think there is any doubt, if there was when this administration began, that the United States is back in Asia, but I want to underscore we are back to stay". Mrs Clinton also made it clear that the US wanted to be "full and leading participants" in "the defining regional institutions" (which should include, in addition to APEC, the ASEAN Regional Forum on East Asian security cooperation and humanitarian actions, and at a leadership level, possibly at the East Asia Summit (see *The Australian* (Daily), 14 January 2010). While in Hanoi attending the ASEAN Regional Forum on 23 July 2010, Clinton strongly advocated for "the South China Sea question" to be posed as "pivotal to regional stability", and called for "multilateral talks" (meaning to involve the US), where hitherto the Paracel and Spratly Islands have always been a bilateral question between China and the countries concerned.
2. The relatively pro-Asia and pro-China Democratic Party of Japan (DPJ) was the first ever party elected to replace the long-governing, highly pro-America Liberal Democratic Party in 2009. Under DPJ, relations with China warmed, and Mr Yukio Hatayama, the party's first ever member to be elected Prime Minister, professed his desire "to deepen economic integration with the East Asia region, pushing for a free trade zone in Asia by 2020", as highlighted in *Wikipedia*. Further, while the Australian Prime Minister, Mr Kevin Rudd, advocated "an overarching East Asia community that has to include the US" on his meeting with Secretary Clinton in January 2010, Hatayama proposed "an economic community excluding the Americans" (*The Australian, ibid.*).

3. See Donald Emmerson, "China's 'frown diplomacy' in Southeast Asia", in *East Asia Forum* (Australian National University), 8 October 2010. Emmerson is director of the Southeast Asia Forum at Stanford University.
4. See Nouriel Roubini, "Our G-Zero World" (Project syndicate, 2011). Roubini's challenging thesis was closely taken up at the World Economic Forum's annual conference in the Swiss resort of Davos.
5. Thus far, currency swap agreements have been signed with Indonesia, Argentina, Malaysia, Hong Kong, South Korea, Belarus, Brazil, Singapore, and lately (in October 2010) with Thailand as well. As of the first quarter of 2011, only 7% of China's external trade was settled in renminbi, mostly through banks based in Hong Kong, and according to the Hong Kong Monetary Authority, overwhelmingly involving mainland Chinese buyers paying for imports in yuan (*SCMP*, 9 July 2011).
6. Some Washington officials categorically rejected Zhou's idea (put forth in March 2009) as "impractical". Perhaps as a token of US courtesy (the largest stakeholder in the IMF), in November 2010, the IMF agreed to realign its quota shares (voting rights) in favour of a marginal increase for China (from 2.77% to 4.42%), elevating the country's status to the third largest member country (next to the US and Japan) effective 2012. However, together with other BRIC countries, the D&TC (developing and transition countries) will only be given a combined total of 47% of the votes. The US alone retains 17% of the votes.
7. *SCMP*, 17 August 2011, p. B3. As of 30 June 2011, China, being the largest creditor of the US, had parked in total two-thirds of the country's stockpile of foreign currencies in US-dollar denominated assets (see also *China Daily*, 4 August 2011).
8. China's concern over the security of her foreign exchange reserves has lately increased greatly with the historical downgrading on 5 August 2011 of the long-term sovereign credit rating of the US by Standard and Poor's. The downgrading followed the approval by the US Congress on 2 August 2011 of the bipartisan bill to raise the government's debt ceiling by US$2.4 trillion to US$16.7 trillion and to cut the fiscal budget deficit by US$2.1 trillion (*China Daily*, 4 and 7 August 2011; see also *New York Times*, 6 August 2011, for what it regards as the "harshest" comments from official Chinese media made just hours after the S&P's downgrading).
9. It is widely reported, e.g., that China's "aircraft carrier killer" DF-21D anti-ship ballistic missiles already have "initial operational capability".
10. See *The China Post*, 6 February 2010.
11. The term "soft power" is coined by Harvard professor Joseph Nye Jr. in his 2004 book, *Soft Power: The Means to Success in World Politics*. It is reminiscent of the Chinese political philosophy of *wuweierzhi* (literally, "ruling by doing nothing") by Laozi (the ancient Chinese philosopher). However, the practical approach for achieving political goals by "co-option and attraction" as advocated by Professor Nye seems still not rid of the conventional American

or Western traces of realist-materialism. How should "attraction" (by material incentives, e.g.) exactly be distinguished from "financial coercion"? Would the latter approach be enforced, should the former fail? What would happen should the US fail to "attract" by virtue of her propagated values of "democracy" and "freedom"? By contrast, Laozi's "not doing anything" implies not anarchism, but positive "role-modelling in peaceful pursuit of enduring convergence, integration and harmony". This clearly stands in sharp contrast to the American aspiration for hegemonic dominance, check and balance (often targeted at an imaginary enemy), and reprisal and retaliation to end up in spiralling armament competition. Secretary Clinton's provocative speech in Hanoi on 23 July 2010 (supra note 1), followed by the US-Vietnamese naval rehearsal in the South China Sea in August 2010, and again in summer 2011, is a clear case in point.

12. After the manuscript was completed in September 2011, geopolitics that was remarkably aggressive on the part of the United States vis-à-vis China erupted once again in conjunction with the 2011 APEC summit and East Asia Summit held in November, respectively in Honolulu and Bali, Indonesia just a week apart; hence this postscript to capture the latest development, as it may bear on the regional and global affairs.
13. The official US argument for involvement is based essentially on the reason of "navigational security" as it may bear on US interests. The established Chinese stance towards the matter, however, is that any controversial territorial claims on the disputed South China Sea islets should be resolved exclusively between the parties concerned. Curiously, while progress has recently been made on the bilateral negotiations between China and Vietnam in this respect, the Philippines as a non-involved party feverishly raised objection to the settlement, backing up the consistent US position for multilateral negotiation.
14. Various media reports including *SCMP*, *China Daily*, and *Xinbao*, November 2011, various days from the countdown to the APEC summit on 13–14 November through to the East Asia Summit a week later and in early December.
15. See *China Daily* (Hong Kong edition), 14 November 2011. Clinton said even more explicitly, "Just as the US played a central role in shaping that architecture across the Atlantic, we are now doing the same across the Pacific", *ibid.*
16. Cf. Bates Gill, "Shanghai Five: An attempt to counter US influence in Asia?" (4 May 2001), article made available on the Brookings Institution website, 2 December 2011.
17. One may also note that China has now been with WTO for more than a decade, but the Russian Federation, perhaps due to its being loaded with Soviet remnants, still remains outside of the orbit pending WTO approval of her membership application, which was submitted nearly two decades ago.
18. See list of acronyms and glossary for explanation. According to the US Department of State website (as of 3 December 2011), Myanmar at the Upper Mekong "accounts for no more than 2% of the total water volume in the Mekong; . . . (while) the Lower Mekong region is defined as those countries who share a common dependence on the Mekong River".

19. It seems premature to examine media comments on the possible regional implications of the latest US approach to Myanmar, but some have already noted that just a few days ahead of Clinton's visit to Myanmar, China's Vice President Xi Jinping hosted in Beijing an official visit by Myanmar's National Defence Minister for enhancing military exchange and cooperation between the two countries. In a press commentary, Professor Li Xiguang from the prominent Tsinghua University in Beijing referred to "increased uncertainty involved in the prospect for China to develop the 'new silk road' through Myanmar to the Indian Ocean, as a result of increased influence of the United States in the region"; see *Xinbao*, 2 December 2011. In fact, the US-led LMK Initiative of 2009 is seen by many as a tacit challenge to the Greater Mekong Subregion (GMS) cooperation programme established in 1992 by China and the five Mekong countries (Cambodia, Laos, Myanmar, Thailand and Vietnam) under the auspices of the Asian Development Bank. Interestingly, hardly three weeks after Clinton's visit to Myanmar, the fourth GMS summit was held in Naypyidaw, capital of Myanmar, on 20 December 2011, and ended with a declaration for launching the new (second) 10-year Strategic Framework for economic cooperation and development in the areas; See *China Daily*, 21 and 22 December 2011.
20. Massive protests by farmers erupted in Seoul when the Korean National Assembly convened on 22 November 2011 to ratify the latest round of FTA agreement signed with the US (on 10 February). Japan is still hesitating, as among other things, TPP for many, especially for representatives from the agriculture sector, would spell a "total collapse" of the country. The removal of the highly protective import tariff of 778% would result in overwhelming import influx from the US. See *Xinbao*, 15 November 2011 for a concise and good commentary by Ma Ting, a lecturer in political economy at Waseda University, Tokyo.
21. Consult the USTR Office website (accessed 4 December 2011) for a highlight of the economic importance of TPP to the US: "As a group, TPP countries are the fourth largest goods and services export market of the United States. US goods exports to the broader Asia Pacific totaled $775 billion in 2010, a 25.5% increase over 2009 and equal to 61% of total US goods exports to the world. US exports of agricultural products to the region totaled $83 billion in 2010 and accounted for 72% of total US agricultural exports to the world. US private services exports totaled $177 billion in 2009 (latest data available), 37% of total US private services exports to the world. America's small-and medium-sized enterprises alone exported $171 billion to the Asia Pacific in 2009 (latest data available)."
22. Note supra 20, for Ma Ting's summary of major Japanese political stances on TPP.
23. Note supra 3.

Name Index

For names of Mainland Chinese origin (romanized according to the pinyin system) entries comprise surname followed by the first and middle name(s), without a comma after the surname (for example, Deng Xiaoping and Jiang Zemin). In entries for other Chinese names (Hong Kong, Taiwan and overseas Chinese, spelled according to the Wade-Giles or another system) the surname is followed by a comma (for example, Chai, Joseph C. H. and Lo, Fu-chen). Exceptions to the latter rule are certain non-Mainland Chinese celebrities, such as Lee Kuan Yew and Tung Chee Hwa.

Names mentioned in endnotes are not indexed separately if they appear in that part of the main text, to which the note number refers. Index entries to names that occur in endnotes comprise the page number followed by the letter 'n' and the note number, viz: 401n16.

Although not a normal practice, in the absence of a bibliography, the names of sources cited in footnotes and endnotes have also been indexed. To avoid long strings of page references, only the page and, where relevant, the note number, relating to the first citation of the source are included in the index entry.

Subject Index

Subjects mentioned in endnotes are not indexed separately if they appear in that part of the main text, to which the note number refers. Index entries to subjects that occur in endnotes comprise the page number followed by the letter 'n' and the note number, viz: 409n8.